BLACKS IN THE NEW WORLD

Series Editor

August Meier

THE WORKING CLASS IN AMERICAN HISTORY

Editorial Advisors

David Brody

David Montgomery

Alice Kessler-Harris

Sean Wilentz

Lists of books in the series Blacks in the New World and The Working Class in American History appear at the end of this volume.

COAL, CLASS, AND COLOR

COAL, CLASS,
and
COLOR

Blacks in Southern West Virginia
1915–32

JOE WILLIAM TROTTER, JR.

UNIVERSITY OF ILLINOIS PRESS

Urbana and Chicago

© 1990 by the Board of Trustees of the University of Illinois
Manufactured in the United States of America
1 2 3 4 5 C P 5 4 3 2 1

This book is printed on acid-free paper.

Library of Congress Cataloging-in-Publication Data

Trotter, Joe William, 1945–
     Coal, class, and color : Blacks in southern West Virginia, 1915–32
  Joe William Trotter, Jr.
     p.   cm.—(Blacks in the New World) (The Working class in
  American history)
     Includes bibliographical references.
     ISBN 0-252-01707-2 (cloth : alk. paper).—ISBN 0-252-06119-5 (paper :
  alk. paper)
     1. Afro-American coal miners—West Virginia—History—20th
  century. 2. Afro-Americans—West Virginia—Social conditions.
  I. Title.   II. Series.   III. Series: The Working class in American
  history.
  HD8039.M62U66943   1990
  331.6'3960730754—dc20   89–20501
                                                                  CIP

For black coal miners in southern West Virginia
in memory of my father, Joe William Trotter, Sr.

5/8/92

To Mike,

WITH

BesT WisHes

IN' YouR

HisToRicAL

CAReeR,

[signature]

Contents

Photographs appear following page 144

List of Maps and Tables

Acknowledgments

It is a pleasure to acknowledge a few of the many people who helped to make this book possible. I wish to thank the Department of History at Carnegie Mellon University, first under the chairmanship of Ludwig F. Schaefer and now under Peter N. Stearns, for its firm support and encouragement of this project. Since moving from the University of California at Davis in 1985, several research grants facilitated my research: annual faculty research awards, faculty development grants, a grant from the Program in Technology and Society, under the direction of Joel Tarr, and a university-sponsored sabbatical leave. This book, however, had its genesis at the University of California at Davis, where my colleague and chair, Rollie E. Poppino, labor historian David Brody, the Office of Research, and a grant from the American Council of Learned Societies aided my initial conceptualization of the project and primary research on it. To both institutions of higher learning and to the ACLS, I am most grateful.

Colleagues at a variety of institutions helped me to break ground, develop, and bring this book to full fruition. They proved over and over again that our field is imbued with a high level of collective consciousness; it values cooperation. Before quite completing my study of blacks in Milwaukee, I wrote letters of inquiry to several scholars, seeking their advice on the feasibility of conducting the kind of study that I envisioned. The response was immediate, enthusiastic, and exceedingly helpful. I especially wish to thank the following people: Kenneth Bailey, vice president, West Virginia Institute of Technology; Stephen Brier, project director, American Working Class History Project, City University of New York; Edward J. Cabbell, folklorist and director, John Henry Memorial Foundation, Princeton, West Virginia; Price V. Fishback, economic historian, University of Georgia; Robert A. Hill, director, Marcus

Garvey Papers, University of California at Los Angeles; John H. M. Laslett, University of California at Los Angeles; Randall Lawrence, director of Sloss Furnaces, Birmingham, Alabama; Ronald L. Lewis, West Virginia University; William H. Turner, then at the University of Kentucky; David Walls, acting director, Appalachian Center, University of Kentucky; and John A. Williams, director, Center for Appalachian Studies, Appalachian State University.

Among these various scholars, however, I owe a special thanks to Ronald Lewis, who not only engaged me in long conversations about the southern West Virginia experience, but who also gave me access to his files on blacks and the United Mine Workers of America. I am also indebted to labor historian David A. Corbin and southern Appalachian historian Ronald D Eller, whose pioneering research on southern West Virginia laid much of the groundwork for my study.

If colleagues proved indispensable to this project, archivists and librarians proved even more so. This study benefited from the able and dedicated services of archivists and librarians at several institutions: Jerry Hess of the Scientific, Economic, and Labor Division, National Archives, Washington, D.C.; acting chief, Paul T. Heffron, and chief, James H. Hutson, Library of Congress; George Parkinson, director, and curators John Cuthbert and Peter Gottlieb (now at Pennsylvania State University), West Virginia Collection, West Virginia University; Rodney Pyles, director, West Virginia Department of Culture and History, Division of Archives and History, Charleston, W.Va.; Maier Fox, research coordinator, United Mine Workers of America archives, Washington, D.C.; Louella Dye, director, Craft Memorial Library, Bluefield, W.Va.; Stuart McGehee, archivist, Eastern Regional Coal Archives, Bluefield, W.Va.; Melissa Delbridge, intern, William R. Perkins Library, Duke University; and Erica C. Linke, acquisitions librarian, Carnegie Mellon University. Holders of private collections also gave me access to their files: Mrs. Jessie Froe Thomas of Gary, McDowell County, and retired U.S. Air Force Captain Nelson L. Barnett, Jr., of Huntington, Cabell County, both in West Virginia.

For the sources upon which this book is based, however, I am most indebted to the coal miners and their families. They kindly granted me interviews, revealed their life stories, and permitted their use herein. The twenty-nine interviewees are mentioned by name in the bibliographical essay. To the people mentioned above, to others like Joe Lawrence of Charleston, Sam and Julia Bundy of Bluefield, and Rosetta Barron Neely of Vallscreek, and to still others too numerous to name individually, I extend collective thanks for helping to make this book a reality.

Understanding the human experience not only requires access to sources, it also requires a forum, where scholars can share ideas, receive criticism, and sharpen their analyses. Fortunately, *Coal, Class, and Color* benefited from presentations and critical comments at a variety of professional meetings, colloquia, and symposia involving the following: the Organization of American Historians, the American Historical Association (both the national body and the energetic Pacific Coast Branch), the Southern Historical Association, the Oral History Association, the Martin R. Delany Lecture Series at West Virginia University, the Southern Labor History Institute at the University of Florida at Gainesville, the West Virginia Conference on Black History in Charleston (especially Dr. Ancella Bickley), the Symposium on the History and Culture of Coal Mining in West Virginia at the Huntington Museum of Art and Coalways, Inc., and the Social History Conference of the Minnesota Humanities Commission. Similar meetings took place at the University of California at Santa Cruz, at Santa Barbara, and at Los Angeles, Indiana University of Pennsylvania, Cleveland State University, the University of Chicago, Ohio State University, the University of Pittsburgh, and the Pittsburgh Center for Social History.

Among the numerous commentators on my work, I would like to thank David M. Katzman, University of Kansas; Marlene Rikard, Samford University; James A. Borchert, Cleveland State University; William L. Van Deburg, University of Wisconsin at Madison; Ronald Schatz, Wesleyan University; Robert Zeiger, University of Florida at Gainesville; Kenneth Sullivan, West Virginia Department of Culture and History; and my friend Earl Lewis, then at the University of California at Berkeley, now at the University of Michigan. Other scholars in a variety of institutions also provided positive reinforcement for this study, through their own scholarship, helpful suggestions, and good conversation: Albert S. Broussard, Texas A&M University; Spencer Crew, Smithsonian Institution; Douglas Daniels, University of California at Santa Barbara; Jacqueline Goggin, Library of Congress; James Grossman, then at the University of Chicago, now at the Newberry Library; Darlene Clark Hine, Michigan State University; James Horton, George Washington University; Kenneth L. Kusmer, Temple University; Lawrence Levine, University of California at Berkeley; Robert Maxon, West Virginia University; Nell I. Painter, Princeton; Henry L. Taylor, State University of New York at Buffalo; Quintard Taylor, California Polytechnic

State University at San Luis Obispo; and George C. Wright, University of Texas at Austin.

In faculty research forums and in other ways as well, my colleagues Andrew E. Barnes, Lizabeth Cohen, Edward W. Constant, John Modell, Richard L. Schoenwald, and others at Carnegie Mellon University offered helpful comments and encouragement on various phases of this project. For their input on this book, I am very appreciative. Moreover, through their enthusiasm and critical responses, in countless ways graduate and undergraduate students contributed to this project. To them I also wish to say thanks. For various administrative and clerical services in connection with this book, I thank Judy Kane, the secretarial staff of the CMU department of history, and my graduate assistant Lori Cole.

Indeed, scholarship builds on the interest, enthusiasm, and commitment of countless people, including and especially editors at university presses. I owe a huge debt to Richard Wentworth, director of the University of Illinois Press, and series editor, August Meier, for their faith in this project from its early conceptualization to completion. For approving the cross-listing of my book, I thank the editorial advisors of the Working Class in American History series, including David Brody, Alice Kessler-Harris, David Montgomery, and Sean Wilentz. Since university presses must increasingly balance their deep humanistic concerns with the hardheaded arithmetic of sales, I am particularly gratified by the editors' commitment to this project. I also wish to extend my appreciation to assistant editor Beth Bower for her editorial services on this book.

I owe my greatest debt to my wife, LaRue. From beginning to end, she has given unyielding intellectual and spiritual support to this project. Her confidence in this book was repeatedly reinforced by a host of relatives, including my mother, sisters, brothers, cousins, and a growing number of nieces and nephews. This book, however, owes its existence to the lives of hundreds of black coal miners and their descendants in the southern West Virginia coalfields. Therefore, I respectfully dedicate this book to them in memory of my father, Joe William Trotter, Sr., a coal miner.

Introduction

Since the late 1970s and early 1980s, our knowledge of life and labor in the southern Appalachian coalfields has dramatically expanded. Scholars of American social, labor, and economic history are carefully charting the rise of the bituminous coal industry during the late nineteenth and early twentieth centuries. They focus on labor-management relations and especially on the remarkable tradition of interracial unionism that developed in the Knights of Labor and the United Mine Workers of America.[1] While it is true that Afro-American coal miners were often union men, at the same time that they were workers in a multi-ethnic labor force, they were also southern blacks making the complicated transition from rural and semirural life to life in a new industrial setting. The socioeconomic and political dynamics of class, race, and region shaped their experiences. By focusing explicitly on black coal miners in southern West Virginia between 1915 and 1932, this study seeks to address important gaps in our knowledge, giving a fuller, and hopefully more satisfying, portrait of the interplay of race, class, culture, and power in the coalfields.

Key to this portrait is the process of black industrial working-class formation—proletarianization. This study systematically traces the rise of the black coal-mining proletariat and the impact this development had on the larger community life of coal-mining towns. Proletarianization is here defined simply as the process by which southern rural and semirural blacks became new industrial workers and crystallized into a new class.[2]

First and foremost, this process involved not just the interaction between white capital, labor, and the state, all of which, to varying degrees, practiced racial discrimination against blacks, but the dynamic actions of blacks themselves. While the social boundaries be-

tween blacks and whites in southern West Virginia were hostile and
rigid, they were by no means impermeable. Proletarianization was
affected by existing patterns of de jure and de facto racial discrimination, but it influenced them in turn. Second, over time proletarianization led to improved housing, education, and social welfare
services for blacks as well as better wages—a decided upward shift
in their material conditions, although it did take place within a solid
framework of class and racial inequality. Finally, in crucial ways, the
proletarianization of blacks in southern West Virginia played a part
in the gradual transformation of black culture and consciousness
there, as reflected in the rise of the black middle class, the expansion of black institutions, and the rise of vigorous new political and
civil rights initiatives. Especially evident here is the role of blacks in
shaping their own experience.

This study of the transformation of black life covers nine counties
in the south-central section of West Virginia. This region offers several advantages as a case study of Afro-American life in both the
coal industry and Appalachia, which stretches "through parts of
thirteen states from New York to Alabama." First, West Virginia is
the only state falling completely within Appalachia.[3] Second, with
the exception of a brief revival during World War II and its early
aftermath, West Virginia reached its peak as a coal-producing state
during the 1915–32 period. It increased its share of the nation's bituminous coal production from 7 percent in 1890 to 26 percent in
1930, while production in the leading northern Appalachian state of
Pennsylvania dropped from 33 percent to roughly 25 percent of total
national output. Moreover, between World War I and 1930, southern West Virginia produced between two-thirds and three-quarters
of the state's coal, employed over 80 percent of the state's black miners, and enabled West Virginia to displace Alabama as the dominant employer of Afro-American coal miners.

During World War I and the postwar years, however, the coal
industry entered a period of relative stagnation. Large and small
firms alike confronted frequent downturns in the business cycle. In
addition, small companies faced increasing pressure from competitive monopolistic combinations, the growing mechanization of productive processes, and the spreading use of alternative fuels.
During the early postwar years of 1919–21, and again under the onslaught of the Great Depression of the late 1920s and early 1930s,
the coal industry experienced sharp downturns that resulted in substantial unemployment. At the same time, especially during periods of economic recovery and expansion, the largest and most

successful firms followed prevailing trends in American industrial ideology and practice. Seeking to stem the rising tide of working-class militance, they initiated welfare capitalism and other paternalistic programs providing a broader array of employee benefits. The 1915–32 period, then, offers an unusual opportunity to observe the social impact of industrialization and proletarianization on Afro-American life under a diverse range of economic and political conditions.[4]

In comparative terms, the study of southern West Virginia offers an important chance to develop an alternative to the usual southern-rural or northern-urban understanding of black life.[5] While the region underwent a dramatic industrial transformation, it did not undergo a concomitant urban transformation. The coal industry in Alabama, Pennsylvania, and parts of Ohio and Illinois developed in or near cities, including large industrial cities like Birmingham, Pittsburgh, and Cincinnati. In addition, as an extractive mineral industry, coal mining's hazards and skill requirements diverged from those of both southern agriculture and northern industry. Rather than the relatively predictable seasonal calendar that dominated rural labor, fluctuating business upturns and downturns dictated the labor demands of the coal industry. Yet, unlike the urban factory system, coal mining's peculiar, dispersed underground terrain precluded the growth of direct and intensive supervision of the labor force. Instead, the highly touted "miner's freedom" reigned. Moreover, since southern Appalachian whites were invariably stereotyped as inferior by the dominant national culture, much as blacks were, research on blacks in southern West Virginia promises fresh insights into the comparative dynamics of race, class, and region in American society.[6]

Black life in West Virginia, as in other border states, differed significantly from life in the Deep South. Blacks in the Mountain State faced fewer incidents of mob violence, fewer debilitating forms of labor exploitation, and, since they retained the franchise, fewer constraints on their exercise of political power.[7] For example, West Virginia's legislature, like northern legislatures, rejected Jim Crow proposals to disfranchise blacks and to segregate them on common carriers. Blacks in southern West Virginia, however, unlike northern blacks, confronted a state-mandated system of racial segregation in the state's schools and social welfare institutions. They also faced relatively greater injustice before the law and a comparatively more hostile social environment, which often threatened to erupt in mob violence when they allegedly violated segregationist norms.

Although black life in southern West Virginia took on unique characteristics, this study suggests that proletarianization was an experience that black coal miners shared with other industrial workers, black and white, in different regional, national, and international settings. Like industrial workers elsewhere in America and the world, black coal miners faced the vicissitudes of wage labor in a rapidly industrializing economy. Yet, their experiences were by no means the same throughout the region. Rather than company-owned towns, incorporated commercial centers, though small, provided the most lucrative prospects for homeownership, better schools, and a wider range of cultural and recreational activities. Incorporated towns served as magnets for black miners from the smaller surrounding coal-mining operations and company-owned towns. Also, the coal industry penetrated the region at different points in time, with varying results. For example, the United Mine Workers achieved its greatest success near the capital city of Charleston in the Kanawha–New River Field, which was the oldest and most urban-oriented of the coal subfields. In contrast, the Pocahontas, Williamson-Logan, and Winding Gulf fields opened later and remained nearly impregnable bastions of anti-union operators. Although lack of data prevents a systematic analysis of all intra-regional differences, this study documents their importance where possible.

By the early twentieth century, McDowell County, located in the rich Pocahontas Field, had emerged as the principal center of black life in southern West Virginia, and in the entire state. It was here that black miners were most heavily concentrated and here that black life gained its most characteristic expression. Black coal-mining communities dramatically expanded, replete with a rich array of churches, fraternal orders, mutual benefit societies, weekly newspapers, and a variety of political and civil rights organizations. This expansion involved the emergence and growth of the black middle class and the increasing stratification of the black community, symbolized by such organizations as the National Association for the Advancement of Colored People (NAACP) and the Universal Negro Improvement Association (UNIA), or Garvey movement.

Part 1 of the book establishes the prewar parameters of proletarianization, emphasizing the rise of a large black coal-mining proletariat during a period when most blacks worked in agriculture, and its impact on the social, economic, and political life of coal-mining towns. Part 2 analyzes wartime and postwar patterns of migration, work, and industrial change, noting both the continuation of earlier patterns and the emergence of new ones. It focuses especially on the transfer of coal-mining skills, the intensification of racial stratification in the workplace, and the escalating struggle of blacks against racial and class exploitation. Part 3 explores the impact of proletarianization on race relations, social welfare services, and the educational system and investigates the connection between the formation of the black working class and the intensification of racial inequality in the life of the region. It also examines the dynamic interrelationship between the rise of the black working class and the growth of the black elite. Focusing on black religious, fraternal, and political organizations, part 4 traces the complex interaction between the black working class and middle class in the building of black institutions; the industrial transformation of black culture and consciousness; and the black community's energetic political and civil rights struggles. Each part treats gender as an integral thread, along with color and class.

The conclusion discusses the larger historiographical, methodological, and theoretical implications of the black experience in southern West Virginia. It calls for more cross-disciplinary research and exchange on all levels of American and Afro-American social, labor, and economic history. Only then will we be able to advance toward a proletarian synthesis in research on the American and Afro-American experience.

NOTES

1. Ronald D Eller, *Miners, Millhands, and Mountaineers: Industrialization of the Appalachian South, 1880–1930* (Knoxville: University of Tennessee Press, 1982); David A. Corbin, *Life, Work, and Rebellion in the Coal Fields: The Southern West Virginia Miners, 1880–1922* (Urbana: University of Illinois Press, 1981); Ronald L. Lewis, *Black Coal Miners in America: Race, Class and Community Conflict, 1780–1980* (Lexington: University Press of Kentucky, 1987); Gary M. Fink and Merle E. Reed, eds., *Essays in Southern Labor History* (Westport, Conn.: Greenwood Press, 1977); William H. Turner and Edward J. Cabbell, eds., *Blacks in Appalachia* (Lexington: University Press of Kentucky, 1985); Price V. Fishback, "Employment Conditions of Blacks in the Coal Industry, 1900–1930" (Ph.D. diss., University of Washington, 1983); James C. Klotter, "The Black South and White Appalachia," *Journal of American History* 66, no. 4 (Mar. 1980): 832–49. For a recent debate on the legacy of Herbert Gutman and the role of race and class in the coalfields, see Herbert Hill, "Myth-Making as Labor History: Herbert Gutman and the United Mine Workers of America," *International Journal of Politics, Culture and Society* 2, no. 2 (Winter 1988): 132–200, and Stephen Brier, "In Defense of Gutman:

The Union's Case," *International Journal of Politics, Culture, and Society* 2, no. 3 (Spring 1989): 382–95.

2. A theoretical perspective on my use of *proletarianization* is in Joe William Trotter, Jr., *Black Milwaukee: The Making of an Industrial Proletariat, 1915–45* (Urbana: University of Illinois Press, 1985), preface, chap. 7, and app. 7.

3. Betty P. Crickard, "The Mountain State," in B. B. Maurer, ed., *Mountain Heritage* (Parsons, W.Va.: McClain Printing Company, 1980), 199–215. For documentation of the following analysis, see the relevant chapters following in this book.

4. Although some studies of black and white coal miners adopt sweeping time frames that span over a century, few examine in detail the tremendous changes of World War I and its aftermath. See, for example, Lewis, *Black Coal Miners*, and Corbin, *Life, Work and Rebellion in the Coal Fields.*

5. Kenneth L. Kusmer, "The Black Urban Experience in American History," in Darlene Clark Hine, ed., *The State of Afro-American History: Past, Present, and Future* (Baton Rouge: Louisiana State University Press, 1986), 91–122; August Meier and Elliott Rudwick, *Black History and the Historical Profession, 1915–80* (Urbana: University of Illinois Press, 1986), especially chaps. 3 and 4; Harold D. Woodman, "Economic Reconstruction and the Rise of the New South, 1865–1900," in John B. Boles and Evelyn T. Nolen, eds., *Interpreting Southern History: Historiographical Essays in Honor of Sanford W. Higginbotham* (Baton Rouge: Louisiana State University Press, 1987), 254–307.

6. Keith Dix, *Work Relations in the Handloading Era, 1880–1930* (West Virginia University, Institute for Labor Studies, 1977), and *What's a Coal Miner to Do?: The Mechanization of Coal Mining and Its Impact on Coal Miners* (Pittsburgh: University of Pittsburgh Press, 1988); Carter Goodrich, *The Miner's Freedom* (1925; rpt. New York: Arno Press, 1971); Klotter, "The Black South and White Appalachia."

7. In his recent study of blacks in Louisville, Kentucky, urban historian George C. Wright adopts the notion of "polite racism," in order to highlight the nature of race relations in that border city compared to patterns further south. See G. C. Wright, *Life Behind a Veil: Blacks in Louisville, Kentucky, 1865–1930* (Baton Rouge: Louisiana State University Press, 1985).

PART
1

The Prewar Years, 1880–1914

1

The Genesis of the Black Working Class

The rise and expansion of the bituminous coal industry stimulated the emergence of the black proletariat in southern West Virginia. Blacks were largely excluded from the northern industrial labor force between 1880 and World War I, but coal companies recruited "native whites," European immigrants, and blacks for the expanding bituminous labor force.[1] The rise of the black coal-mining proletariat was nonetheless a complex process; it was rooted in the social imperatives of black life in the rural South as well as in the dynamics of industrial capitalism. In their efforts to recruit and control black labor, coal operators employed a blend of legal and extralegal measures, reinforced by the racist attitudes and practices of white workers and the state.

On the other hand, black workers, using their network of family and friends, largely organized their own migration to the region. In this way they facilitated their own transition to the industrial labor force and paved the way for the rise of a new black middle class, which helped to gradually transform the contours of Afro-American community life in coal-mining towns. To understand the maturation of these processes during World War I and the 1920s, an understanding of the prewar era is indispensable. Drawing upon the limited amount of data available on this era, this chapter and the following one outline the major prewar processes that would transform black life even more during the war and postwar years.

Under the impact of the rapidly expanding coal industry, southern West Virginia underwent a dramatic transformation during the late nineteenth and early twentieth centuries. While West Virginia produced only five million tons of coal in 1887, coal production in the state's southern region alone increased to nearly forty million tons in 1910, nearly 70 percent of the state's total output. As coal companies increased production, the region's population increased by nearly 300 percent, from about 80,000 in 1880 to nearly 300,000 in 1910 (see table 1.1).[2] The region's immigrant population, mainly from Southern, Central, and Eastern Europe, jumped from nearly 1,400 in 1880 to around 18,000 in 1910, increasing from less than 2 percent of the total population in 1880 to 6 percent in 1910. The black population increased from almost 4,800 in 1880 to over 40,000 in 1910 (table 1.1). With 6 percent of the total in 1880, by 1910 the black population had reached nearly 14 percent, more than twice the percentage who were immigrants. At the same time, the southern region increased its proportion of all blacks in the state from 21 to 63 percent. In order to cut costs and keep wages down, some coal operators preferred a mixed labor force of immigrants, blacks, and American-born whites.[3]

Although the coal industry soon dominated the regional economy, its development was not uniform. From the 1870s through the early 1900s, at least four major geographically interlocking coalfields emerged in southern West Virginia: (1) the Kanawha–New River Field, including Kanawha, Fayette, and Boone counties and part of Raleigh County; (2) the Winding Gulf Field, covering most of Raleigh and Wyoming counties; (3) the Pocahontas Field of McDowell and Mercer counties; and (4) the Williamson-Logan Field, covering Logan and Mingo counties and part of Wyoming County (see map 1).

Basic to the development of the various coalfields was the rapid expansion of railroads into the area. In 1873, linking the Ohio Valley to the Virginia tidewater region, the Chesapeake and Ohio was the first major rail line to penetrate the southern West Virginia coalfields. It opened the Kanawha–New River Field and helped to stimulate development farther south. In 1892, located 60 to 100 miles south of the Chesapeake and Ohio, and running parallel to it, the Norfolk and Western Railroad opened the renowned "Billion Dollar" Pocahontas and Williamson-Logan coal seams. It established rail connections across the southernmost portion of the state, linking what were the richest coal seams in the region to Norfolk Harbor in Virginia. Running in a north-south direction, the Virginian Railroad opened in 1909 and stimulated the development of the Winding Gulf Field, completing the region's major railroads. Later developments were largely extensions of established patterns (map 1). By the early twentieth century, labor historian David A. Corbin aptly states, "West Virginia had a massive network of tunnels, bridges, and iron rails—and the coal rush was on."[4]

TABLE 1.1.
Population of Southern West Virginia
by Race and Ethnicity, 1880–1910

	1880		1890	
	Number	Percent	Number	Percent
Blacks	4,794	6.0	11,114	9.2
Foreign-born whites	1,375	1.7	2,662	2.2
American-born whites/ Foreign-born parentage	—	—	3,889	3.2
American-born whites/ American-born parentage[a]	74,615	92.3	102,806	85.4
Other	—		—	
Total[b]	80,784	100.0	120,471	100.0

	1900		1910	
	Number	Percent	Number	Percent
Blacks	19,670	11.1	40,503	13.5
Foreign-born whites	2,776	1.5	18,061	6.0
American-born whites/ Foreign-born parentage	5,470	3.1	8,978	2.9
American-born whites/ American-born parentage[a]	147,857	84.3	232,276	77.6
Other	—		32	
Total[b]	175,773	100.0	299,850	100.0

Sources: U.S. Census Office, *Report on the Population of the United States, Eleventh Census, 1890* (Washington, 1895), 1:435; U.S. Bureau of the Census, *Thirteenth Census of the United States, 1910* (Washington, 1913), 3:1032–41.

Note: Southern West Virginia is comprised of nine counties—McDowell, Mercer, Mingo, Logan, Fayette, Kanawha, Raleigh, Boone, and Wyoming.

[a]All American-born whites.

[b]Includes a small number of other nonwhites in 1900.

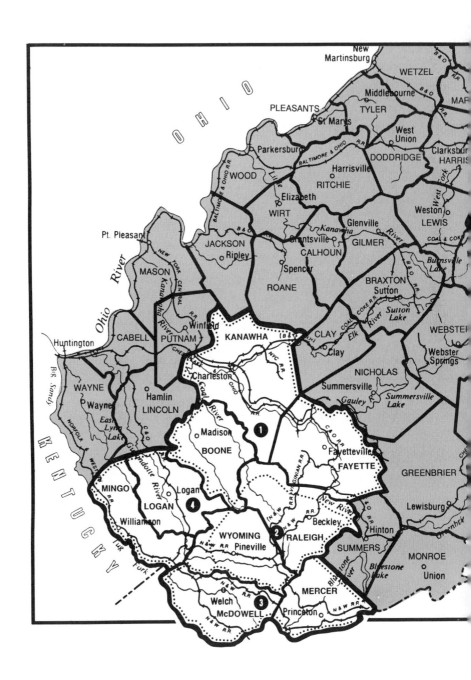

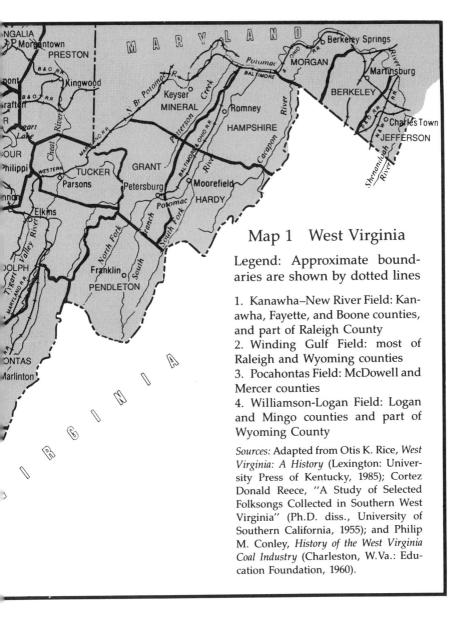

Map 1   West Virginia

Legend: Approximate boundaries are shown by dotted lines

1. Kanawha–New River Field: Kanawha, Fayette, and Boone counties,
and part of Raleigh County
2. Winding Gulf Field: most of
Raleigh and Wyoming counties
3. Pocahontas Field: McDowell and
Mercer counties
4. Williamson-Logan Field: Logan
and Mingo counties and part of
Wyoming County

Sources: Adapted from Otis K. Rice, *West
Virginia: A History* (Lexington: Univer-
sity Press of Kentucky, 1985); Cortez
Donald Reece, "A Study of Selected
Folksongs Collected in Southern West
Virginia" (Ph.D. diss., University of
Southern California, 1955); and Philip
M. Conley, *History of the West Virginia
Coal Industry* (Charleston, W.Va.: Edu-
cation Foundation, 1960).

Industrialization in West Virginia was based mainly on northern, western, and foreign capital. The California railroad magnate Collis P. Huntington financed the Chesapeake and Ohio. In 1873 the line's first train traveled west via Charleston to Huntington (named after the financier). Led by Frederick J. Kimball of Germantown, Pennsylvania, a group of Philadelphia capitalists built the Norfolk and Western railway. Henry H. Rogers, using profits from his affiliation with the Standard Oil Company, constructed the forty-million-dollar Virginian Railroad "on his own resources." As West Virginia historian Otis K. Rice has noted, the Virginian soon "became a formidable competitor of both the Chesapeake and Ohio and the Norfolk and Western." By 1911, Elbert H. Gary and William Edenborn, both linked to the U.S. Steel Corporation, and the local banker Isaac T. Mann of Greenbrier County, purchased the properties of the Flat Top Coal Land Association. The firm soon acquired an estimated 80 percent of the Pocahontas Field, which it then leased to coal-producing companies. Among its most prominent lessees was the U.S. Coal and Coke Company, a subsidiary of U.S. Steel Corporation. For the next thirty years, U.S. Steel secured its coal and coke supplies through its southern West Virginia operations.[5]

As was the case with industrialization in other southern states, coal mining helped to transform the region's largely subsistence economy into a dependent industrial economy, with growing links to national and international markets. The coal economy was increasingly harnessed to the economic interests of northern industrialists like John D. Rockefeller of the Standard Oil Company, Andrew Carnegie, the financier J. P. Morgan, and the Guggenheim family, among others. The British banking firms of Vivian, Gray and Company and T. W. Powell of London also acquired access to valuable southern West Virginia coal, oil, and timber lands. Indigenous mountaineers resisted the sale of their homesteads as long as possible, but they were ultimately defeated as the capitalists gained control of the land, laid track for railroads, and opened the mines.[6]

Gradually coal companies adopted new mining technology. Introduced during the 1880s and 1890s, the undercutting machine was the most significant new technological development until the mid-1920s. By 1910 nearly 40 percent of West Virginia coal was undercut by machines. While pairs of miners working without machines took up to three hours to undercut 120 square feet, the electric cutting machines could undercut 180 square feet in less than one hour. Since the new technology demanded less-skilled workers, it also enabled coal operators to tighten their control over the coal-mining labor force. The undercutting machine, however, was of little help in loading the coal, and handloaders remained the primary mainstay of the industry.[7] In fact, by speeding coal production, the undercutting machine actually necessitated an expanding handloading labor force.

Technological change tightened the coal operators' control over the work force, but only slowly; it was company-owned towns that most gave the operators increasing sway over the economics and politics of coal mining. Coal companies built and rented houses to their employees under contracts that gave management broad powers of search, seizure, and eviction without prior notice; in reality, these contracts established a relationship of "master and servant" rather than "landlord and tenant."[8] The miner's occupancy of company housing was contingent upon his regular and acceptable employment in the mines. In addition, company stores, with their stiff credit policies, reinforced the operator's control over the miner's wages, hours, and working conditions. Although wages were supposedly paid in cash, for example, the widespread use of the scrip system, based on company-printed and only company-honored currency, symbolized the miner's dependence on the company store.[9]

Control over life and labor in the coalfields underlay the operators' control over the larger political machinery of the state. Because they were unincorporated areas, the company-owned towns lacked political officials like mayors, aldermen, and ward politicians. Through the control of jobs, the press, police, and even local postmasters, coal companies monitored the political behavior of workers. In county, state, and national elections, the companies' privately employed guards often served as pollsters, diligently working to regulate the political activities of miners. These conditions gave a kind of feudal quality to political life in the coal-mining towns.[10]

At the local level the operators' political authority was most complete, yet, as elsewhere in industrializing America, West Virginia experienced the erosion of traditional patterns of politics and the rise of a new political order. As the coal industry expanded, small West Virginia cities and towns registered brisk population growth. In 1888, Bluefield, Mercer County, was merely a flag station on a local farm; a year later it was incorporated, with a population of 600, and it increased to over 11,000 by 1910. Welch, McDowell County, was likewise transformed from a forty-dollar purchase of "wild lands" in 1885 to the county seat in 1891. The site of a corn-field in 1891, Williamson, Mingo County, was incorporated in 1892 and soon became "one of the largest coal shipping centers in the state." Similar growth characterized the small towns and cities of Keystone, McDowell County, Bramwell, Mercer County, Logan, Logan County, and Charleston, Kanawha County, which increased from about 3,000 in 1870, when it first became the state capital, to nearly 23,000 in 1910. As one historian of Mountain State politics has noted, West Virginia moved beyond "the preindustrial political culture with its regional networks of kinship and influence to a modern politics dominated by pressure groups, mass media, and professional organizations."[11]

Working through allies in commercial centers as well as in company-owned coal towns, by 1900 West Virginia's leading industrialists had gained control over the Democratic and Republican parties. Democrats like Johnson N. Cambden and Henry G. Davis, and Republicans like Stephen B. Elkins and Nathan Goff, all worked to subdue local competitors for power. Making extensive use of what contemporaries called "a barrel," the new political men issued free railroad passes, delivered free coal for home consumption, and offered private loads to local business and professional men, including newspaper editors. Deeply enmeshed in this statewide system of patronage and political favors, as West Virginia historian John Williams notes, the "local men were usually only too happy to do favors for the industrialists in return, just as Cambden, Davis, and Elkins often ran errands in Washington for such national business leaders as John D. Rockefeller, Andrew Carnegie, and Collis P. Huntington."[12]

As thorough as the industrialists' economic and political influence may have been, it is insufficient to judge the workers' experiences solely against the awesome public and private power of the owners and their political allies. Many mountaineers, rural whites, and immigrants—and especially blacks—who entered coal mining came from depressed socioeconomic backgrounds. Therefore, for large numbers of new recruits, coal mining represented an upward shift in mobility, even if that shift was slight. Moreover, as elsewhere in industrial America, in southern West Virginia the triumph of industrial capitalism was never entirely complete. It was consistently hampered by the vagaries of the business cycle, intra-industry competition, and, most of all, the persistent resistance of coal miners, who protested the most debilitating conditions under which they were expected to live and work.[13]

Under the leadership of the Knights of Labor in the 1880s and the United Mine Workers of America in the 1890s and early 1900s, coal miners launched several unified confrontations with organized capital. In the celebrated Paint Creek–Cabin Creek coal strike of 1912–13, white mountaineers, immigrants, and blacks won an important victory, including recognition of their union at the Kanawha–New River Field. Seeking to vitiate the appeal of the organized labor movement, coal operators modified some of their most oppressive labor policies and practices. In addition to improved housing, health, and recreational conditions, the workers saw an increase in company-supported educational and religious facilities.[14] Nevertheless, although workers resisted the inequitable demands of industrial capitalism with united action, they failed to develop a durable alliance across ethnic and racial lines. American-born whites usurped the most favored supervisory positions in the coalfields, enjoyed the major fruits of welfare capitalism (especially expanding educational opportunities), and placed critical ethnic and racial limits on the progress of immigrants and blacks.[15]

The growth of the black coal-mining proletariat in southern West Virginia unfolded within the foregoing context of socioeconomic and political change, but the black working class also had roots in antebellum Virginia. In 1850 over 3,000 slaves resided in Kanawha County, making up the majority of the county's coal-mining labor force. Slave labor filled the coal demands of the Kanawha Valley salt industry. Although the number of blacks in Kanawha County dropped during the Civil War, in the postwar years their numbers slowly increased. By 1885, blacks made up 90 percent of the miners in the expanding New River portion of the coalfields.[16] Booker T. Washington was among the former slaves who worked in the mines of the Kanawha–New River Field. In his autobiography he described his tenure in the mines: "Work in the coal mines I always dreaded. . . . There was always the danger of being blown to pieces by a premature explosion of powder, or of being crushed by falling slate. Accidents from one or the other of these causes were frequently occurring and this kept me in constant fear."[17]

Although blacks entered the coal mines in the antebellum and Reconstruction eras, it was not until the railroad expansion of the 1890s and early 1900s that their numbers dramatically increased, giving rise to a new industrial proletariat. Black workers helped to lay track for every major rail line in the region. According to sociologist James T. Laing, black laborers from Virginia largely built the Chesapeake and Ohio (and produced the folk hero John Henry). One contemporary analyst, J. M. Callahan, suggested that the "full story of the work done would tell of hardships and dangers bravely borne," and of the faith, patience, skill, and intelligence of the black

workers. Upon completion of the Chesapeake and Ohio in 1873, many
blacks remained behind to work in the New River district. Blacks
played fully as large a part in the building of the Norfolk and Western Railroad as they had in the construction of the Chesapeake and
Ohio. When the Norfolk and Western was finished in 1892, many
black railroad men "remained to work in the coal fields" of the Pocahontas division. Black laborers on the Virginian Railroad similarly
responded to the subsequent opening of the Winding Gulf Field.[18]

As the railroads completed laying track in rapid succession, black
coal miners entered the Kanawha–New River, Winding Gulf, Pocahontas, and Williamson-Logan fields. By 1890, the black population
in Kanawha County reached 3,402, regaining and exceeding its pre–
Civil War level. During the same decade, the number of Afro-
Americans in Fayette County more than doubled, increasing from
1,122 to 3,054. In McDowell and Mercer Counties the black population increased from a negligible size in 1880 to 1,631 and 2,023, respectively, in 1890 (tables 1.1, 1.2). Although growing numbers of
immigrants soon modified the impact blacks were having on the
coal industry, immigrant miners remained outnumbered by black
ones over the next two decades. The number of black miners increased from no more than 3,000 in the entire state in 1890 to over
11,000 in southern West Virginia alone in 1910. Black miners in the
southern region now made up over 90 percent of the state's black
miners, and over 20 percent of the region's total coal-mining labor
force.[19] At the turn of the century, however, the newer Pocahontas
district had supplanted the older Kanawha–New River district as
the principal employer of black miners (tables 1.3, 1.4).

Rural Virginia, contributing over 40 percent of West Virginia's
black population in 1910, was the major source of male and female
black migrants to southern West Virginia. Other sources at that
time were North Carolina, Kentucky, Tennessee, and Maryland,
supplemented by Ohio and Pennsylvania. South Carolina, Georgia,
and Alabama also sent small numbers of blacks, bringing the proportion of the black population born out of state in 1910 to over
50 percent. The black newcomers were mostly young men between
the working ages of 20 and 44, and black men in general outnumbered black women. Although the black sex ratio dropped during
the first decade of the twentieth century, in 1910 it remained high
at 145 males to every 100 females. In contrast, black women outnumbered black men in the migration streams to prewar New York
and Philadelphia, where they gained access to domestic-service
jobs in middle-class white households, which were on the increase.

TABLE 1.2
Population of Southern West Virginia by County, Race, and Ethnicity, 1880–1910

Year	Blacks		Foreign-Born Whites		American-Born Whites/ Foreign or Mixed Parentage		American-Born Whites/ American-Born Parentage		Other		Total	
	Number	Percent	Number	Percent	Number	Percent	Number	Percent	Number	Percent	Number	Percent
McDowell County												
1880	3	0.1	4	0.1	—	—	3,071	99.8	—	—	3,078	100.0
1890	1,631	22.2	306	4.1	143	2.0	5,260	71.7	—	—	7,347	100.0
1910	14,667	30.7	6,260	13.1	1,730	3.6	25,196	52.6	3	—	47,856	100.0
Mercer County												
1880	366	4.9	22	0.2	—	—	7,101	94.9	—	—	7,489	100.0
1890	2,023	12.7	398	2.5	315	1.9	13,267	82.9	—	—	16,003	100.0
1910	5,960	15.6	1,148	3.0	743	1.9	30,515	79.5	5	—	36,371	100.0
Mingo County												
1880	—	—	—	—	—	—	—	—	—	—	—	—
1890	—	—	—	—	—	—	—	—	—	—	—	—
1910	1,236	6.4	1,197	6.1	371	1.9	16,627	85.6	—	—	19,431	100.0
Logan County												
1880	109	1.5	5	0.1	—	—	7,220	98.4	—	—	7,334	100.0
1890	685	6.0	306	2.8	46	0.4	10,267	90.8	—	—	11,304	100.0
1910	532	3.7	927	6.4	220	1.6	12,792	88.4	5	—	14,476	100.0
Fayette County												
1880	1,122	9.3	406	3.3	—	—	10,438	87.4	—	—	11,966	100.0
1890	3,054	16.2	398	2.0	1,077	5.3	15,547	77.5	—	—	20,076	100.0
1910	9,311	17.9	4,466	8.6	2,386	4.6	36,736	68.9	4	—	51,903	100.0

TABLE 1.2 (Continued)

Year	Blacks Number	Percent	Foreign-Born Whites Number	Percent	American-Born Whites/ Foreign or Mixed Parentage Number	Percent	American-Born Whites/ American-Born Parentage Number	Percent	Other Number	Percent	Total Number	Percent
					Kanawha County							
1880	2,870	8.6	857	2.6	—	—	29,596	88.9	—	—	33,323	100.0
1890	3,402	8.1	—	—	2,150	6.1	36,257	86.8	—	—	41,809	100.0
1910	6,476	7.9	2,512	3.1	3,009	3.7	69,446	85.3	15	—	81,457	100.0
					Raleigh County							
1880	71	1.0	43	0.5	—	—	7,296	98.6	—	—	7,410	100.0
1890	79	0.9	29	0.1	99	1.0	8,390	98.0	—	—	9,597	100.0
1910	2,052	8.0	1,525	6.9	459	1.8	21,597	84.3	—	—	25,633	100.0
					Boone County							
1880	189	3.3	34	0.5	—	—	6,636	96.2	—	—	6,868	100.0
1890	170	2.5	12	0.1	55	0.8	6,648	96.6	—	—	6,885	100.0
1910	164	1.6	9	—	37	0.4	10,121	98.0	—	—	10,331	100.0
					Wyoming County							
1880	64	1.4	4	0.1	—	—	4,258	98.6	—	—	4,326	100.0
1890	70	1.1	3	0.1	4	0.1	6,170	98.7	—	—	6,247	100.0
1910	106	1.0	17	0.2	23	0.2	10,247	98.6	—	—	10,392	100.0

Note: In 1880 only persons of foreign or American birth were listed.

Source: U.S. Census Office, *Report on the Population of the United States, Eleventh Census, 1890* (Washington, 1895), 1:435; U.S. Bureau of the Census, *Thirteenth Census of the United States, 1910* (Washington, 1913), 3:1032–41.

Although black women were slightly outnumbered by men in Chicago and Detroit, they nonetheless found significant economic opportunities there. In southern West Virginia the case was the opposite: the coal industry offered few opportunities for female employment outside the home.[20]

Compared to southern agriculture, coal mining offered black workers greater prospects for making money, along with a greater measure of individual and collective autonomy. Despite frequent payment in scrip, in southern West Virginia black workers had substantial opportunities to make cash—enough so that they could spend or save their wages, whichever they desired, and leave when they wished.[21] Yet black workers also faced new forms of coercion and discrimination. Along with paying for advertisements in the local black weekly to attract black workers from nearby Virginia,[22] coal operators employed professional labor agents. Doubling as privately employed "Baldwin-Felts guards," some labor agents were heavily armed, given extensive amounts of cash, and sent to neighboring Virginia and farther south to recruit among rural blacks. After employing black assistants, the white agents frequently disappeared, while the black recruiters, chosen for their eloquence and described as "spellbinders," extolled the advantages of West Virginia mines in glowing terms. Coal operators enthusiastically advanced the miners' transportation costs, then deducted them later from the miners' earnings. Once the new recruits decided to leave the South and boarded the train, according to social historian Kenneth Bailey, the Baldwin-Felts men locked the doors to keep the men from changing their minds.[23]

TABLE 1.3
Coal-Mining Labor Force of Southern West Virginia by Race
and Ethnicity, 1907–10

	1907		1910	
	Number	Percent	Number	Percent
Blacks	9,246	24.0	11,621	23.8
Foreign-born whites	6,466	16.8	11,769	24.3
American-born whites	13,261	34.3	20,759	42.6
Unknown	9,594	24.9	4,498	9.3
Total	38,567	100.0	48,647	100.0

Source: West Virginia Department of Mines, *Annual Reports, 1907, 1910* (Charleston, W.Va.).

TABLE 1.4

Coal-Mining Labor Force of Southern West Virginia by County, Race, and Ethnicity, 1907–10

Year	Blacks		Foreign-Born Whites		American-Born Whites		Unknown		Total	
	Number	Percent	Number	Percent	Number	Percent	Number	Percent	Number	Percent
McDowell County										
1907	4,300	36.1	3,167	26.6	2,286	19.2	2,144	18.1	11,897	100.0
1910	5,276	33.0	6,429	34.0	4,471	34.0	822	5.1	15,997	100.0
Mercer County										
1907	1,022	39.5	598	23.1	761	29.4	205	8.0	2,586	100.0
1910	1,155	31.8	649	23.4	1,086	30.0	536	14.8	3,625	100.0
Mingo County										
1907	123	4.8	109	4.1	604	23.2	1,767	67.9	2,603	100.0
1910	224	9.5	385	16.3	1,670	66.6	179	7.6	2,358	100.0
Logan County										
1907	23	2.2	105	10.4	347	34.5	530	52.9	1,005	100.0
1910	253	12.0	666	31.3	792	37.5	409	19.2	2,120	100.0

	Fayette County									
1907	2,781	23.7	1,964	16.7	4,682	40.3	2,266	19.3	11,693	100.0
1910	3,209	23.8	2,692	19.9	6,185	45.7	1,438	10.6	13,524	100.0
	Kanawha County									
1907	693	9.8	343	4.8	3,863	54.7	2,155	30.7	7,054	100.0
1910	777	10.3	932	12.4	4,970	66.3	816	11.0	7,495	100.0
	Raleigh County									
1907	304	17.5	180	10.4	718	41.5	527	30.6	1,729	100.0
1910	715	21.0	812	23.5	1,672	48.5	244	7.0	3,443	100.0
	Boone County									
1907	N/A	N/A	N/A	N/A	N/A	N/A	N/A	N/A	N/A	N/A
1910	13	16.4	4	4.7	14	16.4	54	63.5	85	100.0
	Wyoming County									
1907	N/A	N/A	N/A	N/A	N/A	N/A	N/A	N/A	N/A	N/A
1910	N/A	N/A	N/A	N/A	N/A	N/A	N/A	N/A	N/A	N/A

Source: West Virginia Department of Mines, *Annual Reports, 1907, 1910* (Charleston, W.Va.).

Some black men, like the legendary gambler John Hardy, entered the coalfields without the slightest intention of working in the mines. When Hardy was hanged for murder at Welch, McDowell County, in 1894, his exploits became the subject of numerous folk songs. While most black migrants to southern West Virginia spent their days loading coal, "John Hardy could fill his days drinking, seeing women, and gambling." Keeping the likes of Hardy out of the coalfields was undoubtedly one reason why some companies manipulated the transportation system in ways designed to retain their black labor force at very low cost. Their manipulations sometimes gave rise to conditions resembling peonage. Some analysts argue that blacks went from the "cotton plantation" to the "coal plantation," and they point to the coercive tactics of the coal operators, such as their use of company detectives.[24]

While employers and their professional recruiters played a leading role in the early recruitment of black labor, black migrants soon established their own migration networks. When Booker T. Washington escaped from slavery and followed Union soldiers into the Kanawha Valley, his stepfather, Washington Ferguson, paved the way for him to work in the mines. After the Civil War, "Wash" Ferguson sent for his wife Jane and her children, including the young Booker T., "who made the trip overland in a wagon, there being no railroad connection as yet with old Virginia." In 1893, former slave James Henry Woodson migrated with his family from nearby Virginia to Huntington, Cabell County, West Virginia. He took a job on the labor crew of the Chesapeake and Ohio Railway, enabling his young son Carter G. Woodson to get mining work at the Kanawha–New River Field. Woodson soon moved out of coal mining, eventually earning a Ph.D. degree from Harvard University and founding the Association for the Study of Negro Life and History.[25]

At the turn of the twentieth century, some black families were still migrating intact, while single men, who often lived in groups in company houses, "were related, or from the same southern town, or in some fashion previously acquainted." During the late 1890s, Leonard Joiner left sharecropping in Sparta, North Carolina, for coal mining in McDowell County and eventually brought three of his brothers, one by one, into the coalfields. When farm laborer Sam Beasley heard that West Virginia was a good place to make money in 1905, he moved from Roxboro, North Carolina, to Gary, McDowell County. After getting a job with the U.S. Coal and Coke Company, he sent for his wife and three children. At about the same time, sharecroppers Walter and Mary Jane Campbell moved with their six children from Statesville, North Carolina, to Maybeury, McDowell County. On the eve of World War I, John W. and Mary Turner left farming in Floyd County, Virginia, for the Winding Gulf coalfields in Raleigh County, where John found work at the Winding Gulf Collieries Company.[26]

Family migration was a difficult process, requiring cooperation and sacrifice. Married men invariably left their families behind for a time when they sought work in the coalfields. Black women maintained the homestead until the family could move. While a few individuals, like Carter G. Woodson and Booker T. Washington, quickly left coal mining, gained substantial education, and eventually became part of the black elite, most black miners finished out their careers as part of the expanding black industrial proletariat. During World War I, working-class black kin and friendship networks would intensify, bringing a new generation of southern black workers into the coal industry.[27]

Coal mining transformed Afro-American life and labor. As rural black men entered the coal mines in growing numbers, their seasonal rhythms of planting, cultivating, and harvesting gradually gave way to the new demands of industrial labor. The techniques of dynamiting coal, a variety of mine safety procedures, and the mental and physical requirements of handloading tons of coal all increasingly supplanted black workers' agricultural skills and work habits. Since coal mining evolved in a semirural area, the transformation was not as radical as it might have been; black coal miners regularly shifted back and forth between farming and work in the coal mines. Moreover, not all black miners faced the same amount of transition. While the black proletariat was primarily comprised of agricultural workers, it also included diverse nonagricultural laborers, particularly railroad men.[28] The black proletariat would come to also include a growing number of veteran miners from other coal regions of the South, but this type of diversification would gain fuller expression during World War I and the 1920s.

Like whites, most blacks entered the mines as manual coal loaders; however, the effects of racial inequality compounded the exploitive impact of the class system blacks experienced. White workers often resisted the hiring of blacks, claiming that "it is a class of labor that meets the approval of the operators here," because "they are used to low wages."[29] When white miners at nearby Raymond City, Putnam County, struck for higher wages in 1891, the black labor leader Richard L. Davis of Ohio rebuked them for having excluded blacks from work in the past. In response to the company's threat to use black strikebreakers, some white miners resolved to use violence. One striker declared, "Mr. Negro, we are ready for the place to be painted red."[30] In several violent incidents between 1890 and 1910, whites attempted to drive blacks out of Mercer County. Another form of white violence, lynchings, also increased, reaching a peak of twelve in 1896 before declining in the early twentieth century. These took place in Mercer, Logan, Fayette, and McDowell counties, although not on the scale that lynchings did elsewhere in the South. As late as 1913, the local black weekly the _McDowell Times_ bitterly denounced the lynching of a black man in Mercer County.[31]

While coal companies overruled the white workers' objections to black employment, they enforced their own brand of ethnic and racial stratification in the workplace. Along with immigrants, employers hired Afro-Americans for the most hazardous underground or "inside" positions, while placing disproportionate numbers of American-born whites in the less dangerous surface or "outside" jobs. Thus, compared to native whites, blacks filled underground positions in nearly the same proportion as immigrants, holding from 85 to 88 percent of them, compared with 85 to 93 percent for immigrants, between 1907 and 1914. While blacks and whites apparently received the same wages for the same job, blacks received a somewhat lower average daily wage than both immigrants and indigenous whites. In 1909, according to available wage data, American-born whites, white immigrants, and blacks, respectively, earned $2.18, $2.14, and $2.10 per day in West Virginia mines.[32]

These lower average earnings for blacks suggest racial discrimination in the assignment and allocation of both inside and outside work. In 1907 in McDowell, Mercer and Mingo counties (and parts of Tazewell County, Virginia), blacks averaged 36 hours per week, compared to 39 for American-born whites and 43 for immigrants. Blacks who gained outside jobs worked mainly in the coke yards— the least desirable of the outside positions, characterized by low pay and unusually hot and arduous labor.[33] Although some blacks gained access to skilled and semiskilled outside jobs on the coal cars such as machine operator or motorman, they were heavily clustered in the brakeman position, the most hazardous one. Between 1911 and 1915, according to economic historian Price V. Fishback, blacks in West Virginia accounted for about 27 percent of all brakemen, but only 14 percent of machine runners, 6 percent of motormen, and 4 percent of foremen. Black foremen, who were described as "honest," "capable," and "efficient," were nonetheless restricted to supervising predominantly black work crews. As for higher managerial and supervisory positions, Afro-Americans were uniformly blocked from them by the discriminatory attitudes of white employers and workers alike. As Fishback succinctly concludes, "Native whites would not work for black bosses."[34] Immigrants also gradually adopted anti-black attitudes and practices, and black miners eventually complained of foreign workers seeking to "Jim Crow" them in the coalfields.

Discriminatory state legislation also blocked black occupational mobility. In 1910, for example, the West Virginia legislature established written examinations for mine foremen and regulations that reduced the significance of practical experience and lengthened educational and training requirements. In 1913–14 West Virginia University established mining extension classes exclusively for white miners, which prepared them for supervisory positions and institutionalized their advantage over blacks. State law mandated that "white and colored persons shall not be taught in the same school."[35] Black workers would not receive similar classes until the 1930s in the midst of the Great Depression, when job opportunities for all miners had dramatically declined.

The precarious employment status of black miners was reinforced by the vagaries of the business cycle. During the depression of the 1890s, the average number of days worked dropped for all miners in West Virginia from 226 in 1890 to a low of 171 in 1894. Average annual earnings likewise dipped from $390 to $301. On the eve of World War I, the average annual days worked dropped from 232 in 1913 to 195 in 1914, and average annual earnings dropped from $461 to $390. In southern West Virginia, racism undoubtedly heightened the impact of downturns such as these on black workers. In the fall of 1913, coal operators in McDowell and Mercer Counties reduced their labor forces by nearly six hundred men. Others introduced short shifts or reduced work time from five or six days per week to between two and four days per week. Many black miners had left the state by November, and others were "leaving daily," the *McDowell Times* reported.[36]

Class and race also shaped black life in the coal-mining community. In housing, public accommodations, education, and social welfare services, black miners were increasingly segregated from immigrants and American-born whites. In the 1880s and 1890s coal companies frequently had placed miners in housing "with little regard to ethnicity, and sometimes little regard to race." As late as 1907, for example, the Standard Pocahontas Coal Company of

Capels, McDowell County, constructed "one long row of houses," where, one immigrant miner recalled, "lots of Italians and colored people lived." This pattern, however, was apparently short-lived, for by 1900 a Washington correspondent reported that Italians in a southern West Virginia mining town lived in a segregated area and "hardly spoke" to or "associated" with blacks. The owner of the Winding Gulf Company town of Tams, Raleigh County, segregated the town along racial and ethnic lines from its beginning in 1909. In the owner's words, "The houses above the tipple were occupied by the Negroes, the section below the tipple by white Americans, and still further down a section for the foreign miners."[37]

Segregation of all kinds had deep roots in the Reconstruction era, and the expansion of the coal industry reinforced and intensified it in the institutional life of the coal-mining community. As new coalfields opened during the late nineteenth and early twentieth centuries, operators upheld the principle of segregation in public schools; supported the continuation of state prohibitions on interracial marriage; and either segregated or excluded blacks from rooming houses, cafes, poolrooms, and theaters. Most coal companies provided the minimum of separate baseball fields for black and white miners, but the most advanced ones maintained a segregated "clubhouse" combination of pool hall, small restaurant, and movie theater.[38]

At the turn of the century, the Raleigh Coal and Coke Company initiated the Raleigh Mining Institute. With funds earned from the company's racially segregated theater, the institute soon sponsored black and white baseball teams and racially segregated community bands. The Island Creek Coal Company (the U.S. Oil Company until 1915) built the town of Holden, Logan County, and provided a segregated "theater, clubhouse and other amenities." By 1912, according to the late historian Robert F. Munn, it was perhaps the best-known model town in the southern West Virginia coalfields. Segregated facilities were also instituted at the Winding Gulf coal town of W. P. Tams. Indeed, one recent historian suggests that the emergence of model town building during the early twentieth century gave a powerful impetus to racial and ethnic segregation. The housing and institutional patterns of "the first coal towns," he argues, "should be carefully distinguished from the enforced segregation of ethnic and racial groups common in company towns of later years."[39]

The expansion and consolidation of the coal industry also reinforced racial segregation in public schools and social welfare institutions. West Virginia's constitution of 1872, drawn up under the control of the Democratic party, mandated racially segregated schools, and in 1873, 1881, and 1901, state law required a minimum of 25, 15, and 10 students respectively, before a community could establish a separate black school. Not only were educational facilities segregated, but the construction and staffing of black schools lagged behind those of their white counterparts. Before World War I, white miners' children gained increasing access to new public high schools, for example, but there were none for blacks in the entire state. In 1868 West Virginia University was founded as a Morrill land grant college for whites, but no separate equivalent university was established for blacks.[40] Although Storer College, founded at Harpers Ferry in 1867, had served the educational needs of blacks from the early postbellum years, blacks in southern West Virginia would not gain access to high and normal school training until the 1890s.[41] The perpetuation of racial discrimination in the state educational system was not merely the result of the attitudes and practices of white capital and labor, but, more profoundly, was a consequence of the discriminatory activities of the state.

Ironically, although racial inequality undermined black miners' access to a better life for themselves and their families, it stimulated the emergence and expansion of a black middle class, particularly its small elite. The number of West Virginia blacks in professional, business, and clerical occupations increased from less than 1,000 in 1900 to over 1,600 in 1910, an increase of over 60 percent. Dominated by a small but slowly expanding upper class of physicians, attorneys, ministers, newspapermen, and educators, the black bourgeoisie responded to the needs of the expanding black proletariat. The *McDowell Times* frequently commented on the "phenom[e]nal success" of black business and professional people in the "southern tier counties of the state."[42] In 1911, Dr. R. G. Harrison, a postgraduate of Howard University's medical school, opened a private hospital in Kimball, McDowell County. Within eighteen months the hospital had performed over three hundred major operations and was described as standing "head and shoulder above any thing of its kind in the state." Including Harrison, seven of the state's most prominent black physicians served on the hospital's staff: James M. Whittico of Williamson, brother of the editor of the *Times;* E. L. Youngue of Welch; D. L. Hilton of Wilcoe; G. N. Marshall of Bluefield; S. A. Viney of Northfork; and W. H. Ambrose Barnett of Keystone. By late 1913, Dr. E. W. Lomax and Dr. N. L. Edwards had developed similar hospitals to serve black patients in Bluefield.[43]

Racial segregation strengthened the bond between black miners and black professionals. In late 1913, Dr. L. Hilton was not only appointed health inspector of "Colored schools" for the Adkins district, McDowell County, but was selected by the U.S. Coal and Coke Company "to give instruction in first aid work" to black miners and their families. "The colored patients are highly pleased with his work," the *Times* reported.[44] Excluded from the larger white medical fraternity, Afro-American physicians had founded the West Virginia Medical Society in 1906. The Flat Top Medical Association, located in the Pocahontas Field, soon emerged as its most important constituent body. In 1913 the state association elected Dr. Roscoe Harrison of Kimball to the presidency. The following year another southern West Virginia physician replaced Harrison, and the city of Keystone hosted the eighth annual meeting of the state body.[45]

Although the number of black attorneys lagged behind that of black physicians, during the 1890s and early 1900s black lawyers gradually increased their practices among black miners in southern West Virginia. The most well known of the early practitioners was the former slave James Knox Smith, who was perhaps the first black lawyer to settle in McDowell County. Apparently he opened his practice in Keystone as early as the late 1880s. Advertising his services as an attorney and "National Jail Robber," Smith emphasized his license to practice in "all criminal courts in the United States 'when my fees are secured.' "[46] Although little is known about his educational background, Smith was apparently less well trained and educated than the growing number of Howard University–trained lawyers who established their practices in southern West Virginia in the prewar years. These Howard law graduates included E. Howard Harper and Tyler Edward Hill of Keystone, McDowell County; James M. Ellis of Oak Hill, Fayette County; Thomas Gillis Nutter of Charleston, Kanawha County; and Harry Jheopart Capehart of Keystone and Welch, McDowell County.[47] Black attorneys S. B. Moon of Wilcoe, McDowell County; William F. Denny of Lester, Raleigh County; W. H. Harris of Bluefield, Mercer County; and Thaddeus E. Harris of Northfork, McDowell County also advertised their services as attorneys at law in southern West Virginia before World War I. Although other prewar black attorneys failed to promote their services in the black press, some, like Arthur G. Froe of Welch, nonetheless figured prominently among black lawyers in the region.[48]

Even more than black physicians, black attorneys combined their professional practice with entrepreneurial activities and appealed directly to black coal miners for business. Under the proprietorship of attorney Harry J. Capehart, one black real estate firm prodded black coal miners: "WHY not own a home in the coalfields where you earn your money?" Capehart offered lots for sale in and near Keystone, Bluefield, Princeton, and other towns in Mercer and McDowell County. Attorney W. H. Harris became an agent for the Pacific Life Insurance Company. In mid-1913 he moved his office from Bluefield to Northfork, McDowell County, "nearer the cent[e]rs of his operations and more convenient for the majority of his policyholders." "Mr. Harris," the *Times* reported, "is doing a big business in the coal fields and offers miners one of the best policies in existence." One prominent black attorney rose directly from the ranks of black coal miners. Born in Tazewell County, Virginia, in 1864, attorney E. H. Harper had served as a coke yard boss at the Houston Coal Company at Elkhorn, McDowell County.[49] The careers of men like Harper who became professionals and served the black proletariat illuminate yet another dimension of the complex relationship between proletarianization and the rise of the black elite.

On the eve of World War I, the black entrepreneurs Archie McKinney and Matthew Buster founded the Eagle Coal Company. In light of the company's dependency on black labor, the Eagle Coal Company's history explicitly illustrates the interrelationship between the rise of the black proletariat and the emergence of the black elite. With McKinney serving as president and Buster serving as secretary-treasurer, the company leased about two hundred acres of coal land in Montgomery, Fayette County, and soon started producing coal for domestic consumption and the steamship market. In 1913 during the Fiftieth Anniversary Celebration of the Emancipation Proclamation in Chicago, the company proudly exhibited a huge piece of its coal, described as having "a very high quality," "especially adapted to steaming uses." McKinney and Buster, a Montgomery news reporter later exclaimed, were "accustomed to handling large affairs," and every indication pointed to "the success of this effort by these progressive Negroes."[50]

Black-owned restaurants, hotels, theaters, and undertaking establishments also catered to the expanding and increasingly segregated Afro-American market. With the exception of the capital city of Charleston, where black businessmen like the grocer C. H. James served a predominantly white clientele, the new black middle class in southern West Virginia did not face competition from an established old elite. Unlike its counterparts elsewhere in America, from the outset the black middle class in southern West Virginia catered to a predominantly black clientele. As one student of West Virginia's black population concluded, "This group began to assist in building a society of Negroes on the pattern of separation . . . and sought to make its position equal."[51]

The expansion of the black coal-mining proletariat that gave rise to the black elite was a dynamic process. It engendered a growing race consciousness among both black miners and the nascent black elite, especially the latter. In an address before the Golden Rule Beneficial and Endowment Association, a local black fraternal and mutual benefit society, President Rev. R. H. McKoy articulated this growing consciousness, declaring that, "if we are to play our part in the great plan of race building and race progress, we must influence, first, ourselves, then others to have confidence in the race."[52] In this atmosphere, under the energetic leadership of Matthew Thomas Whittico, blacks of both classes in southern West Virginia supported the development of the local black weekly the *McDowell Times*.

A graduate of Lincoln University in Pennsylvania, Whittico was born in Ridgeway, Virginia, in 1867. In 1900, in order to edit the *Times*, already underway in McDowell County, he migrated to Keystone, and he went on to purchase the paper in 1904. By 1913, the *Times* served an estimated five thousand subscribers, had purchased a new printing press for $1,600, and had "moved across the street into the Whittico Building recently built and owned by Editor M. T. Whittico." He envisioned the black press as an alternative to the racist reporting of the white press. "The white press champions the cause of all people except the Negro, and upon the question of his rights and privileges with few exceptions the white papers are silent; so it is left for the Negro papers to wage an unceasing warfare upon the enemies of the Negro." In his unrelenting quest for racial solidarity, pride, and social justice in southern West Virginia, Whittico soon popularized the phrase "The Free State of McDowell."[53]

Other black newspapers in the prewar era also promoted the theme of racial solidarity. These included the *Charleston Defender* (later the *Register-Defender*), under the editorship of Rev. George E. Fountain; *Fountain's Digest*, also edited by Rev. Fountain; the *Bluefield Weekly News*, edited by H. Eugene Richardson, a former employee of the *McDowell Times*; and the *Advocate* of Charleston, owned by J. C. Gilmer. Under the editorship of B. F. M. Scott, another former employee of the *Times*, the *Blaze* of Huntington, Cabell County, also vied for the patronage of blacks in southern West Virginia. As new black publications entered the field, editor M. T. Whittico praised his rivals for serving the race "by conducting clean fearless newspapers."[54] Unlike the *McDowell Times*, however, they were all short-lived publications, but they nonetheless added to the Afro-American quest for racial unity, pride, and equity.

By World War I, despite its fragile socioeconomic foundation, the black coal-mining proletariat had fully emerged and given rise to a substantial, although weak black elite. Most of all, the black proletariat had played a major role in its own transformation and settlement in the coalfields. Within the context of the dynamics of coal production, the nature of black life in the rural South, and the hostile white response to its arrival, the black proletariat would also influence the internal institutional, cultural, and political life of blacks in southern West Virginia.

NOTES

1. William H. Harris, *The Harder We Run: Black Workers since the Civil War* (New York: Oxford University Press, 1982), 29–50; Philip S. Foner, *Organized Labor and the Black Worker, 1619–1973* (New York: International Publishers, 1974), pp. 64–135; Sterling D. Spero and Abram L. Harris, *The Black Worker: The Negro and the Labor Movement* (1931; rept., New York: Atheneum, 1968), pp. 53–115.

2. Ronald D Eller, *Miners, Millhands, and Mountaineers: Industrialization of the Appalachian South, 1880–1930* (Knoxville: University of Tennessee Press, 1982), pp. 128–40; David A. Corbin, *Life, Work, and Rebellion in the Coal Fields: The Southern West Virginia Coal Miners, 1880–1922* (Urbana: University of Illinois Press, 1981), pp. 1–7; Darold T. Barnum, *The Negro in the Bituminous Coal Mining Industry* (Philadelphia: University of Pennsylvania Press, 1970), pp. 1–24; Spero and Harris, *The Black Worker*, pp. 206–45; Ronald L. Lewis, *Black Coal Miners in America: Race, Class, and Community Conflict, 1770–1980* (Lexington: University Press of Kentucky, 1987), chap. 7; West Virginia Department of Mines, *Annual Reports, 1909, 1910* (Charleston, W.Va.).

3. Corbin, *Life, Work, and Rebellion*, pp. 8, 43–52; Eller, *Miners, Millhands, and Mountaineers*, pp. 129, 165–75; Barnum, *The Negro in the Coal Industry*, pp. 1–24; Randall G. Lawrence, "Appalachian Metamorphosis: Industrializing Society on the Central Appalachian Plateau, 1860–1913" (Ph.D. diss., Duke University, 1983), pp. 224–28; Price V. Fishback, "Employment Conditions of Blacks in the Coal Industry, 1900–1930" (Ph.D. diss., University of Washington, 1983), pp. 44–51; Lewis, *Black Coal Miners in America*, chap. 7; Kenneth R. Bailey, "A Judicious Mixture: Negroes and Immigrants in the West Virginia Mines, 1880–1917" *West Virginia History* 34 (1973): 141–61;

U.S. Census Office, Report on the Population of the United States, Eleventh Census, 1890 (Washington, 1895), 1:435; U.S. Bureau of the Census, *Thirteenth Census of the United States, 1910* (Washington, 1913), 3:1032–41.

4. W.Va. Department of Mines, *Annual Reports, 1907–14;* Philip M. Conley, *History of the West Virginia Coal Industry* (Charleston, W.Va.: Education Foundation, 1960), pp. 92–150, 202–13, 223–39, and 241–65; W. P. Tams, *The Smokeless Coal Fields of West Virginia: A Brief History* (Morgantown, W.Va.: West Virginia University, 1963), chap. 1; Lawrence, "Appalachian Metamorphosis," pp. 34–42; Eller, *Miners, Millhands, and Mountaineers,* pp. 132–40; James T. Laing, "The Negro Miner in West Virginia" (Ph.D. diss., Ohio State University, 1933), pp. 41–53; Corbin, *Life, Work, and Rebellion,* p. 2; Jerry Bruce Thomas, "Coal Country: The Rise of the Southern Smokeless Coal Industry and its Effect on Area Development, 1872–1910" (Ph.D. diss., University of North Carolina, 1971).

5. John A. Williams, *West Virginia and the Captains of Industry* (Morgantown, W.Va.: University of West Virginia, 1976), pp. 109–29; Charles Kenneth Sullivan, "Coal Men and Coal Towns: Development of the Smokeless Coalfields of Southern West Virginia, 1873–1923" (Ph.D. diss., University of Pittsburgh, 1979); Otis K. Rice, *West Virginia: A History* (Lexington: University Press of Kentucky, 1985), pp. 184–204 (quote is on p. 186); Corbin, *Life, Work, and Rebellion,* pp. 3–4.

6. Williams, *West Virginia and the Captains of Industry,* pp. 109–29; Rice, *West Virginia,* pp. 184–204; Corbin, *Life, Work, and Rebellion,* pp. 2–4; Eller, *Miners, Millhands, and Mountaineers,* pp. 132–40, 165–68; Lawrence, "Appalachian Metamorphosis," pp. 28–42, 64–81.

7. Thomas, "Coal Country," pp. 205–31; Keith Dix, *Work Relations in the Coal Industry: The Handloading Era, 1880–1930* (Morgantown: West Virginia University, 1977), chap. 1; Dix, *What's A Coal Miner To Do?: The Mechanization of Coal Mining and Its Impact on Coal Miners* (Pittsburgh: University of Pittsburgh Press, 1988), chaps. 1 and 2; and Carter Goodrich, *The Miner's Freedom* (1925; rept., New York: Arno Press, 1971), chap. 2.

8. Corbin, *Life, Work, and Rebellion,* pp. 8–10; Fishback "Employment Conditions," pp. 317–19, 359–68; Eller, *Miners, Millhands, and Mountaineers,* pp. 182–86; Lawrence, "Appalachian Metamorphosis," pp. 162–82; Margaret Ripley Wolfe, "Putting Them in Their Places: Industrial Housing in Southern Appalachia, 1900–1930," *Appalachian Journal* 7, no. 3 (Summer 1979): 27–36.

9. Fishback, "Employment Conditions," pp. 90–95, 147–71, 330–68; Eller, *Miners, Millhands, and Mountaineers,* pp. 175–82; Corbin, *Life, Work, and Rebellion,* pp. 8–10, 30–32; Lawrence, "Appalachian Metamorphosis," pp. 228–44.

10. Williams, *West Virginia and the Captains of Industry,* pp. 1–67; Eller, *Miners, Millhands, and Mountaineers,* pp. 210–19; Fishback, "Employment Conditions," pp. 383–421.

11. Rice, *West Virginia,* pp. 163, 184–86; Corbin, *Life, Work, and Rebellion,* pp. 12–13; U.S. Bureau of the Census, *Thirteenth Census of the United States*

1910 (Washington, 1913), 3:1043–44; John A. Williams, *West Virginia: A History* (1976; rept. Nashville, Tenn.: American Association for State and Local History, 1984), p. 116.

12. Williams, *West Virginia and the Captains of Industry*, pp. 115–29; Rice, *West Virginia*, pp. 205–16.

13. Stephen Brier, "Interracial Organizing in the West Virginia Coal Industry: Participation of Black Mine Workers in the Knights of Labor and the United Mine Workers, 1880–1894," pp. 18–43, in Gary M. Fink and Merle E. Reed, eds., *Essays in Southern Labor History* (Westport, Conn.: Greenwood Press, 1977); Corbin, *Life, Work, and Rebellion*, pp. 99–100, 117–45; Hoyt N. Wheeler, "Mountaineer Mine Wars: An Analysis of the West Virginia Mine Wars of 1912–13 and 1920–21," *Business History Review* 50 (Spring 1976): 69–91; Lewis, *Black Coal Miners in America*, chap. 7.

14. Corbin, *Life, Work, and Rebellion*, chaps. 4 and 5.

15. Fishback, "Employment Conditions," especially chap. 6.

16. Laing, "The Negro Miner," chap. 2.

17. Booker T. Washington, *Up From Slavery* (1901; rept., New York: Bantam Books, 1967), pp. 26–28; R. G. Hubbard et al., Malden Homecoming Committee, to Booker T. Washington, 29 May 1913, in B. T. W. Tuskegee Records, Lecture File, Boxes 811 and 816, Booker T. Washington Papers, Manuscript Division, Library of Congress; Louis R. Harlan, *Booker T. Washington: The Making of a Black Leader* (New York: Oxford University Press, 1972), pp. 28–29.

18. Laing, "The Negro Miner," pp. 64–69; J. M. Callahan, *Semi-Centennial History of West Virginia* (Charleston, W.Va., 1913), quoted in Laing, p. 64; A. A. Taylor, *The Negro in the Reconstruction of Virginia* (Associated Publishers, 1926), cited in Laing, pp. 64–65.

19. Laing, "The Negro Miner," chaps. 2 and 3; U.S. Census Office, *Compendium of the Eleventh Census, 1890*, pt. 1, *Population* (Washington, 1892), pp. 660–61; U.S. Bureau of the Census, *Thirteenth Census of the United States, 1910* (Washington, 1914), 4:529.

20. Lawrence, "Appalachian Metamorphosis," pp. 48–64, 90–105; Corbin, *Life, Work, and Rebellion*, pp. 62–63; Laing, "The Negro Miner," pp. 41–72; Eller, *Miners, Millhands, and Mountaineers*, pp. 168–72; Fishback, "Employment Conditions," pp. 72–88; Spero and Harris, *The Black Worker*, pp. 206–45; Thomas, "Coal Country," chap. 6; Lewis, *Black Coal Miners in America*, chap. 7; Charles W. Simmons et al., "Negro Coal Miners in West Virginia, 1875–1925," *Midwest Journal* 61 (Spring 1954): 60–69; U.S. Bureau of the Census, *Negroes in the United States, 1920–32* (Washington, 1935), p. 45; U.S. Bureau of the Census, *Negro Population, 1790–1915* (Washington, 1918), p. 85.

21. Lawrence, "Appalachian Metamorphosis," pp. 48–64, 90–105.

22. See various issues of the *McDowell Times*, 1913–14, especially "New River and Pocahontas Consolidated Collieries Company," 16 May 1913, and "The Flat Top Coal Field: Advantages Offered Laborers—Conditions Good," 30 May 1913.

23. Bailey, "A Judicious Mixture," pp. 141–61 (quote is on p. 157); Eller, *Miners, Millhands, and Mountaineers*, pp. 169–71; Lewis, *Black Coal Miners in America*, chap. 7; Spero and Harris, *The Black Worker*, pp. 206–45.

24. Lawrence, "Appalachian Metamorphosis," pp. 104–5; Simmons et al., "Negro Coal Miners in West Virginia," pp. 63–64.

25. Washington, *Up From Slavery*, pp. 18–19; Louis R. Harlan, *Booker T. Washington*, pp. 28–29; Harlan, ed., *The Booker T. Washington Papers*, vol. 1, *The Autobiographical Writings* (Urbana: University of Illinois Press, 1972), pp. 13, 15–19; Tim R. Massey, "Carter G. Woodson," *Goldenseal* 13 (Winter 1987), pp. 31–32; Laing, "The Negro Miner," p. 68; Lawrence, "Appalachian Metamorphosis," pp. 98–99; Lewis, *Black Coal Miners in America*, chap. 7.

26. Lawrence, "Appalachian Metamorphosis," pp. 98–99; interviews with William M. Beasley, 26 July 1983, Andrew Campbell, 19 July 1983, Walter and Margaret Moorman, 14 July 1983, and Preston Turner, 26 July 1983; Massey, "Carter G. Woodson," pp. 31–32. Cf. Nell I. Painter, *Exodusters: Black Migration to Kansas after Reconstruction* (1976; rept., Lawrence: University Press of Kansas, 1986), especially chap. 15.

27. Corbin, *Life, Work, and Rebellion*, pp. 64–65; Lewis, *Black Coal Miners in America*, chap. 7. See also chap. 3 below.

28. Gilbert C. Fite, *Cotton Fields No More: Southern Agriculture, 1865–1980* (Lexington: University Press of Kentucky, 1984); James C. Cobb, *Industrialization and Southern Society, 1877–1984* (Lexington: University Press of Kentucky, 1984); C. Vann Woodward, *Origins of the New South, 1877–1913* (1951; rept., Baton Rouge: Louisiana State University Press, 1971); Pete Daniel, "The Crossroads of Change: Cotton, Tobacco, and Rice Cultures in the Twentieth-Century South," *Journal of Southern History* 50, no. 3 (1984): 428–56. Simmons et al., "Negro Coal Miners in West Virginia," pp. 62–64; Bailey, "A Judicious Mixture," pp. 156–61; Lewis, *Black Coal Miners in America*, chaps. 7, 8; Lawrence "Appalachian Metamorphosis," pp. 101–3; Corbin, *Life, Work, and Rebellion*, p. 41.

29. Corbin, *Life, Work and Rebellion*, p. 63.

30. Brier, "Interracial Organizing in the West Virginia Coal Industry," pp. 18–43.

31. Laing, "The Negro Miner," pp. 493–94; John R. Sheeler, "The Negro in West Virginia before 1900" (Ph.D. diss., West Virginia University, 1954), pp. 262–63, 288; Lawrence, "Appalachian Metamorphosis," pp. 183–86; "Sensitive Police," 25 July 1913, "Bluefield Police," 18 July 1913, "Grim Tragedy Follow[s] Tragedy," 7 Nov. 1913, "Wanton Murder of Negro by Two White Men," 4 July 1913, in *McDowell Times*.

32. Fishback, "Employment Conditions," table 22, p. 149, and table 50, p. 283; George T. Surface, "The Negro Mine Laborer: Central Appalachian Coal Field," *Annals of the American Academy of Political and Social Sciences* 33 (1909): 120–21; Simmons et al., "Negro Coal Miners in West Virginia," pp. 65–66; West Virginia Department of Mines, *Annual Reports, 1907, 1910* (Charleston, W.Va.).

33. Fishback, "Employment Conditions," table 22, p. 149, and table 50,

p. 283; Surface, "The Negro Mine Laborer," pp. 120–21; Simmons et al., "Negro Coal Miners in West Virginia," pp. 65–66.

34. Fishback, "Employment Conditions," table 22, p. 149, and table 50, p. 283, chaps. 4 and 7, especially pp. 309–10; Memphis T. Garrison, newspaper clipping, *Welch Daily News*, 21 Sept. 1926, in U. G. Carter Papers, West Virginia Collection, West Virginia University.

35. Fishback, "Employment Conditions," table 22, p. 149, and table 50, p. 283; and Garrison, newspaper clipping. For historical data on mining extension work in West Virginia, see West Virginia State College Mining Extension Service, *Annual Report, 1942–43*, in U. G. Carter Papers, West Virginia Collection, Morgantown, W.Va.; Homer L. Morris, *The Plight of the Bituminous Coal Miner* (Philadelphia: University of Pennsylvania Press, 1934), pp. 207–8; and Sheeler, "The Negro in West Virginia," chaps. 8 and 9, especially pp. 232–45.

36. Fishback, "Employment Conditions," pp. 94–179; "Coal Companies: Reducing Forces, Working Shifts," *McDowell Times*, 28 Nov. 1913; W.Va. Department of Mines, *Annual Reports, 1913, 1914*.

37. Lawrence, "Appalachian Metamorphosis," p. 179; Lewis, *Black Coal Miners in America*, p. 150; Tams, *The Smokeless Coal Fields*, p. 67. For commentary on prewar shanty dwellings, see W. H. Harris, "Exceptional Opportunities . . . At Olga Shaft Coalwood, W.Va.," 8 Sept. 1916, and Ralph W. White, "Weyanoke: The Eldorado of the Coal Fields," 13 July 1917, in *McDowell Times*.

38. Sullivan, "Coal Men and Coal Towns," pp. 29, 162, 194.

39. Sullivan, "Coal Men and Coal Towns," pp. 29, 162, 194. Robert F. Munn, "The Development of Model Towns in the Bituminous Coal Fields," *West Virginia History* 40, no. 3 (Spring 1979): 243–53; Tams, *The Smokeless Coal Fields*, pp. 51–67.

40. William P. Jackameit, "A Short History of Negro Public Higher Education in West Virginia, 1890–1965," *West Virginia History* 37, no. 4 (July 1976): 309–24; Sheeler, "The Negro in West Virginia," pp. 203–8, 218–34; Charles H. Ambler, *A History of Education in West Virginia: From Early Colonial Times to 1949* (Huntington, W.Va.: Standard Printing and Publishing Company, 1951), p. 409.

41. Rice, *West Virginia*, pp. 244–46; Sheeler, "The Negro in West Virginia," pp. 203–8, 223–61; Ambler, *A History of Education in West Virginia*, p. 409; Jackameit, "A Short History of Negro Public Higher Education," pp. 309–24; John C. Harlan, *History of West Virginia State College, 1890–1965* (Dubuque, Iowa: Wm. C. Brown Company, 1968); "Storer College," Box 1, Storer College Papers, West Virginia Collection, West Virginia University.

42. "Locals," 9 May 1913, "New Surgeon Dentist in Keystone," 7 Nov. 1913, "Dr. S. A. Viney is Claimed by Death," 7 May 1915, "Hospital Moved to New Location," 7 Jan. 1916, and "Dr. Crichlow's Hospital Doing Good Work," 19 Oct. 1917, all in *McDowell Times*.

43. "The Harrison Hospital," 9 May 1913, "The Lomax Hospital," 7 Nov, 1913, "Bluefield," 12 Dec. 1913, "Williamson Notes," 30 May 1913, "J. E. Hereford: Physician and Surgeon," 23 Jan. 1914, in *McDowell Times*.

44. "Bridgeford Pharmacy Doing Big Business," 16 May 1913, "News," 26 Sept. 1913 and 3 Oct. 1913, "Wilcoe News," 19 Dec. 1913, in *McDowell Times*.

45. "West Virginia Medical Society," 13 June 1913, "Meeting of the Flat Top Medical Association," 24 Oct. 1913, "West Virginia Medical Society: Great Meeting," 22 May 1914, in *McDowell Times*.

46. West Virginia Bureau of Negro Welfare and Statistics (WVBNS), *Biennial Report, 1925–26* (Charleston, W.Va.), pp. 51–52; "Jas. Knox Smith," 16 May 1913, "An Ex-Slave is Very Successful Attorney," 26 Feb. 1915, "J. K. Smith Ready to Help Unfortunate," 3 Sept. 1915, in *McDowell Times*.

47. C. W. Swisher, ed., *Manual of the State of West Virginia, 1907–1908* (Charleston, W.Va.: The Tribune Printing Company, 1907), p. 114; John T. Harris, ed., *West Virginia Legislative Hand Book and Manual* (Charleston, W.Va.: The Tribune Printing Company, 1917), p. 737, (1920), p. 258, (1928), pp. 220–21, and (1929), p. 201; "Howard Harper for Legislature," 16 June 1916, and "Negro Elected to the Legislature," 24 Nov. 1916, in *McDowell Times*.

48. Harris, ed., *West Virginia Legislative Hand Book, Manual and Official Register*, (1920), p. 241; "Secretary of Colored Organization Passes Bar Examination," 13 June 1913, "S. B. Moon," 14 Nov. 1913, "William F. Denny," 19 June 1914, "Our Raleigh County Representative," 18 Sept. 1914, "Special Agent, Pacific Life Insurance Company," 5 Nov. 1915, editorial page, 2 Jan. 1914, "Raising the Standard," 11 July 1913, and "Thaddeus E. Harris," 25 July 1913, all in *McDowell Times*; presidential case file no. 51, Commissioners of the District of Columbia, folder no. 39, Arthur Froe, Warren G. Harding Papers, Manuscript Division, Library of Congress.

49. "Bargains in M'Dowell Co. Real Estate," 22 Aug. 1913, "William F. Denny," 26 June, 3 July, and 10 July 1914, "W. H. Harris Moves Down to Northfork," 18 July 1913, in *McDowell Times*; Harris, ed., *West Virginia Legislative Hand Book* (1917), p. 737.

50. "Negro Operating Coal Mine," 27 Aug. 1915, "Montgomery," 28 July 1916, in *McDowell Times*.

51. "New Hotel to be Built in Keystone," 28 Nov. 1913, "Bluefield," 12 Dec. 1913, and advertisement page, 9 May 1913, *McDowell Times*; Sheeler, "The Negro in West Virginia," pp. 267–69. For a comparative discussion of the black middle class, see Joe William Trotter, Jr., *Black Milwaukee: The Making of an Industrial Proletariat, 1915–45* (Urbana: University of Illinois Press, 1985), chaps. 3 and 7.

52. "Address of Rev. McKoy," *McDowell Times*, 3 July 1914.

53. "Editor Mr. Whittico," 23 Feb. 1917, "Whittico Dead," 23 June 1939, "The Fight Will Go On," 8 Aug. 1913, "McDowell Times Moves," 13 June 1913, and "M'Dowell Congratulated by the Pioneer Press," 27 June 1913, in *McDowell Times*.

54. "The W.Va. Register-Defender," 23 May 1913, "Will Working for the Common Good Pay?," 1 Aug. 1913, "The Blaze," 23 May 1913, "Locals," 1 Aug. 1913, and "The Advocate," 17 Oct. 1913, in *McDowell Times*.

2

Class, Race, and Community

The emergence of the black coal-mining proletariat played a pivotal role in the rise of the black community in southern West Virginia. Black religious, fraternal, and political organizations dramatically expanded. Afro-American institution-building activities not only reflected growing participation in the coal economy, rapid population growth, and the effects of racial discrimination (discussed in chapter 1), but also both reflected and stimulated the rise of a vigorous black leadership. As elsewhere, however, although the black community developed a high level of racial solidarity in the process, it failed to fully surmount internal conflicts along class lines. As a prelude to understanding the shifting war and postwar patterns of Afro-American culture, community, and power in the coalfields, this chapter analyzes their prewar development. The black church, fraternal orders, and state and local politics offer the most sensitive barometers of change in these areas within the black coal-mining community.

The independent Afro-American churches in southern West Virginia had their roots in the early emancipation era. Until the Civil War, blacks had worshipped in the same congregations as whites, but on a segregated basis. Following the Civil War, as elsewhere in the South, Afro-Americans increasingly separated from white religious institutions. Under the leadership of Rev. Lewis Rice, for example, the African Zion Baptist Church at Tinkerville (Malden), Kanawha County, spearheaded the independent black Baptist movement in southern West Virginia. Belonging to the Providence Association of Ohio, formed in 1868, the African Zion Baptist Church stimulated the rise of new "arms of the African Zion Church" in West Virginia. By 1873, as a result of the church's vigorous organizing activities, West Virginia's black Baptists seceded from the Ohio conference and formed the Mt. Olivet Baptist Association. Until he left the region in 1880, Booker T. Washington was a member, Sunday School teacher, and clerk of the "mother church" at Malden.[1]

As the processes of black migration, proletarianzation, and institutional racism converged during the late nineteenth and early twentieth centuries, black religious institutions dramatically expanded. Black membership in West Virginia religious organizations increased by 100 percent, from over 7,000 in 1890 to nearly 15,000 in 1906. Although blacks developed a thriving Presbyterian church in McDowell County, and although the number of African Methodist Episcopal churches increased to over 35 at the turn of the century, Baptists dominated the region's black religious life. In 1906 the United States *Census of Religious Bodies* reported a total of 148 black Baptist churches in the Mountain State. New congregations were initiated and new associations rapidly emerged in McDowell, Mercer, Raleigh, Fayette, Mingo, and Logan counties. The Mt. Olivet Baptist Association was soon followed by the New River Baptist Association (1884), the Flat Top Baptist Association (1896), and the Guyan Valley Association (1913). The Flat Top Baptist Association, located in the Pocahontas Field, became the largest and financially richest in West Virginia.[2]

Black religious life both mirrored and stimulated the growth of an energetic black ministry. The number of black ministers increased from 93 in 1900 and to 150 a decade later. Black ministers played a major role in harnessing working-class financial resources to pay church debts, although some preached for months without pay. Sometimes their fund-raising efforts were quite successful. In May 1913, for example, under the pastorship of Rev. R. H. McKoy, the Bluestone Baptist Church at Bramwell, Mercer County, "closed one of the most successful [financial] rallies in its history," raising $330 over a two-week period. Under the pastorship of Rev. R. V. Barksdale, in July 1913 the First Baptist Church of Anawalt, McDowell County, raised $400 in a special rally.[3] When a fire destroyed the St. James Baptist Church in Welch, Rev. W. R. Pittard and his congregation launched a spirited rebuilding campaign. Within six months, they had raised nearly $500.[4] As suggested in chapter 1, coal companies often gave financial support to black and white churches, but their assistance was not enough to sustain black churches. Only the persistence of black coal miners, their families, and their ministers in contributing to the churches fully explains their success in the coalfields. Black religious life would gain even greater importance in the wake of World War I and the Great Migration.

If the resources of black coal miners underlay the material well-being of the church, their spiritual and cultural needs shaped patterns of church worship and participation. Rooted deeply in the religious experience of southern blacks, the black church in southern West Virginia helped to sustain and reinforce the black workers' spiritual and communal beliefs and practices through sermons, revival meetings, baptismal ceremonies, and funeral rites. At a May 1914 revival meeting, Rev. C. H. Rollins of the Slab Fork Baptist Church "preached two able sermons to an appreciative audience." Taking his texts from Matthew 7:7 and Zechariah 13:1, he "preached so powerful that we were made to say within ourselves as one of the apostles of old, 'Did not our hearts burn within us as he talked by the way.' "[5] At the Wingfield Baptist Church in Eckman, McDowell County, a huge crowd gathered at the river's edge to witness "the 'plunging under' or the 'Burial in Baptism' " of the new converts. "People from all over the county hearing of the occasion . . . came on every train, both east and west. A densely packed crowd of men and women, boys and girls . . . were there."[6] In mid-1913 a funeral for a black miner who died in a slate fall was conducted at the Mt. Ebenezer Baptist Church near Gilliam, McDowell County, where he was a member in good standing. Rev. L. A. Watkins preached the funeral sermon to a host of "friends and relatives," selecting his text from St. John 19:30, "When Jesus therefore had received the vinegar, he said, It is finished: and he bowed his head, and gave up the ghost." The choir sang the deceased miner's favorite hymn, "Will the Waters Be Chilly?"[7] Moreover, besides attending funerals and other local church functions, through frequent visits to their old southern homes, black workers renewed their ties with the established religious customs of their past.[8]

As blacks entered the southern West Virginia coalfields in greater numbers, although they retained important cultural links with their rural past, their religious beliefs and practices underwent gradual transformation. Although the evidence is quite sparse, apparently an educated black ministry gradually emerged in the prewar years. Under its leadership, emotional services increasingly gave way to ones featuring rational and logical sermons often concerned with improving temporal social, economic, and political conditions, and above all, with the proper attitude and behavior for racial progress in the new industrial age.[9] These emphases undoubtedly had antecedents in the southern black religious experience, but they emerged clearly within the socioeconomic, political, and cultural environment of southern West Virginia.

The growing pool of educated black preachers included school-teachers who doubled as ministers such as Rev. J. W. Robinson, principal of the Tidewater Grade School. In November 1913, Rev. Robinson was installed as pastor of the First Baptist Church of Kimball. "He is one of the best known and ablest men in the state, an advocator of note and a preacher of great ability," the *McDowell Times* reported. But perhaps the best example of the rising educated black ministry was Rev. Mordecai W. Johnson, who took the pastorship of the First Baptist Church of Charleston, West Virginia, in 1913. Born in 1890 in Paris, Henry County, Tennessee, Rev. Johnson received a B.A. degree from Morehouse College in Atlanta in 1911, where he taught economics and history for a while, and another from the University of Chicago in 1913. In the postwar years he would leave the First Baptist Church for a position at Howard University, where, in 1926, he would become its first black president. Before leaving, though, Rev. Johnson played an important role not only in the religious life of the community, but also in the civil rights struggle.[10]

Some influential ministers in southern West Virginia were self-taught. The pastor of several black churches in Kanawha County, Rev. Nelson Barnett of Huntington, Cabell County, was perhaps the most gifted. Born a slave in Buckingham County, Virginia, in 1842, Barnett migrated to West Virginia in 1873 and eventually became the pastor of churches in St. Albans, Longacre, and Raymond City. Upon his death in 1909, the *Huntington Dispatch* wrote: "He lacked the learning of the schools because he was born a slave. But he was of a studious turn of mind, gifted in speech, could expound the scriptures with an insight truly remarkable, and his preaching was wonderfully effective in bringing men to Christ."[11] The funeral sermon for Barnett, preached by the educated black minister Rev. I. V. Bryant of Huntington, was even more eloquent. "If by education we mean the drawing out of the latent powers and spreading them in glowing characters upon the canvas of the mind, if by education we mean the proper cultivation of all the faculties, the symmetrical development of the head, the heart, and the hand, together with those combined elements that make the entire man, I positively deny that he was uneducated. . . . he was taught by the Great God."[12]

Both formally and informally educated black ministers helped to transform black workers' religious beliefs and practices. By appealing to the intellect, rather than merely the emotions, of their congregants, they helped to rationalize black religious services. Rev.

Barnett, his eulogizer stated, "preached industry as well as religion, and had accumulated considerable property, owning two or three houses and lots in the city. He was active in all interests for the betterment of his race, and took particular interest in the education of young people who regard him as a father."[13] In his sermon before the Seventeenth Annual Meeting of the Flat Top Baptist Association, Rev. G. W. Woody stressed "the fact that men must work for this world's goods." "In conclusion, Rev. Woody grew more forceful and urged upon the brethren to be patient in the small details of their life's work." Before World War I, Rev. J. H. Hammond of Jenkinjones became an agent of the *McDowell Times* and received praise for helping the "educational uplift of his race." And in late 1914, the Baptist minister Rev. J. W. Crockett was elected to the Northfork District School Board of McDowell County.[14]

As black ministers broadened their interest in the here and now, their sermons before their coal-mining congregations underwent a gradual change. In two sermons at Giatto, a black Baptist minister was both "forceful and practical." At the First Baptist Church of Kimball, Rev. R. D. W. Meadows "preached one of the most profound and scholarly sermons." Another sermon "showed much thought in preparation" and delivery. Still another Baptist minister "preached a strong and scholarly sermon." At a meeting of the Winding Gulf Ministerial and Deacons Union, Rev. T. J. Brandon "gave a high class lecture to preachers and congregation on how they should act in church." On the same occasion, another minister delivered an "able" and "instructive" sermon on the subject, "Behave." When the "spirit" threatened to overcome him, another Baptist minister took "pains as to control his voice." Yet however rational and controlled black sermons may have become, black ministers worked to retain contact with the traditional black culture and consciousness of black workers. At the Baptist church in Keystone, Rev. Brown of Kimball preached "quite a deep sermon," but he nonetheless emphasized, "It matters not how much learning one may have, unless they have the Spirit of God they cannot have power to do the best work of life."[15]

Unlike the Baptist church, both the Methodist Episcopal and the African Methodist Episcopal churches were more hierarchical in their administrative structures. Their hierarchies exercised greater control over ministers and congregations—in particular, controlling the mandatory movement of ministers from one church to another—and vigorously promoted an educated black ministry. These two churches were nonetheless deeply enmeshed within the spiritual traditions of southern blacks. Utilizing Baptist ministers, for example, the Methodists often conducted revivals and engaged in spirited meetings similar to the Baptists'. In April 1914 the Northfork Methodist Episcopal Church conducted a revival that resulted in 51 accessions, 26 new converts, and 25 more converts by letter. Under the pastorship of Rev. W. R. Burger, the *McDowell Times* suggested, the Methodists, like the Baptists, understood how "to shout, sing, preach and pray."[16] Yet over time, black Methodists and Presbyterians in southern West Virginia, as elsewhere, gradually shed the spiritual and emotional aspects of their religious traditions more rapidly than the Baptists. Within three years after Rev. James Gipson's transfer from the AME Kentucky Conference to Williamson, West Virginia, Gipson developed a reputation as "a hard worker, constructive in mind and progressive in spirit." Under his leadership, the congregation grew from eight members to forty members and moved from an inadequate public hall near the railroad tracks to a new brick building in a previously all-white area; the church's assets grew from a mere 44 cents to over $800, the minister's salary not included; and, starting with no church auxiliaries, a "flourishing" array of them was begun.[17]

Under the pastorship of Rev. R. P. Johnson, the small Presbyterian church of Kimball developed a more energetic social orientation. In December 1913, the church held a sacred concert. The program featured a variety of guest speakers who addressed a broad range of religious, political, and social issues. In his speech, attorney H. J. Capehart, the *Times* reported, emphasized the need to make "services so varied and instructive that they will appeal to all classes. He spoke of the gymnasium, the swimming pool, reading room, sewing circle and settlement work as examples of the work being done by adher[e]nts of the new school of thought in religious worship."[18] In an address titled "My Dream of the Future Church," attorney T. E. Hill looked forward to a church that practiced the principles of social justice and equality. "In this institution there will be no color line, the brotherhood of man will be a fact instead of a catch phrase and it will seek to save the bodies as well as the souls of mankind." In another example of the black church's growing social bent, the pastor Rev. R. P. Johnson developed a vigorous ministry among black convicts on the road crews of McDowell County and also a Sunday School Relief Department, which was designed to aid the working-class "poor of our town, especially children whose parents are not able to keep them in school and Sunday school."[19]

In addition to joining churches, black coal miners participated in an expanding network of fraternal organizations and mutual benefit societies. By World War I black fraternal orders included the Elks, the Knights of Pythias, the Odd Fellows, the Independent Order of St. Luke, and the Golden Rule Beneficial and Endowment Association.[20] The Golden Rule Association emerged as one of the most energetic of the prewar black fraternal orders. Formed in 1903 under the leadership of Rev. R. H. McKoy, the order established headquarters at Bramwell, Mercer County, and served blacks in southern West Virginia and parts of Kentucky and Virginia. Within one decade the organization proudly celebrated its success: fifty-four subordinate lodges, twenty-six nurseries serving young people aged three to sixteen, over 5,280 members, and over $13,000 paid out in death and sick claims. In numerous churches in the coalfields, Rev. McKoy and officers of the Golden Rule Association publicly paid benefits in ceremonies replete with speeches—indeed, sermons—on the value of the order. In July 1913, for example, the organization paid the endowment of one member "before an overflowing congregation."[21] With God's help, McKoy stated, "The continued progress of the Golden Rule Association means the actual progress of the race in a tangible form.[22]

Within the framework of black religious culture, the fraternal orders offered black coal miners an opportunity to protect their material interests. The obituary for John Panell, who lost his life in a slate fall at Gilliam, McDowell County, noted Panell's membership in the Grand United Order of Odd Fellows. Samuel Blackwell, who died of injuries sustained in a slate fall, belonged to the Shining Light Association of the Golden Rule Beneficial and Endowment Association. The 1913 obituary of A. H. Hudle described him as "a consistent Christian, a member of the A. M. E. Church . . . [and] a member of the Grand United Order of Odd Fellows and also a Knight of Pythias."[23] All these black fraternal orders offered mutual aid and insurance plans to their members that promised to cushion them and their families against hard times.

At the same time as fraternal orders addressed the material welfare of black workers, they repeatedly reinforced the communal and spiritual aspects of their culture. In company and noncompany towns, the fraternal parade, replete with marching band in full regalia, and the annual thanksgiving sermon emerged as prominent features of Afro-American life in the coalfields. In May 1913, for example, at Keystone and Eckman, McDowell County, the Grand United Order of Odd Fellows held their Thirteenth Annual Thanksgiving Parade and Services. Led by Lord's Cornet Band, the order assembled at Lord's Opera House, in Keystone, marched up Main Street, and wound its way to Eckman, where the Odd Fellows then assembled at the Wingfield Baptist Church. There Rev. L. E. Johnson called the service to order, Rev. William Manns read the scripture, and Rev. Dabney "preached one of the most forceful sermons ever heard here." Taking his text from the 133rd Psalm, Rev. Dabney exclaimed, "Behold how good and how pleasant it is for brethren to dwell together in unity." Over one thousand people witnessed the parade and services.[24]

If the fraternal orders helped to reinforce the religious culture of black workers, they also helped to link black miners to the larger Afro-American political and civil rights campaign. The fraternal orders invited major political figures to speak at the annual thanksgiving services and parades.[25] In 1913 the Keystone and Eckman Odd Fellows secured Republican Governor H. D. Hatfield as their guest speaker. Similarly, at the Twenty-first Annual Meeting of the West Virginia Knights of Pythias, held at Charleston's First Baptist Church, Mayor J. F. Bedell addressed the gathering.[26] In this manner, blacks used the fraternal orders to subtly and not so subtly advance their political aims.

More important, unlike most of their counterparts in other southern states, Afro-Americans in West Virginia received the franchise in 1870 and retained it throughout the period between Reconstruction and World War I. During the 1890s and early 1900s, at a time when other southern blacks were being disfranchised, black coal miners in southern West Virginia exercised a growing impact on state and local politics. West Virginia blacks developed a highly militant brand of racial solidarity, marked by persistent demands for full equality, albeit on a segregated basis.[27]

Afro-American unity across class lines was most evident in protests against racial violence. When whites lynched a black man at Hemphill, McDowell County in 1896, an aroused black community, workers and elite members alike, confronted local authorities with demands for justice and protection. Under the leadership of prominent middle-class blacks, an estimated five to eight hundred blacks held a mass meeting in the company town of Elkhorn, McDowell County. The group petitioned both county and company officials, demanding an investigation. Although the guilty parties were apparently never brought to justice, the blacks involved did secure public announcements from government and company officials promising an investigation to determine the guilty parties.[28]

Black coal miners and their elite allies supplemented their protest activities with electoral politics. As early as 1873, Charleston appointed its first black public official, Ernest Porterfield, who served as a regular policeman. In 1877 the former coal miner Booker T. Washington began his public speaking career as a Kanawha County Republican. According to biographer Louis R. Harlan, Washington played a major role in mobilizing the black vote in the successful campaign to relocate the state capital from Wheeling to Charleston. Washington not only supported the relocation of the capital, a change backed by powerful white Republicans in the state, but also joined other blacks in tying the capital campaign to the issue of equity for blacks within the party and the state. "Washington began his speeches for the capital on June 27, at a rally in Charleston of 'the colored citizens of Kanawha.' . . . A resolution of the meeting claimed 'the right to a fair portion of the public institutions' in their part of the state." Although Washington later abandoned this vigorous political tradition, most blacks in southern West Virginia did not. Even so, the state's powerful Democratic party, which called itself the "white man's party," reinforced by the Ku Klux Klan in the early post–Civil War years, kept black Republican influence at bay.[29]

For the next two decades Democrats controlled West Virginia's political machinery. The party's constituency included voters in counties that were predominantly agricultural, workers in the industrial centers of northern West Virginia, and, increasingly, the state's powerful industrialists. By the early 1890s the Democrats not only regularly returned their candidate to the governor's mansion, but returned majorities to the state legislature as well.[30] The increasing migration of blacks into the region, however, set the stage for the resurgence of the Republican party during the late 1890s. By 1910 blacks made up over 17 percent of the state's voting-age (male) population. Immigrants made up 13 percent, but their voting potential was actually much lower, for only 11.5 percent of voting-age immigrants were naturalized and eligible to vote. Thus, the rise of the black coal-mining proletariat gave Afro-Americans the decisive balance of power in Mountain State politics. As early as the gubernatorial election of 1888, for example, the Republican candidate defeated his Democratic opponent by a narrow margin of 110 votes. Democrats contested the vote, arguing that several hundred black migrants in Mercer and McDowell Counties "had voted without the required period of residence and that many of them were, in fact, migratory or transitory workers with no fixed abode." More than a year later, a special session of the legislature awarded the office to the Democratic candidate by a margin of 237 votes. In the gubernatorial election of 1896, however, the Republican candidate George W. Atkinson courted black voters and won the governorship by more than 12,000 votes. Although the Democratic party continued to control the legislature, Republicans made increasing inroads there as well.[31]

Despite the increasing role of black voters in Republican victories, blacks fought an uphill battle for recognition within the party. As one state historian has noted, in addition to courting the black vote, Republicans appealed to mountain whites for vital support by rejecting "unpopular national issues, especially federal intervention in racial matters." Thus they were able to "overcome identification with the black population and hated Reconstruction policies," which included the enfranchisement of blacks. For example, even as G. W. Atkinson campaigned for black votes, he loudly proclaimed his belief in white supremacy. In a letter to the *New York World*, Governor Atkinson affirmed his Southern roots and racial beliefs: "I am a Virginian, and am therefore 'to the manor born.' . . . Southern people will not submit to negro rule. 'They will die first.' This is an old Southern expression, and they mean it when they say it." Within this racist framework, however, Atkinson and similar Republicans made room for an alliance with West Virginia blacks around the issue of education. Atkinson delivered a scathing attack on Mississippi Senator James K. Vardaman, who sought to deprive blacks of the right to an education: "When he says it is folly to attempt to advance the negro race by education, and in any way qualify them for responsibility and power . . . because by so doing we spoil corn-field hands and make 'shyster' professional men,—he simply loses sight of good judgment and fair dealing, and seeks to vent his narrowness, prejudice and spleen against his 'brother in black.' "[32]

In order to push for greater influence in the Republican party, forty-nine black delegates met in Charleston in 1888. They attacked the Republicans for "absolutely" refusing to give blacks "the recognition" to which they were "entitled, notwithstanding the fact that there are eleven thousand colored voters in the state, nearly all of whom are Republicans." These black voters were not merely Republicans; more fundamentally, they were coal miners. They added substance to the Afro-American protests against racial injustice within the party of their allies. It was the black coal miners' vote that enabled middle-class black politicians to gain increasing access to public office in southern West Virginia.

Over the next decade the expanding proletarian electorate fueled the Afro-American campaign for elective and appointive office. In 1896 Republicans elected the first Afro-American, Christopher Payne, to the state legislature. Born in Monroe County, West Virginia, Payne was, in turn, a teacher, preacher, and attorney. Allied with Nehemiah Daniels, a powerful white Republican and county sheriff, Payne entered the statehouse from Fayette County, signaling the gradual rise of black power in southern West Virginia. Payne's election also inaugurated a long tradition of black Republican legislators in West Virginia. Attorney James M. Ellis of Oak Hill, Fayette County, succeeded Payne in the legislative sessions of 1903, 1907, and 1909, while the educator H. H. Railey of Fayette County served in the 1905 session.[33]

In 1904 blacks in the Pocahontas district formed the McDowell County Colored Republican Organization (MCCRO). Over the next decade, the MCCRO claimed credit for a growing number of black elected and appointed officials. In November 1913 the organization celebrated its achievements: six deputy sheriffs, three guards on the county road, constables and justices of the peace in four districts, members of school boards in three districts, and the state librarian, a post first held by the influential schoolteacher and Grand Chancellor of the West Virginia Knights of Pythias L. O. Wilson. Open to "All Negro Republicans," the officers of the MCCRO in 1913 included the deputy sheriff Joe E. Parsons, president; the attorney S. B. Moon, recording secretary; the educator E. M. Craghead, corresponding secretary; and attorney A. G. Froe, treasurer.[34] Black coal miners were a powerful springboard for the political ascent of educated blacks in southern West Virginia.

Nowhere did the political alliance of black workers and black elites in the region produce greater results than in the educational system. Afro-Americans ranked education as their first priority. In their expanding electoral activities, they increasingly demanded equal access to the state's educational resources. In rapid succession during the 1880s and 1890s, the state funded black public schools in Fayette, McDowell, Mercer, and Kanawha counties. In 1891 the state legislature established West Virginia Colored [Collegiate] Institute, a Morrill land grant college for the training of blacks in "agricultural and mechanical arts." Four years later, the legislature created the Bluefield Colored [Collegiate] Institute by "an act to establish a High Grade School at Bluefield, Mercer County, for the colored youth of the State."[35]

Storer College was the earliest institution to offer West Virginia blacks an education "above the common school grades." Founded in 1867 at Harpers Ferry, Jefferson County, for the next twenty-five years Storer would remain the only such school.[36] Following the establishment of the Bluefield Colored Institute and the West Virginia Colored Institute, though, Storer declined as a major provider of educational services to blacks in southern West Virginia.[37] This decline was yet another indication of the shifting center of black life from northern to southern West Virginia as the black coal-mining proletariat expanded.

Although the educational strides of blacks in southern West Virginia proceeded on a segregated and unequal basis, they still symbolized a victorious black community. As suggested by Howard Rabinowitz in his study of race relations in the urban South, whites increasingly accommodated themselves to black access to, rather than exclusion from, fundamental resources and human services. Racial separation was not a static phenomenon: it was not entirely externally imposed by white racism, and it was not uniformly negative in its results. Within the segregationist framework, the rise of the black coal-mining proletariat spurred the Afro-American struggle for racial equity, facilitated the winning of new concessions, and made racial discrimination in the institutional life of the region less demeaning than it might have been.[38]

Through membership in national black religious, fraternal, and political organizations, southern West Virginia's black coal miners and small black elite also participated in a larger national black community. The National Baptist Convention, the Colored Bureau of the Republican party, and the nationwide bodies of the Elks, Masons, Knights of Pythias, and Odd Fellows all helped to create bonds between the region's blacks and their southern and northern counterparts. Through black ministers like the self-educated Rev. Barnett of Huntington, blacks in southern West Virginia were intimately linked to blacks in northern West Virginia, Ohio, and parts of Kentucky. In addition to pastoring churches in West Virginia, such as the First Baptist Church in Huntington, Barnett also served as pastor of a variety of black Baptist churches in southern Ohio, including the Tried Stone Baptist Church in Ironton as well as others in Gallipolis, Glouster, Providence, and other cities. Upon Barnett's death, the New Hope Baptist Church of Ashland, Kentucky, adopted a resolution expressing its "admiration of the many fine qualities of our departed leader." "For a hundred miles around," the *Huntington Dispatch* proclaimed, "Rev. Barnett's name is a household word in [N]egro homes."[39]

Based upon their firm support within the black coal-mining community, black elites from southern West Virginia sometimes took prominent leadership positions in national organizations. At its 1913 annual meeting in Atlantic City, New Jersey, and for several years thereafter, for example, the Improved Benevolent Protective Order of the Elks of the World elected Charleston attorney T. G. Nutter as its Grand Exalted Ruler. In 1913 Nutter defeated the incumbent, Armand Scott, of Washington, D.C. It was the mass migration of working-class blacks to southern West Virginia, along with their rich pattern of visiting states farther south and north, that fundamentally underlay Nutter's victory and the growing participation of southern West Virginia blacks in the creation of a national black community. These national linkages were to intensify during World War I and its aftermath.[40]

Although extensive evidence attests to the strength of Afro-American unity across class lines, this unity had its limits. Although the *McDowell Times* worked for Afro-American solidarity, for example, it also supported the class interests of coal operators and the small black elite. The editor encouraged black miners to provide regular and efficient labor and repeatedly warned them against joining unions. In a mid-1913 letter to the editor, one reader dropped his subscription, emphasizing the editor's anti-union position as the reason. The *Times* not only worked to mold workers' behavior to meet their employers' demands, but also worked to shape working-class behavior to fit middle-class cultural norms. In an editorial titled "Clean Up and Swat the Flies," the editor admonished black coal miners to keep their surroundings sanitary, downplaying the failure of operators to pay higher wages or to provide necessary repairs and sanitation facilities.[41]

As black coal miners faced the limitations of their alliance with the black elite, they developed distinct strategies of their own. While they did seek to endear themselves to employers by providing regular and efficient labor, they frequently shunned other elite injunctions. Seeking to improve the terms of their labor, black coal miners often moved from one mine to another, either within southern West Virginia or farther north and south, and often switched between coal mining and farming in nearby southern agricultural areas, especially Virginia. In the early 1890s, and again in the Paint Creek–Cabin Creek strike of 1913–14, against the advice of middle-

class leaders, numerous black miners joined white miners in organized confrontations with management. The Paint Creek–Cabin
Creek confrontation produced the heroic exploits of "Few Clothes"
Dan Chain, a black union man. Recently portrayed by James Earl
Jones in the popular film *Matewan,* "Few Clothes" was a big man of
over 250 pounds, according to available evidence. Labor historian
Ronald Lewis claimed that "Dan Chain's size, nerve, and fighting
ability made him a favorite among strikers." In 1887, however, when
whites lynched a black man in Fayette County, black miners initiated their own mass-march of some 1,000 men, by some estimates
3,000, vowing to retaliate in kind. Although they disbanded without
confrontation, James T. Laing noted, "Whites at the mines in the
New River Valley were terrified, for the report was sent to them
that the Negroes expected to 'clean out' every white person along
the river."[42]

While cleavage along class lines was the most prominent division
within the black community, gender inequality was also a significant problem. Emphasizing the home as women's proper sphere,
McDowell Times editor Whittico sought to regulate the behavior of
black women, endorsed the removal of married women from teach-
ing positions, and opposed woman's suffrage. In an editorial titled
"Split Skirts," the editor urged black women to shun the "split
skirt," and maintain codes of "modesty." The injunction, however,
was directed mainly at black women in coal-mining families: "Only
a few of the vulgar variety have been seen in Keystone and none
are worn at present by the better class of Colored [women]."[43] On
another occasion, the editor threatened to publish a gossip list if
black women failed to attend to their own "home work, social affairs and individual business and stop going from house to house,
store to store carrying messages and . . . stirring up strife and generally making trouble."[44] On gender issues, the views of black elite
men, expressed by the editor, converged with those of the black
proletariat.

Yet, as with class conflicts within the black community, gender
conflict tended to give way to the imperatives of racial solidarity.
Black women perceived their class and gender interests in essentially racial terms.[45] Black Baptist, Methodist, and Presbyterian
women, through their regional, state, and local auxiliaries, figured
prominently in black religious activities, especially fund-raising
campaigns, sacred concerts, musicals, and literary programs.[46]
Moreover, under the energetic leadership of Mrs. Malinda Cobbs,

by World War I black women dominated the Independent Order of St. Luke, which diligently worked "to benefit the race."[47]

Although racial hostility, along with an expanding black consciousness, helped to forge Afro-American unity across class and gender lines, substantial interracial cooperation went on as well. At both the elite and working-class levels, as discussed above, blacks and whites in southern West Virginia developed interracial alliances. As early as the 1880s, black miners in the Kanawha–New River Field joined the Knights of Labor. They served on integrated committees and, during strikes, helped persuade black strikebreakers to leave the area.[48] As the United Mine Workers of America supplanted the Knights in the early 1890s, it attracted blacks from the Pocahontas Field as well as the Kanawha–New River area. Blacks soon gained recognition in the union, not only as members, but as officers, too. In 1893 when the white president of District 17 died in office, the black miner J. J. Wren of Fayette County filled the position. At Freeman, Mercer County, a white official exclaimed, "The Colored miners have been in the lead in this district until they have shamed their white brethren."[49]

Despite the dramatic display of interracial working-class unity during the 1880s and early 1890s, interracial unionism declined during the mid-1890s and resurged only briefly during the 1913–14 coal strikes.[50] Even during periods of intense interracial organizing, black members and officers of local unions frequently complained that they were not accorded equal treatment with white unionists. During the 1880s, for example, the Knights of Labor established segregated units, while white members of the UMWA (formed later) sometimes blatantly resisted black leadership. Such resistance led one black labor leader to complain that, "If your vice president is a Negro . . . he must be treated the same as a white man and unless you do there is going to be a mighty earthquake somewhere." Although interracial working-class unity remained highly volatile, it was nonetheless important in the lives of black workers.[51]

Black elites developed a corresponding relationship with white elites, mainly coal operators, within the political framework of the Republican party. As noted earlier, through alliances with black coal miners, on the one hand, and white Republicans, on the other, black professional and business people gained election to the West Virginia legislature, appointments to prestigious positions like state librarian, and membership on the board of regents of all-black colleges.[52] Likewise, in McDowell County coal operators supported

M. T. Whittico's black weekly, the *McDowell Times*, which became a preeminent promoter of the McDowell County Colored Republican Organization. No less than the alliance between black and white miners, however, the alliance between black elites and the coal operators was inequitable, as indicated by the companies' demand that black leaders like Whittico help to discipline the black coal-mining labor force. In the hostile class and racial climate of southern West Virginia, neither black elites nor black workers could fully articulate their interests in class terms.

Linked to each other through both color and culture, black workers and black elites forged their strongest bonds with each other across class lines. They developed a distinct Afro-American community in the coalfields. In the ongoing struggle between white capital and labor, however, Afro-Americans developed their most consistent alliances with coal operators and their corporate and political representatives, rather than organized labor. For example, Republican Governor H. D. Hatfield, speaking in a local black church in 1913 before a gathering of black Odd Fellows, declared his "uncompromising purpose to see that every man gets a square deal."[53] Unfortunately, no corresponding white labor leader developed such a close bond with the black community.

As the black coal-mining proletariat expanded following the Civil War through the early twentieth century, it established the socioeconomic and demographic foundation for the emergence and growth of the black middle class, the rise of black communities in coal-mining towns, and, most important, the emergence of a viable political and civil rights struggle. These processes, rooted in the prewar rise of the black industrial working class, involved the complex dynamics of class, race, and region. Along with new developments, they would reach their peak during World War I and the 1920s.

NOTES

1. John R. Sheeler, "The Negro in West Virginia before 1900" (Ph.D. diss., West Virginia University, 1954), pp. 256–57; Booker T. Washington, *Up From Slavery* (1901; rept., New York: Bantam Books, 1967), pp. 57–58; Louis R. Harlan, *Booker T. Washington: The Making of a Black Leader, 1856–1901* (New York: Oxford University Press, 1972), pp. 33–51, 84–85, and 137–38.

2. U.S. Bureau of the Census, *Religious Bodies, 1906* (Washington, 1910), p. 140; U.S. Bureau of the Census, *Religious Bodies, 1926* (Washington, 1929), pp. 133, 998; "Sacred Concert," 5 Dec. 1913, "Services at Keystone" and

"Locals," 15 May 1914, "The Presbyterian Sunday School Relief Department," 16 Oct. 1914, "The Mt. Olivet Baptist Ass'n," 18 July 1913, "The Flat Top Baptist Association," 9 May 1913, in *McDowell Times*. Sheeler, "The Negro in West Virginia," pp. 251–74; Washington, *Up From Slavery*, pp. 57–58; Harlan, *Booker T. Washington*, pp. 33–51, 84–85, and 137–38.

3. U.S. Census Office, *Twelfth Census, 1900: Special Reports, Occupations* (Washington, 1904), pp. 410–14; U.S. Census Bureau, *Thirteenth Census of the United States, 1910* (Washington, 1913), 4:529–30; "Bluestone Baptist Church Rally," 9 May 1913, "Rally at Anawalt," 4 July 1913, and "Welch News," 13 June 1913, in *McDowell Times*.

4. "Welch News," *McDowell Times*, 13 June 1913.

5. "McAlpin Notes," 1 May 1914, "Locals," 23 May 1913, "Coalwood News," 22 May 1914, and "Slabfork," 11 Dec. 1914, in *McDowell Times*. For insight into black religion during the industrial era, see Lawrence Levine, *Black Culture and Black Consciousness: Afro-American Folk Thought from Slavery to Freedom* (Oxford: Oxford University Press, 1977), chap. 3; E. Franklin Frazier, *The Negro Church in America* (New York: Shocken Books, 1963), chaps. 3, 4, 5; and Elizabeth R. Bethel, *Promiseland: A Century of Life in a Negro Community* (Philadelphia: Temple University Press, 1981), pp. 69–91, 136–44.

6. "Baptizing at Wingfield Baptist Church: Fifteen Hundred People . . . Witness Ceremony," 9 May 1913, "Bramwell News," 28 Nov. 1913, "Giatto News," 12 Dec. 1913, "Kimball Notes," 23 Oct. 1914, in *McDowell Times*.

7. "Death at Gilliam," *McDowell Times*, 4 July 1913.

8. See various issues of the *McDowell Times*, 1913–14; Randall G. Lawrence, "Appalachian Metamorphosis: Industrializing Society on the Central Appalachian Plateau, 1860–1913" (Ph.D. diss., Duke University, 1983), pp. 133–35.

9. For works on black religion in the South, see n. 5 above.

10. "The Flat Top Baptist Association Holds Successful Session in City," 25 July 1913, and "Pastor Installed at First Baptist Church," 14 Nov. 1913, in *McDowell Times*; Joseph J. Boris, *Who's Who in Colored America*, vol. 1, *1927* (New York: Who's Who in Colored America Corp., 1927), pp. 108–9; Mary M. Spradling, ed., *In Black and White: A Guide to . . . Black Individuals and Groups* (Detroit: Gale Research Company, 1980), p. 517; Wilhelmina S. Robinson, *Historical Afro-American Biographies* (Cornwells Heights, Penn.: The Publishers Agency, Inc., under the auspices of the Association for the Study of Afro-American Life and History, 1978), pp. 215–16.

11. "In Memory: Rev. Nelson Barnett," and Rev. I. V. Bryant, "Funeral Sermon of Rev. Nelson Barnett," both in private files of Captain Nelson L. Barnett, United States Air Force (retired), Huntington, West Virginia (copies in author's possession).

12. Ibid.

13. Ibid.

14. "The Flat Top Baptist Association Holds Successful Session in City," 25 July 1913, "Rev. Coger Preaches Able Sermon," 25 July 1913, "Jenkin-

jones Notes," 8 Aug. 1913, and "Colored Member Elected," 30 Oct. 1914, in *McDowell Times*.

15. "Giatto News," 12 Dec. 1913, "Rally at First Baptist Church, Kimball," 10 Apr. 1914, "Services at Keystone," 1 May 1914, "Great Baptist Meeting at Tams," 24 July 1914, "Glen White," 2 Oct. 1914, "Religious Services at Keystone," 20 Mar. 1914, in *McDowell Times*.

16. For spirited revivals at African Methodist Episcopal churches, see "A Voice from the A.M.E. Church," 8 May 1914, "Locals," 15 May 1914, and "Great Revival at Landgraff," 16 May 1913, *McDowell Times*. Black Presbyterians in West Virginia also retained important links to the spiritual traditions of southern blacks. See especially "Back from Vacation," *McDowell Times*, 5 Sept. 1913.

17. "Successful Evangelistic Services Conducted at Northfork," 24 Apr. 1914, and "Rev. Gipson and His Church Work," 25 Sept. 1914, *McDowell Times*.

18. "Sacred Concert," *McDowell Times*, 5 Dec. 1913.

19. T. E. Hill, "My Dream of the Future Church," reprinted in full in the *McDowell Times*, 12 Dec. 1913. Also see "The Prisoners' Friend," 5 June 1914, "The Presbyterian Sunday School Relief Department," 16 Oct. 1914, and "McDowell County Applies for 150 State Convicts," 20 June 1913, in *McDowell Times*.

20. See the *McDowell Times*, 1913–14 passim.

21. "Golden Rule News," 9 May 1913, "Address of Rev. R. H. McKoy, D. D.," 13 June 1913, "2000 Wanted," 16 Jan. 1914, and "Golden Rule Association: Hold 10th Annual Meeting in Tazewell," 12 June 1914, in *McDowell Times*.

22. "Golden Rule News," "Address," and "2000 Wanted," in *McDowell Times*.

23. "John Panell Killed by Falling Slate," 5 Sept. 1913, "Death at Gilliam," 4 July 1913, and "Landgraff Loses a Good Citizen," 25 July 1913, in *McDowell Times*.

24. "Colored Odd Fellows Parade: Hold Great Thanksgiving Service," *McDowell Times*, 16 May 1913.

25. "Keystone Lodge A.F. and A.M. Hold Services," 27 June 1913, and "Pythian Anniversary Ceremonies Held," 3 Apr. 1914, in *McDowell Times*.

26. "Colored Odd Fellows Parade: Hold Great Thanksgiving Service," 6 May 1913, and "Mayor: Delivers Address of Welcome to Colored Pythians of State," 8 Aug. 1913, in *McDowell Times*.

27. Sheeler, "The Negro in West Virginia," pp. 191–94. For patterns of black disfranchisement in other parts of the South, see Joel Williamson, *The Crucible of Race: Black-White Relations in the American South since Emancipation* (New York: Oxford University Press, 1984).

28. Lawrence, "Appalachian Metamorphosis," pp. 183–86.

29. Sheeler, "The Negro in West Virginia," pp. 202–3; Washington, *Up From Slavery*, pp. 64–65; Harlan, *Booker T. Washington*, pp. 93–96.

30. Otis K. Rice, *West Virginia: A History* (Lexington: University Press of

Kentucky, 1985), pp. 165–73, 204–16; John A. Williams, *West Virginia: A History* (New York: W. W. Norton and Company, 1984), pp. 115–29; David A. Corbin, *Life, Work, and Rebellion in the Coal Fields: The Southern West Virginia Miners, 1880–1922* (Urbana: University of Illinois Press, 1981), pp. 10–18.

31. Sheeler, "The Negro in West Virginia," pp. 207–12; U.S. Census Bureau, *Thirteenth Census of the U.S., 1910* (Washington, 1913), 3:1032–41; Rice, *West Virginia,* pp. 172, 206, 208.

32. Rice, *West Virginia,* p. 207; Williams, *West Virginia,* pp. 115–19; Corbin, *Life, Work, and Rebellion,* pp. 10–18; quote in *New York World,* 23 July 1899, reprinted in *Public Addresses, etc., of Governor G. W. Atkinson,* courtesy of Gary L. Weiner, Clarksburg, W.Va.

33. Williams, *West Virginia,* pp. 115–29; Corbin, *Life, Work, and Rebellion,* pp. 10–18; Sheeler, "The Negro in West Virginia," pp. 207–12; U.S. Census Bureau, *Thirteenth Census, 1910* (Washington, 1913), 3:1032–41; C. W. Swisher, ed., *Manual of the State of West Virginia, 1907–1908* (Charleston, W.Va.: The Tribune Printing Company, 1907), p. 114; "Great Meeting of the McDowell County Colored Republican Organization," 21 Nov. 1913, "Republicans Together," 31 July 1914, and "Prof. Sanders Promoted," 31 July 1914, in *McDowell Times;* West Virginia Bureau of Negro Welfare and Statistics (WVBNWS), *Biennial Report, 1921–22* (Charleston, W.Va.), p. 67.

34. "Great Meeting of the McDowell County Colored Republican Organization," 21 Nov. 1913, "Republicans Together," 31 July 1914, "Prof. Sanders Promoted," 31 July 1914, in *McDowell Times;* "State Librarian," in John T. Harris, ed., *West Virginia Legislative Hand Book* (Charleston, W.Va.: The Tribune Company, 1916), p. 809.

35. Sheeler, "The Negro in West Virginia," pp. 223–26, 230–46; "The School Attendance," 9 May 1913, and "West Virginia Colored Institute," 27 June 1913, *McDowell Times;* John C. Harlan, *History of West Virginia State College, 1890–1965* (Dubuque, Iowa: Wm. C. Brown Book Company, 1968).

36. Sheeler, "The Negro in West Virginia," pp. 234–39; "Storer College" and "State of W.Va. Correspondence on Appropriations to Storer, 1914–1941," Box 1, Storer College Papers, West Virgnia Collection, West Virginia University.

37. See Storer College to Governor H. D. Hatfield, Feb. 1915, Box 1, Storer College Papers.

38. "Interracial Racial Relations," WVBNWS, *Biennial Report, 1925–26,* pp. 118–20.

39. Sheeler, "The Negro in West Virginia," pp. 251–60, 207–13; "In Memory" and "Funeral Sermon," in private files of Captain Nelson L. Barnett, Huntington, W.Va.; "Pythians Capture the City of Baltimore," 5 Sept. 1913, "National Baptist Convention," 26 Sept. 1913 and 25 Sept. 1914, and "Locals," 5 Sept. 1913, in *McDowell Times;* Harris, ed., *West Virginia Legislative Hand Book* (Charleston, W.Va.: The Tribune Printing Company, 1916), p. 809, (1928), p. 220, and (1929), p. 201.

40. "Elks Hold Great Meeting" and "Nutter Elected Grand Exalted Ruler," 5 Sept. 1913, "Convention of Elks," 17 July 1914, " Elks Hold Big

Meeting," 4 Sept. 1914, "Fifteenth Annual Session of the I.B.P.O.E. of the World," 11 Sept. 1914, in *McDowell Times*; Louis R. Harlan, *Booker T. Washington: The Wizard of Tuskegee, 1901–1915* (New York: Oxford University Press, 1983), pp. 125–27; and chap. 2 below.

41. For the *Time's* anti-union position, see "We Still Adhere to Our Policy," 4 July 1913, "Illimitable as the Wind: We Blow on Whom We Please," 11 July 1913, "Unfair Attitude of Union Men Toward the Negro," 18 July 1913, Rev. M. L. Shrum to M. T. Whittico, 20 June 1913, reprinted, 4 July 1913, and "Clean Up and Swat the Flies," 9 May 1913, in *McDowell Times*. See also Corbin, *Life, Work, and Rebellion*, pp. 75–79.

42. Corbin, *Life, Work, and Rebellion*, pp. 41, 77–105; Lawrence, "Appalachian Metamorphosis," pp. 63, 133–38, 184–85, 262–63, 288; Ronald L. Lewis, *Black Coal Miners in America: Race, Class and Community Conflict, 1770–1980* (Lexington: University Press of Kentucky, 1987), chaps. 7 and 8, especially pp. 141–42; John Sayles, *Thinking in Pictures: The Making of the Movie Matewan* (Boston: Houghton Mifflin Company, 1987); Sterling D. Spero and Abram L. Harris, *The Black Worker: The Negro and the Labor Movement* (1931; rept., New York: Atheneum, 1968), chap. 7; James T. Laing, "The Negro Miner in West Virginia" (Ph.D. diss., Ohio State University, 1933) pp. 493–96.

43. "Split Skirts," *McDowell Times*, 4 July 1913.

44. "Attend to Your Duties," *McDowell Times*, 25 July 1913.

45. "Literary Program," 13 Mar. 1914, and "Woman's Auxiliar[y] National Baptist Convention," 5 Sept. 1913, *McDowell Times*.

46. "St. Luke News," 9 May 1913; "Mrs. Malinda Cobbs: A Successful Deputy," 10 Aug. and 31 Aug. 1917 (includes a photo and summary of Cobbs's lodge activities), "Woman's Auxiliar[y] National Baptist Convention," 5 Sept. 1913, *McDowell Times*.

47. "Bluefield Police," 18 July 1913, and "Brave Colored Woman Defends Her Honor and Home—Shoots at Cops," 18 July 1913, "Colored Odd Fellows," 16 May 1913, "The Annual Thanksgiving Services," 30 May 1913, and "The Ninth Annual Meeting," 13 June 1913, in *McDowell Times*.

48. Stephen Brier, "Interracial Organizing in the West Virginia Coal Industry: Participation of Black Mine Workers, 1880–1894," in Gary M. Fink and Merle E. Reed, eds., *Essays in Southern Labor History* (Westport, Conn.: Greenwood Press, 1977), pp. 18–43; Lewis, *Black Coal Miners in America*, pp. 136–40.

49. Brier, "Interracial Organizing in the West Virginia Coal Industry," p. 29.

50. For the upsurge of interracial unionism in 1913–14, see Corbin, *Life, Work, and Rebellion*, pp. 87–101; Lewis, *Black Coal Miners in America*, pp. 140–42; Richard D. Lunt, *Law and Order versus the Miners: West Virginia, 1907–1933* (Hamden, Conn.: Archon Books, 1979); Hoyt N. Wheeler, "Mountaineer Mine Wars: An Analysis of the West Virginia Mine Wars of 1912–13 and 1920–21," *Business History Review* 50 (Spring 1976): 69–91.

51. Brier, "Interracial Organizing in the West Virginia Coal Industry," pp. 32–33.

52. See n. 31 above, especially Sheeler, "The Negro in West Virginia," pp. 207–12, and *McDowell Times*, 21 Nov. 1913, 31 July 1914, and 16 May 1913. See also "Editor Mr. Whittico," 23 Feb. 1917, and "Whittico Dead," 23 June 1939, *McDowell Times*.

53. "Colored Odd Fellows Parade: Hold Great Thanksgiving Service," *McDowell Times*, 16 May 1913.

PART
2

Migration, Work, and Industrial Change, 1915–32

3

The Expansion of the Black Coal-Mining Proletariat

The black coal-mining proletariat gained its fullest development during World War I and the 1920s. It was shaped by the continuing interplay between changes in the coal industry, the imperatives of black life in the rural South, and the activities of black miners themselves. As the black proletariat expanded in the war and postwar years, it continued to lead a precarious existence. Sharp cyclical swings in the coal market, the persistence of racial inequality in the workplace, and the discriminatory policies of the state all served to press Afro-Americans downward in the occupational hierarchy. Nonetheless, despite the debilitating impact of these forces on their lives, black coal miners in southern West Virginia played an expanding role in their own transition from rural and semirural workers to industrial laborers. As with the prewar era, however, in order to understand changes in Afro-American life during this period, an assessment of the larger regional context is essential.

Between World War I and 1930, southern West Virginia's population nearly doubled, increasing from close to 300,000 in 1910 to an estimated 600,000 in 1930. Unlike the case in the prewar years, though, the immigrant population declined due to the effects of World War I and immigration restriction legislation passed during the 1920s. Between 1910 and 1930, the immigrant population dropped from 6 to nearly 3 percent, while the black population remained stable at about 13 percent (tables 3.1, 3.2). As in the prewar years, the region's population expansion was tied to the growth of the coal industry, which increased production from an estimated 37 million tons in 1910 to 57 million tons in 1916. Following a brief postwar decline, production increased to 122 million tons in 1925 (about 70 percent of the state's total output), before dropping at the onset of the Great Depression.[1]

TABLE 3.1
Population of Southern West Virginia by Race and Ethnicity, 1910–30

	Number	Percent of Regional Total	Percent of State Total
		1910	
Blacks	40,503	13.5	63.1
Foreign–born whites	18,061	6.0	31.6
American–born whites/ Foreign–born or mixed parentage	8,978	2.9	15.5
American–born whites/ American–born parentage	232,276	77.6	22.2
Other	32		24.8
Total	299,850	100.0	24.5
		1920	
Blacks	58,819	13.5	68.1
Foreign-born whites	18,388	4.1	29.6
American–born whites/ Foreign–born or mixed parentage	18,346	4.1	22.2
American–born whites/ American–born parentage	342,960	78.3	27.8
Other	41		33.8
Total	438,504	100.0	29.9
		1930	
Blacks	79,007	13.2	68.7
Foreign-born whites	15,472	2.6	30.0
American–born whites/ Foreign–born or mixed parentage	23,584	4.0	23.3
American–born whites/ American–born parentage	473,699	80.1	32.4
Other	194	—	51.3
Total	591,956	100.0	34.2

Sources: U.S. Bureau of the Census, *Thirteenth Census of the United States, 1910* (Washington, 1913), 3:1032–41; *Fourteenth Census, 1920* (Washington, 1922), 3:1105–9; *Fifteenth Census, 1930*, vol.3, pt.2 (Washington, 1932), pp. 1268–72.

The percentage of West Virginia coal mined by undercutting machines increased from 45 percent in 1910 to 72 percent in 1920, then to over 80 percent by the mid-1920s. Thereafter, mine mechanization signaled the decline of the handloading era, as companies began to install coal-loading machines that loaded blasted coal onto mechanized conveyors and shuttle cars. With increasing mechanization, giant corporate entities like U.S. Steel, Standard Oil, and J. P. Morgan increased their hold on West Virginia's valuable coal and timber lands. By the early 1920s, large corporations accounted for an estimated 80 percent of the state's total value of products.[2]

Although southern West Virginia coal operators increased their control over the political economy, it remained incomplete. Mechanization gave large producers an advantage over small regional competitors, but the operators' control in general was undercut by the increasing shift to alternative sources of fuel like gas, oil, and hydroelectricity, as well as by the individual and collective demands of coal miners.[3] In the violent coal strikes of 1919–22, for example, coal miners joined the United Mine Workers of America and submerged their ethnic and racial differences in a broad display of class unity.[4] More important, however, unlike factory workers, who were spatially concentrated and subjected to the close supervision of foremen, coal miners usually worked alone in widely dispersed underground tunnels, and eluded the strict day-to-day supervision of mine foremen. Nonetheless, much like factory workers in search of better working conditions during good and bad times, miners constantly moved from mine to mine, still working for the same employer, and from job to job in different coalfields. By the mid-1920s, according to the U.S. Coal Commission, southern West Virginia's mines had the highest labor turnover rates of any in the nation's bituminous coal industry.[5]

The workers' struggle for a better life lies behind not only the incomplete authority of the operators, but also their growing use of welfare capitalism. In their growing efforts to stem the tide of working-class militancy and discontent, the major coal companies sponsored mine safety programs, hired social workers, and subsidized the public school system, as well as supporting private churches, social clubs, and fraternal organizations. During the war years, for example, an advertisement by a company in the Williamson-Logan Field emphasized the ideology of welfare capitalism: "Miners Wanted: The Ideal Mining Town of the State. YMCA, Three Schools, Splendid Churches, Shower Baths, Playground, [and] Baseball Parks. . . ."[6]

TABLE 3.2
Population of Southern West Virginia by County, Race, and Ethnicity, 1910–30

Year	Blacks Number	Blacks Percent	Foreign-Born Whites Number	Foreign-Born Whites Percent	American-Born Whites/ Foreign or Mixed Parentage Number	American-Born Whites/ Foreign or Mixed Parentage Percent	American-Born Whites/ American-Born Parentage Number	American-Born Whites/ American-Born Parentage Percent	Other Number	Other Percent	Total Number	Total Percent
McDowell County												
1910	14,667	30.7	6,260	13.1	1,730	2.0	25,196	52.6	3	—	47,856	100.0
1920	18,157	26.5	5,416	7.9	4,175	6.1	40,822	59.5	1	—	68,571	100.0
1930	22,558	25.0	3,528	3.9	4,930	5.5	59,432	65.6	31	—	90,479	100.0
Mercer County												
1910	5,960	15.6	1,148	3.0	743	1.9	30,515	79.5	5	—	36,371	100.0
1920	6,427	13.0	914	1.9	1,225	2.4	40,985	82.7	7	—	49,558	100.0
1930	7,587	12.4	761	1.3	1,451	2.3	51,520	84.0	4	—	61,323	100.0
Mingo County												
1910	1,236	6.4	1,197	6.1	371	1.9	16,627	85.6	—	—	19,431	100.0
1920	2,191	8.4	698	2.7	605	2.2	22,869	86.7	1	—	26,364	100.0
1930	3,768	9.9	759	1.9	997	2.7	32,791	85.5	4	—	38,319	100.0
Logan County												
1910	532	3.7	927	6.4	220	1.6	12,792	88.4	5	—	14,476	100.0
1920	4,737	11.6	2,710	6.6	1,815	4.4	31,744	77.4	—	—	41,006	100.0
1930	6,993	12.0	2,822	4.9	3,032	5.1	45,637	78.0	50	—	58,534	100.0

	Fayette County											
1910	9,311	17.9	4,466	8.6	2,386	4.6	36,736	68.9	4	—	51,903	100.0
1920	9,636	16.0	3,203	5.4	3,418	5.6	44,120	73.0	—	—	60,377	100.0
1930	11,607	16.2	2,213	3.1	3,521	4.8	54,687	75.9	22	—	72,050	100.0
	Kanawha County											
1910	6,476	7.9	2,512	3.1	3,009	3.7	69,446	85.3	15	—	81,457	100.0
1920	8,929	7.5	2,735	2.3	5,007	4.2	102,948	86.0	31	—	119,650	100.0
1930	12,671	8.2	2,715	1.7	6,048	3.8	136,199	86.3	34	—	157,667	100.0
	Raleigh County											
1910	2,052	8.0	1,525	6.9	459	1.8	21,597	84.3	—	—	25,633	100.0
1920	6,393	15.2	2,270	6.3	1,694	3.9	32,122	75.6	—	—	42,479	100.0
1930	11,116	16.4	2,094	3.1	2,835	4.2	51,985	76.3	42	—	68,072	100.0
	Boone County											
1910	164	1.6	9	—	37	0.4	10,121	98.0	—	—	10,331	100.0
1920	759	5.0	230	1.6	251	1.6	14,078	91.8	1	—	15,319	100.0
1930	746	3.2	341	1.3	448	1.8	23,047	93.7	4	—	24,586	100.0
	Wyoming County											
1910	106	1.0	17	0.2	23	0.2	10,247	98.6	—	—	10,392	100.0
1920	1,590	10.5	182	1.1	156	1.0	13,272	87.4	—	—	15,180	100.0
1930	1,961	9.4	239	1.2	322	1.5	18,401	87.9	3	—	20,926	100.0

Source: U.S. Bureau of the Census, Thirteenth Century of the U.S., 1910 (Washington, 1913), 3:1032–41; Fourteenth Census, 1920 (Washington, 1922), 3:1105–9; Fifteenth Census, 1930, vol. 3, pt. 2 (Washington, 1932), pp. 1268–72.

As employers turned toward new labor management techniques, they nonetheless continued to hold traditional notions of labor control. As late as 1930, despite the declining immigrant population, some coal operators continued their preference for a mixed labor force, "where one class [ethnic or racial group] is looked upon by the others and try to get advantage of the other class in the way of good places and responsible positions which pay more."[7] Although ethnic and racial competition and conflict did hamper working-class solidarity, above all it was the company town through which coal companies retained their control over labor. The company towns enabled owners to dominate the Republican and Democratic parties, control state and local law enforcement officials, and relegate miners to the bottom of the political economy, denying them access to collective bargaining until the 1930s.[8]

The foregoing war and postwar developments shaped the black experience in southern West Virginia. Spurred by the labor demands of World War I, the black population increased by nearly 50 percent, from just over 40,000 in 1910 to nearly 60,000 in 1920 (tables 3.1, 3.2). At the same time, the black coal-mining proletariat increased from about 11,000 in 1915 to over 16,000 during the war years (table 3.3). The percentage of blacks living in southern West Virginia increased from 63 percent in 1910 to nearly 70 percent in 1920 (table 3.1), and over 80 percent of the state's black miners resided there.[9] Black workers increased from 20 percent of the real labor force in 1915 to nearly 25 percent in 1919, as immigrants declined from 31 to about 20 percent (tables 3.3, 3.4). Located in the rich Pocahontas Field, McDowell and Mercer counties consistently housed and employed over 37 percent of all black miners and their families, followed by the counties of the Winding Gulf Field, the Kanawha–New River Field, and the rapidly expanding, though small, Williamson-Logan Field (map 2).

Migration from other southern states was the major factor behind West Virginia's black population growth. In 1910, blacks born in other states made up nearly 60 percent of West Virginia's black population (see table 3.5). As elsewhere, the majority were young men between the primary working ages of 20 and 44. Although the black sex ratio evened out over time (as did the white ratio), substantial imbalance continued through the war years, standing at 125:100 in 1920. Led by blacks from Virginia, who comprised over 34 percent of West Virginia's total black population in 1920, blacks from upper South states made up 56 percent of the state's total (table 3.5). Black migration to southern West Virginia was part of the first wave of

TABLE 3.3
Coal-Mining Labor Force of Southern West Virginia by Race and Ethnicity, 1915–29

	1915		1917		1919		1925		1929	
	Number	Percent	Number	Percent	Number	Percent	Number	Percent	Number	Percent
Blacks	11,035	20.0	16,572	26.2	15,180	24.7	20,272	27.2	19,648	26.7
Foreign-born whites	17,192	31.0	12,095	19.1	12,105	19.7	10,338	13.8	8,819	11.9
American-born whites	27,080	48.9	34,497	54.6	34,214	55.5	43,811	58.8	45,151	61.2
Other or unknown	69	0.1	111	0.1	76	0.1	191	0.2	17	—
Total	55,376	100.0	63,275	100.0	61,575	100.0	74,612	100.0	73,635	100.0

Source: West Virginia Department of Mines, *Annual Reports, 1915–29* (Charleston, W.Va.).

TABLE 3.4
Coal-Mining Labor Force of Southern West Virginia by County, Race, and Ethnicity, 1915–31

Year	Blacks		Foreign-Born Whites		American-Born Whites		Unknown		Total	
	Number	Percent	Number	Percent	Number	Percent	Number	Percent	Number	Percent
					McDowell County					
1915	4,354	28.0	5,911	38.0	5,280	34.0	14	—	15,559	100.0
1917	6,914	36.3	4,786	24.9	7,417	38.6	53	0.2	19,170	100.0
1919	5,897	34.6	4,243	24.7	6,986	40.7	2	—	17,128	100.0
1921	6,440	33.4	4,424	23.0	8,384	43.4	41	0.2	19,289	100.0
1923	5,937	33.2	3,350	18.6	8,637	48.1	26	0.1	17,950	100.0
1925	6,726	34.3	3,021	15.2	9,970	50.4	31	0.1	19,748	100.0
1927	6,594	34.5	2,550	13.3	10,034	52.2	10	—	19,188	100.0
1929	6,861	35.4	2,408	12.4	10,147	52.2	8	—	19,424	100.0
1931	6,092	34.5	2,503	14.2	9,027	51.2	24	0.1	17,646	100.0

Source: West Virginia Bureau of Mines, *Annual Reports, 1915–29* (Charlestou, W.Va.).

TABLE 3.4 (Continued)

Year	Blacks		Foreign-Born Whites		American-Born Whites		Unknown		Total	
	Number	Percent	Number	Percent	Number	Percent	Number	Percent	Number	Percent
Mercer County										
1915	1,176	34.7	823	24.2	1,397	41.1	—	—	3,398	100.0
1917	1,185	35.8	553	16.7	1,573	47.5	—	—	3,311	100.0
1919	975	31.0	509	16.2	1,665	62.8	—	—	3,149	100.0
1921	1,008	27.4	651	17.6	2,031	65.0	—	—	3,690	100.0
1923	978	26.6	360	9.7	2,354	63.7	—	—	3,692	100.0
1925	919	27.8	267	8.0	2,122	64.2	—	—	3,308	100.0
1927	873	27.2	205	6.5	2,118	66.3	—	—	3,196	100.0
1929	1,022	27.5	169	4.6	2,526	67.9	2	—	3,719	100.0
1931	965	27.8	237	6.9	2,273	65.3	1	—	3,476	100.0
Mingo County										
1915	281	9.4	859	28.7	1,856	61.8	4	—	3,000	100.0
1917	487	14.5	558	16.4	2,338	69.1	—	—	3,383	100.0
1919	490	15.4	525	16.4	2,178	68.2	3	—	3,193	100.0
1921	518	17.7	704	23.8	1,716	58.2	9	0.3	2,947	100.0
1923	832	19.0	597	13.7	2,950	67.3	—	—	4,379	100.0
1925	867	20.3	553	13.0	2,839	66.5	12	0.2	4,271	100.0
1927	850	18.3	574	12.4	3,215	69.1	10	0.2	4,649	100.0
1929	744	17.7	503	11.9	2,973	70.4	—	—	4,220	100.0
1931	610	16.5	322	8.8	2,766	74.7	—	—	3,698	100.0

					Logan County					
1915	480	7.9	2,446	40.0	3,163	51.6	32	0.5	6,121	100.0
1917	1,395	17.7	1,798	22.5	4,735	69.4	37	0.4	7,965	100.0
1919	1,605	17.0	2,410	25.6	5,411	57.3	18	0.1	9,444	100.0
1921	2,068	15.9	4,110	31.4	6,842	52.3	59	0.4	13,079	100.0
1923	2,415	18.1	3,816	28.4	7,160	53.4	15	0.1	13,406	100.0
1925	2,764	21.3	2,991	22.9	7,199	55.0	116	0.8	13,070	100.0
1927	2,894	21.7	3,029	22.7	7,413	55.3	50	0.3	13,886	100.0
1929	2,372	21.3	2,292	20.5	6,516	58.2	—	—	11,180	100.0
1931	2,212	20.5	2,135	19.8	6,443	59.7	4	—	10,794	100.0
					Fayette County					
1915	2,610	20.2	3,702	28.7	6,611	51.1	—	—	12,923	100.0
1917	3,213	26.9	1,826	15.0	7,038	58.1	11	—	12,109	100.0
1919	2,955	24.9	1,916	16.1	7,011	58.9	15	—	11,896	100.0
1921	3,260	24.4	2,264	16.8	7,895	58.7	23	0.1	13,442	100.0
1923	3,204	25.4	1,658	13.1	7,698	61.1	14	0.1	12,574	100.0
1925	3,138	26.6	1,123	9.5	7,545	63.9	1	—	11,807	100.0
1927	3,177	24.7	1,478	11.5	8,235	63.8	10	—	12,900	100.0
1929	3,316	26.5	1,181	9.4	8,036	64.1	3	—	12,536	100.0
1931	3,060	25.6	1,355	11.3	7,553	63.1	6	—	11,974	100.0

TABLE 3.4 (Continued)

Year	Blacks		Foreign-Born Whites		American-Born Whites		Unknown		Total	
	Number	Percent	Number	Percent	Number	Percent	Number	Percent	Number	Percent
					Kanawha County					
1915	690	8.9	1,315	16.8	5,801	74.3	—	—	7,806	100.0
1917	890	11.7	728	9.5	6,019	78.8	—	—	7,637	100.0
1919	844	12.2	640	9.2	5,463	78.5	12	0.1	6,959	100.0
1921	1,190	13.9	650	7.6	6,686	78.0	44	0.5	8,570	100.0
1923	1,482	18.7	458	5.7	6,011	75.4	16	0.2	7,967	100.0
1925	1,360	21.5	451	7.0	4,538	71.3	13	0.2	6,362	100.0
1927	1,391	17.8	550	7.0	5,894	75.0	19	0.2	7,854	100.0
1929	971	15.7	332	5.3	4,920	79.0	—	—	6,223	100.0
1931	1,054	17.5	355	5.9	4,626	76.6	—	—	6,035	100.0
					Raleigh County					
1915	1,255	22.2	1,964	34.7	2,424	42.8	19	0.3	5,662	100.0
1917	1,923	26.6	1,634	21.5	4,018	52.9	10	0.1	7,585	100.0
1919	1,799	26.2	1,430	20.7	3,650	53.0	7	0.1	6,886	100.0
1921	2,608	26.6	2,312	22.5	6,328	51.9	16	0.1	10,264	100.0
1923	2,994	29.6	1,606	15.9	5,515	54.3	30	0.2	10,145	100.0
1925	3,166	30.5	1,441	13.8	5,804	55.6	15	0.1	10,426	100.0
1927	3,449	30.1	1,525	13.3	6,513	56.6	9	—	11,496	100.0
1929	3,451	29.5	1,541	13.1	6,730	57.4	2	—	11,724	100.0
1931	3,632	30.2	1,561	13.0	6,848	56.8	—	—	12,047	100.0

Boone County

Year										
1915	114	16.8	120	17.6	448	65.6	—	—	682	100.0
1917	95	8.9	121	11.2	859	79.9	—	—	1,075	100.0
1919	207	12.1	206	12.1	1,282	74.7	19	1.1	1,714	100.0
1921	298	11.3	281	10.4	2,103	78.2	4	0.1	2,686	100.0
1923	426	15.5	343	12.5	1,984	72.0	2	—	2,755	100.0
1925	431	13.9	329	10.6	2,347	75.5	—	—	3,107	100.0
1927	393	11.6	277	8.2	2,727	80.2	—	—	3,397	100.0
1929	316	11.8	216	8.0	2,167	80.2	—	—	2,699	100.0
1931	289	11.6	346	13.8	1,877	74.6	1	—	2,513	100.0

Wyoming County

Year										
1915	75	33.1	52	22.9	100	44.0	—	—	227	100.0
1917	449	43.2	95	9.0	500	47.8	—	—	1,044	100.0
1919	408	34.0	227	18.8	568	47.2	—	—	1,203	100.0
1921	737	39.5	194	10.3	939	50.2	—	—	1,870	100.0
1923	895	36.2	263	10.6	1,321	53.2	—	—	2,479	100.0
1925	901	35.9	162	6.5	1,447	57.5	3	—	2,513	100.0
1927	976	34.5	205	7.3	1,645	58.1	5	—	2,831	100.0
1929	595	31.2	177	9.1	1,136	59.4	2	—	1,910	100.0
1931	589	32.9	151	8.4	1,053	58.7	—	—	1,793	100.0

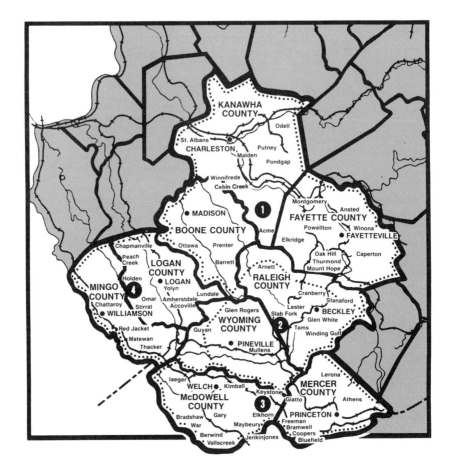

Map 2 Southern West Virginia

Legend: Approximate boundaries are shown by dotted lines

1. Kanawha–New River Field: Kanawha, Fayette, and Boone counties, and part of Raleigh County
2. Winding Gulf Field: most of Raleigh and Wyoming counties
3. Pocahontas Field: McDowell and Mercer counties
4. Williamson-Logan Field: Logan and Mingo counties and part of Wyoming County

Sources: Adapted from Otis K. Rice, *West Virginia: A History* (Lexington: University Press of Kentucky, 1985); Cortez Donald Reece, "A Study of Selected Folksongs Collected in Southern West Virginia" (Ph.D. diss., University of Southern California, 1955); and Philip M. Conley, *History of the West Virginia Coal Industry* (Charleston, W.Va.: Education Foundation, 1960).

TABLE 3.5
West Virginia Blacks by State of Birth, 1910–30

	Number	Percent
	1910	
Born in West Virginia	27,160	42.3
Born in other states	36,573	57.0
Virginia	26,565	41.4
North Carolina	4,522	7.2
Ohio	1,176	1.8
Kentucky	907	1.4
Pennsylvania	554	0.9
Tennessee	554	0.9
Maryland	526	0.8
South Carolina	461	0.7
Georgia	275	0.4
Alabama	206	0.3
District of Columbia	143	0.2
All other states	584	0.9
Other American-born	358	0.6
Foreign-born	82	0.1
Total living in West Virginia	64,173	100.0
	1920	
Born in West Virginia	33,347	39.0
Born in other states	52,226	61.0
Virginia	29,315	34.2
North Carolina	6,512	7.6
Alabama	5,144	6.0
Tennessee	1,827	2.1
Kentucky	1,648	1.9
Georgia	1,623	1.8
Ohio	1,471	1.7
South Carolina	1,179	1.3
Mississippi	543	0.6
Maryland	527	0.6
All other states	2,437	2.8
Total living in West Virginia	85,573	100.0

TABLE 3.5 (Continued)

	Number	Percent
	1930	
Born in West Virginia	46,834	40.9
Born in other states	67,724	59.1
Virginia	31,401	27.4
Alabama	10,560	9.2
North Carolina	8,304	7.2
Georgia	2,905	2.5
Tennessee	2,794	2.4
Kentucky	2,467	2.2
South Carolina	2,441	2.1
Ohio	1,822	1.6
Pennsylvania	1,369	1.2
Mississippi	796	0.7
Maryland	548	0.5
Florida	334	0.3
District of Columbia	222	0.2
Louisiana	211	0.2
Illinois	199	0.2
Missouri	168	0.1
All other states	1,183	1.0
Total living in West Virginia	114,558	100.0

Sources: Adapted from U.S. Bureau of the Census, *The Negro Population in the United States, 1790–1915* (1918; rpt., New York, 1968); *Negroes in the United States, 1920–1932* (1935; rpt., New York, 1966); *Fourteenth Census of the U.S.: Population, 1920,* vol. 2 (Washington, 1922), pp. 636–40.

the Great Migration of blacks northward out of the South. One contemporary observer, Ralph W. White, argued that the Mountain State received not only the earliest but also the "best" of the migrants. "We got the vanguard. . . . those who came voluntarily and were not encouraged to leave on account of strained [race] relations or the strain of living." This was a version of the "talented tenth" theory of black migration later popularized by the pioneer black historian Carter G. Woodson. In reality, however, the majority of blacks who migrated to West Virginia did so precisely because of the "strain of living" and the often "strained [race] relations" in other parts of the South.[10]

    In the upper South and border states, black farmers abandoned the land in growing numbers. During World War I, John Hayes moved his family from rural North Carolina to McDowell County, his daughter tersely recalled, "because he got tired of farming." For similar reasons, in 1917 John Henry Phillips moved his family from a small farm in Floyd County, Virginia, to Pageton, McDowell County. During World War I, Salem Wooten's family owned a farm in Henry County, Virginia, near Martinsville. The family raised wheat, corn, some livestock, and especially tobacco for the market. Tobacco farming, Wooten recalled, was "back-breaking labor." "Tobacco is a delicate crop and it's a lot of hard work. . . . If you did that all day, it was very tiresome." With thirteen boys and five girls in the family, the Wootens managed to make ends meet during the war and early postwar years, but the boys "wanted to get away from the farm." In the face of the growing attraction of coal mining in southern West Virginia, the elderly Wooten fought in vain to keep his sons on the land. The eldest son, shortly after being discharged from the army in 1918, migrated to West Virginia, setting in motion a process that soon brought seven of his younger brothers into the coalfields.[11]

The rising labor demands of the coal industry, combined with the disastrous effects of the boll weevil and destructive storms on southern farms, led hundreds of black sharecroppers and farm laborers from the Deep South to also migrate to southern West Virginia. Alabama, Georgia, South Carolina, and Mississippi sent increasing numbers of black migrants to West Virginia. In 1920 Alabama ranked third among all states that were sources of migrants, accounting for 6 percent of West Virginia's black population (table 3.5). Under the deteriorating agricultural conditions in the Deep South, some white landowners eased their tenacious grip on the black farm labor force and helped to stimulate out-migration. In a revealing letter to the U.S. Department of Justice, Alexander D. Pitts, federal attorney for the southern district of Alabama, explained: "In 1914 the cotton crop in Dallas County amounted to 64,700 bales. . . . in 1916, which is this year, . . . there are not five thousand bales in the entire county. All of the surrounding counties are in the same condition. . . . There has been no corn made and [since] this country only raises cotton and corn, you can readily see that the negroes have nothing to eat. The planters are not able to feed them and they are emigrating."[12] By contrast, black miners averaged $3.20 to $5.00, and even more, per eight-hour day, compared to a maximum of $2.50 per nine-hour day for southern industrial workers. Black southern farm laborers made even less—as little as 75 cents to $1.00 per day. It is no wonder, as one migrant recalled, that blacks moved to southern West Virginia, when "they heard that money was growing on trees."[13]

In 1916, sharecropper Thornton Wright and his family moved from Montgomery, Alabama, to the coal-mining community of Accoville, Logan County. In the same year, a Union Springs, Alabama, migrant wrote from Holden, Logan County: "I make $80 to $90 per mo. with ease and wish you all much success. Hello to all the people of my home town. I am saving my money and spending some of it." Another Alabama migrant wrote from Omar, Logan County, "You can make 1 dollar heaire quicker than you can 20 ct theaire in Alla."[14]

Important social, cultural, and political factors reinforced West Virginia's attractiveness to black migrants. Lynchings were fewer, educational opportunities were greater, and voting was not restricted to whites, unlike elsewhere in the South. In a letter to home, one migrant, W. L. McMillan enclosed a flyer that announced a political rally in bold printing: "Republican Speaking - Mr. Colored Man Come Out And Bring Your Friends To Hear." "Now listen," McMillan concluded. "I will vote for the president on the 11 of this mont Collered man tick[e]t stands just as good as white man heare." During the 1920s, the state agency the Bureau of Negro Welfare and Statistics (BNWS), although it frequently overstated the case, repeatedly emphasized the political and social attractions of West Virginia: "His political rights . . . and educational advantages in West Virginia make a strong appeal to the Negro's sense of justice and fair play."[15]

Though most blacks who moved to West Virginia came from agricultural backgrounds, many had already made a substantial break with the land. As opportunities in southern agriculture had steadily declined, rural blacks had increasingly moved into non-farm industries, especially lumber, coal, and railroad work. Before bringing his family to Pageton, McDowell County, John Henry Phillips had alternated between working in a local saw mill and doing farm labor. Salem Wooten recalled that one of his brothers had worked in a furniture factory in Martinsville, Virginia, before migrating to southern West Virginia. Before migrating to Coalwood, McDowell County, Pink Henderson and his father had been coal miners in the Birmingham district of Alabama. Alabama coal operators were infamous for using a highly unjust contract labor system and also the convict lease system of employment. Together these systems placed miners, mainly blacks, at a severe disadvantage, protected management, and helped to drive numerous Alabama miners to

West Virginia. Commenting on the low wages in Alabama mines, Henderson explained: "That's why we came to West Virginia. They wasn't paying nothing. They was paying more here in West Virginia mines than they was down there."[16] Blacks who entered mining from industrial or semi-industrial backgrounds, like the Hendersons, Phillips, and Wooten, experienced less radical change than farm laborers did.

The advertising campaigns of coal companies were an important stimulant to black migration. In the spring of 1916, the U.S. Coal and Coke Company, a subsidiary of U.S. Steel Corporation, advertised for workers at Gary, McDowell County: "Wanted at once/ 1000 Miners and Coke Drawers/ 11 mines and 2000 coke ovens working Six Days Per Week/ Five Percent Increase in Wages/ Effective May 8, 1916." At the height of World War I such advertising intensified. In the summer of 1917, the King and Tidewater Coal and Coke Company at Vivian, McDowell County, frantically announced: "10 Automobiles Free/ Men Wanted! Miners and Day Men Money without limit to be made with Ten Automobiles given away free."[17]

Professional labor recruiters for the coal companies also spurred southern blacks to move to the coalfields. During World War I, recruiter E. T. McCarty, whose office was in the Jefferson County Bank Building, Birmingham, Alabama, had major southern West Virginia coal producers as his clients, including the New River Coal Company and the New River and Pocahontas Coal Company. The renowned Jones and Maddox Employment Agency, headquartered in Bessemer, Alabama, also served a variety of southern West Virginia coal companies. The recruiters carefully calculated messages such as these: "Do you want to go North where the laboring man shares the profits with the boss? Are you satisfied with your condition? Are you satisfied with your pay envelope? Are you making enough wages [to] take care of you in the times of distress? If you are not satisfied we want you to come to see us."[18]

Coal companies also enlisted the support of middle-class black leaders to boost their labor recruitment campaigns. Especially important was the local black weekly (the sole one at the time), the *McDowell Times*, which circulated in West Virginia and nearby communities in Virginia. During World War I its editorial page proclaimed, "Let millions of Negroes leave the South, it will make conditions better for those who remain." In lengthy articles, the *Times* celebrated the movement of blacks into the various coal camps like those at Glen White, Raleigh County. "The old saying that 'All roads lead to Rome' surely has its modern analogy. . . . 'All railroads seem to lead to Glen White' for every train drops its quota of colored folks who are anxious to make their homes in the most beautiful spot in the mining district of West Virginia." The *Times* columnist Ralph W. White stated simply: "To one and all of them we say WELCOME."[19]

Despite the weekly's optimistic portrayals, a substantial degree of private and public coercion underlay the recruitment of black labor. Operators often advanced migrants' transportation fees, housing, and credit at the company store, putting them in debt from the start. After securing black labor for their mines, some coal operators were notorious for their violent control of black workers through the Baldwin-Felts detectives they employed. One black miner recalled: "I can show you scars on my head which were put in there by the Baldwin-Felts men in 1917. There was four of them jumped me until they thought me dead, but I didn't die. They kicked two or three ribs loose—two or three of them—on Cabin Creek."[20]

The operators' autonomy over company-owned land was strengthened in 1917 when the West Virginia legislature enacted a law to "prevent idleness and vagrancy . . . during the war and for six months thereafter." "All able-bodied men between 18 and 60 years of age, regardless of color, class or income, must toil 35 hours each week to support themselves and their dependents."[21] Failure to work as prescribed could result in arrests and sentences to work for the county or city for six months. Because the law was ostensibly neutral regarding race and class, however, it received the enthusias-tic endorsement of middle-class black leaders like T. Edward Hill. "So the boys who 'toil not' in McDowell county have 30 days to make up their minds [to work in the mines or on public road crews]. . . . Don't crowd boys."[22]

Moreover, West Virginia had passed a prohibition law in 1914. Some of the arrests and convictions under the law—and sentences to hard labor on county road projects—were scarcely veiled efforts to discipline and exploit the black labor force. Even the *McDowell Times* soon decried the injustice, if condescendingly. It condemned the authorities for arresting "a lot of ignorant men and depriving their families of support for months and in some cases years." According to the State Commissioner of Prohibition, southern West Virginia had the highest incidence of arrests, convictions, and sentences to hard labor on county road projects.[23]

Although some black migrants felt the impact of public and private coercion, most chose southern West Virginia voluntarily, using their network of kin and friends to get there. After arriving, they often urged their southern kin and friends to join them. In his investigation of the Great Migration, the U.S. attorney for the southern district of Alabama reported that at least 10 percent of those who had left had returned, but half of the returnees had come back for relatives and friends. "It is the returned negroes who carry others off."[24]

Coal companies soon recognized the recruitment potential of black kin and friendship networks and hired black miners to recruit among relatives and friends. During World War I, the Rum Creek Collieries Company hired Scotty Todd as a labor recruiter. For one of his trips back to Alabama, Todd was given enough money to bring fifty men to West Virginia. Several relatives and friends returned to the state with him, including his younger brother Roy. At Hollow Creek, McDowell County, the company added a second and then a third shift. When one newcomer asked why, the superintendent's reply, although highly paternalistic, revealed the familial pattern of black migration: "If you stop bringing all your uncles and . . . aunts and cousins up here we wouldn't have to do that. We got to make somewhere for them to work. . . . They can't all work on day shift. They can't all work on evening shift."[25]

Coal mining was an overwhelmingly male occupation, with few opportunities for black women outside the home. Yet black women made great sacrifices in the black migration to southern West Virginia. Catherine Phillips lived in rural western Virginia, where her husband, John Henry, worked in a nearby sawmill. Catherine raised crops for home consumption, performed regular household chores, and gave birth to at least three of the couple's eight children. In 1917 she took care of the family by herself for several months while John Henry traveled to southern West Virginia to work in the coal mines. He finally returned for her and the children.[26] Nannie Bolling, more than a decade before she moved with her family to southern West Virginia, married Sam Beasley in rural North Carolina. Sam eventually traveled to Gary, McDowell County, and worked in the mines for several pay periods, leaving Nannie to take care of the couple's four children by herself until he returned for them. Vallier Henderson, in a family group that included her husband, four children, and one grandparent, traveled from Jefferson County, Alabama, to McDowell County during World War I. The Hendersons traveled with three other Alabama families, along with their household furnishings, and the trip took nearly seven days by rail. Upon reaching McDowell County, the families made a long and arduous horse-and-wagon trip into the mountains of Coalwood.[27] Black women—desiring to hold their families together, escape rural poverty, and gain greater control over their destinies—played a key role in the migration to southern West Virginia.[28]

Entangled in a web of legal snares and debts, some black sharecroppers found it more difficult than others to escape the South. Notwithstanding deteriorating southern economic conditions, southern landowners and businessmen often resisted black migration, fearing the permanent loss of their low-wage labor pool. Thus, many blacks had to use a great deal of careful planning, and even secrecy, to leave. In his effort to ascertain the character and extent of black migration from Mississippi, Jasper Boykins, a U.S. deputy marshal, reported: "It is very difficult to get the names and addresses of any of the negroes going away. It seems that this movement is being conducted very quietly."[29] Another investigator likewise observed: "I, myself, went to see the families of several negroes who have left and they are loath to tell where these people have gone. Of course, I did not tell them what I wanted to know. . . . they are secretive by nature."[30] Black migrants were by no means "secretive by nature," but many of them were secretive by design, and for good reason. The coercive elements of the southern sharecropping system would die hard.

Yet not all black migrants to southern West Virginia received the blessings of their kin. Some young men moved despite the opposition of their fathers, who sought to keep them on the land. Scotty Todd and his brother moved to West Virginia when their father rejected their effort to bargain with him: they had requested a car in exchange for staying on the farm.[31] Salem Wooten's father also fought a losing battle to keep his sons on the land. The oldest son "slipped away," and his brother later vividly recalled the occasion: "My father sent him over in the field to do some work. . . . And he packed his clothes, what few he had, and slipped them over there at the edge of the field and worked a little bit, well something like a half an hour in the field. Then he went to the cherry tree, ate all the cherries he could eat. Then he came down the tree and got his little suit case and he had to cross Smith River to get what we called the Norfolk and Western Railroad train . . . into Roanoke, [Va.] from there into West Virginia. . . . He had money enough. . . . He came to McDowell County."[32] Such family disputes undoubtedly touched the lives of numerous blacks who made their way to the coalfields.

In contrast to the vigorous recruitment of black mine workers that characterized the war years, rising unemployment plagued them during the early 1920s. The Bureau of Negro Welfare and Statistics (BNWS) reported that the two years from July 1, 1921, to June 30, 1923, "were the most unsettled and dullest in the coal industry of this state for many years." Numerous black miners like John Henry Phillips moved to farms in Virginia and North Carolina until work in West Virginia was "more plentiful and wages higher." Other black miners left the state for Pennsylvania and other northern industrial centers.[33]

More important, as the United Mine Workers of America accelerated its organizing activities in the early years after World War I, coal companies intensified their efforts to retain a solid cadre of black labor. As early as June 1920, the Williamson Coal Operators Association addressed a full-page advertisement to black workers that emphasized "the discrimination practiced against their race in the unionized fields" where the United Mine Workers held contracts with the operators of the northern Appalachian mines. Logan County coal operators developed a pamphlet for black workers that exaggerated the virtues of coal mining in the area. "You are now living in the best coal field in the country, working six days a week in perfect harmony and on the seventh day resting, where there are churches and schools furnished by the coal company, while in the so-called Union fields, churches and schools are not furnished. . . . You are getting better pay than any other field and better coal."[34]

During the early postwar years, the BNWS reinforced the operators' lively campaign to keep black workers. Under its black director, T. Edward Hill, an attorney and business manager of the *McDowell Times*, the bureau often served the labor needs of the coal industry. In 1921–22, for example, the bureau proudly proclaimed credit for deterring over one hundred black men from joining the violent "Armed March" of miners on Logan and Mingo Counties. Equally important, the bureau recognized how destabilizing the cyclical swings of the coal economy were. When work was "irregular and wages reached a certain minimum," the bureau observed, hundreds of black miners moved to nearby southern farms until work resumed at higher wages. In an effort to help stabilize the black labor force, the BNWS advocated the permanent resettlement of southern blacks on available West Virginia farm land: "If this can be done, it will not only add to the fixed productive population of the state but will keep a large body of workers convenient to the industry. When business resumes, after the periodical shutdowns, operators can locate workers near at hand without the necessity of sending to Virginia, North Carolina, Alabama, and other Southern states for them."[35]

As the coal industry recovered, roughly between 1923 and 1928, black migration to southern West Virginia also resumed. The black population there increased from close to 60,000 in 1920 to nearly 80,000 in 1930 (tables 3.1, 3.2). By 1925 the black coal-mining labor force had increased to nearly 20,300, about 27 percent of the labor force, and the proportion of immigrants had declined to less than 14 percent (tables 3.3, 3.4). The black workers who had left the area during the economic downturn and coal strikes of the early postwar years had slowly been replaced by other blacks, some of whom had served as strikebreakers. It was during this period that black migrants from the Deep South states of Alabama, Georgia, and South Carolina dramatically increased in number. Alabama moved up from third to second place as a source of black migrants. In 1924 blacks born in Alabama made up nearly 10 percent of the total number of West Virginia blacks born in other states. Unlike the case with black migration to the industrial North, however, the upper South and border states of Virginia, North Carolina, Tennessee, and Kentucky continued to dominate the migration stream to West Virginia (table 3.5).[36]

Established black kin and friendship networks played a key role in stimulating the new cycle of black migration into southern West Virginia's coalfields. Born in Leesville, Virginia, Sidney Lee had worked since the age of fifteen, alternating between work on the Virginian Railroad and farm labor. He visited relatives in southern West Virginia for several months off and on before moving to Omar, Logan County, in 1926 to take his first permanent job, loading coal. Lester Phillips (son of Catherine and John Henry) returned to southern West Virginia to work in the mines shortly after his sister's marriage to a Pageton, McDowell County, man during the late 1920s. Salem Wooten's oldest brother, after migrating to southern West Virginia from Virginia in the early postwar years, assisted seven of his younger brothers to enter the coalfields, most of whom arrived during the mid-to-late 1920s. The youngest, Salem, was the last to arrive; he migrated during the early 1930s. According to Elizabeth Broadnax, she and her mother moved from North Carolina to Capels, McDowell County, during the 1920s because her brother lived and worked there.[37]

The growing importance of black kin and friendship networks was also reflected in the rising number of West Virginia–born black miners. In increasing numbers, southern-born miners taught their West Virginia–born sons how to mine coal. This process gained momentum during the 1920s. In 1923, the Virginia–born miner, James B. Harris took his fifteen-year-old son into the mines at Giatto, Mercer County. Charles T. Harris, member of a coal-mining family, recalled how he became a miner: "I never even thought about it. Just coal mining was all I knew. My father was a coal miner." In 1926, Preston Turner, with his father and cousin, loaded his first ton of coal at the Winding Gulf Colliery Company. Under the shadow of the impending depression, Lawrence Boling entered the mines of Madison, Boone County, in 1930. While Gus Boling had hoped to educate his son, he now relented and carried the young man into the mines. Lawrence recalled: "My dad and I talked it over. . . . Things were tough in the mines. . . . I seen I didn't have a chance to go to college even if I finished high school. So I decided at that point that I wanted to work in the mines and would be helping him too. I went in with him. . . . He was responsible for me for a certain length of time."[38]

During the 1920s, like most of their white counterparts, Afro-Americans entered the mines primarily as unskilled coal loaders. As before the war, they worked mainly in underground positions, called "inside labor," as opposed to doing outside or surface work. In 1921, and again in 1927, the BNWS reported that more than 90 percent of black miners worked as manual coal loaders or as common day laborers. The percentage of black laborers declined during the Great Depression. Yet, according to Laing's survey of twenty coal-mining operations—covering McDowell, Mercer, Fayette, Raleigh, Kanawha, and Logan counties—75 percent of black miners still worked in these positions in 1932 (tables 3.6, 3.7, and 3.8).[39]

Coal loading was the most common, difficult, and hazardous inside job and thus was more readily available. Yet blacks often preferred it because it paid more than other manual labor jobs and "provided the least supervision with the greatest amount of personal freedom in work hours." As one black miner recalled, because coal loaders were paid by the ton, they could increase their wages simply by increasing their output.[40] On the other hand, while the average wage rates for coal loading were higher than most outside jobs, like other inside work, it was subject to greater seasonal fluctuations and presented greater health hazards.

Although coal loading was classified as unskilled work, it did require care and skill. For the novice especially, the apparently simple act of loading coal into a waiting train car could not be taken for

granted. Watt Teal's father taught him important techniques for pre-
serving his health as well as his life such as carefully pacing his
work. As Watt Teal concluded:

> There is a little art to it. . . . He taught me to load the coal. . . . After
> all you could load it the wrong way and get broke down and you
> couldn't do business. . . . First of all [when] a young man go in he
> want to fill his shovel up so full he can't pick it up which is
> wrong. . . . So [at first] you get so much on the shovel and start off
> and get used to it and then you can gradually pick up more on the
> shovel.[41]

Coal loading involved much more than merely pacing the work,
though. It took over an hour of preparation before the miner could
lift his first shovel of coal. The miner deployed an impressive range
of knowledge and skills: the techniques of dynamiting coal, including knowledge of various gases and the principles of ventilation;
the establishment of roof supports to prevent dangerous cave-ins;
and the persistent canvassing of mines for potential hazards. Referring to the training he received from his brother, Salem Wooten recalled: "The first thing he taught me was . . . my safety, how to set
props and posts. Wood posts were set up to keep the slate and
rocks from caving in on you . . . safety first."[42]

Wooten's brother also taught him the techniques for blasting
coal: how to drill holes with an auger and place sticks of dynamite
in them properly, how to judge atmospheric conditions and be
acutely sensitive, not only to his own safety, but to the safety of

TABLE 3.6
Black Coal Miners in West Virginia by Job Classification, 1921

	Number	Percent
Loaders	2,876	44.4
Inside and outside men (mainly common laborers)	3,376	52.1
Motormen	182	2.8
Skilled mechanics (mainly undercutting machine)	36	0.5
Foremen and other bosses	7	0.1
Officers and welfare workers	6	0.1
Total	6,483	100.0

Source: West Virginia Bureau of Negro Welfare and Statistics, *Biennial Report, 1921–22*
(Charleston, W.Va.), pp. 57–58.
Note: Table sample was 6,483.

TABLE 3.7
Black Coal Miners in West Virginia by Job Classification 1927

	Number	Percent
Day laborer[s]	2,233	29.4
Coal loaders	4,674	61.4
Drivers	125	1.6
Brakemen	34	0.4
Trappers	10	0.1
Motormen	321	4.2
Machine operators	215	2.8
Carpenters	8	0.1
Fire boss	1	—
Total	7,621	100.0

Source: West Virginia Bureau of Negro Welfare and Statistics, *Biennial Report, 1927–28* (Charleston, W.Va.) pp. 17–19.
Note: Table sample was 7,621.

TABLE 3.8
Mining Occupations by Race and Ethnicity in Twenty Coal Operations of
Five Southern West Virginia Counties, 1932

	Blacks		Immigrants		American-Born Whites	
Occupation	Number	Percent	Number	Percent	Number	Percent
Coal loaders	1,410	76.8	626	87.6	1,329	52.7
Machinemen	36	1.9	18	2.5	172	6.5
Motormen	85	4.6	16	2.2	199	7.6
Brakemen	128	6.9	7	0.9	169	6.4
Trackmen	109	5.9	36	5.0	177	6.7
Tipplemen	24	1.3	6	0.8	293	11.2
Other	43	2.3	5	0.7	224	8.5
Totals	1,835	100.0	714	100.0	2,613	100.0

Source: James T. Laing, "The Negro Miner in West Virginia" (Ph.D. diss., Ohio State University, 1933), p. 195
Note: The table included the following counties: McDowell, Mercer, Raleigh, Fayette, Kanawha, and possibly Logan.

fellow workers as well. Salem also learned the miner's distinctive vocabulary of terms like "bug dust" (particles of coal remaining after machines undercut the coal), "kettlebottom" (a huge fossilized type of rock that could injure and even kill workers if dislodged from the roof of a mine), and the frequently shouted "Fire! Fire in the Hole!" warning to fellow workers of an impending dynamite blast.[43]

Coal loading was not the only job that blacks entered. Small numbers of them worked in skilled positions as machine operators, brakemen, and motormen. In its 1921–22 report, the BNWS proudly announced its success, although modest, in placing "three machine men, two motormen . . . [as well as] 57 coal loaders and company men." Labor advertisements sometimes specified the broad range of jobs available to Afro-Americans: "Coal Miners, Coke Oven Men, Day Laborers, Contract Men and Helpers, Motormen, Track Layers. Machine Runners, Mule Drivers, Power Plant Men, and other good jobs to offer around the mines." According to statewide data, the number of black motormen and machinemen (or mechanics) increased nearly 50 percent, from 218 in 1921 to 536 in 1927 (tables 3.6, 3.7). Although their numbers declined thereafter, some blacks retained their foothold in skilled positions through the 1920s, with machine running being the most lucrative. Between 1926 and 1929, for example, Roy Todd and his brothers worked as machine operators at the Island Creek Coal Company, at Holden, Logan County. On this job, Roy Todd recalled, he made enough money to buy a new car, bank $100 monthly, pay his regular expenses, and still have "money left over."[44]

However skillful black coal loaders may have become, coal loading took its toll on their health. Some men literally broke themselves down loading coal. Pink Henderson painfully recalled: "My daddy got so he couldn't load coal. He tried to get company work [light labor, often on the outside], but the doctor turned him down, because he couldn't do nothing. He done broke his self down. . . . My brothers done the same thing. They used to be the heavy loaders." Moreover, all coal loaders, black and white, careful and careless, were subject to the inherent dangers of coal mining such as black lung disease, then commonly called "miners' asthma," a slow killer of miners caused by constant inhalation of coal dust. Explosions were the most publicized and dramatic cause of miner's deaths, but roof and coal falls were the largest and most consistent killer (tables 3.9, 3.10). All coal miners and their families had to learn how to live with the fear of death, although few fully succeeded. As one black miner and his wife recalled, reminiscent of Booker T. Washington's experience in the early prewar years: "That fear is always there. That fear was there all the time, because . . . you may see [each other] in the morning and never [see each other] any more in the flesh."[45]

As Afro-Americans abandoned southern life and labor for work in the coalfields, the foregoing evidence suggests, their rural and semirural work culture gradually gave way to the imperatives of industrial capitalism. New skills, work habits, and occupational hazards moved increasingly to the fore, gradually supplanting their

TABLE 3.9
Two Selected Inside Fatal Accidents by Race and Ethnicity,
West Virginia, 1917–27

	Roof and Coal Falls		Mine Cars	
	Number	Percent	Number	Percent
1917				
Blacks	41	18.9	14	27.5
Foreign-born whites	73	33.4	14	27.5
American-born whites	104	47.7	23	45.0
Total	218	100.0	51	100.0
1921				
Blacks	45	23.0	12	22.7
Foreign-born whites	52	26.5	11	20.7
American-born whites	99	50.5	30	56.6
Total	196	100.0	53	100.0
1925				
Blacks	67	18.8	24	23.6
Foreign-born whites	90	25.1	13	12.7
American-born whites	201	56.1	65	63.7
Total	358	100.0	102	100.0
1927				
Blacks	59	22.1	19	23.8
Foreign-born whites	60	22.3	8	10.0
American-born whites	149	55.6	53	66.2
Total	268	100.0	80	100.0

Source: West Virginia Department of Mines, *Annual Reports, 1917,* p. 228, *1921,* p. 346, *1925,* p. 238, and *1927,* p. 207.

older rural work patterns and rhythms of "alternating periods of light and intensive labor." With the dramatic expansion of their numbers during World War I and the 1920s, black miners increasingly experienced southern West Virginia as a permanent place to live and labor.[46]

The working lives of black women also underwent change in southern West Virginia, but it was less dramatic. Along with their regular domestic tasks, working-class black women nearly universally tended gardens. Although the men and boys cleared and

TABLE 3.10
Fatal and Nonfatal Mine Accidents by Race and Ethnicity,
West Virginia, 1917–27

	Fatal		Nonfatal	
	Number	Percent	Number	Percent
		1917		
Blacks	74	18.8	176	17.8
Foreign-born whites	115	29.2	237	23.8
American-born whites	205	52.0	580	58.4
Total	394	100.0	993	100.0
		1919		
Blacks	72	20.9	137	16.3
Foreign-born whites	86	24.8[a]	203	24.3
American-born whites	188	54.3	500	59.0
Total	346	100.0	842	100.0
		1925		
Blacks	128	18.7	645	19.1
Foreign-born whites	138	20.1	617	18.1
American-born whites	420	61.2	2,132	62.8
Total	686	100.0	3,394	100.0
		1927		
Blacks	168	28.5	644	18.8
Foreign-born whites	96	16.3	554	16.0
American-born whites	326	55.2	2,245	65.2
Total	590	100.0	3,443	100.0

Source: West Virginia Department of Mines, *Annual Reports, 1917–27* (Charleston, W.Va.).

[a]Includes three unknowns.

broke the ground, women and children planted, cultivated, harvested, and canned the produce: corn, beans, cabbage, and collard and turnip greens. The family's diet was supplemented by a few hogs, chickens, and sometimes a cow.[47] Gardening not only nourished the family, but also symbolized links with their rural past and soon became deeply entrenched in the region's economic and cultural traditions. Not yet eleven years old, while confined to a local hospital bed, a young black female penned her first verse, illuminating the role of black women in the life of the coalfields:

> When I get [to be] an old lady,
> I tell you what I'll do,
> I'll patch my apron, make my dress
> And hoe the garden too.[48]

Although black women maintained gardens and worked mainly in the home, when compared to their white counterparts, they had a higher rate of wage-earning domestic service employment. Based on state-level data, in 1920, when 19.8 percent of black women were gainfully employed, only 10.8 percent of American-born white women, 15.5 percent of American-born white women of foreign or mixed parentage, and merely 8.2 percent of immigrant women were so employed. Recalling her mother's experience during the 1920s, Margaret Moorman opined, "No matter how poor white people are, they can always find a little change to hire a black woman in their home, and [my mother] did that, she would work occasionally for some of the bosses."[49] When Mary Davis's husband lost a leg in a mining accident during the 1920s, she opened a boardinghouse restaurant, serving black miners in the area. She rented an eight-room facility, where her family of nine boys and seven girls resided. To supplement Mary's restaurant activities, the family purchased a mule and cultivated a relatively large hillside plot behind the restaurant. In addition to a variety of vegetable crops, the family raised several hogs, chickens, and cows.[50]

Part and parcel of the material services that black coal miners' wives provided their families were indispensable emotional encouragement and support. Even if exaggerated, the obituaries of black women suggest their successful interweaving of material and spiritual roles. The 1916 obituary of Maggie E. Matney, wife of a black miner and a teacher by training, testified: "Her aim in life was the comfort and happiness of her home. She worked day and night to have these conditions exist there. It was indeed a place where each

absent member longed to be. . . . [She planned] minutely the cost
and use of every item that entered the family budget."[51]

Matney's teacher's training must have enabled her to systematize
her parental role. Yet working-class black women placed a high
value on children and family; some sought to adopt children when
they could not have their own. In 1928, for example, a black woman
in the coal town of Hiawatha, McDowell County, wrote to W. E. B.
Du Bois seeking his aid in adopting a child: "I would love for you
all to look out for a girl are [sic] a boy [w]ho have not got a good
home. . . . We have not got children and we would be so glad
to. . . . they would really have a good home." When one black
woman married a coal miner who had recently lost his wife and
had two sons, she dreaded the task of stepmothering, until one day
she overheard one of her stepsons say to the other, "There is a
dusty seat in Heaven waiting for a good stepmother and I believe
Mrs. Lulu will get it; for she is a good step-mother."[52]

Family and gender relations in the black coal-mining community
were by no means unproblematic, though. The son of one miner
who remarried following the death of his first wife recalled that his
stepmother "was very antagonistic toward her three stepsons." As
tension built between the children and the stepmother, one of the
sons left home at an early age, he said, "in order to avoid the conflict between us." When it came to defining gender roles, working-
class black men endorsed the home as woman's proper and special
sphere. In an ad for a wife, one black miner sought a woman who
could "cook, iron, feed his children and hogs, milk his cows, patch
his pants, darn his socks, sew buttons on his shirt and in a general
way attend to the domestic duties of his palatial home." Working-
class black men were acutely aware of their own tremendous labor
value in the coalfields, as well as the small ratio of black female
wage earners. Unfortunately, this awareness, in part, often led
black miners to undervalue the black woman's contributions to the
household economy. "My mother never hit a lick at a snake," exclaimed one second-generation miner when asked if his mother
worked outside the home.[53] Nonetheless, in the hostile racial environment of southern West Virginia, black men and women pooled
their resources in the interest of group survival and development.

Although Afro-American coal-mining families gained a significant foothold in the coal industry, not all blacks who entered the
coalfields were equally committed to coal-mining life. Some of the
men were actually gamblers, pimps, and bootleggers, reminiscent
of John Hardy of prewar fame. Middle-class black leaders attacked

these men as "Jonahs" and "kid-glove dudes," who moved into the coalfields, exploited the miners, and then often moved on.[54] Other black men, like European immigrants, used coal mining as a means of making money to buy land and farms in other parts of the South. On the eve of World War I, for example, Ike Mitchell came to West Virginia from South Carolina. After two years, he had saved $2,000 in cash from his job in the Kanawha–New River Field. During the early war years he returned his family to South Carolina, used his savings to buy land, and began raising cotton for market. The 1921–22 report of the BNWS noted that some black miners continued to work, sacrifice, and save in order "to buy a farm 'down home,' pay the indebtedness upon one already purchased or, after getting a 'little money ahead,' return to the old home." The 1923–24 report observed that several hundred blacks in the mines of McDowell, Mercer, and Mingo counties either owned farms in Virginia and North Carolina or else had relatives who did. In order to curtail the temporary, and often seasonal, pattern of black migration and work in the mines, the BNWS accelerated its campaign for the permanent resettlement of blacks on available West Virginia farm land.[55]

If some black workers entered the region on a temporary or seasonal basis, shifting back and forth between southern farm work and mine labor, it was the upswings and downswings of the business cycle that kept most black miners on the move. Although there was an early postwar economic depression in the coal economy, as noted above, it was the onslaught of the Great Depression that revealed in sharp relief the precarious footing of the black coal-mining proletariat. In December 1930, the black columnist S. R. Anderson of Bluefield reported that "more hunger and need" existed among Bluefield's black population "than is generally known. It is going to be intensified during the hard months of January and February."[56] In the economic downturn that followed, the region's black miners dropped from 19,648 in 1929 to 18,503 in 1931, though the percentage of blacks in the labor force fluctuated only slightly, hovering between 26 and 27 percent. Before this, the BNWS had advocated black farm ownership as a mode of labor recruitment for the coal industry; now it advocated farming as a primary solution to the permanent unemployment that affected a growing number of black miners: "The most helpful solution is found in the soil. Mother Earth alone will offer the only secure refuge against suffering and starvation for the army of unemployed and their families."[57]

As unemployment increased during the late 1920s and early 1930s, the advice of the BNWS notwithstanding, intraregional movement accelerated. Unlike during the earlier downturn, when many black miners moved to nearby southern farms and to northern industrial centers, most miners now struggled to maintain their foothold in the coal-mining region. Their desperation is vividly recorded in the "Hawk's Nest Tragedy" of Fayette County. In 1930 the Union Carbide Corporation commissioned the construction firm of Rinehart and Dennis of Charlottesville, Virginia, to dig the Hawk's Nest Tunnel, in order to channel water from the New River to Union Carbide's hydroelectric plant near the Gauley Bridge. As local historian Mark Rowh noted, "Construction of the tunnel would mean hundreds of jobs, and many saw it as a godsend. Unfortunately, it would prove the opposite."[58]

Requiring extensive drilling through nearly four miles of deadly silica rock, in some areas approaching 100 percent, the project claimed the lives of an estimated five hundred men by its completion in 1935. Afro-Americans were disproportionately hired for the project, and they were the chief victims. They made up 65 percent of the project's labor force and 75 percent of the inside tunnel crew. Official company reports invariably underestimated the number of casualities on the project, but, even so, they highlight the disproportionate black deaths among the work crews. According to P. H. Faulconer, president of Rinehart and Dennis, for example, "In the 30 months from the start of driving to the end of 1932, a total of 65 deaths of all workmen, both outside and inside the tunnel occurred, six whites and fifty-nine colored." Although the firm was aware of a safer, wet drilling method, it selected to use the more efficient, but lethal, dry drilling process, allowing workers to use water "only when state inspectors were expected at the scene."[59] The Depression was not only a period of extensive unemployment, but, as the Hawk's Nest calamity demonstrates, also a time of extraordinary labor exploitation.

If unemployment pressed some men into the lethal Hawk's Nest project, it also required substantial sacrifice from black women. Pink Henderson recalled that while he worked on a variety of temporary jobs during the early depression years, his wife "canned a lot of stuff," kept two or three hogs, raised chickens, and made clothing for the family. In 1930 the U.S. Census Bureau reported that 57.6 percent of black families in West Virginia were comprised of three persons or less, compared to 37.5 percent for immigrant families and 40.8 percent for American-born white ones; but the difference in household size was offset by the larger number of boarders taken in by black families. During the late 1920s and early 1930s, for example, Mary Davis not only enabled her own family to survive hard times, but also aided the families of unemployed coal miners with her boardinghouse restaurant. "We were pretty fortunate," her son later recalled, "and helped a lot of people."[60]

Black coal miners and their families, the foregoing evidence suggests, were inextricably involved in the larger proletarianization process. As in the prewar years, through their southern kin and friendship networks, black coal miners played a crucial role in organizing their own migration to the region, facilitating their own entrance into the industrial labor force and, to a substantial degree, shaping their own experiences under the onslaught of industrial capitalism. Yet their socioeconomic footing remained volatile, as reflected in the significant economic contributions of black women, the Hawk's Nest tragedy, and the miner's substantial geographical mobility.

Moreover, as the coal industry entered the postwar era, racial and ethnic competition intensified. In their persistent efforts to move up in the job hierarchy, blacks faced increasing racial and class barriers, erected by discriminatory employers, workers, and the state. Even as manual coal loaders they confronted growing economic discrimination. Patterns of class and racial discrimination in the workplace, the energetic responses of black miners, and the growing alliance between black workers and black elites are explored in the following chapters.

NOTES

1. West Virginia Department of Mines, *Annual Reports, 1910–30* (Charleston, W.Va.); Philip M. Conley, *History of the West Virginia Coal Industry* (Charleston, W.Va.: Education Foundation, 1960), pp. 92–266; W. P. Tams, *The Smokeless Coal Fields of West Virginia: A Brief History* (1963; rept., Morgantown: West Virginia University Press, 1983), p. 107; Ronald D Eller, *Miners, Millhands, and Mountaineers: Industrialization of the Appalachian South, 1880–1930* (Knoxville: University of Tennessee Press, 1982), pp. 132–40.

2. West Virginia Department of Mines, *Annual Reports, 1910–30*; Keith Dix, *Work Relations in the Coal Industry: The Handloading Era, 1880–1930* (Morgantown: West Virginia University, Institute for Labor Studies, 1977), pp. 20–29; Dix, *What's A Coal Miner To Do?: The Mechanization of Coal Mining and Its Impact on Coal Miners* (Pittsburgh: University of Pittsburgh Press, 1988), pp. 1–27; Price V. Fishback, "Employment Conditions in the Coal Industry, 1900–1930" (Ph.D. diss., University of Washington, 1983), pp. 44–51; Eller, *Miners, Millhands, and Mountaineers*, pp. 132–49, 153–160; Darold T.

Barnum, *The Negro in the Bituminous Coal Mining Industry* (Philadelphia: University of Pennsylvania Press, 1970), pp. 7–8; David A. Corbin, *Life, Work, and Rebellion in the Coal Fields: The Southern West Virginia Miners, 1880–1922* (Urbana: University of Illinois Press, 1981), pp. 3–5; Conley, *History of the West Virginia Coal Industry*, pp. 92–266.

3. West Virginia Department of Mines, *Annual Reports, 1916–30*; Eller, *Miners, Millhands, and Mountaineers*, pp. 153–60; Corbin, *Life, Work, and Rebellion*, chaps. 7, 8, and 9; Fishback, "Employment Conditions," pp. 72–82, 116–20; "How the Unorganized Colored Miner and Foreigner Are Exploited for Low Wages," *United Mine Workers Journal* (hereafter cited as *UMWJ*), 15 Jan. 1924; Van A. Bittner, "Wages in Bituminous Coal Mines as Viewed by the Miners," *Annals of the American Academy of Political and Social Sciences* 3 (1924): 32–38.

4. Corbin, *Life, Work, and Rebellion*, chaps. 2, 7, 8, 9; Eller, *Miners, Millhands, and Mountaineers*, pp. 197–98; Daniel P. Jordan, "The Mingo War: Labor Violence in the Southern West Virginia Coal Fields, 1921–1922," in Gary M. Fink and Merle E. Reed, eds., *Essays in Southern Labor History*, (Westport, Conn.: Greenwood Press, 1977), pp. 102–43; "Civil War in West Virginia," excerpts of articles from the *New York Evening Post*, Feb. 7–Mar. 3, in Kanawha Coal River files, Box 6, Record Group No. 68, U.S. Coal Commission, National Archives, Washington, 1923; "West Virginia Militia Drives Representatives of the United Mine Workers from the State," *UMWJ*, 1 Aug. 1921; "Mingo County Operators Admit That They Pay Salaries of Gunmen Serving as Deputy Sheriffs," *UMWJ*, 15 Aug. 1921; U.S. Senate, *West Virginia Coal Fields: Hearings Before the Committee on Education*, (Washington, 1921), 1:26–38, 469–82.

5. Eller, *Miners, Millhands, and Mountaineers*, pp. 159–60; Corbin, *Life, Work, and Rebellion*, pp. 30–31; Fishback, "Employment Conditions," pp. 187–89; and Dix, *Work Relations in the Coal Industry*, chap. 1.

6. Eller, *Miners, Millhands, and Mountaineers*, pp. 190–98; Corbin, *Life, Work, and Rebellion*, chap. 5; Charles H. Ambler and Festus P. Summers, *West Virginia: The Mountain State*, 2d ed. (Englewood Cliffs, N.J.: Prentice Hall, 1958); U.S. Agricultural Extension Service, *Annual Reports, 1921–26* (Morgantown, W.Va.); *The New River Company Employees' Magazine*, 1924–30, vols. 2–5, in the West Virginia Collection, Morgantown, W.Va., especially S. A. Scott, vice president and general manager, "What Our Garden and Yard Contest is Accomplishing," 3, no. 1 (Sept. 1925); Mining Schedule A, Boxes 28 and 29, Record Group No. 68, U.S. Coal Commission; Parke P. Deans, "Coal Mining and Workmen's Compensation (with discussion)," in U.S. Bureau of Labor Statistics, *Bulletin* 91 (1930): 279–91.

7. James T. Laing, "The Negro Miner in West Virginia" (Ph.D. diss., Ohio State University, 1933), p. 266.

8. Corbin, *Life, Work, and Rebellion*, chaps. 7, 8, and 9; Eller, *Miners, Millhands, and Mountaineers*, pp. 156–60; Jordan, "The Mingo War," in Fink and Reed, eds., *Essays in Southern Labor History*, pp. 102–43; Richard D. Lunt, *Law and Order versus the Miners: West Virginia, 1907–1933* (Hamden, Conn.:

Archon Books, 1979); Hoyt N. Wheeler, "Mountaineer Mine Wars: West Virginia Mine Wars of 1912–13 and 1920–21," *Business History Review* 50 (Spring 1976): 69–91; Dix, *Work Relations in the Coal Industry*, chap. 2; Matt Witt and Earl Dolter, "Before I'd Be a Slave," in *In Our Blood* (New Market, Tenn.: Highlander Research Center, 1979), pp. 23–47.

9. West Virginia Department of Mines, *Annual Reports, 1910–20*.

10. Ralph W. White, "Another Lesson from the East St. Louis Lynching," *McDowell Times*, 20 July 1917; Carter G. Woodson, *A Century of Negro Migration* (1918; rept., New York: AMS Press, 1970), pp. 147–66; U.S. Bureau of the Census, *Thirteenth Census of the United States, 1910* (Washington, 1913), 3:1032–41; *Fourteenth Census, 1920* (Washington, 1922), 3:1105–9; *Fifteenth Census, 1930*, vol. 3, pt. 2 (Washington, 1932), pp. 1268–72.

11. Interviews with Lester and Ellen Phillips, 20 July 1983 and Salem Wooten, 25 July 1983. See also Reginald Millner, "Conversations with the Ole Man: The Life and Times of a Black Appalachian Coal Miner," *Goldenseal* 5 (Jan.-Mar. 1979): 58–64; Tim R. Massey, " 'I Didn't Think I'd Live to See 1950': Looking Back with Columbus Avery," *Goldenseal* 8 (Spring 1982): 32–40; Eller, *Miners, Millhands, and Mountaineers*, pp. 153–98; Corbin, *Life, Work, and Rebellion*, chaps. 7, 8, 9; Fishback, "Employment Conditions," pp. 72–82, 116–20.

12. Robert N. Bell, U.S. Attorney, Northern District of Alabama, to U.S. Attorney General, 25 Oct. 1916, and Alexander D. Pitts, U.S. Attorney, Southern District of Alabama, to Samuel J. Graham, Assistant Attorney General, 27 Oct. 1916, both in Department of Justice, Record Group No. 60, Straight Numerical File No. 182363, National Archives; interview with Thelma O. Trotter, 1 Aug. 1983, and conversation with Solomon Woodson, 9 Nov. 1985.

13. Florette Henri, *Black Migration: Movement North, 1900–1920* (Garden City, N.Y.: Anchor Press/Doubleday, 1975), pp. 132–73; Laing, "The Negro Miner," chap. 4; Eller, *Miners, Millhands, and Mountaineers*, pp. 168–72; Corbin, *Life, Work, and Rebellion*, pp. 61–63; interview with Roy Todd, 18 July 1983.

14. Interview with Thornton Wright, 27 July 1983; W. L. McMillan, Omar, W.Va., to R. L. Thorton, Three Notch, Ala., 2 Nov. 1916, in Record Group No. 60, Department of Justice, Straight Numerical File No. 182363; "Migration Study Negro Migrants, Letters Fr. (Typescript), 1916–18," in Series 6 Box 86, National Urban League Papers, Library of Congress.

15. McMillan to Thorton, 2 Nov. 1916; West Virginia Bureau of Negro Welfare and Statistics (WVBNWS), *Biennial Reports* (Charleston, W.Va.), *1921–22*, p. 5, *1925–26*, p. 8.

16. Interviews with Lester and Ellen Phillips, 20 July 1983, Salem Wooten, 25 July 1983, and Pink Henderson, 15 July 1983; Ronald L. Lewis, *Black Coal Miners in America: Race, Class, and Community Conflict, 1770–1980* (Lexington: University of Kentucky, 1987), chaps. 3 and 4; McMillan to Thornton, 2 Nov. 1916; "From Alabama: Colored Miners Anxious for Organization," *UMWJ*, 1 June 1916; Rev. T. H. Seals, "Life in Alabama," *UMWJ*,

15 Sept. 1924; "The Horrors of Convict Mines of Alabama," *UMWJ*, 19 Aug. 1915. See also Bell to U.S. Attorney, 25 Oct. 1916, Pitts to Graham, 27 Oct. 1916, "Memorandum: Willie Parker," and "Statement of Tom Jones," all in Department of Justice, Record Group No. 60, Straight Numerical File No. 182363.

17. "Wanted at Once," 12 May 1916, and "10 Automobiles Free," 25 May 1917, in *McDowell Times*; "Safety First," "Go North," "Wanted," and "Employment Office," in Box 2, Folder 13/25, Record Group No. 174, U.S. Department of Labor, National Archives.

18. From the Department of Justice, Record Group No. 60, Straight Numerical File No. 182363: Bell to Attorney General, 25 Oct. 1916; Pitts to Graham, 27 Oct. 1916; "Labor Agents Succeed in Inducing Negroes to Leave Southern Farms" (news clippings from the *Atlanta Constitution*); "Memorandum: Willie Parker," recorded by Edwin Ball, General Manager, Tennessee Coal, Iron, and Railroad Company; and "Statement of Tom Jones." See also "Early Surveys: Migration Study, Birmingham Summary," Series 6, Box 89, National Urban League Papers; "Safety First," "Go North," "Wanted," and "Employment Office," in Box 2, Folder 13/25, Record Group No. 174, U.S. Department of Labor.

19. "The Exodus," 18 Aug. 1916, "Southern Exodus in Plain Figures," 1 Dec. 1916, Ralph W. White, "Another Lesson From the E. St. Louis Lynching," 20 July 1917, and "Colored Folks Enjoying Universal Industrial and Social Advancement," 28 July 1917, in *McDowell Times*.

20. U.S. Senate, Committee on Interstate Commerce, *Conditions in the Coal Fields of Pennsylvania, West Virginia, and Ohio* (Washington, 1928). For excerpts of the committee hearings, see *UMWJ*, 1 Mar. 1928; testimony of J. H. Reed, in U.S. Senate, *West Virginia Coal Fields*, pp. 479–82.

21. "Idlers Between Ages of Eighteen and Sixty will be Forced to Work," *McDowell Recorder*, 25 May 1917; T. Edward Hill, "Loafers and Jonahs," *McDowell Times*, 25 May 1917; "Dig Coal or Dig Trenches is the Word to the Miner," *Raleigh Register*, 12 July 1917.

22. Hill, "Loafers and Jonahs," *McDowell Times*, 25 May 1917.

23. "Educate All the People," 16 April 1915, "To Whom it May Concern," 29 Jan. 1915, "Good People of McDowell County Outraged," 17 May 1918, in *McDowell Times*; State Commissioner of Prohibition, *Fourth Biennial Report, 1921–22* (Charleston, W.Va.).

24. Interviews with Salem Wooten, 25 July 1983. See also Pitts to Graham, 27 Oct. 1916, and Bell to U.S. Attorney General, 25 Oct. 1916, both in Record Group No. 60, Department of Justice, Straight Numerical File No. 182363.

25. Interviews with Roy Todd, 18 July 1983, and Watt B. Teal, 27 July 1983; Laing, "The Negro Miner," chap. 4.

26. Interviews with Lester and Ellen Phillips, 20 July 1983, and Andrew Campbell, 19 July 1983; Bell to U.S. Attorney General, 25 Oct. 1916, and Pitts to Graham, 27 Oct. 1916, both in Department of Justice, Record Group No. 60, Straight Numerical File No. 182363; WVBNWS, *Biennial Report*,

1923–24, pp. 22–23; "Adams-Russel," 14 July 1916, and "Gannaway-Patterson," 22 Dec. 1916, in *McDowell Times; The New River Company Employees' Magazine* 2, no. 3 (Nov. 1924): 9–10.

27. Interviews with William M. Beasley, 26 July 1983, and Pink Henderson, 15 July 1983; Thomas D. Samford, U.S. Attorney, Middle District of Alabama, to U.S. Attorney General, 2 Nov. and 21 Oct. 1916, in Department of Justice Record Group, No. 60, Straight Numerical File No. 182363.

28. See interview with Thornton Wright, 27 July 1983.

29. Jasper Boykins to U.S. Attorney General, 16 Oct. 1916, Department of Justice Record Group No. 60, Straight Numerical File No. 182363. For a discussion of coercion in southern agriculture, see Jay R. Mandle, *The Roots of Black Poverty: The Southern Plantation Economy after the Civil War* (Durham, N.C.: Duke University Press, 1978).

30. Pitts to Graham, 27 Oct. 1916, Department of Justice, Record Group No. 60, Straight Numerical File No. 182363.

31. Interview with Roy Todd, 18 July 1983.

32. Interview with Salem Wooten, 28 July 1983.

33. WVBNWS, *Biennial Reports, 1921–22*, pp. 57–58, and *1927–28*, pp. 17–19; interview with Lester and Ellen Phillips, 20 July 1983; James T. Laing, "The Negro Miners in West Virginia," *Social Forces* 14 (1936): 416–22; Laing, "The Negro Miner," chap. 5.

34. "Discrimination Against the Negro," *Bluefield Daily Telegraph*, 20 June 1920; "Negro Tricked into Logan County," *UMWJ*, 15 June 1921 (includes extensive excerpts of the operator's pamphlet to black workers).

35. WVBNWS, *Biennial Reports, 1921–29*, especially *1921–22*, pp. 38–41, and *1923–24*, pp. 29–35.

36. WVBNWS, *Biennial Report, 1923–24*, pp. 39–45; Children's Bureau, U.S. Department of Labor, *The Welfare of Children in Bituminous Coal Mining Communities in West Virginia* (Washington, 1923), p. 5.

37. Interviews with Sidney Lee, 19 July 1983, Lester and Ellen Phillips, 20 July 1983, and Salem Wooten, 25 July 1983; Randall G. Lawrence, interview with Eliza Broadnax, " 'Make a Way Out of Nothing': One Black Woman's Trip from North Carolina to the McDowell County Coalfields," *Goldenseal* 5, no. 4 (Oct.-Dec. 1979): 27–31.

38. Interviews with North Dickerson, 28 July 1983, Charles T. Harris, 18 July 1983, Preston Turner, 26 July 1983, and Lawrence Boling, 18 July 1983.

39. Laing, "The Negro Miner," p. 195.

40. Laing, "The Negro Miners in West Virginia," pp. 416–22; Laing, "The Negro Miner," chap. 5; interview with North Dickerson, 28 July 1983.

41. Interview with Watt B. Teal, 27 July 1983; Laing, "The Negro Miner," chap. 5. For general insight into the miner's work, see Carter G. Goodrich, *The Miner's Freedom* (1925; rept., New York: Arno Press, 1971) and Dix, *Work Relations in the Coal Industry*, chaps. 1, 2.

42. Interviews with Salem Wooten, 25 July 1983, Charles T. Harris, 18 July 1983, and Leonard Davis, 28 July 1983.

43. Interview with Salem Wooten, 25 July 1983. While some scholarly accounts refer to the particles left by the undercutting machine as "buck dust," black miners used the term "bug dust." It was even the nickname of one black miner. See Laing, "The Negro Miner," p. 171; Dix, *What's a Coal Miner to Do?*, chap. 1; and Goodrich, *The Miner's Freedom*, p. xx.

44. WVBNWS, *Biennial Report, 1921–22*, p. 59; "Safety First," "Go North," "Wanted," and "Employment Office," in Box 2, Folder 13/25, Record Group No. 174, U.S. Department of Labor; "Wanted: Sullivan Machine Men," *Logan Banner*, 8 June 1923; interviews with Roy Todd, 18 July 1983, and William M. Beasley, 26 July 1983. See also Dix, *Work Relations in the Coal Industry*, chap. 1; Laing, "The Negro Miner," pp. 264–65; and Fishback, "Employment Conditions," chap. 6.

45. Interview with Pink Henderson, 15 July 1983; Fishback, "Employment Conditions," pp. 182–229; Eller, *Miners, Millhands, and Mountaineers*, pp. 178–82; interview with Walter and Margaret Moorman, 14 July 1983. For reports of black casualties, see "Six Miners Killed in Explosion at Carswell," *Bluefield Daily Telegraph*, 19 July 1919; "Gary (Among the Colored People)," 11 Dec. 1923, 2 Jan. 1924, "Compensation for Six Injured Miners," 10 Dec. 1923, "Russel Dodson Killed Monday by Slate Fall," 14 July 1925, and "Walter McNeil Hurt in Mine," 22 July 1925, all in the *Welch Daily News*; "Negro Miner is Killed at Thorpe," 12 June 1929, "Colored Miner Killed Friday in Slate Fall," 5 Mar. 1930, "McDowell County Continues Out in Front in Mine Fatalities," 24 July 1929, "Negro Miner Electrocuted in Tidewater Mines," 9 Oct. 1929, and "Hemphill Colored Miner Killed in Mining Accident," 8 Jan. 1930, all in the *McDowell Recorder*.

46. For a discussion of these processes in the urban-industrial context, see Peter Gottlieb, *Making Their Own Way: Southern Blacks' Migration to Pittsburgh, 1916–30* (Urbana: University of Illinois Press, 1987); James R. Grossman, *The Land of Hope: Chicago, Black Southerners, and the Great Migration* (Chicago: University of Chicago Press, 1989); Earl Lewis, *At Work and At Home: Blacks in Norfolk, Virginia, 1910–1945* (Berkeley: University of California Press, forthcoming); and Joe William Trotter, Jr., *Black Milwaukee: The Making of an Industrial Proletariat, 1915–45* (Urbana: University of Illinois Press, 1985).

47. Interviews with Lawrence Boling, 18 July 1983, Andrew Campbell, 19 July 1983, William M. Beasley, 26 July 1983, and Charles T. Harris, 18 July 1983; "Annual Garden Inspection at Gary Plants," 17 and 23 July 1925, "Annual Inspection of Yards and Gardens: Consolidation Coal Company," 27 July 1925, all in *Welch Daily News*; Agricultural Extension Service, *Annual Reports, 1921–32*, especially "Negro Work" and "Extension Work with Negroes" (Morgantown, W.Va.); "The Annual Garden and Yard Contest Complete Success," *The New River Company Employees' Magazine* 3, no. 1 (Sept. 1925): 3–4, and vol. 2, no. 2 (Oct. 1924): 8–9; "55 Individual Awards Made Today in Yard and Garden Contests," *McDowell Recorder*, 31 July 1929.

48. The Peters Sisters, *War Poems* (Beckley, W.Va., 1919), p. 7.

49. WVBNWS, *Biennial Report, 1923–24*, pp. 25–28; interview with Walter and Margaret Moorman, 14 July 1983; Women's Bureau, U.S. Department of Labor, *Home Environment and Employment Opportunities of Women in Coal Mine Workers' Families* (Washington, 1925), p. 47; interviews with Thornton Wright, 27 July 1983, and Andrew Campbell, 19 July 1983; "Goes South on Vacation," 5 Mar. 1915, and "Giatto Rapidly Progressing," 29 May 1915, in *McDowell Times.*

50. Interview with Leonard Davis, 28 July 1983.

51. Obituaries, *McDowell Times*, 1915–18, especially 28 Jan. 1916 and 13 Aug. 1915.

52. Susie Norwell to W. E. B. Du Bois, 10 Jan. 1928; Du Bois to Norwell, 16 May 1928, reel no. 27, W. E. B. Du Bois Papers, Library of Congress; Minnie Holly Barnes, *Holl's Hurdles* (Radford, Va.: Commonwealth Press, 1980), pp. 24–27; interviews with Thornton Wright, 27 July 1983, Walter and Margaret Moorman, 14 July 1983, Lester and Ellen Phillips, 20 July 1983, Watt Teal, 27 July 1983, and Leonard Davis, 28 July 1983.

53. Reginald Millner, "Conversations with the 'Ole Man': The Life and Times of a Black Appalachian Coal Miner," *Goldenseal* 5 (Jan.-Mar., 1979): 58–64; " Looking for a Helpmate," *McDowell Times*, 19 Nov. 1915; "Among Our Colored People," *The New River Company Employees' Magazine* 2, no. 3 (Nov. 1924): 11–12; interviews with Charles T. Harris, 18 July 1983, and Walter and Margaret Moorman, 14 July 1983.

54. See n. 21 above, especially T. Edward Hill, "Loafers and Jonahs."

55. "How a Coal Miner Can Save Money," *McDowell Times*, 19 Feb. 1915; Laing, "The Negro Miner," chaps. 2, 3, and 4. Also see "Local Items," *McDowell Times*, 26 Mar. 1915; WVBNWS, *Biennial Reports, 1921–22*, pp. 5–11, 38–41, *1923–24*, pp. 8–10, 39–45; "Kimball (Colored News)," *Welch Daily News*, 28 Jan. 1924; "Among Our Colored," in various issues of the *The New River Company Employees' Magazine, 1924–30*; "Agricultural Extension Work in Mining Towns," in Agricultural Extension Service, *Annual Reports, 1921– 26.*

56. S. R. Anderson, "News of the Colored People," *Bluefield Daily Telegraph*, 28 Dec. 1930; WVBNWS, *Biennial Reports, 1929–32*, pp. 12–14.

57. West Virginia Department of Mines, *Annual Reports, 1929, 1931*; WVBNWS, *Biennial Reports, 1929–32*, pp. 4–7; Laing, "The Negro Miner" pp. 254, 503–4.

58. Martin Cherniack, *The Hawk's Nest Incident: America's Worst Industrial Disaster* (New Haven: Yale University Press, 1986), pp. 18–19, 89–91; Mark Rowh, "The Hawk's Nest Tragedy: Fifty Years Later," *Goldenseal* 7, no. 1 (1981): 31–32.

59. Cherniack, *The Hawk's Nest Incident*, pp. 18–19, 90–91; Rowh, "The Hawk's Nest Tragedy," pp. 31–32.

60. Interviews with Pink Henderson, 15 July 1983, and Leonard Davis, 28 July 1983; U.S. Bureau of the Census, *Fifteenth Census of the United States 1930* (Washington, 1933), 6:1428.

4

Racial Discrimination
in the Workplace

As the coal industry entered the postwar era, racial and ethnic competition increased. Afro-Americans found it increasingly difficult to retain the small foothold they had acquired in supervisory and skilled positions. As manual coal loaders they also faced growing discrimination in the assignment of work, which made it hard to keep pace with the production and wage levels of their white counterparts. For the most disagreeable tasks, employers sought blacks over immigrants and American-born whites, and their discriminatory policies were repeatedly reinforced by the racist attitudes and behavior of white workers and the state. Operating on the precarious middle ground between these hostile forces, black coal miners developed strategies for fighting them. A look at the economic obstacles black miners faced reveals both the depth of their grievances and the complexity of their responses under the impact of industrial capitalism.

Hired during the prewar and war years, black foremen increasingly lost ground during the postwar era. In the 1916–20 period, nearly 10 percent of the supervisory personnel killed or seriously injured were black men. Over the next five years no black fatalities or injuries were reported in this category; rather than an improvement in their status, however, this indicated a drop in the numbers of blacks holding supervisory positions. As early as 1916, attorney W. H. Harris, a *McDowell Times* columnist, complained: "It has been the practice not to employ Colored men as bosses in the mines. This has been . . . a sort of unwritten law as it were—no matter how capable or efficient they were."[1]

In its 1921–22 survey of black miners, the Bureau of Negro Welfare and Statistics recorded only seven black foremen and other bosses in the entire state. A similar survey in 1927 produced "only one fire boss." "In late years, many or all of these places were filled by native whites or foreigners," wrote the teacher and political activist Memphis T. Garrison in 1926.[2] Sociologist James T. Laing found only eleven blacks at the onset of the Depression "in positions which, even by the most liberal stretch of the term, could be called positions of authority." Two of the eleven were assistant mine foremen; five worked as stable bosses in mines that still used mules; and the remainder held a miscellaneous set of jobs, including foreman over a slate dump, a boss mule driver, and head of a "Negro rock gang." In practice employers modified their traditional position that "a Negro is a very good boss among his own color." One contemporary observer noted an emerging pattern: "Even foreigners are given these positions in preference to native Colored men."[3]

The discriminatory attitudes and practices of the state reinforced the exclusion of blacks from supervisory and managerial jobs. To help miners meet the new state standards for the job of foreman that had been set on the eve of World War I, West Virginia University expanded its mining extension classes—for whites only. Enrollment reached over 4,500 during the war years, accelerated during the 1920s, and by 1930 climbed to over 20,000. These classes represented increased state support of a racially stratified labor force. Only in the late 1930s would blacks receive similar classes, and then only on a segregated and inadequate basis.[4] In the war and postwar years, as in the prewar era, racial restrictions continued to limit the occupational mobility of black workers.

If blacks found it nearly impossible to get supervisory jobs, they had somewhat less trouble becoming machine operators and motormen. The employment of blacks in skilled jobs was highly sensitive to the specific labor demands of the coal industry. During the coal strikes of the early 1920s, for example, company officials hired growing numbers of black machine operators and frequently praised them for their efficient labor. In 1921–22, according to the BNWS, employers of skilled black workers stated that "they are as efficient, more loyal, as regular and take a greater personal interest in their work and in the success of the business than workers of other races." Likewise, during the economic upswing of the mid-1920s, the bureau enthusiastically reported, "Not only has the Negro made for himself a permanent place as miner and laborer about the mines, but he is being sought . . . by mine owners to fill positions requiring skill and training."[5]

Although some blacks gained skilled positions, their path was nonetheless fraught with difficulty. During the war years, for example, a Logan County engineer informed operators that "where ever one finds a Colored motorman having a white brakeman or a machineman a white helper, he may be sure that there is more or less friction between the two. . . . A white man doesn't care to have a Colored for his buddy."[6] Black workers found it especially difficult to secure jobs as mainline motormen, who transported loaded coal cars from underground working areas to the surface. In the mines of Hemphill and Coalwood, McDowell County, Pink Henderson bitterly recalled, during the 1920s, "the mine foremen wouldn't let the black[s] . . . run the motor. . . . A white man ran the motor." When the foreman assigned blacks to motorman jobs, he was careful to specify that they were "running the motor extra," as a temporary expedient, giving whites a proprietary right to the job. "When a white man came there and wanted the job," Henderson concluded, "you had to get down. . . . A black man had to get down and let the white run." Another black miner, Charles T. Harris, agreed. At the Weyanoke Coal and Coke Company in Mercer County, he said, "There were no black motormen."[7]

The exclusion of blacks from jobs as mainline motormen was underscored by their employment as brakemen and mule drivers. Among skilled and semiskilled jobs, blacks gained their strongest foothold in the dangerous brakeman job, which paralleled the hazardous coupling job on the old railroad cars. The black brakemen provided empty cars for the loaders and removed them as soon as they were filled. They usually worked behind white motormen. In the reverse case, blacks continually complained, white brakemen "would not brake behind a black motorman." Although the use of draft animals steadily declined after the war with the rise of mechanization, some mines continued to use mules in the underground transportation of coal. During the 1920s, Oscar Davis, and later, his son Leonard, drove mules at the New River and Pocahontas Consolidated Coal Company in McDowell County.[8] Disproportionately black, the mule drivers worked between the miners' individual workplaces and the mainline rails, where the "mainline motor," usually operated by white men, pulled the cars to the tipple and the outside preparation and shipment facilities. According to the accident reports of the State Bureau of Mines, between 1916 and 1925 Afro-Americans were involved in over 35 percent of the state's 124 fatal and serious nonfatal accidents involving mule drivers.[9] Gradually, however, "gathering motors" replaced the mules. Subordinate to the mainline motor, the gathering motor gave blacks an increased opportunity to become motormen after World War I.

As the coal-mining economy recovered during the mid-1920s, white resistance to blacks' employment as skilled workers grew. As the coal industry entered the late 1920s and the Depression, white opposition became intense. Employers increasingly asserted that " 'the negro is not much good with machinery,' " while white workers increased their resistance to the hiring of blacks as machinist's helpers, which would have put blacks one step away from machinist jobs. When asked if his black helper was a good worker, one machinist replied, " 'Yes, he will do his work and half of mine if I want him to.' He said that he never 'gets familiar' and 'keeps in his place.' " The same machinist nonetheless expressed his preference for a white helper; and, as blacks lost helper jobs, those who remained worked under reluctant and blatantly exploitative white bosses.[10] Racism obviously shaped the white workers' responses toward blacks: white machinists desired white helpers not because blacks were "lazy," inefficient, or uncooperative, but because they were apparently the opposite and thus presented a competitive threat to whites.[11]

In the aftermath of World War I, racial discrimination not only excluded blacks from important skilled, semiskilled, and supervisory positions, but also blocked their progress in unskilled jobs. As coal loaders, blacks faced increasing discrimination in the assignment of workplaces. Although all coal loaders shared low wages, hazardous conditions, and hard work, racism intensified their impact on blacks. "A lot of those mines had unwritten policies. The blacks would work a certain section of the mines. The [American-born] whites would work a certain section. The Italians and the foreigners would work a certain section," recalled Leonard Davis. Recalling his father's experience during the 1920s and his own later on, Davis also related that "at times . . . in certain conditions blacks would have a good place to load coal. But mostly they were given places where there was a lot of rock, water, and some days you worked until you moved the rock. You didn't make a penny because they weren't paying for moving rock then. You didn't make anything."[12]

During the mid-1920s, black miners repeatedly complained of poor working conditions. They sometimes loaded three to four cars of rock before reaching the "good" coal. From the mid-1920s through the early 1930s, Roy Todd recalled, black miners lost a lot of time and money through "dead work." If there was a rockfall in

your area, "you had to clean it up for nothing." The cleanup sometimes took two or three days.[13] Work in excessive water was a ubiquitous problem. Numerous observers claimed that West Virginia
mines tended to be water-free because the mountainous terrain provided relatively good drainage; nevertheless, some men loaded coal
in hip boots. Where water was no problem, black miners faced disproportionately low seams, frequently as low as two or three feet,
and they had to load coal on their knees. "I like it high. . . . I don't
like it low," black miner Lester Phillips exclaimed. "You got to crawl
in there."[14] Although miners used knee pads to load the low coal,
some men developed such callouses on their knees, they "looked
like they had two knee caps." According to Lawrence Boling, poor
ventilation was also a problem: "Sometimes the circulation of air or
no air would be so bad you'd have to wait sometimes up to two
hours before you could get back in there to load any coal. . . . I
have been sick and dizzy off of that smoke many times. . . . that
deadly poison is there. . . . It would knock you out too, make you
weak as water."[15]

Compounding the problems of bad air, low coal seams, and water was the difficulty of pick-and-shovel mining, that is, undercutting coal and loading it by hand. While few mines used pick mining
exclusively, it persisted in portions of mines where machines were
difficult and unprofitable to use. During the late 1920s, in one of the
few mines relying upon the laborious pick method, black miners
outnumbered the combined total of immigrants and American-born
white workers. Describing his father's employment as an occasional
pick-and-shovel miner, one black miner recalled, "My dad would
tell me many times that I was sleep when he went to work and
sleep when he came back." Another black miner, Willis Martin of
Gary, McDowell County, recalled, "We used to go to work so early
in the morning and come home so late that on Sunday morning
you'd see a little baby start to crying when he saw the strange man
in the house."[16]

Surveys of employer attitudes and practices during the late 1920s
confirm the role of racism in shaping the black coal loader's experience. "The best points of the colored coal loader are that he
will work in wet places and in entries where the air is bad with
less complaint than the white man," claimed an employer in the
Kanawha–New River Field. Another employer declared, "In this
low coal I would rather have a negro than any other loader."[17]

Yet another employer revealed how immigrants were able to out-
bid blacks for better working areas: "If they [immigrants] do not get

the best places in the mine they will not work. . . . That is one thing about the colored man—he will work anywhere." Like American-born whites, in their competition with black workers, immigrants increasingly adopted anti-black attitudes and practices. According to blacks, some of them exceeded "native whites in this respect." When an immigrant foreman lost his job, black miners rejoiced, one of them stating, "I just can't stand being Jim-Crowed by one of these fellows."[18]

Few miners held outside positions, which were relatively safe from the dangers of explosions, coal dust, poisonous gases, and rockfalls. During World War I and the postwar period, racial stratification increased in the outside labor force more than it did in the inside labor force. Blacks held most of the jobs in the coke yards, which were hot and difficult and the most disagreeable of the outside positions, while whites dominated the less demanding outside jobs such as preparing and shipping coal. In 1910, blacks made up 47 percent of the state's coke workers, but in southern West Virginia during World War I and the 1920s, black made up between 67 to 86 percent of all coke workers, with immigrants and American-born whites each making up fewer than 26 percent (see table 4).

Table 4
Ethnic Distribution of Southern West
Virginia Miners in Coke Yards, 1915–25

	1915		1917	
	Number	Percent	Number	Percent
Blacks	715	67.3	2,315	86.8
Immigrants	275	25.8	216	8.1
American-born whites	72	6.9	136	5.1
Total	1,062	100.0	2,667	100.0

	1921		1925	
	Number	Percent	Number	Percent
Blacks	621	67.0	313	80.6
Immigrants	226	24.3	23	5.9
American-born whites	81	8.7	52	13.5
Total	928	100.0	388	100.0

Source: West Virginia Department of Mines, *Annual Reports, 1915–25* (Charleston, W.Va.)

Racial discrimination was also apparent in the lower average earnings of black miners. The racial wage gap, comparatively small in the prewar era, widened during the economic downturn of the late 1920s. In 1929 the average semimonthly wage at three coal companies was $118.30, and the average semimonthly earnings of whites, both immigrants and Americans, exceeded those of blacks by nearly $20.00.[19] Although comparative statistics for the downturn of the early postwar years are not available, given the strength of racial discrimination in the labor force, a comparable wage differential probably existed for that period as well.

Despite the debilitating effects of class and racial inequality, black miners took a hand in shaping their own experience, developing strategies to deal with the discriminatory practices of white employers, workers, and the state. At times their actions appeared contradictory and at cross-purposes. Yet, within the highly volatile class and racial environment of southern West Virginia, the black coal miners' responses had an underlying coherence and logic of their own.

Job performance emerged as one of the black miners' most telling survival mechanisms. To secure their jobs, they resolved to provide cooperative, efficient, and productive labor.[20] After more than fifty years of coal mining, one black miner set a record for handloading—90,000 tons of coal, the equivalent of a seventeen-mile-long train of 1,750 cars, each containing fifty tons.[21] Average black coal miners also related with pride the number of tons they loaded in a day or week, and finally, over a lifetime. Lawrence Boling offered crucial insight into the black miner's mentality and use of productivity as a strategy of survival. "As far as I am concerned back in those days, the black miner was the backbone of the mines. . . . I am proud of my life. . . . I may have worked hard. It was honest."[22]

Throughout the job hierarchy, black miners exhibited a similar resolve to perform well. At the Weyanoke Coal Company, Charles T. Harris transformed the dangerous brakeman's job into a status symbol as well as a mechanism of survival. "I liked the brakeman best . . . because the guys . . . would get together in the pool rooms . . . to see who was the best brakeman and [to] show off. . . . In fact I done it mostly for a name. . . . They said that I was one of the best brakemen . . . and they called me 'Speed Harris.' " Harris even developed a joke around his job, which captured the interracial, and even intraracial, competition in the coal-mining labor force. "I said, 'Very few colored people can do what I do, but no white at all.' "[23]

In the face of white competition, black machine cutters and motormen also worked to improve their productivity. Between 1921 and the early 1920s, William Beasley alternated between jobs as a motorman and machine cutter. During the late 1920s, using an old standard Goodman machine, he set a record on the undercutting machine, cutting twenty-eight places in eight hours. On occasion, coal operators even set standards for white workers partially based on the performance of black men. The general manager of a large company in McDowell County related: "We try to standardize our work as much as possible. One day one of the groups of [white] coal cutters at a certain mine decided that five places were all that any one man could cut in a day. I went to one of my Negro cutters and told him to go down to that place and we would give [him] all the places he wanted and a $100 [bill] besides. That night this Negro cut twenty-five places. We standardized at seven."[24]

Black miners worked to increase tonnage, but they aimed to do so with minimal damage to their health. Even as they pushed to increase output, they worked to avoid lost-time accidents. Through company-sponsored safety contests, but most of all through day-to-day attention to their own safety, black miners developed their survival skills. Roy Todd recalled that he worked in the mines "forty-seven years without a lost-time accident." Another black miner recalled that his father worked in the mines "fifty-one years, and he never had a lost-time accident." Charles T. Harris recalled that his father, after over fifty years of coal mining, "never was what you might say sick, and he didn't have no bad back, and he didn't have no beat-up hands. . . . That's right. I am telling you the truth now."[25] Harris's claim is probably exaggerated, but it nonetheless suggests the importance that black miners' placed on their health and safety. Some simply refused to work in the most dangerous places. Columbus Avery recalled: "I'd go into a place in the morning and inspect it. If it was bad, I wouldn't have anything to do with it. I never was hurt. I just wouldn't go into a dangerous place. They could fire me if they wanted to, but I wouldn't risk my life on a bad top."[26]

The refusal of black miners to work in dangerous places suggests that their transiency was sometimes a survival strategy. "They fired me at Pidgeon Creek once because I refused to go into a place I thought was dangerous," Avery said. Black miners, like their white counterparts, frequently moved from one mine to another to improve their working conditions, increase their wages, and gain greater recognition of their humanity as workers and blacks. They also moved from southern West Virginia mines to farms in other parts of the South and back. Gradually their job wanderings included the mines and steel mills of northern West Virginia, Pennsylvania, and Ohio. "I moved once ten times in ten years," North Dickerson recalled. "I was high-tempered. I would not take nothing off of anyone. I had a lot of pride." Another black miner stated, "I would always be looking for the best job and the most money."[27]

To be sure, as noted in chapter 3, a great deal of the black miners' geographic mobility was necessitated by cyclical swings in the coal economy. Moreover, even during good times, coal operators and their supervisory personnel could be quite ruthless in their exercise of hiring and firing prerogatives. As Walter Moorman recalled, when miners complained about pay once, one foreman retorted, "Don't grumble and stay, grumble and be on your way." In both good and bad times, many black miners took his advice. One time a foreman tried to bully black brakeman Charles T. Harris by claiming he had brakemen tied up outside "with a paper string. If it rain, they'll come in." Harris reached up on the motor board, got his lunch bag, and said, "You get 'em."[28]

Roy Todd's career offers insight into the transiency of black miners. In 1919 he took his first job at the No. 1 mine of the McGregor Coal Company at Slagle, Logan County. He worked at McGregor for one year, then moved on to the Island Creek Company at Holden, Logan County, where he began at the firm's No. 1 mine and soon moved to the company's No. 8 mine. He quit to go to Trace Hollow for six months, where he worked as a brace carrier on a company-constructed high-school building. During the mid-1920s, he worked at several mines in McDowell County, including the Carswell Coal Company and the Houston Colliery Company at Kimball. During the late 1920s and early 1930s, Todd spent short periods mining in the Pittsburgh region, in the Fairmont District of northern West Virginia, and in Lance and Wheelwright, Kentucky.[29] Todd's career demonstrates how black miners not only moved from one company to another, but also from mine to mine within the same company (these sometimes varied in quality) and, eventually, how they went from mines in southern West Virginia to mines in adjacent regions.

At times, black coal miners developed close bonds with white miners, especially during crises such as explosions. Echoing the sentiments of many, Charles T. Harris declared: "When that mine [explosion or accident] come everybody seem like they were brothers. . . . If one man got killed, it throwed a gloom over the whole mine." Under ordinary circumstances as well, sometimes black and white miners slowly developed bonds that cut across racial and ethnic lines. These ties were apparently most prominent between blacks and Italian immigrants, whom blacks called "Tallies." Pink Henderson recalled that a "certain bunch of whites would not work with a black man," but that immigrants and blacks got along "pretty well." American-born whites, North Dickerson said, "didn't accept the immigrants as peers . . . so they turned to blacks for companionship . . . [and] we got along well." "They seemed like they'd rather be with the blacks than with the whites," Lawrence Boling recalled. While black coal miners made few comparable remarks about relationships with American-born white miners, Harris suggested that blacks got along better with the West Virginia "mountain whites" than with white workers from Mississippi and other Deep South states.[30]

However uneven the relationship between black and white coal miners may have been, a substantial degree of interracial solidarity emerged among the southern West Virginia coal miners. During World War I, Districts 17 and 29 of the United Mine Workers of America (UMWA) expanded dramatically. Covering the Kanawha–New River and Williamson-Logan fields, District 17 increased its membership from 7,000 in early 1917 to over 17,000 within a few months. By the war's end, District 17 claimed over 50,000 members. At the same time, membership in District 29—covering the southernmost Pocahontas and Winding Gulf fields—increased from fewer than 1,000 to over 6,000. Although there are no available quantitative data on the proportion of black members and officers in UMWA locals, black coal miners served on the executive boards of Districts 17 and 29, worked as district organizers, served as delegates to the national biennial meetings, and frequently held local office.[31]

Because of language barriers, immigrants sometimes deferred to black leadership. At the 1921 meeting of the national body, the black delegate Frank Ingham eloquently addressed the gathering on conditions in his area:

> "I will first say that I am happy to be permitted to speak, not for myself, but for Mingo county. . . . The real truth has never been told of Mingo county. It cannot be told. The language has not been coined to express the agonies the miners of Mingo county are enduring today. The world is under the impression that martial law exists there. That is not true. What exists in Mingo is partial law, because it is only brought to bear upon the miners that have joined the union."

Even T. Edward Hill, the staunch anti-union director of the BNWS, confirmed the positive character of interracial unionism in the area.

"Negro members of the Executive Board . . . were elected in conventions in which white miner delegates outnumbered negroes more than five to one. The Negro union miners . . . are as staunch and faithful supporters of their organization as any other class of workers."[32]

George Edmunds of Iowa, an international black organizer, played a key role in unionizing black miners in southern West Virginia. From a jail cell in Polk County, Iowa, in 1916, Edmunds wrote to his West Virginia comrades, expressing intimate knowledge of conditions in the region. "I know so many of you, brothers. We have had some good times and hard times together. On Paint Creek and Cabin Creeks; from Gauley to the Ohio River, I have passed and repassed among you and . . . I always did my best for you and your cause." On one occasion Edmunds addressed "a large and enthusiastic gathering" at Bancroft, West Virginia, where there were miners from several other mining towns in the Kanawha–New River district. On another occasion he helped to organize a "rousing meeting" at Winnifrede, in the same area. In the early postwar years Edmunds continued to appear among the slate of speakers at UMWA membership drives in the region.[33]

The immediate postwar years produced the most dramatic expression of working-class solidarity, which culminated in the coal strike of 1921 and the "Armed March" of white and black miners on Logan and Mingo counties. When coal companies denied workers the right of collective bargaining, armed conflict erupted between more than 5,000 union miners and over 1,200 Logan and Mingo defenders (local law officers, company-employed private detectives, and some black and white strikebreakers). The conflict resulted in more than 100 deaths and led to the declaration of martial law on three different occasions, once in 1920 and twice in 1921. Only the intervention of federal troops brought an end to the hostilities. By standard accounts, the march included an estimated 2,000 black miners, mainly union men from the Kanawha–New River Field. The movement gradually attracted the support of blacks in the violently anti-union strongholds of Mingo, Logan, and McDowell Counties as well.[34]

In their violent confrontation with capital, black and white miners developed mutual loyalties, and sometimes their commitment to each other was demonstrated in dramatic ways. When law officers and Baldwin-Felts guards dispersed a meeting of union men at Roderfield, McDowell County, leaving four dead and four wounded, black miner R. B. Page organized a contingent of 75 men "and started for Roderfield to help his union brothers." Although his plans were aborted by a force of over 100 policemen, his actions were a testament to the interracial character of the mine workers' struggle. At the height of the class warfare, "One of the [white] deputies who was killed was John Gore. He was scouting through the woods near Blair [Mountain] and encountered a Negro scout. The negro opened fire on Gore and the latter fired in return. The negro was killed." When a white miner "came upon Gore who was bending over the body of the negro searching for identification marks," he shot the officer "through the heart." In an enthusiastic letter to the *United Mine Workers Journal*, a white miner summed up the interracial character of the miners' struggle in southern West Virginia. "I call it a darn solid mass of different colors and tribes, blended together, woven, bound, interlocked, tongued and grooved and glued together in one body."[35]

The testimony of black coal miners themselves before a U.S. Senate investigation committee headed by Senator William S. Kenyon of Iowa is the most potent evidence of black participation in the "Mingo War." Black miners not only stood firmly with white workers, but, as is evident from their testimonies, the Mingo War involved a complicated blending of class and racial consciousness. It is also apparent that black union men suffered a large, perhaps disproportionate, share of the violent reprisals during and after the war from law enforcement officers and private Baldwin-Felts guards. Frank Ingham lost his job and house on several occasions for his union activities. A veteran miner of fourteen years, in the early postwar years he resisted efforts to divide workers along racial lines. "The reason that he [the superintendent of the Howard Collieries Company in Chattaroy, Mingo County] gave for discharging me the last time was that all of the white men that had joined the union, he had discharged them and he said that he was going to put all of the colored fellows back to work. . . . He told me to get out when I told the colored people not to take the white people's places."[36]

Arrested several times, under both state and local authorities, Ingham was brutally beaten and denied visiting privileges while in jail. He testified that on one occasion a local officer suggested that "what we ought to do with him is not take him to jail, but to riddle his body with bullets." At midnight law officers removed him from the jail, stole his money and belongings, took him to an isolated place, and beat him nearly to death. Ingham received no better treatment from state authorities. Major Thomas Davis, acting adjutant general for the state, denied him visitors, informing his wife, relatives, and friends, "The next nigger that came over and asked him anything about me that he would put them in [jail] as well." Through out his testimony Ingham emphasized his working-class activities as the fundamental cause of the attacks upon him. Even following his brutal beating, he testified, "They asked me what I had been in the hands of the mob for, and I told them because I belonged to the Union."[37]

On the other hand, underlying Ingham's support of the union was racial solidarity. When Ingham joined the union and resisted the use of black strikebreakers, his judgment revealed both race and class consciousness. "I did not think that would be a very safe thing to do, from the fact that it would terminate in a race riot, and I would not like to see my people in anything like that, because they were outnumbered so far as Mingo County." Ingham further reasoned, "My motive in advising the people was, I am a pioneer colored man in that part of the country. I worked for two years in the mine before any more colored people went to work on that creek. Before that they had been denied the privilege of working in these mines, and since they have got well established in there, many of them had found employment there. I did not want them to make enemies of the white race by taking their places."[38]

Other black miners confirmed Ingham's commitment to working-class solidarity within the framework of black unity. George Echols, a union miner, local UMWA officer, and striker, declared: "The United [Mine] Workers of America have privileges which are guaranteed by the United States, [and] we have rights to protect us, both the black and white, but they [operators and law officers] do not regard those rights at all. They take those privileges away from us. Now we are asking you to give them back to us. Let us be free men. Let us stand equal."[39] Echols's union activities were intertwined with the peculiar Afro-American legacy of slavery. "I was raised a slave," Echols related. "My master and my mistress called me and I answered, and I know the time when I was a slave, and I feel just like we feel now." Another black miner, J. H. Reed, likewise expressed the blending of class and racial consciousness. Reed linked his arrest, incarceration, and mistreatment to his activities as a union man and as a black: "The thing here is that a man is the same as being in slavery."[40]

Unfortunately, as suggested by the black workers' expressions of class and racial consciousness above, working-class solidarity was a highly precarious affair. To be sure, white miners drew inspiration from black bondage, using the symbolism of slavery to help buttress the mine workers' case against the operators. Later, one white miner even put the issue in verse: "The boss said stand up boys— And drive away your fears, You are sentenced to slavery—For many long years."[41] Yet the white miners' own heritage of racism placed critical limits on their ability to identify with black workers.

White workers and employers coalesced to a substantial, even fundamental, degree around notions of black inferiority. The Carbon Fuel Company, in its contract with employees, stipulated under a provision on workmanship and methods "the miner shall load his coal in every case free from shale, bone, *niggerhead* [worthless coal] and *other impurities* [my italics]."[42] When the *UMWJ* reprinted a racist joke from the operators' *Coal Age*, the racial consensus between white operators and coal miners was made even more explicit: "Sambo, a negro [mule] driver . . . was able to gather his trips without speaking to his mule. . . . Mose, another driver [presumably black] . . . went to Sambo for help and asked Sambo what was needed to teach such tricks. Sambo said all that was necessary was to know more than the mule."[43]

Further highlighting the white racist consensus were the distasteful and often vicious stereotypes of black women held by whites of all classes. White men articulated and practiced clear-cut notions of gender inequality along racial lines, placing white women of any class background on a social plane above their black counterparts. On the final page of its labor contract, a local coal company apparently amused white managers and workers alike with a racist, sexist joke that promoted the image of black women as lewd sexual objects.[44]

White unity helped to engender a growing bond between black workers and black elites. The activities of the BNWS, the black press (especially the *McDowell Times*), and the McDowell County Colored Republican Organization, all reflected aspects of the growing black worker–black elite alliance. Through the strikebreaking activities of T. Edward Hill of the BNWS, for example, some blacks gained jobs during the massive coal strikes of the early 1920s. The bureau proudly claimed credit for deterring over one hundred black miners from joining the "Armed March," but nonetheless pursued its strikebreaking function with care, seeking to avoid racial violence. As an added measure of protection for black workers, Hill advocated, with some success, small interracial contingents of strike-

breakers. "The coal companies that are bringing in workers are having them sent in bunches of not more than 25 and in all crowds
brought in to date there have been whites as well as negroes."[45]

Hill not only sought to avoid racial violence in the short run, he
also promoted long-run job security for the black miner. Keenly
aware of the traditional dismissal of blacks after strikes, Hill sought
protective agreements from the operators. In a letter to the local secretaries of the Coal Operators' Association and the president of the
West Virginia Coal Association, Hill wrote, "It would be manifestly
unfair to use negro miners in this crisis and then displace them
when workers of other races are available."[46] During the coal strikes
of 1921–22, Hill secured an agreement from owners and managers
"that, however the strike is settled, the negro miners now being
employed" would be retained; or, if they voluntarily left their jobs
or were "discharged for cause," their places would be filled by
other blacks. In case operators could not secure other blacks to take
the vacant places, the BNWS would "be requested to supply qualified Negroes." M. S. Bradley, president of the West Virginia Coal
Association, promised to "lend his personal assistance in seeing
that justice is done." The secretaries of the Kanawha and New River
Coal Operators' Associations endorsed the agreement. Hill believed
the operators would keep their word; and, until the Great Depression, most of them undoubtedly did.[47]

These economic concessions, however, were purchased at a substantial price. They were achieved not only at the expense of interracial working-class unity, but at the expense, to some degree, of
greater racial pride and self-assertion. The relationship between
blacks and coal operators, although based upon the interplay of
concrete class and racial interests, was mediated through the increasingly common rhetoric of welfare capitalism, conditioned by
the operators' paternalistic and racist notions of black dependency.
In a 1920 advertisement titled "Discrimination Against the Negro,"
the Logan County coal operators hoped to convince blacks that
they, not the United Mine Workers of America, were best suited
to protect the interests of black workers. "Colored miners in the
Williamson field who have been induced to become members of the
United Mine Workers," the operators lamented, "were doubtless
not informed about the discrimination practiced against their race
in the unionized fields."[48] In a similar pamphlet the following year,
they asserted that they had the blacks' best interest at heart: "First,
when they open up a new mine they think of the things that will
lead you and your children to the better land. . . . So we can plainly

see how kind and true the operators are to the colored people in Logan fields." As late as 1928, testifying before the U.S. Senate Committee on Interstate Commerce, a local coal operator echoed this rhetoric: "The negro is not responsible for his position in America. It is the duty of the white man to treat him with justice, mercy, and compassion. . . . I do believe in providing the negroes with every economic and industrial [as opposed to social] opportunity possible."[49]

The black press supported the operators' self-portrait of themselves as just and paternalistic employers, partially following a larger progressive tradition that urged corporate America to take a more humane interest in the welfare of its workers. In a detailed description of the Carter Coal Company, the popular *McDowell Times* columnist W. H. Harris presented a telling contrast between what he called the old and new captains of industry. "The old time captain of industry was ob[sessed] with just one idea: to get as much labor as possible for the smallest amount of money. . . . In late years the industrial captains have found that . . . the best investment is an intelligent, satisfied class of employees."[50] During the 1920s, the popular black Bluefield columnist S. R. Anderson reiterated the same theme in his column, "News of Colored People," printed in the white *Bluefield Daily Telegraph.* Anderson once reinforced the idea of welfare capitalism "as an expression of the human element in corporate interest upon which we may rely as a 'savor of life unto life' against the wreck of radicalism in labor and corporate insanity."[51] In exchange for employment, housing, credit at the company store, and a gradually expanding variety of recreational and social welfare programs, discussed in subsequent chapters, employers expected deference from all workers, but especially from blacks.

Under the energetic editorship of M. T. Whittico, paternalism was a recurring theme in the *McDowell Times* that was sometimes taken to extremes. A *Times* columnist described R. D. Patterson, general manager of the Weyanoke Coal Company, as "a father to every man, woman and child on his work—a kind but not overly indulgent one. He gets results because his men believe in him." Moreover, the columnist concluded: "If you will stop to watch him a little, you will see Patterson reflected in everything on that works. . . . Chamelion-like, he has caused everything about him to become PATTERSONIZED." "On the Winding Gulf," another columnist exclaimed, "the men say that Mr. Tams is the working man's 'daddy.' "[52]

The black press's use of subservient language helped to perpetuate notions of racial subordination and superordination, suggesting that there were critical limits to the alliance of black coal miners and black elites. Yet, the exaggerated portraits it drew were undoubtedly designed to elicit, as well as support, the desired corporate behavior. As we will see in chapters 9 and 10, under the leadership of the McDowell County Colored Republican Organization, during World War I and the years following it, Afro-Americans escalated their demands for representation in the state bureaucracy. With the struggle for power dominated by the region's small black elite, the black press's paternalistic tone gave way to a more urgent articulation of black demands, with greater attention to the needs of the black proletariat at work and in the community.

In their efforts to move up in the coal industry, black miners perceived their growing political alliance with black elites to be of great value. It not only promised more jobs in the state bureaucracy to highly trained black miners, but also offered hope for the establishment of that training. By 1927, for example, the State Department of Mines had appointed Osborne Black, a black miner, to the position of safety director. A former fire boss in the mines of McDowell County and a graduate of West Virginia State College, Black was now responsible for instructing black miners (only) in mine safety procedures. According to U. G. Carter, later director of the mine extension service of West Virginia State College, the new safety director was well regarded "in mining circles."[53]

Upon Black's death nearly two years later, the MCCRO, the strongest black political organization in southern West Virginia, passed a resolution "paying a tribute of respect" to Black, who had been an active member. The MCCRO also urged the State Department of Mines to replace him with another black miner, which it did. Upon John Patterson's appointment to the post, a contemporary remarked, "So far as is known, he is the only Negro safety director in the world." Patterson was later described by black mine educators as "the dean of miners." Before passing his state mine safety examination and receiving his appointment, Patterson had prepared himself by taking correspondence courses from Pennsylvania State University and had worked for several years as "a practical miner" and a mine foreman in Raleigh County.[54] (The details of the black worker–black elite alliance in the larger community life of coal-mining towns will be discussed in subsequent chapters.)

Between World War I and the Great Depression, black coal miners in southern West Virginia developed a variety of responses to racial inequality in the workplace. Their strategies included achieving high levels of productivity in the face of white competition, fighting in solidarity with white workers against capitalist exploitation, and, most important, building an alliance with black elites. Involving the complex intersection of the dynamics of class and race, the war and postwar expansion of the black proletariat set the stage for the further institutional, political, and cultural transformation of black life in southern West Virginia.

NOTES

1. "Exceptional Opportunities . . . At Olga Shaft, Coalwood, W.Va.," *McDowell Times*, 8 Sept. 1916; Price V. Fishback, "Employment Conditions in the Coal Industry" (Ph.D. diss., University of Washington, 1983), pp. 284–85.

2. West Virginia Bureau of Negro Welfare and Statistics (WVBNWS), *Biennial Reports, 1921–22*, pp. 58–59, and *1927–28*, pp. 15–17; Garrison, newspaper clipping, *Welch Daily News*, 21 Sept. 1926, in U. G. Carter Papers, West Virginia Collection, West Virginia University.

3. James T. Laing, "The Negro Miner in West Virginia" (Ph.D. diss., Ohio State University, 1933), pp. 182–83, 213; "Exceptional Opportunities," *McDowell Times*, 8 Sept. 1916.

4. Homer L. Morris, *The Plight of the Bituminous Coal Miner* (Philadelphia: University of Pennsylvania Press, 1934), pp. 207–8; Fishback, "Employment Conditions," pp. 308–9; West Virginia State College Mining Extension Service, *Annual Report, 1942–43*, in U. G. Carter Papers.

5. WVBNWS, *Biennial Reports, 1921–22*, pp. 86–87, *1923–24*, pp. 36–37.

6. C. F. Fuetter, "Mixed Labor in Coal Mining," *Coal Age* 10 (22 July 1916): 137, quoted in Ronald L. Lewis, *Black Coal Miners in America: Race, Class, and Community Conflict, 1780–1980* (Lexington: University Press of Kentucky, 1987), pp. 144–45; interview with Pink Henderson, 15 July 1983.

7. "Memorandum, Willie Parker," Straight Numerical Files, No. 182363, Record Group No. 60, U.S. Department of Justice, National Archives; interviews with Pink Henderson, 15 July 1983, and Charles T. Harris, 18 July 1983; Laing, "The Negro Miner," p. 242.

8. "Memorandum, Willie Parker," U.S. Department of Justice; interviews with Leonard Davis, 28 July 1983, and Roy Todd, 18 July 1983.

9. Fishback, "Employment Conditions," pp. 284–85; Laing, "The Negro Miner," pp. 191, 242, 249–50.

10. Laing, "The Negro Miner," pp. 234–36.

11. Tim R. Massey, " 'I Didn't Think I'd Live to See 1950': Looking Back with Columbus Avery," *Goldenseal* 8, no. 1 (Spring 1982): 32–40.

12. Interview with Leonard Davis, 28 July 1983; Laing, "The Negro Miner," pp. 225–28.

13. Interviews with Walter E. and Margaret Moorman, 14 July 1983, and Roy Todd, 18 July 1983.

14. Interviews with Andrew Campbell, 19 July 1983, Pink Henderson, 15 July 1983, and Lester and Ellen Phillips, 20 July 1983.

15. Interviews with North Dickerson (first quote), 28 July 1983, and Lawrence Boling (second quote), 18 July 1983.

16. Interview with Leonard Davis, 28 July 1983; Laing, "The Negro Miner," p. 189; interview with Willis Martin in Matt Witt and Earl Dolter, "Before I'd Be A Slave," in *In Our Blood: Four Coal Mining Families* (New Market, Tenn.: Highlander Research Center, 1979), pp. 23–47.

17. Laing, "The Negro Miner," pp. 225–28.

18. Ibid.

19. Laing, "The Negro Miner," pp. 222–24; Fishback, "Employment Conditions," p. 169.

20. Interviews with Roy Todd, 18 July 1983, and Charles T. Harris, 18 July 1983.

21. Interviews with Roy Todd, 18 July 1983, and Charles T. Harris, 18 July 1983; Lewis, *Black Coal Miners in America,* pp. 179–80, from *Color: A Tip Top World Magazine* 4 (Feb. 1948): 13; "Among Our Colored People," *The New River Company Employees' Magazine* (Apr. 1928): 8, West Virginia Collection, West Virginia University.

22. Interview with Lawrence Boling, 18 July 1983.

23. Interview with Charles T. Harris, 18 July 1983.

24. Interviews with William M. Beasely, 26 July 1983, and Roy Todd, 18 July 1983; quote in Laing, "The Negro Miner," pp. 264–65.

25. Interviews with Roy Todd, 18 July 1983, and Charles T. Harris, 18 July 1983; "First Aid Contest at Gary," 4 June 1915, and "Working Hard to Stop Accidents," 4 Aug. 1916, in *McDowell Times;* "Pocahontas Wins Safety Meet . . . New River–Pocahontas Consolidated Teams of Berwind Jones First Place Among Colored Division," *McDowell Recorder,* 22 Aug. 1929.

26. Quoted in Massey, "Looking Back with Columbus Avery," pp. 32–40; Reginald Millner, "Conversations with the 'Ole Man': The Life and Times of a Black Appalachian Coal Miner," *Goldenseal* 5 (Jan.-Mar. 1979): 58–64.

27. Massey, "Looking Back with Columbus Avery," pp. 32–40; interviews with North E. Dickerson, 28 July 1983, and William M. Beasley, 26 July 1983.

28. Interviews with Walter E. and Margaret Moorman, 14 July 1983, and Charles T. Harris, 18 July 1983.

29. Interview with Roy Todd, 18 July 1983.

30. Interviews with Charles T. Harris, 18 July 1983; Roy Todd, 18 July 1983, Pink Henderson, 15 July 1983, North Dickerson, 28 July 1983, and Lawrence Boling, 18 July 1983.

31. For membership statistics on UMWA Districts 17 and 29, see David A. Corbin, *Life, Work, and Rebellion in the Coal Fields: The Southern West Virginia Miners, 1880–1922* (Urbana: University of Illinois Press, 1981), pp. 76–

77, 184. See also "Roll Call," in *Proceedings of the Re-Convened 28th Consecutive and 5th Biennial Convention of the United Mine Workers of America, Indianapolis, Indiana, 14 Feb. 1922* (Indianapolis, Ind.: Bookwalter-Ball-Greathouse Printing Company, 1922), p. 173.

32. "Delegate [Frank] Ingham," in *Proceedings of the 28th Consecutive and 5th Biennial Convention of the United Mine Workers of America, Indianapolis, Indiana, 20 Sept. to 5 Oct. 1921* (Indianapolis, Ind.: Bookwalter-Ball-Greathouse Printing Company, 1921), 1:538–39; T. Edward Hill, "The Coal Strike and Negro Miners in West Virginia," ca. 1922, in "Early Surveys: Migration Study, Birmingham Summary," Series 6, Box no. 89, National Urban League Papers, Library of Congress; WVBNWS, *Biennial Reports, 1923–24*, pp. 22–24, and *1925–26*, p. 131. For insight into black and white relations in the UMWA tent colonies of striking miners, see Box 2, file folders 9 and 10, Van Amberg Bittner Papers, West Virginia Collection, West Virginia University.

33. "From Iowa: A Word to the West Virginia Miners," *United Mine Workers Journal (UMWJ)*, 1 June 1916; G. H. Edmunds, "West Virginia on Tap," *UMWJ*, 11 Apr. 1917; "District 29 Holds a Splendid Special Convention," *UMWJ*, 1 Feb. 1919; "Assignment of Speakers for 1921 Labor Day," *UMWJ*, 1 Sept. 1921.

34. Heber Blankenhorn, "Marching Through West Virginia," *The Nation* 113 (Sept. 1921): 289, estimated 2,000 blacks among the 8,000 marchers. Daniel P. Jordan, "The Mingo War: Labor Violence in the Southern West Virginia Coal Fields, 1919–1922," in Gary M. Fink and Merle E. Reed, eds., *Essays in Southern Labor History* (Westport, Conn.: Greenwood Press, 1977), pp. 102–43; Corbin, *Life, Work, and Rebellion in the Coal Fields*, pp. 195–224; T. Edward Hill, "The Coal Strike and Negro Miners in West Virginia"; "Confessed Murderer of John Gore is Given Life Sentence," *Logan Banner*, 19 Oct. 1923; and *The Charleston Gazette*, 1 Sept. 1921; Witt and Dolter, "Before I'd Be a Slave," pp. 23–47.

35. Corbin, *Life, Work, and Rebellion in the Coal Fields*, p. 196. "Confessed Murderer of John Gore," *Logan Banner*, 19 Oct. 1923; "From Silush, W.Va.," *UMWJ*, 1 Sept. 1921; and *The Charleston Gazette*, 1 Sept. 1921.

36. Testimony of Frank Ingham, in U.S. Senate, *West Virginia Coal Fields: Hearings Before the Committee on Education* (Washington, 1921), 1:26–38.

37. Ibid.; Richard D. Lunt, *Law and Order versus the Miners: West Virginia, 1907–1933* (Hamden, Conn.: Archon Books, 1979), p. 119.

38. Testimony of Frank Ingham, in U.S. Senate, *West Virginia Coal Fields*, 1:26–38.

39. Testimony of George Echols and J. H. Reed, in U.S. Senate, *West Virginia Coal Fields*, 1:469–82.

40. Ibid.

41. Corbin, *Life, Work, and Rebellion*, p. 77.

42. "Agreement Between Carbon Fuel Company and Its Employees, 1923–25," in "Kanawha/Coal River," Mining Community Schedule-A, Box 28, Record Group No. 68, U.S. Coal Commission, National Archives.

43. "Easy," *UMWJ*, 15 Jan. 1925.

44. "Agreement Between Carbon Fuel Company and Its Employees, 1923–25," U.S. Coal Commission.

45. WVBNWS, *Biennial Report, 1921–22*, pp. 54–60; Hill, "The Coal Strike and Negro Miners in West Virginia."

46. WVBNWS, *Biennial Report, 1921–22*, pp. 54–60.

47. Hill, "The Coal Strike and Negro Miners in West Virginia."

48. "Discrimination Against the Negro," *Bluefield Daily Telegraph*, 20 June 1920.

49. "Negro Tricked into Logan County . . . ," *UMWJ*, 15 June 1921, includes extensive excerpts from the operators' pamphlet directed toward black workers; testimony of Langdon Bell, Director of the Red Jacket Consolidated Coal Company, in U.S. Senate, *Conditions in the Coal Fields of Pennsylvania, West Virginia, and Ohio: Hearings Before the Committee on Interstate Commerce* (Washington, 1928), pp. 1838–41.

50. W. H. Harris, "Exceptional Opportunities," *McDowell Times*, 8 Sept. 1916. Also see Agricultural Extension Service, *Annual Reports, 1922* (Morgantown, W.Va.), pp. 40–47, *1923*, pp. 98–110.

51. S. R. Anderson, "News of Colored People," *Bluefield Daily Telegraph*, 2, 9, 22, and 23 Sept. 1920, 15 Nov. 1924, 1 Jan. 1925.

52. Ralph W. White, "Weyanoke: The Eldorado of the Coal Fields in its Section of State," 13 July 1917, "Lynwin Coal Company Offering Great Extra Inducements," 11 May 1917, "Lynwin Coal Company: Offering Great Opportunities for Money," 4 May 1917, "Sycamore C. Company: Located in Mingo County, W.Va.: Doing Good Work," 23 July 1915, "The Coal Miners Provided For," 26 Feb. 1915, Lawson Blenkinsopp, "The Colored Miner: 'Don'ts' for Safety First," 15 Jan. 1915, "Improved Conditions in the Winding Gulf Fields," 17 Sept. 1917, all in *McDowell Times*. See also S. R. Anderson, "News of Colored People," *Bluefield Daily Telegraph*, 23 Sept. 1920, and Yvonne S. Farley, "Homecoming," *Goldenseal* 5, no. 4 (Oct.-Dec. 1979): 7–16.

53. U. G. Carter, "Public Address" and "Speech to New River Colored Mining Institute, Fayette County," in Box 1, Folder 8, U. G. Carter Papers; "McDowell County Colored Republican Organization," *McDowell Recorder*, 23 Oct. 1929; Fishback, "Employment Conditions," p. 231, n. 9; Lewis, *Black Coal Miners in America*, p. 223, n. 18; Laing, "The Negro Miners," pp. 180–82.

54. U. G. Carter, "Public Address," and "Speech"; *McDowell Recorder*, 23 Oct. 1929; Fishback, "Employment Conditions," p. 231, n. 9; Lewis, *Black Coal Miners in America*, p. 223, n. 18; and Laing, "The Negro Miners," pp. 180–82.

PART
3

*The Dynamics of Class and Race in
Coal-Mining Towns, 1915–32*

5

Race Relations, Housing, and Social Conditions

Along with racial stratification in the labor force after World War I, black miners in southern West Virginia confronted growing inequality in the community life of coal-mining towns. In addition to informal manifestations of public and private racial hostility, legal forms of racial segregation expanded, especially in the state's educational and social welfare institutions. Nevertheless, compared to the status quo in the contemporary South and in prewar West Virginia, race relations and social conditions in the postwar years in southern West Virginia improved. In the Mountain State, unlike other parts of the South, the black vote not only persisted but increased in significance, lynchings declined, and black institutions expanded, filling needs left unmet under the earlier pattern of exclusion.

The racial subordination of Afro-Americans in coal-mining towns, perhaps even more than their unequal treatment in the mines, sharply differentiated the lives of black coal miners from those of their white counterparts. As in the prewar era, racism played a major role in shaping the housing, health, educational, and legal status of blacks in southern West Virginia. Its most extreme public and private manifestations included the persistence of lynching sentiment, the resurgence of the Ku Klux Klan, and the intensification of racial discrimination in a broad range of public accommodations.

As elsewhere in industrial America, the Great Migration of blacks to southern West Virginia and their growing participation in the coal economy precipitated white violence against blacks. On 15 December 1919, a white mob lynched two black coal miners at Chapmanville, Logan County. Employed at the Island Creek Colliery Company, Ed Whitfield and Earl Whitney were lynched for allegedly murdering a white construction foreman. The mob seized the two men from local deputies, backed them up against a railroad box car, riddled their bodies with bullets, and tossed them into a river. Although the governor wired the local prosecutor, Don Chafin, to ensure a full investigation, and although national and local officers of the National Association for the Advancement of Colored People vigorously pushed for one, the county prosecutor and county judges refused to cooperate. Moreover, the white press downplayed the lynching, printing headlines asserting "No evidence warranting indictments." The lynching of Whitney and Whitfield, the Charleston NAACP concluded, "places West Virginia in the class with other communities who believe in mob rule, the Charleston branch feeling keenly the disgrace."[1]

Although lynchings virtually disappeared from the coalfields during the 1920s, throughout the period lynching sentiment seethed just below the surface. Nowhere was this more evident than in the cases of black men accused of crimes against white women. Reflecting West Virginia's strong cultural prohibition of interracial sexual relations, the state retained its statute forbidding interracial marriage, and its white citizens jealously guarded the vaunted integrity of white women. In 1921 when Leroy Williams faced rape charges in Charleston, Kanawha County, a lynching atmosphere developed, reinforced by inflammatory reporting by the local press, making it necessary for authorities to transport the accused from Charleston to Huntington, Cabell County. The threat of mob violence dictated a speedy trial and the death sentence. Despite the change of venue, Williams was quickly tried, convicted, and sentenced to be hanged. Evidence of Williams's innocence, including the highly inconsistent testimony of the woman involved, was ignored.

Williams's hanging took place in early 1922. Republican Governor Ephraim F. Morgan denied the NAACP's plea for clemency and a reduced sentence of life imprisonment, despite blacks' strong support of the Republican party. On 7 September of the same year, Harry Lattimar of Williamson was arrested "on the charge of rape, indicted, tried, convicted and sentenced to hang, by one o'clock of the next day and the same day placed on a train leaving for the state penitentiary." "The actual trial," the Charleston NAACP reported, "only lasted about thirty minutes." At the initial hearing Lattimar pleaded "not guilty" without the advice of legal counsel. When he later received a court-appointed attorney, the public defender assigned "seemed as anxious to have Lattimar convicted as did the prosecuting attorney, and no effort whatever was made in defense of Lattimar," according to the NAACP. Fortunately, under the vigorous protests of blacks and the legal defense activities of the Charleston NAACP, Governor Morgan commuted Lattimar's sentence to twenty years' imprisonment.[2]

Similar cases continued to occur until the latter part of the decade. When Henry Grogan was accused of raping a white woman in 1928, an intense lynching atmosphere developed and largely dictated the outcome of his case. To elude various lynching mobs, law officers transported Grogan from Beckley, Raleigh County, to Charleston, Kanawha County, and finally to Huntington, Cabell County. While a lynching was avoided, the transfers interfered with Grogan's defense, culminating in his summary conviction and sentence to hang. To no avail, Brown W. Payne, Grogan's black defense attorney, bitterly petitioned the Raleigh County Court for a writ of error, primarily basing his plea on the failure of officials to inform him of his client's whereabouts when lynching sentiment had required his speedy transfer from county to county. Without contact between the defendant and his lawyer, a proper defense could not be prepared, and racial injustice prevailed.[3]

As suggested above, with its racially biased, inflammatory reporting, the white press worsened the volatile racial climate blacks faced in coal-mining towns. In the Williamson, Mingo County, rape case, "the local daily paper ran for several days screaming headlines in which the race of the accused was over-emphasized," complained T. Edward Hill, director of the Bureau of Negro Welfare and Statistics. In a similar case, involving a sixteen-year-old black male and a thirteen-year-old white female, the local press played up the alleged crime as "the most heinous that could be committed." The white press painted a criminal portrait of blacks in general, and of the black coal miner in particular, under a plethora of racially explicit headlines: "Negro Murders White Man," "Negro Attacks Girl," "Miner Shot to Death and Murderer Escapes: Both Victim and Slayer are Colored," and "Three Negro[e]s are Dead . . . Whiskey, Pistols and Politics Hold High Carnival," to list only a few.[4]

Racism also intensified during the postwar years with the revival of the Ku Klux Klan. As the Klan expanded nationally in the wake of World War I, important branches emerged in Logan, Mercer, and Kanawha counties. In 1923, when the evangelist Billy Sunday completed a series of revival meetings in Logan County, the local Klan presented him with $1,000 in cash, along with a prepared statement emphasizing its stature as a white supremacist "organization con-

sisting of several hundred of the leading citizens of this country."
Until the mid-1920s, the Logan Klan held extensive public meetings,
demonstrations, and celebrations—all testimony to its growing
strength.[5] In 1924 the Bluefield KKK opened its office and held its
first mass meeting at the city's Colonial Theater. "The theatre was
packed from pit to dome and many were standing in the aisles," the
Bluefield Daily Telegraph reported. When the curtains opened, there
sat in full regalia a host of local Klan, joined by W. H. Thomas, city
mayor. After receiving the mayor's cordial welcome, H. L. Burham,
a grand officer of the West Virginia Klan, outlined the organization's white supremacist ideology and its goal of segregation and
disfranchisement. "The Klan believes in white supremacy, and will
not compromise on this issue," the principal speaker proclaimed.
After the Klan led parades through black sections of some towns,
and after several threatening notes to black homeowners, churches,
fraternal orders, and civil rights organizations, the BNWS targeted
the Klan as the "greatest apparent danger to the peace and good-
will between the races in West Virginia."[6]

In the war and postwar years, racial segregation of public accommodations persisted and even intensified. Black coal miners vividly
recalled, for example, how theaters in company and non-company
towns alike continued to segregate black and white patrons. Andrew Campbell remembered "separate sides" for blacks and whites
at the Hippodrome Theater in Keystone, McDowell County. The
Weyanoke Theater in Mercer County, Charles T. Harris recalled,
had a single floor with a partition dividing the races. In Bluefield,
another black miner recollected, the Granada Theater reserved the
balcony for black patrons and forced them to use a back-alley entrance. Disgusted, they made fun of the balcony, calling it the "buz-
zard's roost." In addition, whites in the company town of Gary,
McDowell County, claimed another black miner, had better public
accommodations and recreational facilities than blacks. And when
segregated public places like theaters became overcrowded, "whites
could use the black section, but blacks could not cross into white
territory."[7]

Hotels excluded blacks, and restaurants either barred them or
served them on a carry-out basis only. In Bluefield in 1917, black
visitors to the Twenty-eighth Annual Meeting of the Bluestone Baptist Sunday School Union lodged with black families. In the same
year, when the Primitive Baptist Association held its second annual
meeting in Keystone, out-of-town guests did the same. In fact, every major black gathering faced the same problem. As for restaurants, those that were white-owned and operated excluded blacks,

or, as Pink Henderson recalled, they "served you, but you couldn't come in." These patterns of racial segregation persisted into the mid-1920s.[8]

Such clear-cut manifestations of racism increased in southern West Virginia in all areas of public life, including housing, education, and legal and medical services. Like white miners, as a condition of their employment, blacks miners lived in company-owned housing mainly consisting of inadequately constructed wooden homes. Unlike their white counterparts, however, black miners were increasingly relegated to the worst structures. Black coal miners invariably recall a pattern of segregated and unequal housing, a decided reversal of the earlier pattern of blacks and whites at least sometimes receiving similar-quality housing. As noted in chapter 1, in the company town of Capels, McDowell County, blacks and immigrants at first lived in the same newly constructed rows of houses. Then, in the early 1920s, the company constructed a new group of houses. At the same time, one Italian miner recollected, "The company began moving white families from the older section of the town into the newer town, and all new Black miners hired were assigned houses in the older section of town. In a few years, the town's housing was completely segregated."[9] In 1921 North Dickerson recalled, when he moved to Stanaford, Raleigh County, "White foreigners and blacks lived up here until another superintendent came along, and he forced segregation of the camp." In this case, segregation expanded to "protect" immigrant whites as well as American-born whites. Black miners recalled always living in segregated company housing throughout the 1920s despite their frequent movement from one company town to another.[10]

Black miners often complained that housing was not only segregated but unequal as well. The housing needs of whites, they believed, received the operator's closer attention. In some places, Preston Turner recalled, white miners received "better materials" and "better-built" houses. Substantial evidence suggests that management placed blacks at the bottom of its list of housing repairs and other amenities. In the early 1920s, black men at the Winding Gulf Colliery Company "took offence" when the company painted and repaired the houses of whites, but overlooked those of blacks. When black miners threatened to leave, company officials promised them new housing the next year, when materials would be cheaper.[11]

Obie McCollum of the New York Urban League recalled working with his father, a carpenter, in the company town of Jenkinjones, McDowell County. "In practically all cases, housing for Negroes

[was] segregated and inferior. . . . When a Negro asked for flooring instead of rough boards for his porch, he was told that everything must be as it was originally."[12] In his close examination of black housing of the late 1920s and early 1930s, sociologist James T. Laing concluded that "where segregation is the policy of the company the Negroes are likely to be found in the less favorable locations and in the less desirable houses." Located close to coal tipples and railroad tracks, the worst houses inhabited by black coal miners and their families were "loosely-built, unpainted, board and batten type with leaking roof affording scant protection from winter drafts." In her survey of company housing in the southern Appalachian region, Margaret Wolfe also concluded that "the inherently unequal concept of 'separate but equal' prevailed during World War I and its aftermath."[13]

Inadequate living conditions plagued both black and white coal-mining families in the region. According to the U.S. Department of Labor, in 1923 only 11.2 percent of company-owned homes in West Virginia had running water; only 2.5 percent had bathtubs or showers; and only 3.9 percent had inside flush toilets. Of the 402 company-controlled towns in West Virginia, only 28 had a single water outlet for every family; an almost equal number had only a single outlet for every seven families.[14] None of the towns had a complete sewer system, and over 60 percent had outside privies. Large numbers of them were without cesspool equipment, too.[15] Although these conditions confronted working-class black and white families alike, the dynamics of racial discrimination intensified their impact on blacks.[16]

While coal-town housing for blacks was inferior to that for whites, it would be misleading to leave the comparison at that level. Compared to blacks' prewar experience, and especially compared to conditions farther south, housing gradually improved for blacks in southern West Virginia during World War I and the 1920s. The *Mc-Dowell Times* noted a shift from shanties for single men to family dwellings at the Sycamore Coal Company at Cinderella, Mingo County. "There are 83 houses all well built and of the two-story kind. There is not a shanty upon the operation because the company wants men with families to do their work, therefore they prepared the best accommodations for them."[17] One columnist contrasted the war housing of blacks at Giatto, Mercer County, to prewar housing. "Houses at that time . . . were mainly rude constructed shelters thrown up here and there on the mountainside. . . . Thirteen years hence visit the same place again and what a wonderful transformation."[18] The employment manager at the Winding Gulf Colliery Company, George Wolfe, informed the owner that only six houses were available at the Superior Mines for new workers and added, "To be frank with you the six empty houses that we have are not fit for any one to live in, they are houses only by the courtesy of the name." Wolfe recommended a vigorous building program to upgrade the company's housing stock.[19]

In the years following World War I, the U.S. Coal Commission found that nearly 80 percent of miners' homes in West Virginia were supplied with electricity, the highest percentage of any mining region in the country. Partly as a device to control labor, and also in a response to growing worker power, coal companies intensified their sanitary housing and garden campaigns among black and white miners. The U.S. Coal and Coke Company emerged at the forefront of these efforts, but with ulterior motives, as revealed by this statement by a company official: "When employees of a company are made to take a great interest in their homes and to have pride in the appearance of them, there is but one result—they become happy and contented, and are not so susceptible to 'hard times' and anarchistic propaganda."[20]

Eventually, some black coal miners were able to escape dependence on company-owned housing and purchase their own homes outside the company towns. Although West Virginia had one of the lowest rates of black homeownership in the nation, an estimated 18 to 19 percent of blacks owned their homes in 1920 and 1930. While some blacks purchased homes within established municipal areas, most bought them in new unincorporated segregated developments on the edges of towns and cities. During World War I and the 1920s, an increasing number of Afro-Americans bought homes in and around various coal-mining towns including Keystone, Welch, and Bluefield in the Pocahontas Field; Beckley in the Winding Gulf Field; Charleston in the Kanawha–New River Field; and Williamson in the Williamson-Logan Field. The nearly all-black town of Giatto, Mercer County, was described as "a very independent town . . . largely owned by colored people. Fifty or more persons own their own property and quite a number of persons are e[x]cavating for the foundation of [new] residences."[21] In the fall of 1916, a number of black families moved from McDowell County to a settlement near Beckley, Raleigh County. More than thirteen families moved from Eckman, the *Times* reported, "where they made their first money [in the coal mines of] . . . the Pulaski Iron Company." These people, the reporter concluded, "are proud of their homes and suffice it to say they are at home."[22] The *Times* consistently urged black miners to save their money and buy homes in Keystone, described as the "Mecca of the Coal Fields." Also, throughout the 1920s the BNWS urged black workers to buy homes with their savings and earnings as protection against downturns in the economy.[23]

Although some black miners managed to heed the injunction, black homeownership was a highly precarious affair. Located in the least desirable areas, black privately owned homes were invariably "without modern improvements, such as paving, sewer, water or gas." Less than 40 percent of the black-owned lots, the BNWS reported, were located in areas with established and stable real estate values. Some real estate sales actually reflected the blatant entrapment of blacks in fraudulent land deals, in which blacks purchased "mythical lots in subdivisions which never existed." Still others purchased lots and found it impossible to save or borrow the money necessary to build. During the late 1920s and early 1930s, blacks increasingly lost both lots and homes as the Depression got underway. Buying property, even at bankrupt sales, the *Times* had earlier discovered, was "out of reach" of most blacks. In an effort to pay mortgages, a growing number of black homeowners took in boarders, even though their homes could "safely accom[m]odate only a half or a third as many." Making matters worse, coal companies preferred workers who lived in company-owned houses, and frequently laid off homeowners first during economic downturns.[24]

Poor housing, as part of poor living conditions, took a disproportionate toll on the health of black miners and their families according to a 1927–28 health survey by the BNWS. The survey covered twelve counties, seven of which were located in southern West Virginia. It found that mine accidents were responsible for nearly 9 percent of black deaths, versus roughly 4 percent for whites, but that tuberculosis was a far worse cause of black deaths. "The great scourge of the Negro race," tuberculosis was a greater killer than heart disease, pneumonia, nephritis, and premature births, accounting for 13 percent of black health-related deaths compared to less than 8 percent for whites. In McDowell County, the only southern county tabulated by race, tuberculosis accounted for 12 percent of black deaths, compared to less than 4 percent for whites.[25] The BNWS concluded that to improve the black miner's health it would be "necessary to improve his economic position which alone will enable him to improve his living conditions—proper housing, wholesome food and sanitation are prerequisites of good health."

The agency reflected the views of black health professionals like Dr. B. A. Crichlow, superintendent of the all-black Denmar Sanitarium for tuberculosis patients.[26]

Another factor behind the poor health status of black miners was the discriminatory health care provided by the coal companies. The *McDowell Times*, the BNWS, and black miners themselves frequently complained of medical mistreatment of blacks by the coal companies and their physicians.[27] In 1929 North Dickerson suffered a broken back and two broken ribs in a slate fall. Dickerson was immediately transported from the mine at about 3:00 P.M., but it was not until 7:00 P.M. that he was hospitalized. Upon admittance to the hospital, however, Dickerson bitterly recalled, for three days the medical staff did little to aid his recovery. The doctors believed that he would die, he said, and wished to avoid "the trouble of traction and everything if he was going to die." At one mine, according to interviews conducted by James T. Laing, the company president had a physician son-in-law on the staff of the local hospital who frequently dismissed injured men instead of treating them, ordering them back to work and preventing their full recovery.[28] To be sure, medical abuses like these were perpetrated against white as well as black miners, but racial discrimination certainly heightened their impact on blacks.

The segregationist policies of the state reinforced the poor health status of black workers. In the state-supported medical facilities, blacks and whites were decidedly separated by race. In McDowell County at Welch Hospital Number 1, formerly "Miners' Hospital No. 1," the superintendent reported, "On the first floor are two entrances—one for white patients and one for colored. The south wing is used exclusively for white patients. . . . The north wing is used exclusively for colored patients." Likewise, in Fayette County at the McKendree Hospital Number 2, formerly "Miners' Hospital No. 2," "the first floor consist[ed] of white and colored wards."[29] Although racially segregated health services were discriminatory, their emergence represented an advance over the earlier system of exclusion and neglect.[30]

While the white press ignored discrimination against blacks, it exaggerated black criminality. Nevertheless, black criminal behavior significantly affected the lives of black coal miners. Blacks comprised less than 7 percent of the state's population throughout the postwar period, but they made up an estimated 25 to 30 percent of the state's prison population. Most of them came from southern West Virginia, but, in fact, a disproportionate number came from the urban areas of northern West Virginia.[31] As elsewhere in industrial America, the most frequently committed crimes by blacks were larceny, homicide, malicious wounding, and bootlegging.

In early 1915 the *Times* reported that the prohibition law was "helping to fill up the jails" in Raleigh County, but had not yet ended the thriving bootlegging business among blacks. "The bootleggers of 'colored hill' seem to have been making good here of late," the *Times* asserted. Southern West Virginia had the state's highest incidence of prohibition arrests, convictions, and sentences to hard labor on county roads. As mentioned earlier, although some of the arrests and convictions were unfairly made to obtain labor for county road projects, some did involve blacks who were genuine bootleggers.[32] During the mid-1920s, in addition to importing "moonshine" from as far away as Detroit, blacks made home brew. The BNWS reported: "Many persons make small quantities in their homes. They do not peddle it in bottles, but 'sell, enough to pay expenses' by the drink. It is more frequently in homes of this kind at such 'liquor parties' that crime[s] of violence are committed or trouble is started which lead to crimes among Negroes."[33]

However common prohibition violations may have been, it was homicide that was the most serious criminal problem for blacks in southern West Virginia. More than any other crime, homicide reflected the development of intraracial and intra–working class conflicts within the black community. Along with the white press, the *Times* consistently reported black-on-black homicides, which usually involved firearms and knives. Homicide offenders usually eluded arrest and trial by escaping into the mountains. "On the least provocation," the *Times* reported, "a human life is snuffed out, the 'bad man' backs up the mountain with his smoking revolver until he has had time to make good his escape."[34] However, some homicides involved men of good reputation who were not known for fighting.[35] Still others involved gender conflict within the black working class. For example, in 1915 one miner shot and killed a woman, and severely wounded her friend, when she refused to move into his shanty. The miner escaped into the mountains, eluded police bloodhounds, and caught a freight train out of the area.[36]

Black leaders repeatedly emphasized the connection between black crime and poverty. Poor blacks were not only more likely to commit crimes such as larceny and bootlegging, they believed, but were less likely to get professional legal counsel upon arrest.[37] Although blacks achieved greater access to protection before the law in West Virginia than elsewhere in the South, by the mid-1920s no more than three West Virginia counties impaneled racially mixed juries. Moreover, white offenders were more likely than blacks to have "interested friends and relatives" among justice officials.[38] Furthermore, the frequency with which black homicide offenders escaped the law not only demonstrated the difficulties of law enforcement in the mountains, but also revealed the laxity of law officers in addressing black-on-black crime.[39] Thus the racially discriminatory justice system encouraged black-on-black crime and inflated the criminal record of blacks.

As black miners faced the problems of crime, health, and housing, southern West Virginia experienced a postwar educational boom.[40] With only 10 black high schools in the entire state on the eve of World War I, southern West Virginia alone boasted 13 black high schools in 1923, and by 1932 the the state total had increased to 32.[41] The total state funds spent on the annual salaries of black public schoolteachers increased from an estimated $160,000 in 1914 to nearly $400,000 in 1920, $700,000 in 1925, $800,000 in 1926, and over $1.2 million in 1929. By the late 1920s, West Virginia had almost fully complied with its educational statute, which required at least an elementary school in any community with ten or more black students.[42]

Unfortunately, although black educational facilities increased, they did not keep pace with the rapid expansion of the black working class. As the black migration to southern West Virginia accelerated during and after World War I, the number of school-aged black youth (from 5 to 20 years old) also rose, increasing from about 19,800 in 1910 to 26,400 in 1920, to 35,600 in 1930. The number of black youth attending schools likewise increased, from nearly 10,000 in 1910 to 15,000 in 1920, to nearly 23,500 in 1930. With their parents, the BNWS reported, most black youth had migrated to West Virginia from other southern states, especially from rural areas and small towns, where schools were few and far between and only met from two to five months each year. Typically these schools were taught by poorly prepared teachers who were seldom paid more than twenty dollars a month. In fact, many of the children had received no schooling whatever.[43]

The state's exclusion of Afro-Americans from the West Virginia state university system and its segregation of them at all other levels of public education hampered the training of black teachers and administrators. From the outset, then, the educational advancement of blacks lagged behind that of whites. Scholars often note that, compared to other southern dual school systems of the period, West Virginia's blacks received a relatively equal, and sometimes disproportionately high, percentage of state aid. In 1918, for example, with about 6 percent of the state's black population, black colleges received nearly 8 percent of the state's total appropriations for higher education. What figures such as this ignore, though, is that until the late 1920s black colleges maintained vigorous high-school departments because some school districts refused to finance high-school training for black students. As the education historian William P. Jackameit has recently noted, "This situation . . . was, in effect, a shifting of the burden of financing the secondary education of Negroes from the local to the state level."[44]

Local school boards set education for white children as their top priority. Blacks invariably saw white high schools established before black ones reluctantly were. From the beginning, some counties excluded blacks from the school construction boom. In early 1915 the state supervisor of free schools reported that several new high schools for whites in McDowell County had been built, ranging in cost from $20,000 to $90,000. At Mt. Hope, Fayette County, school authorities built "a handsome new High School building, a large graded school and a kindergarten." Although white children of "various nationalities" could be found in the town's schools, blacks were excluded. Where counties failed to establish black schools, especially high schools, black parents were forced to send their children elsewhere for post-secondary education, sometimes even out of state. Few black coal-mining families could afford to, though.[45]

The unequal education of blacks and whites persisted into the 1920s. In his 1921–22 biennial report, the state supervisor of black schools reported that West Virginia was "far behind in its building program for Negro schools," and that only a few districts had provided adequate facilities. Some of the school buildings for black children were "unsanitary, poorly built and utterly unsuited for school use," and blackboards, seats, maps, books, and suitable playgrounds were generally in short supply. Black teachers were often compelled to hold school in the same public halls as those used by churches, lodges, and the miners' union. The superintendent further lamented: "There seems to be an 'unwritten rule' that whenever a building is to be erected for a Negro school a hill-side site must be selected. Usually these sites are almost inaccessible on account of the steep hill upon which they are located."[46]

Even in the capital city of Charleston, where black schools were generally better staffed and better equipped, black education stood on a grossly unequal footing with that of whites. In 1925, upon investigating conditions at the black Garnet Senior High School, a member of the Charleston Board of Education, Mrs. H. D. Rummel, was "mortified beyond expression at the conditions existing there." Rummel "expressed the hope that no visitors would visit the school before conditions could be corrected" and roundly condemned the state, declaring, "I can't understand why we should be building a million-dollar school for the white children and allow such conditions to exist among the colored children."[47] In 1927, in a vigorous attempt to extend the institutional segregation of blacks and whites, the Charleston Board of Education sought to establish a segregated black branch library and barred blacks from the city's public library. Although a highly aroused and politically active black community defeated the board's resolution and blacks retained access to the main building, the board was able to continue segregating black and white patrons within the building.

Although West Virginia statutes prohibited racial differentials in the payment and training of teachers, some school districts blatantly violated the law. In his 1921–22 report, the state supervisor of black schools complained of such illegal discrimination being practiced by a few districts, and the BNWS's 1925–26 biennial report noted that some districts were notorious for it. As late as 1929, the McDowell County Colored Republican Organization passed a resolution complaining that "in some districts of McDowell county colored school teachers are not receiving the same salaries as white teachers . . . of equal experience and holding the same credentials."[48]

Black teachers also received unequal training. The state excluded blacks from West Virginia University, yet required high-school teachers to have "college degrees." Until 1915, the state's only black institutions of higher learning, Bluefield State College and West Virginia State College, were ranked such that they could only offer training for elementary teachers. At the same time, state scholarship funds for training elsewhere were insufficient. Not until 1919 did West Virginia State College award its first baccalaureate degrees; Bluefield State College conferred its first bachelor of science degrees in 1929. Although black access to higher education eventually and gradually improved, its slow development hampered the training of black teachers. Moreover, when bachelor-level education finally became available, blacks seeking graduate training had to leave West Virginia to attend school and had to have the funds to do so.[49]

Not only were black schools deficient in providing opportunities for teacher training, but they also lacked vocational training programs. The BNWS, emphasizing the exclusion of blacks from several skilled trades, fought for the addition of vocational training to the black school system. Although over 75 percent of the state's blacks worked in mining, the bureau noted in 1925, "Negroes [were being] taught no trade or profession which has the remotest connection with mining," but white youth were "being taught at the expense of the State all branches of coal mining." Like blacks seeking graduate training, blacks seeking professional training for coal-industry positions had to look elsewhere. In 1926, as noted in chapter 4, in order to pass the state mine foreman and mine safety examinations, black miner John Patterson took correspondence courses from Pennsylvania State University.[50] Although the state offered some segregated mine safety classes to black workers by the late 1920s, not until the 1930s would blacks receive the necessary training to compete for jobs as foremen and for other higher-paying positions requiring formal education and certification.

Although black miners experienced gradual and, in certain areas, dramatic improvements in their social status, racial inequality persisted in housing, and in legal, educational, and health services. Yet, the emergence of segregated public services and institutions represented an advance over the earlier system of exclusion and neglect. Moreover, as we will see in subsequent chapters on the political activities of blacks, the expansion of the color line in the institutional life of the region was not entirely led by whites. Black leaders vigorously pushed for more services, even if on a segregated basis. The war and postwar growth of the black middle class and its small elite would play a crucial role in this process.

NOTES

1. Lillian B. Waller to E. C. Lewis, 18 Feb. 1920, Lewis to John R. Shillady, 16 Feb. 1920, "Bloodthirsty Murder in Thug-Rule Logan," newsclipping, Charleston Federationist, 18 Dec. 1919, "Report of the Charleston Branch," 18 Feb. 1920, all in Charleston Branch Files, Box G-215, Records of the National Association for the Advancement of Colored People (NAACP Papers), Library of Congress; James Weldon Johnson to Howard Sutherland, West Virginia Senator, 16 Dec. 1919, "West Virginia Senators Notified of Lynching in Their State," news release, 17 Dec. 1919, Lewis to Governor John J. Cornwell, 13 Mar. 1920, Shillady to Cornwell, 12 Feb. 1920, Cornwell to Shillady, 17 Feb. 1920, Cornwell to Lewis, 15 Mar. 1920, "Two Negroes Taken Off Train Tied to Freight Car and Shot to Death by Coal Field Mob," newsclipping, New York Herald, 16 Dec. 1919, all in Administrative File, Box C-370, NAACP Papers.

2. Lewis to Walter White, 13 and 19 Dec. 1922, White to Lewis, 19 and 16 Dec. 1922, White to T. G. Nutter, 28 Feb. 1922, "A Negro Woman," letter to editor, *New York Age*, n.d., newsclipping from *Cincinnati Post*, 23 Feb. 1922, all in Charleston Branch Files, Box G-215, NAACP Papers; letter of petition for clemency, Charleston NAACP to Governor E. F. Morgan, 21 Feb. 1922, Nutter to White, 3 Mar. 1922, both in Legal Files, Box D-2, NAACP Papers; First Baptist Church, *The Bulletin*, 28 May 1922, in Charleston Branch Files, Box G-216, NAACP Papers; West Virginia Bureau of Negro Welfare and Statistics (WVBNWS), *Biennial Report 1923–24* (Charleston, W.Va.), pp. 96–98.

3. "Henry Grogan," testimony of plaintiff and the accused, Nutter to Robert Bagnall, 16 Aug. 1928, Albert Kyselka to Roger Baldwin, American Civil Liberties Union, 24 Aug. 1928, Baldwin to Bagnall, 24 Aug. 1928, "State of West Virginia vs. Henry Grogan," defense attorney's petition for a writ of error, all in Charleston Branch Files, Box G-215, NAACP Papers.

4. WVBNWS, *Biennial Reports, 1925–26*, pp. 114–18, *1921–22*, p. 52. See also the following newsclippings in Charleston Branch Files, Box G-216, NAACP Papers: "Has Never Heard of God: Girl Tells Court," 19 Oct. 1923, and "Three Negro[e]s Are Dead," 2 Nov. 1926, both in *Logan Banner;* "Negro is Placed on Trial Today in Assault Case," 25 July 1925, "Jury In Watt Wall Case," 29 July 1925, both in *Welch Daily News;* "Negro Murders White Man," ca. Jan. 1922, "Negro Attacks Girl in Holdup Case: Makes Escape," 22 Jan. 1922, in *Charleston Gazette.*

5. "Billy Sunday Bids Logan Fond Farewell," 22 June 1923, "Ku Klux Klan Gives Billy Pleasant Surprise," 22 June 1923, "Klansmen Celebrate Independence Day," 6 July 1923, "Klan's Greatest Ceremonial Tonight," 2 Nov. 1923, "Klan Ceremonial Was Witnessed by Multitude," 9 Nov. 1923, "Logan Klan Have Special Train," 22 Aug. 1924, "Logan Klan is Prominent at State Meeting," 29 Aug. 1924, "Logan Klan Gives Money to Christian Church," 22 Aug. 1924, all in *Logan Banner*. For the revival of the Ku Klux Klan after World War I, see Kenneth T. Jackson, *The Ku Klux Klan in the City, 1915–1930* (New York: Oxford University Press, 1967) and David M. Chalmers, *Hooded Americanism: The History of the Ku Klux Klan* (Durham: N.C.: Duke University Press, 1981).

6. "Packed Theatre to Hear Speech on Ku Klux Klan," newsclipping, *Bluefield Daily Telegraph*, 6 Mar. 1924, "The Negro Situation," KKK circular letter, in Charleston Branch Files, Box G-215, NAACP Papers; WVBNWS, *Biennial Report, 1921–22*, pp. 52–54.

7. Interviews with Andrew Campbell, 19 July 1983, Charles T. Harris, 18 July 1983, Pink Henderson, 15 July 1983, John L. Page, 13 July 1983, and Lawrence Boling, 18 July 1983. See also Matt Witt and Earl Dolter, "Before I'd Be A Slave," in *In Our Blood: Four Coal Mining Families* (New Market, Tenn.: Highlander Research Center, 1979), pp. 23–47; James T. Laing, "The Negro Miner in West Virginia" (Ph.D. diss., Ohio State University, 1933), pp. 409–11.

8. "Welch Has No Accom[m]odation for Colored People—Hotel Greatly Needed," 31 Aug. 1917, other articles, 6 Apr., 10 Aug., and 12 Oct. 1917, in *McDowell Times;* interview with Pink Henderson, 15 July 1983.

9. Lawrence, "Appalachian Metamorphosis," p. 180; interviews with North Dickerson, 28 July 1983, Andrew Campbell, 19 July 1983, Watt B. Teal, 27 July 1983, and Charles T. Harris, 18 July 1983; "Memorandum: Willie Parker," U.S. Department of Justice, Record Group No. 60, Straight Numerical File No. 182363; Laing, "The Negro Miner," pp. 480–81, 483.

10. Interviews with North Dickerson, 28 July 1983, Andrew Campbell, 19 July 1983, Watt B. Teal, 27 July 1983, and Charles T. Harris, 18 July 1983; "Memorandum: Willie Parker," U.S. Department of Justice; Laing, "The Negro Miner," pp. 480–81, 483.

11. Interview with Preston Turner, 26 July 1983; S. R. Anderson, a black journalist, to Justin Collins, 13 Aug. 1923, Series 1, Box 14, Folder 101, Justus Collins Papers, West Virginia Collection, West Virginia University.

12. Obie McCollum to Walter White, 17 Oct. 1930, Charleston Branch Files, Box G-215, NAACP Papers; "Rich Coal Operator," *United Mine Workers Journal (UMWJ),* 15 Oct. 1930.

13. Laing, "The Negro Miner," pp. 348–49; "Why," *McDowell Times,* 17 Nov. 1916; Margaret R. Wolfe, "Putting Them in Their Places: Industrial Housing in Southern Appalachia, 1900–1930," *Appalachian Journal* 7, no. 3 (Summer 1979): 27–36. Also see "International Convention Goes on Record in Favor of Traditional Policy of Observance of Contracts . . . ," *UMWJ,* 1 Oct. 1921, and "Living Conditions in Many Mine Fields Against Which the Union Continues to Fight," *UMWJ,* 15 Mar. 1924.

14. Women's Bureau, U.S. Department of Labor, *Home Environment and Employment Opportunities of Women in Coal-Mine Workers' Families* (Washington, 1925), pp. 55–59; Children's Bureau, U.S. Department of Labor, *The Welfare of Children in Bituminous Coal Mining Communities in West Virginia* (Washington, 1923), pp. 6–17, 47.

15. Women's Bureau, *Home Environment and Employment Opportunities of Women,* pp. 17, 55–59.

16. Ibid.; Children's Bureau, *The Welfare of Children,* pp. 6–17, 47.

17. "Sycamore Coal Company," *McDowell Times,* 23 July 1915.

18. W. H. Harris, "Exceptional Opportunities . . . At Olga Shaft Coalwood, W.Va.," *McDowell Times,* 8 Sept. 1916; Ralph W. White, "Weyanoke: The Eldorado of the Coal Fields," *McDowell Times,* 13 July 1917.

19. Wolfe to Collins, 25 Aug. 1917, Series 1, Box 15, Folder titled, "August," Wolfe to Collins, 19 Sept. 1918, Series 1, Box 14, Folder 101, both in Justus Collins Papers; "Annual Garden Inspection at Gary Plants," 17 and 23 July 1925, "Gary Colored News," 25 July 1925, "Annual Inspection of Lands and Gardens: Consolidation Coal Company," 27 July 1925, all in *Welch Daily News.*

20. Laing, "The Negro Coal Miner," pp. 340–41; "Mining Community Schedule—A," Record Group No. 68, U.S. Coal Commission, National Archives; "Annual Garden Inspection at Gary Plants," 17 and 23 July 1925,

and "Gary Colored News," 25 July 1925, in *Welch Daily News;* "Agricultural Extension Work in Mining Camps" and "Negro Work" in Agricultural Extension Service, *Annual Reports, 1921–32* (Morgantown, W.Va.).

21. U.S. Bureau of the Census, *Fifteenth Census of the United States, 1930* (Washington, 1933), 6:1427–29. WVBNWS, *Biennial Reports, 1921–32;* "Miners Own Homes and Automobiles," reprint from a Charleston newspaper in *McDowell Times,* 5 Mar. 1915; "Giatto for Judge Ira E. Robinson," *McDowell Times,* 31 Mar. 1916; Laing, "The Negro Miner," pp. 295, 317.

22. "Mt Carbon and Kimberly," 28 July 1916, "McDowell Citizens . . . ," 13 Oct. 1916, "Lilly Land Company," 26 Nov. 1915, and "Great Land Sale," 28 May 1915, all in *McDowell Times.*

23. See the Keystone-based *McDowell Times,* 1915–18; "Lot Sale Going On," *McDowell Recorder,* 18 May 1917; "Housing Conditions" and "Home Ownership" in WVBNWS, *Biennial Reports, 1921–22,* pp. 45–49, and *1925–26,* pp. 59–61.

24. WVBNWS, *Biennial Report, 1923–24,* pp. 47–48; "Evils of Bad Housing," in WVBNWS, *Biennial Report, 1929–32,* pp. 6–10; "Great Land Sale," *McDowell Times,* 28 May 1915; Laing, "The Negro Miner," pp. 295, 317.

25. WVBNWS, *Biennial Report, 1927–28,* pp. 5–14. The BNWS based its study on Federal Registration Area data. Also see WVBNWS, *Biennial Reports, 1921–22,* p. 16; *1923–24,* pp. 14–15; *1925–26,* pp. 10–11; and *1929–32,* p. 49. See also West Virginia State Board of Control (WVSBC), *Biennial Report, 1924–25* (Charleston, W.Va.), pp. 145–63; West Virginia State Health Department, *Annual Reports, 1918–1932* (Charleston).

26. WVBNWS, "Health and Mortality," *Biennial Report, 1927–28,* pp. 5–14.

27. W. H. Harris, "The Negro Doctors Should Be Employed . . . By the Coal Companies," *McDowell Times,* 28 July 1916; WVSBC, "State Tuberculosis Sanitarium," *Biennial Report, 1914–16,* pp. 172–92.

28. Interviews with Walter and Margaret Moorman, 14 July 1983, North Dickerson, 28 July 1983, Thornton Wright, 27 July 1983, and Watt B. Teal, 27 July 1983; Laing, "The Negro Miner," p. 314. For role of black midwives, refer to interviews with Leonard Davis, 28 July 1983, and Andrew Campbell, 19 July 1983.

29. WVSBC, "Welch Hospital," *Biennial Report, 1918–19,* pp. 172–84, and *Biennial Report, 1924–25,* pp. 165–66; WVSBC, "McKendree Hospital Number 2," *Biennial Report, 1924–25,* pp. 185–87. Also see WVSBC, "Weston State Hospital," *Biennial Report, 1916–17,* pp. 48–90.

30. See n. 26 above. For insight into the political dimensions of all-black state-supported institutions, see chaps. 9 and 10.

31. "What is the Cause?" *McDowell Times,* 23 July 1915; WVSBC, "Penitentiary," *Biennial Reports, 1918–19,* pp. 218–35; WVBNWS, *Biennial Reports, 1921–22,* pp. 34–36, *1923–24,* p. 92; WVSBC, "Penitentiary," *Biennial Reports, 1920–30.*

32. W. F. Denny (sometimes misprinted as D. F. Denny), "People Have Rights," 30 Apr. 1915, W. F. Denny, "Criminal Court at Princeton," 9 July

1915, "To Whom It May Concern," 29 Jan. 1915, and "Educate All the People," 16 Apr. 1915, *McDowell Times;* State Commissioner of Prohibition, *Fourth Biennial Report, 1921–22* (Charleston, W.Va.), "Thirty Gallon Still is Found Near Church," 21 Dec. 1923, "Two Plead Guilty to Liquor Charges," 31 Dec. 1923, "Three Give Bond," 5 Jan. 1924, all in *Welch Daily News.*

33. "Negro Has Special Jacket to Carry His Moonshine In," 21 July 1925, "Three Colored Men Pose as Officers and Carry Liquor," 15 Jan. 1925, in *McDowell Recorder;* "Whoopee," 28 May 1915, "Again," 30 July 1915, "Thousands of Dollars Worth of Liquor . . . Destroyed," 30 Mar. 1917, "Still Captured: Fire Water Destroyed," 29 Mar. 1918, all in *McDowell Times;* WVBNWS, *Biennial Report, 1923–24,* p. 92.

34. "What is the Cause?" *McDowell Times,* 23 July 1915.

35. "Man Murdered at Eureka," 19 Mar. 1915, W. H. Harris, "Murder on King's Operation," 26 Mar. 1915, "Murder for Revenge," 7 May 1915, "Murder at Landgraf," 23 July 1915, all in *McDowell Times;* "Miner Shot to Death and Murderer Escapes," *Charleston Daily Mail,* 14 July 1918; *Welch Daily News,* 4 Feb. 1924, 28 July 1925, and 4 Nov. 1926.

36. "Murder at Crumpler: Woman Killed, Another Shot," *McDowell Times,* 30 July 1915, and "Kills Husband," 17 Sept. 1915, in *McDowell Times;* "Bullets Aimed at Fast Moving Auto," 13 Dec. 1923, and "Woman Kills Husband, Another Shoots Hers," in *Welch Daily News;* "Crazed Negro Slays Wife, Shoots Brother," 21 Aug. 1929, and "Negro Inflicts Fatal Wound on Girl," 5 Mar. 1930," in *McDowell Recorder.*

37. WVBNWS, *Biennial Reports, 1925–26,* pp. 110–14, "Crime," *1927–28,* pp. 56–61, and *1929–32,* pp. 55–57.

38. "Why[?]" 17 Nov. 1916, and "The Climax," 10 Sept. 1915, in *McDowell Times;* WVBNWS, *Biennial Report, 1923–24,* pp. 96–98. E. C. Lewis to Walter White, 13 and 19 Dec. 1922, White to Lewis, 19 and 16 Dec. 1922, in Charleston Branch Files, Box G-215, NAACP Papers. Also see n. 32 above.

39. WVBNWS, *Biennial Report, 1923–24,* pp. 96–98.

40. Charles H. Ambler, *A History of Education in West Virginia: From Early Colonial Times to 1949* (Huntington, W.Va.: Standard Printing and Publishing Company, 1951), pp. 503–4; Otis K. Rice, *West Virginia: A History* (Lexington: The University Press of Kentucky, 1985), pp. 239–54.

41. William P. Jackameit, "A Short History of Negro Public Higher Education in West Virginia, 1890–1965," *West Virginia History* 37, no. 4 (July 1976): 309–24; Ambler, *A History of Education in West Virginia,* pp. 454–56, 489–95; John C. Harlan, *History of West Virginia State College, 1890–1965* (Dubuque, Iowa: Wm. C. Brown Book Company, 1968), chaps. 4, 5, and 6; WVBNWS, *Biennial Reports, 1923–24,* pp. 64–67, *1921–32;* State Supervisor of Negro Schools, *Biennial Report, 1921–22* (Charleston, W.Va.), pp. 1–35; "West Virginia Collegiate Institute" and "Bluefield Colored Institute," in WVSBC, *Biennial Reports, 1916–1930.*

42. WVBNWS, *Biennial Reports, 1921–22,* p. 25, *1923–24,* pp. 64–69, and *1929–32,* p. 15; "Ten High Schools Receive State Aid," *Welch Daily News,*

9 Feb. 1923; State Supervisor of Negro Schools, *Biennial Report, 1921–22*, pp. 1–35; State Superintendent of Free Schools, *Biennial Report, 1929–30* (Charleston, W.Va.), p. 88; Jackameit, "A Short History of Negro Public Higher Education," pp. 309–24; Ambler, *A History of Education in West Virginia*, p. 409.

43. U.S. Bureau of the Census, *Fourteenth Census of U.S., 1920* (Washington, 1922), 2:1172; *Fifteenth Census, 1930*, vol. 3, pt. 2 (Washington, 1932), pp. 1263–77; "Education of the Negro," WVBNWS, *Biennial Reports, 1921–22*, p. 25, *1923–24*, pp. 64–69, and *1929–32*, p. 15; State Supervisor of Negro Schools, *Biennial Report, 1921–22*, pp. 1–35; State Superintendent of Free Schools, *Biennial Report, 1929–30*, p. 88; Jackameit, "A Short History of Negro Public Higher Education," pp. 309–24; Ambler, *A History of Education in West Virginia*, p. 409.

44. Jackameit, "A Short History of Negro Public Higher Education," p. 312; WVSBC, *Biennial Report, 1916–18*, pp. 17–18; Ambler, *A History of Education in West Virginia*, pp. 489–95; Harlan, *History of West Virginia State College*, chaps. 4, 5, and 6. Cf. Ronald L. Lewis, *Black Coal Miners in America: Race, Class, and Community Conflict, 1780–1980* (Lexington: The University Press of Kentucky, 1987), p. 155, and David A. Corbin, *Life, Work, and Rebellion in the Coal Fields: The Southern West Virginia Miners, 1880–1922* (Urbana: University of Illinois Press, 1981), p. 70.

45. "Successful School Year," 11 June 1915, "Account of High Schools in McDowell Co.," 15 Jan. 1915, "The Mining Town School System," 5 Mar. 1915, "Prof. W. W. Sanders Makes Statement," 21 June 1916, "Are Fees of High School Pupils Paid by District Boards of Education?" 16 Feb. 1917, all in *McDowell Times*.

46. "Education Made by Teacher," *McDowell Times*, 19 Mar. 1915. Also see *McDowell Times*, 19 Feb. and 6 Oct. 1915, 13 Oct. and 8 Sept. 1916; State Supervisor of Negro Schools, *Biennial Report, 1921–22*, pp. 1–35; "Education of the Negro," WVBNWS, *Biennial Reports, 1921–22*, pp. 22–25, pp. 64–69; WVSBC, "State Aid to Students Outside the State," *Biennial Report, 1930–31*, pp. 530–31.

47. "Colored High School Will be Improved Upon," *Charleston Gazette*, 9 Dec. 1925; WVBNWS, *Biennial Report, 1925–26*, pp. 84–91; "Resolutions, Charleston Board of Education," 13 Oct. 1927, "The Board of Education of the Charleston Independent School District: Minutes of a Special Meeting," 21 Feb. 1928, T. G. Nutter, president of the Charleston NAACP, to William T. Andrews, special legal assistant, NAACP headquarters, 28 Feb. 1928, 15, 20, 28 Mar. 1928, 21 Apr. 1928, and 28 May 1928, R. S. Spillman, member and attorney of Charleston Board of Education," 27 Feb. 1928, and Charleston NAACP, Lewis to National Office, 23 Oct. 1918, all in Charleston Branch Files, Box G-215, NAACP Papers.

48. State Superintendent of Free Schools, *Biennial Report of the State Supervisor of Negro Schools, 1921–22*, pp. 1–35; WVBNWS, *Biennial Report, 1925–26*, pp. 87–91; "McDowell County Colored Republican Organization," *McDowell Recorder*, 23 October 1929; Laing, "The Negro Miner," p. 376.

49. "College Department for Negroes," *McDowell Times*, 8 Jan. 1915; *Biennial Report of the State Supervisor of Negro Schools, 1921–22*, pp. 1–35; WVSBC, Biennial Report, 1930–31, pp. 530–31; WVBNWS, *Biennial Report, 1923–24*, pp. 64–69; Jackameit, "A Short History of Negro Public Higher Education," pp. 309–24; Harlan, *History of West Virginia State College*, chaps. 4, 5, and 6.

50. WVBNWS, *Biennial Report, 1925–26*, pp. 84–91; speeches and correspondence of U. G. Carter, Mining Extension Service, West Virginia State College, in the U. G. Carter Papers, West Virginia Collection.

On a mainline run in Wyoming County. Although some blacks worked as motormen, they usually complained that white men would not brake behind a black motorman.

Unless otherwise acknowledged, the following photographs and commentary are adapted from James T. Laing, "The Negro Miner in West Virginia" (Ph.D. diss., Ohio State University, 1933).

A coal tipple in Raleigh County. Although few miners held the safer and easier outside positions, preparing coal for shipment, the number of blacks with such outside jobs was even less.

Black miners' homes were often relegated to undesirable locations. The houses shown here were located near a tipple.

A board and batten house, the poorest type, in Fayette County.

A front-porch view of a family living in one of the "stilthouses" common to the mountainous terrain of southern West Virginia. The front porch served widely as a home entertainment center—a place for family discussions and sometimes games such as checkers.

Black residences of "the better type," in Raleigh County.

The Omar Elementary School for blacks in Logan County. Although Afro-Americans faced persistent inequality in the allocation of educational resources, during the 1920s black elementary, junior high, and senior high schools expanded dramatically.

A black miner passes one of the "better types of
Negro churches." Although the best facilities were
usually occupied by the African Methodist Episcopal
Church, the above facility was shared by Baptists
and Methodists in Raleigh County.

A coal miner–preacher, Rev. Wilford Dickerson, and his wife, the former Harriet Boone. Working-class ministers played a crucial role in the institutional life of coal-mining towns. (Courtesy of Mr. and Mrs. North Dickerson, Beckley, West Virginia.)

A small junior high school in Kanawha County.

6

The Expansion of the Black Bourgeoisie

Southern West Virginia's black middle class and its small elite expanded during World War I and the 1920s. No less than in the prewar era, however, this historical process was a dynamic one. The black bourgeoisie arose in response to the increasing segregation and discrimination blacks faced in coal-mining towns, a growing sense of Afro-American race consciousness, a continued rise in black migration, and, most of all, the earnings of the expanding black working class. By energetically exploiting entrepreneurial and professional opportunities, the black elite increased its material, political, and social resources. Yet despite its substantial energy, and even ingenuity, in tapping available opportunities, the fortunes of the black middle class rose and fell in cadence with those of the black coal-mining proletariat.

As elsewhere, the black middle class in the southern West Virginia coalfields was comprised of an expanding corps of public schoolteachers, a small number of artisans and clerical employees, and a growing number of proprietors of barbershops and beauty shops, hotels, rooming houses, and drugstores. At its apex was a tiny bourgeois elite of doctors, lawyers, and the wealthiest entrepreneurs. Later chapters discuss black ministers, teachers, and social workers; leaders from their ranks rounded out the black elite.

As the black coal-mining proletariat expanded during World War I, black business and professional opportunities increased. The number of West Virginia blacks in middle-class occupations increased by 30 percent, from 1,515 in 1910 to 2,223 in 1920. Although black enterprise developed in company towns, incorporated commercial centers offered the most promising business prospects. In May 1920, the "Colored News" division of the *Bluefield Daily Telegraph* noted the pattern of business growth: "Among us are sustained . . . two splendid hotels . . . several up to date restaurants, four or five grocery stores, an undertaker's establishment, two splendid barber shops, two creditable drug stores, one steam laundry, three cleaning and pressing shops with modern equipment, two hospitals, two real estate and employment agencies, four doctors, one dentist and one coal dealer. Not a bad showing for a city of this size. It shows that our Colored people have been given an opportunity and have profited."[1] Afro-Americans in Keystone, Kimball, Beckley, Welch, and Charleston, provided a similar range of business and professional services.[2]

Alongside the emerging new businesses, established black enterprises retained and expanded their ties to the black proletarian market. Because of the rising fuel demands of war production, in 1916 the black-owned Eagle Coal Company advertised for "twenty-five more men at once," promising "Good Wages, Good Pay, good man to work for, good town to live in, good water to drink and a good town in which to spend your money." The proprietors of the Eagle Coal Company, Archie McKinney and Matthew Buster, made "some good shipments" and contemplated "a steady run of the mine." Described as having a ready market for its coal (apparently including white, as well as black, customers), the company invested considerable resources in "the erection of a new tipple over which coal is to be loaded for rail shipments, a new stable with a capacity for several head of stock and storing of a large amount of hay and feed, the installation of electric haulage and electric pumps, and the building of a side track from the mainline of the C. & O. to the tipple." In late 1917 the Eagle Coal Company's financial records showed a balance of $11,758. At its height during the war and early postwar years, the company was valued at $100,000 and employed nearly one hundred men.[3] The Eagle Coal Company was perhaps the most telling illustration of the enduring relationship between proletarianization and elite formation within the black coal-mining community.

As in the prewar era, however, the *McDowell Times* persisted as the most well known black enterprise in southern West Virginia. Like the Eagle Coal Company, it is also an example of the continuing connection between the black proletariat and the growth of the black bourgeoisie. Published in Keystone, McDowell County, the *Times* expanded its circulation and influence by adding special columns on a growing number of black coal-mining communities, eventually embracing almost every major company and non-company town in the region.[4] In a revealing article on the miners of the Pulaski Iron Company at Eckman, McDowell County, editor

M. T. Whittico pinpointed the precise relationship between his paper, the coal company, and the black coal miner. "Through the kindness and big heartedness of Hon. Floyd E. Cunningham, superintendent of the Pulaksi Iron Company . . . I was permitted to begin canvassing the above named operation for subscriptions to The McDowell Times. At first, I had no other thought and interest than to increase my subscription list."[5] During his visit, however, R. L. Benton, a black miner, urged Whittico to tour the mine and observe the black miner at work. "When I found out that Benton knew so much about the mines, mining and miners; then it was that . . . my mission became a two-fold proposition—subscriptions and information about the mines."[6]

If the expansion of the black proletariat stimulated the growth of black businesses during World War I, it encouraged the establishment of black professional practices even more. Black professionals in West Virginia increased from less than 600 in 1910 to nearly 1,000 in 1920, an increase of over 70 percent. Most of the increase involved less well paid professionals, though—teachers, social workers, and ministers. Between 1910 and 1920, for example, black teachers (mainly women) and ministers increased by more than 50 percent. By contrast, the number of black attorneys in West Virginia increased only slightly, from 17 in 1910 to 23 in 1920. The number of black physicians also increased, from 46 in 1910 to 56 in 1920 (tables 6.1 and 6.2).

Although their numbers increased slowly, black doctors and lawyers continually dominated the professional life of Afro-Americans in southern West Virginia. During the war years, established black physicians and attorneys expanded their services to black miners, although some professionals, like physicians Drs. S. S. Viney and W. H. Ambrose Barnett of Keystone, either died or left the area. Dr. Roscoe G. Harrison expanded his hospital in Kimball, McDowell County. Under the aegis of the Alpha Hospital Charity Commission, in 1915 Harrison launched a highly successful capital campaign. Described as "one of the finest and perhaps one of the most learned physicians in the state," Harrison sought to raise $5,000 for a new twenty-room hospital. Half of the beds were designated for poor and working-class blacks, who would receive free medical care. Appealing to both blacks and whites, Harrison soon secured enough funds to purchase land for the facility and start its building program.[7]

Similarly, Dr. B. A. Crichlow moved from practices in McDowell and Mercer counties to Charleston in early 1915 and established the

TABLE 6.1
West Virginia Professional, Business, and Clerical Occupations by Race and Ethnicity, 1910–30

	Professional		Business		Clerical	
	Number	Percent	Number	Percent	Number	Percent
1910						
Males						
Blacks	327	3.8	496	3.9	241	1.3
Immigrants	184	2.1	1,520	12.3	738	4.1
Whites/Foreign or mixed parentage	339	4.0	1,151	9.3	1,683	9.5
American-born whites	7,697	90.1	9,250	74.5	15,160	85.1
All groups	8,547	100.0	12,417	100.0	17,822	100.0
Females						
Blacks	237	3.8	197	7.8	17	0.1
Immigrants	93	1.5	438	17.4	112	0.7
Whites/Foreign or mixed parentage	453	7.5	170	6.8	707	4.8
American-born whites	5,318	87.2	1,707	68.0	14,144	94.4
All groups	6,101	100.0	2,512	100.0	14,980	100.0
1920						
Males						
Blacks	536	4.3	674	3.8	258	1.0
Immigrants	439	3.5	2,507	14.2	958	3.9
Whites/Foreign or mixed parentage	695	5.6	1,425	8.0	2,094	8.3
American-born whites	10,735	86.6	13,049	74.0	21,900	86.8
All groups	12,405	100.0	17,655	100.0	25,210	100.0
Females						
Blacks	445	4.4	272	10.8	38	0.3
Immigrants	123	1.2	236	9.3	242	2.1
Whites/Foreign or mixed parentage	569	5.6	160	6.3	1,266	11.2
American-born whites	8,948	88.8	1,856	73.6	9,774	86.4
All groups	10,085	100.0	2,524	100.0	11,320	100.0

TABLE 6.1 (Continued)

	Professional		Business		Clerical	
	Number	Percent	Number	Percent	Number	Percent
			1930			
Males						
Blacks	920	5.2	948	4.1	279	0.7
Immigrants	600	3.3	3,061	13.3	1,103	3.0
American-born						
whites	16,241	91.5	18,916	82.6	35,961	96.3
All groups	17,761	100.0	22,925	100.0	37,343	100.0
Females						
Blacks	863	5.3	413	10.5	105	0.5
Immigrants	252	1.5	341	8.7	317	1.8
American-born						
whites	14,964	93.2	3,154	80.8	17,267	97.7
All groups	16,079	100.0	3,908	100.0	17,689	100.0

Sources: U.S. Bureau of the Census, *Thirteenth Census of the United States, 1910* (Washington, 1913), 4:529–30; *Fourteenth Census, 1920* (Washington, 1923), 4:1039–42; *Fifteenth Census, 1930* (Washington, 1933), 4:1741–43.
*Data not available on whites of foreign or mixed parentage for this year.

Crichlow Hospital there, which was described as "the only hospital for [the] exclusive treatment of Colored people" in the Kanawha–New River Field. Equipped with sixteen beds and administered by a staff of nine trained physicians and surgeons, within three years the Crichlow Hospital had developed an enviable reputation for "accomplishing much good for the race."[8] Drs. N. L. Edwards and E. W. Lomax of Bluefield, James M. Whittico of Williamson, and E. L. Youngue of Welch all continued their services throughout World War I and the 1920s. In the war and postwar years, coal companies gradually came to pay for the treatment of black miners at black-owned hospitals and private practices, thereby reinforcing the link between the black coal miner and the rising black business and professional class in southern West Virginia.[9]

    Like black physicians, established black attorneys expanded their practices among black coal miners and their families during the war and early postwar years. In Northfork, McDowell County, James Knox Smith, continued to advertise his services as the national "Jail Robber." Smith frequently gained appointment as a public defender

TABLE 6.2
West Virginia Blacks in Professional, Business, and Clerical Occupations by Sex, 1910–30

Professional	1910		1920		1930	
	Number	Percent	Number	Percent	Number	Percent
			Males			
Actors, entertainers	—	—	—	—	20	2.2
Clergymen	149	45.7	230	43.0	313	34.2
Chemists	—	—	—	—	1	0.1
Dentists	—	—	12	2.2	22	2.3
Engineers	3	0.9	3	0.5	1	0.1
Journalists, authors	—	—	—	—	3	0.3
Lawyers, judges	17	5.1	23	4.3	20	2.1
Musicians, music teachers	—	—	29	5.4	49	5.3
Physicians, surgeons	46	14.0	56	10.4	65	7.1
Professors[a]	—	—	—	—	44	4.8
Schoolteachers	112	34.3	130	24.3	257	28.0
Others	—	—	53	9.9	125	13.6
Total	327	100.0	536	100.0	920	100.0

	Females					
Librarians	—	—	—	—	2	0.2
Musicians, music teachers	12	5.0	14	3.1	23	2.7
Professors[a]	—	—	—	—	17	2.0
Religious workers	—	—	—	—	6	0.6
Schoolteachers	209	88.3	374	84.2	728	84.5
Social welfare workers	—	—	—	—	6	0.6
Trained nurses	16	6.7	19	4.2	46	5.4
Others	—	—	38	8.5	35	4.1
Total	237	100.0	445	100.0	863	100.1

Sources: U.S. Bureau of the Census, *Thirteenth Census of the United States, Population, 1910* (Washington, 1913), 4:529–30; *Fourteenth Census, 1920* (Washington, 1923), 4:1039–42; *Fifteenth Census, 1930* (Washington, 1933), 4:1741–43.

[a]Data for 1930 include college presidents and probably also some teachers below college rank.

TABLE 6.2 (Continued)

Business	1910		1920		1930	
	Number	Percent	Number	Percent	Number	Percent
			Males			
Bankers, bank officials	—	—	1	0.1	—	—
Barbers, hairdressers, manicurists	329	66.4	317	47.1	343	36.3
Boarding and lodging house keepers	—	—	—	—	—	—
Brokers, moneylenders	—	—	1	0.1	—	—
Cab, truck, and transfer company owners and managers	—	—	—	—	13	1.3
Garage owners, managers	—	—	—	—	3	0.3
Hoteliers[a]	—	—	27	4.0	13	1.3
Hucksters, peddlers	—	—	—	—	—	—
Pool room proprietors[b]	—	—	31	4.5	49	5.1
Restaurateurs[c]	—	—	67	10.0	80	8.4
Retail dealers	82	16.6	118	17.8	134	14.2
Saloonkeepers	—	—	—	—	—	—
Shoemakers, cobblers (not in factory)	36	7.2	47	7.0	47	4.9
Tailors	49	9.8	64	9.4	243	25.8

Undertakers	—	—	—	—	22	2.3
Wholesale dealers, importers, exporters	—	—	1	0.1	1	0.1
Total	496	100.0	647	100.0	948	100.0
Females						
Barbers, hairdressers, manicurists	—	—	—	—	109	26.4
Boarding and lodging house keepers	184	93.5	221	81.3	224	54.3
Hoteliers[a]	3	1.5	45	16.5	9	2.1
Restaurateurs[c]	—	—	—	—	53	12.9
Retail dealers	10	5	6	2.2	18	4.3
Total	197	100.0	272	100.0	413	100.0

[a] For the years 1900 and 1910 only proprietors are represented.

[b] For the year 1930 this category includes dance hall keepers.

[c] For the years 1920 and 1930 this category includes proprietors of cafes and lunchrooms.

TABLE 6.2 (Continued)

Clerical	1910		1920		1930	
	Number	Percent	Number	Percent	Number	Percent
			Males			
Bookkeepers, cashiers[a]	17	7.0	9	3.5	7	2.4
Agents, canvassers, collectors[b]	4	1.6	9	3.4	7	2.5
Clerks, non-store	24	10.0	65	25.3	56	20.2
Commerical travelers	132	54.9	5	1.9	6	2.1
Insurance agents[c]	9	3.8	12	4.7	38	13.6
Mail carriers	19	7.8	17	6.6	28	10.1
Messengers, errand and office boys[d]	—	—	35	13.6	23	8.2
Postmasters	—	—	—	—	1	0.3
Real estate agents, officials	2	0.8	18	7.0	14	5.0
Salesmen, store	28	11.7	50	19.4	60	24.5
Stenographers, typists	—	—	2	0.7	4	1.4
Store clerks	4	1.6	34	13.2	56	20.2
Telegraph operators	2	0.8	2	0.7	—	—
Total	241	100.0	258	100.0	279	100.0

	Females					
Accountants, bookkeepers, cashiers	1	5.8	8	21.0	9	8.6
Clerks, non-store	4	23.6	7	18.5	16	15.2
Insurance agents, managers, officials	—	—	—	—	5	4.8
Postmistresses	—	—	—	—	2	2.0
Saleswomen, store	3	17.6	7	18.5	40	38.1
Stenographers, typists	4	23.6	7	18.5	19	18.0
Store clerks	5	29.4	6	15.7	11	10.5
Other	—	—	3	7.8	3	2.8
Total	17	100.0	38	100.0	105	100.0

[a]Includes male accountant in 1930 (who was also an auditor).
[b]Canvassers not included for the year 1930.
[c]Insurance officials are included for the year 1910.
[d]Includes bundle boys for the years 1920 and 1930.

in area courts and retained an interest in defending the accused in cases where his fees were "secured." In 1916 Smith opened a second office in the heart of Keystone to better serve his "large and growing clientele."[10] Along with Smith, attorneys Ebenezer Howard Harper of Keystone, James M. Ellis of Oak Hill, Thomas G. Nutter of Charleston, Harry J. Capehart of Keystone and Welch, T. Edward Hill of Keystone, W. F. Denny of Lester and Beckley, S. B. Moon of Wilcoe, and Thaddeus E. Harris of Northfork expanded their practices in the region. In 1917 black attorneys formed the West Virginia Negro Bar Association, drafted a constitution that emphasized "professional" goals, and elected James M. Ellis as president. The Negro Bar Association both symbolized and promoted the black lawyers' growing effort to build a working-class clientele in the coalfields of southern West Virginia.[11]

Dependent upon a working-class clientele, black businesses and professional practices were shaped by the economy of the coal industry. During the early postwar years, the Eagle Coal Company was a major casualty of a downturn in the market. In its comprehensive survey of black business activity in 1921–22, the BNWS praised the company for demonstrating "that the Negro is not merely a good practical miner, but can control and direct [the] production of coal." Thereafter, however, the company faded from the agency's biennial reports. Perhaps better than any other enterprise, the Eagle Coal Company highlighted the dependence of black entrepreneurs on the vitality of the coal industry.[12]

Although the black business and professional elite briefly declined during the early postwar years, the black middle class in southern West Virginia, like the black working class, continued to expand during the mid-1920s. The number of West Virginia blacks in professional and business occupations increased from 1,927 in 1920 to 3,144 in 1930, an increase of 63 percent (tables 6.1, 6.2). In 1920 the U.S. Census Bureau counted nearly 140 black hotels, restaurants, and cafes in West Virginia. Even during the economic downturn of 1921–22, the BNWS reported nearly 200 black hotels, restaurants, and cafes; in the next biennium, it reported over 220. As elsewhere, black visitors to West Virginia demanded "better hotel accommodations"; and, in response, the BNWS noted, "farseeing Negro business men are erecting splendid modern structures and opening them to the Negro traveling public."[13] Hotel Capehart of Welch, Hotel Ferguson of Charleston, and Hotel George of Northfork emerged as the best of the new establishments. Individually owned, they represented an investment of $75,000 to

$350,000 each. At the same time, the number of black poolroom keepers increased from 31 in 1920 to 78 in 1923–24. The number of black-owned drugstores also slowly increased from around a half-dozen in 1918 to twelve in 1925–26 (all but three of which operated in southern counties), and to sixteen in 1928.[14]

At the same time, black savings and loan, insurance, and publishing businesses increased their black coal miner clientele. Agents of white companies like the Pacific Mutual Life Insurance Company were increasingly joined, and even displaced, by agents of black insurance companies like the National Benefit Life Insurance Company of Washington, D.C., and the Supreme Life and Casualty Company of Cleveland, Ohio. The Charleston-based Union Insurance Company that emerged in 1924 was the first black life and casualty insurance company in West Virginia. With the active encouragement and support of the BNWS, the company was able to meet the requirements of the state insurance department. Capitalized at $150,000, the Union Insurance Company owned "cash resources of $50,000 and a reserve of equal amount." Owned entirely by West Virginia blacks, the company invested in "first mortgages" on black-owned property in the state. By the end of 1924 it had joined the two black out-of-state companies mentioned above in writing more than three million dollars' worth of insurance on the lives of nearly 9,000 black coal miners and their families; over the next two years, the amount increased to nearly four million dollars on 11,000 blacks.[15]

During the early 1920s, S. R. Anderson, editor of the "Colored News" section of the *Bluefield Daily Telegraph*, intensified his efforts to establish a new black newspaper, the *Clarion*. Like the *McDowell Times*, the *Clarion* received the endorsement of Republican coal operators in the Winding Gulf Field. Anderson encouraged operators to purchase subscriptions to the paper, to be distributed to miners at reduced rates. By December 1923, the Winding Gulf Coal Operators' Association had become Anderson's chief supporter. In a detailed letter to Justus Collins, owner of the Winding Gulf Colliery Company, Anderson related the agreement between his paper and the coal operators' association. "The Winding Gulf secretary, Mr. Wolfe, has given me $700 with which to put on an intense campaign in the Winding Gulf section for subscribers, offering them the first years' subscription for Fifty-cents as an introductory subscription." In another letter to Collins, the manager of the Winding Gulf Collier Company suggested even greater support for the *Clarion*. "As I have stated to you in the past, Anderson is a good man and a real friend of the coal people in this entire section and really does more to keep us posted as to conditions than any other Agent covering the field, and . . . does not receive the support from our people that he merits."[16]

Although the *Clarion* failed to achieve the stature of Whittico's *McDowell Times*, for the short time it existed during the early 1920s it added variety to black media in southern West Virginia. The Winding Gulf Colliery Company helped Anderson to distribute 125 copies per month to each of the company's various operations. Also, for most of the 1920s Anderson continued to edit the "Colored News" column of the *Bluefield Daily Telegraph*. Along with the circulation of national black newspapers like the *Chicago Defender* and the *Pittsburgh Courier*, by the mid-1920s the BNWS reported, "more than two-thirds of the reading Negroes of West Virginia read one or more Negro publications weekly." Moreover, "their attitude toward subjects in which the race is vitally interested is influenced by what they read about them in the Negro press."[17]

As black businesses expanded and diversified during the 1920s, so did black professional practices. The number of West Virginia blacks in proprietary occupations increased by an estimated 44 percent, while their professional counterparts rose by more than 80 percent. Black teachers, preachers, and social workers continued to multiply dramatically and outnumber blacks in the legal and medical professions, whose numbers increased slowly, with the exception of dentists. Black physicians gradually increased from 56 in 1920 to slightly over 60 during the late 1920s; black attorneys rose even more slowly, from 23 to a peak of 25, before declining in 1930. By contrast, black dentists dramatically increased from 12 in 1920 to 24 in 1924, to 28 in 1929 before declining thereafter (tables 6.1, 6.2).[18]

As in the case of the black proletariat, movement into and out of southern West Virginia characterized a portion of the black professional elite. In 1923–24, 11 of the 24 black attorneys in West Virginia resided in McDowell County. During the same biennium, four new attorneys entered the state; two of them set up practices in McDowell County, and one each settled in Kanawha and Mercer counties. New lawyers such as these often replaced black attorneys who had died or moved away. In the next biennium, two black attorneys died and three left the state. Among the deceased was the famous "National Jail Robber," James Knox Smith. "Mr. Smith," the BNWS noted, was known "for his wit, the quaintness of his character and his very unusual manner of examining witnesses and presenting his cases." Among the new lawyers, Stewart A. Calhoun, son of the poolroom operator A. L. Calhoun, was soon to become the most well known. Born in Keystone in 1897, Calhoun received his law degree from Howard University. In July 1925 the young lawyer opened his office in Keystone. By 1930 he had won election to a series of offices—city councilman, city attorney, and state legislator.[19]

Although most black enterprises served the segregated, predominantly working-class Afro-American market, they were not automatically patronized. In company and non-company towns alike, black business and professional people worked diligently to attract clients. They skillfully exploited the class-based and racial limitations on the black miners' access to crucial services and often offered a variety of products or services under the same roof. In Keystone, for example, the Bismark Restaurant and Pool Room provided "Furnished Rooms for Rent by Day or Week," as well as pool tables and "Meals at all hours, day or night." Similarly, in early 1918 when Hotel Dixie opened on the property of the Raleigh Coal and Coke Company (one of the few black establishments in the region that was situated on company-owned property), it advertised "splendid accom[m]odations, meals at all hours, board and lodging, pool room and pressing club connected."[20]

Whatever their combination of services, black businesspeople had the same strategy for attracting working-class customers: low prices, high quality, courteous treatment, modern service, and unique consideration of the race. One restaurateur advertised "Meals at all hours in First Class Style at Reasonable prices. . . . Eat here and ya'll not know the high cost of living is higher." During the early 1920s, when G. E. Ferguson opened his hotel in Charleston, the BNWS exclaimed that Hotel Ferguson "takes rank as one of the foremost modern and elaborately furnished and equipped hotels catering exclusively to Negro patronage in the country." Although smaller, Hotel Capehart in Welch, under the proprietorship of Attorney Harry J. Capehart, and Hotel George in Northfork were also praised as black-owned, "modern high class establishments." Similarly, during the 1920s, the Charleston branch of the NAACP not only celebrated "Negro Business" but promoted it as well. In addition to featuring a brief survey of black businesses in the city, one meeting featured guest speakers on "Business as a Foundation for Negro Advancement," "Reciprocal Obligations of Negro Business and the Negro Public," and "Needed Lines of Business Advance."[21]

No less than black entrepreneurs, black professionals developed energetic campaigns to secure patrons, a fact that suggests that the attitudes and expectations of black coal miners helped to shape the nature and scope of black businesses and professional practices in the region. As noted above, some physicians not only established private practices, but also small hospitals, which were, in effect, business enterprises. The advertisements of black medical professionals repeatedly emphasized high quality and trustworthy service. The dentist Dr. A. S. Adams's advertisement is typical: "I have equipped my office at a cost of more than $2,500 for the benefit of my people. If you care to see a modern equipped Negro Dental office you should visit mine. — I do all classes of dental work satisfactor[il]y. — I administer gas for the extraction of teeth and any other work where necessary."[22] Harrison Hospital in Kimball, Crichlow Hospital in Charleston, and Edwards Hospital in Bluefield all received frequent praise for neat and sanitary conditions as well as expert service.[23]

Even more than physicians, black lawyers combined their professional practices with business enterprises. As studies of black lawyers during this period have noted, black attorneys encountered such difficulty in surmounting racial hostility at the bar that few of them could earn a living from the practice of law alone. William F. Denny of Raleigh County promoted his services as both businessman and lawyer: "Attorney and counselor-at-law—Money to Loan on Real Estate for Improvements, Building, Etc." In another ad Denny promoted real estate and insurance businesses along with legal services. Black attorneys such as James Knox Smith of Keystone combined private practice with service to the poor as public defenders in exchange for secure, government-paid fees. Until his death in 1923–24, attorney Smith habitually remarked that he "especially loves to represent the 'poor' devils, when his fee is insured." Nonetheless, Smith was frequently reported "making some strong efforts at trying to get a poor unfortunate fellow out of prison," sometimes at an apparent personal sacrifice. "It is gratifying as well as praiseworthy to note the unflinching faithfulness and individual sacrifices the 'Jail Robber' is always willing to go in order to help those who happen to be in trouble," the Times reported.[24]

Despite their commendable service to black miners, few black businesses and professional services were up to par with their white counterparts. Several black hotels, the BNWS was at pains to admit, "are merely dignified by the name 'hotel,' . . . others are ramshackle dens and dives, harbors for criminals and bedbugs, breeding places for disease, vice and crime and contributors to the delinquency of girls and boys. This applies to many restaurants and, to a lesser degree, to some pool rooms and barber shops." On one occasion, the BNWS initiated a medical examination of seven persons, "cooks and scullions" in black restaurants, who were suspected of having venereal disease. Three of the seven had recently left the employ of white restaurants, and all were "infected with either syphillis or gonorrhea."[25]

Housed in frame structures in the poorest sections of coal-mining towns, some small black business establishments were firetraps. During World War I, the black business section of Keystone, McDowell County, was the scene of many bad fires. In a fire at Wilcoe, McDowell County, in December 1923, the black grocer Ed Hairston lost his shop, and the black barber C. E. Bailey lost three hundred dollars' worth of property. In early January 1924, a fire consumed the black Riverview Hotel in Clark, under the proprietorship of William Tucker; damages were estimated at $5,000. During the mid-1920s, Keystone continued to suffer fires that destroyed both black and white property; reports invariably focused on the wooden frame structures that prevailed in town. In 1924, for example, the *Welch Daily News* reported, "All of the buildings destroyed were frame structure and burned quickly, so that practically nothing was saved."[26]

Restricted access to capital and training because of class-based and racial discrimination undermined the quality of black businesses and professional services. First and foremost, black business and professional people were constrained by the imperatives of life in company-owned towns. For example, by offering employees credit at the company store and taking automatic payroll deductions for medical services, coal operators invariably discouraged the expansion of alternative commercial and professional services. If white professional and commercial opportunities were hampered by such practices, black ones were discouraged even more. In a highly racist manner, a white Fayette County store manager exclaimed: "If I wanted to make a killin' . . . I'd have nothing but Niggers on the place. You see you can sell them anything . . . and you can make [it] back off them that way." Another official explained: "You see we bring pressure to bear to make the men trade here. Of course, . . . we wouldn't fire a man for not trading at the store—but he could be let out for something else."[27]

Like company store managers, company doctors were invariably whites who identified with the interests of the coal operators. Although their fees were deducted from the miner's payroll, they considered themselves company employees. In McDowell, Mercer, Logan, and Raleigh counties, the BNWS noted, the coal companies contracted white physicians, and black employees had to pay for their services whether they liked it or not. In thirty-eight mining towns in McDowell, Mercer, Raleigh, Fayette, Logan, and Kanawha counties, Laing found that during the early 1930s, "company doctors in the operations visited were without exception white men."[28] Thus black miners found it doubly difficult to patronize black physicians.

Moreover, the training of black physicians and attorneys was hampered by the refusal of West Virginia University to admit black students. When black students gained professional degrees elsewhere, they still faced discrimination in trying to establish their professional practices in West Virginia. When white students received law degrees from West Virginia University, for example, they were automatically admitted to the state bar; black students forced to study out of state were treated the same as out-of-state residents and required to take and pass the state's bar examination.[29]

As economist Abram L. Harris noted for both the North and South during the 1920s and early 1930s in his study of black businesses, in southern West Virginia's incorporated commercial centers, Afro-Americans faced racial discrimination in the capital market.[30] During the war and postwar years, S. R. Anderson lamented Bluefield's lack of available capital for growth, despite the relative success of black businesses there. "In Bluefield . . . there is neither a shoe, clothing nor dry goods store among them, and only one real grocery. There is no kind of loan or financial institution. Yet, the Negroes carry through our city banks annually in deposit and savings over $400,000." Lending institutions discouraged black applications for business loans. "Money for this purpose is not available to Negroes through local banks of many commercial communities," T. Edward Hill of the BNWS frequently complained.[31]

Finally, although most black businesses served a segregated black clientele, they nonetheless faced vigorous white competition. Black agents of white insurance companies actively competed for the black insurance business, making it difficult for some black firms to succeed. For a short period during the early war years, for example, blacks in southern West Virginia organized the South Western Mutual Fire Insurance Company. Owned and operated entirely by blacks, the company was billed as "the first effort of the kind" in West Virginia. The company insured homes and household property and apparently failed before the end of World War I. The expansion of white-owned commercial drug chains and five-and-ten-cent stores represented even worse competition, which cut into the black pharmacist's "sales on sundries and accessories from which he draws much of his profit." As a result, black pharmacists like Dr. S. J. Bampfield frequently changed site, seeking the most lucrative location. By the early 1930s, Bampfield had moved his pharmaceutical business several times before relocating in Logan County.[32]

It was not the failures of the black elite, then, that was so remarkable in southern West Virginia, but rather its successes and optimism in appealing to black miners in the face of great odds. As in the prewar years, a deepening race consciousness helps to explain the success of black enterprises during and following World War I. In his addresses before the Golden Rule Beneficial and Endowment Association, Rev. R. H. McKoy continually asserted the necessity of Afro-American unity. In June 1917 he exhorted: "As a race, we have done well, but let us not be contented with the past, but attempt greater things for the future. WE CAN do more and we MUST do more. As a race we can win more confidence and respect from other races by having more confidence and respect for each other." Similarly, in a letter to the historian Carter G. Woodson, attorney J. M. Ellis of Oak Hill, Fayette County, wrote, "I am yet here in West Virginia trying to do my best for my Race. I have had some hard bumps but have been able to ward them off thus far."[33]

During the early 1920s, Dr. N. L. Barnett of Kansas City contemplated a practice in Logan County. He received encouragement from his uncle, Dr. C. C. Barnett of Huntington, son of the prewar black minister Nelson Barnett. In a letter to his nephew, C. C. Barnett highlighted the difficulties of medical practice in the Logan Field but exclaimed in positive terms that "such experiences make you fit." They teach you "how to make a scalpel out of a rubber cathe-[te]r, a rectal tube a stomach pump, etc." Despite the hardships, Barnett believed, the black medical professional could prosper in the coalfields; and he advised his nephew, "When you do come I want you to drop in on the boys as though a great meteor had fallen among them. [T]hen in one year you will surpass 8 or 10 years of your neighbor whom you thought would be a millionaire before you began."[34]

Although Barnett was unable to convince his nephew to leave the city and join him, other black professional and businesspeople like him found a variety of strategies to surmount the obstacles in their way. At the very least, black entrepreneurs relied upon the support of their wives, as available records repeatedly emphasize. In May 1918 at Montcalm, the *Times* reported, Mr. and Mrs. J. B. Brown of Brown's Restaurant were "holding their own feeding the hungry travelers, sheltering the weary and worn pedestrians and in [a] general way are . . . full of accommodation to mankind." At Hotel Liberty in Welch, the day-to-day management of the facility was in the hands of Mesdames Lowry and Morton, the proprietors' wives.[35] The forming of partnerships was another common strategy, useful for securing the necessary capital to start new businesses and professional practices. Young black lawyers and physicians ordinarily began their practices in partnership with established practitioners, later moving on to establish their own offices.[36]

In order for black enterprises to succeed, they often required some form of white support or sufferance, especially when they were located on company-owned property. Thus cultivating white support became an important component of black entrepreneurial development. J. T. White and his wife ran a restaurant on the premises of the Raleigh Coal and Coke Company, with the owners' support. A local reporter thought that the Whites were "fortunate in having such able and painstaking men at their back and to be so thoroughly their friends." The *McDowell Times* was perhaps the most outstanding recipient of aid from local coal operators. As noted elsewhere, the *Times* vigorously advertised the labor requirements of local industries, received company permission to sell subscriptions among the miners, and repeatedly printed its heartfelt gratitude for the coal operators' endorsement of its efforts. Similarly, when the Pocahontas Collieries Company provided dental clinics for blacks at Maybeury and Jenkinjones, it equipped two offices and paid the salaries of two black dentists.[37]

Despite important constraints on its development, the black elite increasingly systematized its business, professional, and social interactions and deepened its class consciousness. While establishing new organizations like the West Virginia Negro Bar Association in 1917 and a growing number of Negro Business Leagues, the black elite revitalized and extended old organizations like the West Virginia Medical Society. Formed during the prewar era, the West Virginia Medical Society was a chapter of the National Medical Association, which spearheaded black physicians' quest for racial solidarity in the medical field. The society continued its development as the strongest black professional organization in the region, and the Flat Top Medical Association, covering southern West Virginia, persisted as its foremost constituent body.[38]

Emphasizing the virtues of racial solidarity, thrift, and economic development, the ideology of progress emerged at the center of black middle-class consciousness. Black elites, men and women alike, continually worked to promote their values among black workers. During the war years, in a letter to Governor John J. Cornwell, black attorney T. Edward Hill, secretary of the West Virginia Negro Bar Association, wrote, "We are making an effort to get the miners to work regularly and load more coal, to somewhat make up for the loss of the services of nearly 400 coal miners."[39] Predominantly women, black teachers were perhaps the chief harbingers of the new industrial ideology and culture. Nowhere were their efforts more apparent than in their energetic promotion of student banks, honor rolls, and regular attendance. In the discipline of working-class students, editor Whittico emerged as the teachers' most ardent defender. Also a truant officer, Whittico promoted the vigorous, even callous, enforcement of attendance laws for the children of black coal miners.[40]

Black coal miners were by no means silent partners in the rise and expansion of the black bourgeoisie. They were highly conscious of the working-class basis of the bourgeois class's livelihood and even regarded it with a measure of suspicion, resentment, and distrust. For example, one black miner recalled that a prominent black attorney gave "more favors to whites" than to blacks. Other blacks insisted that black professionals guarantee their services, such as the client of attorney H. J. Capehart who insisted, "If you ain't going to beat this case, don't you take money, because . . . if you're going to get my money, you're going to guarantee my money." In a strongly worded letter to attorney T. E. Harris, Ella W. Robinson, apparently the wife of a black coal miner, urged the attorney to bring her up-to-date on the status of her insurance case: "Now listen lawyer have you heard anything from the . . . policy that I got you to see after[?] . . . Now I want you to write strait back & tell me whether you herd from them or not & I will be down to see you a bout it."[41]

During the early Depression years, in one coal town black miners complained that relief was being distributed discriminatorily. Yet the miners refused to approach the local branch of the NAACP, apparently because it was headed by a local black attorney. " 'What he care 'bout us?' " they asked James T. Laing. " 'Why he's a rich man—he don't worry none about us people up here. He'll take our cases . . . but he does it for the money in it. He don't care about us po' folks.' " Laing's extensive survey of black coal miners during the late 1920s and early 1930s found that they exhibited "extreme suspicion of the sincerity of Negro leaders and successful men."[42]

While an important undercurrent of antagonism characterized the black miners' attitude toward the black elite, in the hostile racial environment of southern West Virginia they more often expressed appreciation for the services the black middle class provided and voiced pride in its accomplishments. Referring to a black coal mine proprietor as "the first black millionaire in West Virginia," North Dickerson proudly recalled that Matthew Buster "owned a whole block in Montgomery, a filling station, [and] a coal mine." Lawrence Boling described attorney H. J. Capehart as "a big-time lawyer," and another miner described him as "a thoroughbred Republican," emphasizing the "favors" that blacks received from the Republican party. Still another recalled Capehart and Leon Miller as "about the best two colored lawyers we had in McDowell County." Recalling the vitality of black businesses and professional practices in Kimball, McDowell County, Roy Todd asserted that blacks "owned Kimball" and got "better breaks with the law." While some black miners had no memory of editor M. T. Whittico and the McDowell Times, others enthusiastically placed the editor in "the big league" in McDowell County.[43]

During World War I and the 1920s, black workers turned increasingly toward the black middle class for a wide range of services, but especially for the pursuit of leisure-time activities. To take advantage of town living, many black coal miners moved to commercial centers and commuted to their jobs. They recalled the poolrooms, restaurants, and rooming houses of Keystone, Giatto, Bluefield, and other mining towns with great pleasure. They were places for black workers to "show off," drink moonshine, gamble, and tell "down-home jokes." At this end of the middle-class spectrum, some black businessmen, especially poolroom keepers, were miners or ex-miners.[44] The foregoing evidence suggests that, together with the pressures of living and working in a racist society, the modest ascent of some black miners into the black middle class may have helped to mute working-class antagonism toward the black elite. Nonetheless, it also demonstrates that the expansion of the black middle class entailed some intraracial class conflict.

Afro-Americans faced not just cleavages along class lines, but gender inequality as well. Although women were often vital to the success of black professional practices and businesses, black men appropriated the top positions as physicians, attorneys, and administrators of black educational and social welfare institutions. Women were relegated to the least prestigious and most poorly paid positions as teachers, social workers, and nurses. Restricted in their professional aspirations, black women sometimes keenly felt the force of intraracial gender inequality. When Professor Arthur Barnett resigned as principal of the Gary Grade School, Phyllis W. Waters filled the vacancy, "very effectively carrying on the work," until a man could be appointed.[45]

Sexism was often evident in the columns of the *McDowell Times*. Editor M. T. Whittico entered the war years in a fighting mood against women's suffrage. For women, "the ballot: no, never," he said. When New Jersey rejected woman's suffrage, he editorially exclaimed: "Hurrah for New Jersey! . . . Hit 'em again men and hit 'em hard. Make the women stay at home, tend to the babies, educate them, [and] teach them politeness." Undergirding the editor's opposition to woman's suffrage was the notion of female inferiority to men: "Leave the affairs of state and nation to the men." "Men are wanted, needed and alone depended upon to fight battles, explore, discover, manage, boss, dictate, rule and invent."[46]

Although sex discrimination divided black men and women, interracial discrimination muted its effects. Even as black men and women clashed and divided, they continually reached out to each other, creating intimate bonds across gender lines within the hostile racial environment of southern West Virginia. The BNWS and local chapters of the NAACP repeatedly protested the negative public treatment of black women compared to the positive treatment of white women. From its beginning in the early 1920s, the BNWS bitterly assailed white newspapers for downplaying white sexual assaults against black women while promoting a lynching atmosphere in the case of alleged black male assaults against white women. The bureau also launched a campaign to ban the term "Negress," urging that it "never be used" as a synonym for black women. "Papers never use the term 'Jewess,' 'Italianess,' 'Hungarianess,' and 'Caucasianess,' and no linguistic dissertation can convince us that the use of 'Negress' is ever necessary in referring to our women."[47]

Although the data are weak on this issue, evidently discrimination based on skin color divided the black community, even dictating a differential opportunity structure for light- and dark-skinned blacks. In February 1924, a glowing article on black life in West Virginia by T. G. Nutter appeared in the radical black publication, *The Messenger*, edited by A. Philip Randolph and Chandler Owens. Re-

plete with a photo display of 21 prominent West Virginia black business and professional men (17 of whom resided in the southern
counties) and 7 outstanding professional and business women, the
article extolled the accomplishments of the black elite. An estimated
40 to 50 percent of the men and all of the women seemed to be
light-skinned.

Some of the women featured in the article as teachers, social
workers, and secretaries were the wives or employees (or both) of
prominent black men. As late as 1930, Laing found that intraracial
color differences had the greatest impact on black women. "In West
Virginia as elsewhere a woman with a dark skin is at a disadvantage in the marriage mart." Successful black men in southern West
Virginia apparently preferred light-skinned women. In fact, color
distinctions apparently permeated the entire Afro-American class
structure. In his description of "Babe," the black labor recruiter at
his mine, one black miner was quite emphatic: "He was real light."
"Babe" would work for a week, then depart for two weeks and return with new black recruits. Although few black coal miners chose
to discuss the issue, their efforts to move up and out of the coal-
mining labor force into business and professional careers, as elsewhere in black America, were undoubtedly influenced by skin
color.[48]

Place of origin also divided Afro-Americans in the coalfields. The
strongest cleavage appears to have emerged between West Virginia–
born and Virginia–born blacks, on the one hand, and Deep South
blacks, especially Alabamans, on the other. While some West Virginia–born black miners like North Dickerson perceived little conflict along these lines, others developed negative attitudes toward
Deep South blacks, who were sometimes considered too docile.
Lawrence Boling recalled that his West Virginia–born father was a
strong defender of his rights; but, as for Alabama blacks, "those
guys were brainwashed to start with," and they feared losing their
jobs too much. William Beasley was born in North Carolina, but
moved to West Virginia when he was ten years old. Beasley said
that he disliked "most blacks from the South," because "the biggest
majority . . . were scared of white people." "They done just what
they tell them to do . . . [and] wouldn't talk back to them. . . . I
wasn't that type."[49]

In what was perhaps the most prejudiced view, some West Virginia blacks perceived their Deep South counterparts as too aggressive. Charles T. Harris placed the Deep South black newcomer and
the European immigrant in the same category. "I always said that it

wasn't but two people in the world you couldn't tell anything, and that was a man from the old country and a man from Alabama. . . . That's what we said up here." In his interviews with black miners during the late 1920s, Laing found that West Virginians considered "the southerner 'crude,' emotional, [and] 'mean,' and tended to avoid them." Alabamans were particularly "objectionable."[50]

As important as regional, color, and gender differences may have been, blacks in southern West Virginia would face their greatest challenges from cleavages along class lines. From the rise of the black coal-mining proletariat in the prewar years through its expansion during World War I and the 1920s, developments in the black community corresponded to the growth of the black proletariat and the black bourgeoisie. Unlike the old elite in black America, with its tradition of service to a white clientele, from the beginning black business and professional people in the southern mountains catered to an essentially working-class black clientele. Through its business, professional, and social interactions, the black elite sought its own class interests, deepened its class consciousness, and in substantial ways developed a world of its own. Conversely, the dynamics of class-based and racial discrimination limited the elite's aspirations, intensified its racial consciousness, and strengthened its identification with black workers.

NOTES

1. U.S. Bureau of the Census, *Thirteenth Census of the United States, 1910* (Washington, 1913), 4:529–30; *Fourteenth Census, 1920* (Washington, 1923), 4:1039–42; "The Colored People," *Bluefield Daily Telegraph,* 20 May 1920, and The First Baptist Church of Charleston, *The Bulletin,* 28 May 1922, in Charleston Branch Files, Box G-216, NAACP Papers; *The Bulletin,* newsclipping, ca. Jan. 1921, in Charleston Branch Files, Box G-215, NAACP papers; interviews with Andrew Campbell, 19 July 1983, Charles T. Harris, 18 July 1983, Pink Henderson, 15 July 1983, John Page, 13 July 1983, and Lawrence Boling, 18 July 1983.

2. *Thirteenth Census,* 1910, 4:529–30; *Fourteenth Census,* 1920, 4:1039–42. For data on black business and professional activities in Keystone, Welch, Kimball, Beckley, Williamson, and other towns in southern West Virginia, see the *McDowell Times,* 1 and 8 Jan. 1915; 29 Sept. 1916; 25 May 1917; 1, 8, 22, and 29 June 1917; 7 Sept. 1917; 30 Nov. 1917; 18 Jan. 1918; 20 and 27 Sept. 1918. Also useful is the occupational profile of the Mt. Hope branch of the NAACP in "Application for Charter of Mt. Hope, W.Va. Branch," 16 Mar. 1921, in Mt. Hope/MacDonald Branch Files, Box G-218, NAACP Papers; interviews with Charles T. Harris, 18 July 1983, Pink Henderson, 15 July 1983, and Roy Todd, 18 July 1983.

3. "Montgomery," 28 July 1916, "Negro Operating Coal Mine," 27 Aug. 1915, both in *McDowell Times*; "Business," in West Virginia Bureau of Negro Welfare and Statistics (WVBNWS), *Biennial Report, 1921–22*, pp. 84–86; interview with North Dickerson, 28 July 1983.

4. See "Editor Mr. Whittico," 23 Feb. 1917, and "Whittico Dead," 23 June 1939, in *McDowell Times*. Other relevant issues of the *Times* include the following: 11 June 1915; 31 Mar. 1916; 7 Apr. 1916; 9 and 30 June 1916; 5 and 26 Jan. 1917; 13 Apr. 1917; and 24 May 1918. See also interview with Charles T. Harris, 18 July 1983.

5. "Editor Mr. Whittico," *McDowell Times*, 23 Feb. 1917.

6. Ibid.

7. "The Alpha Hospital Charity Commission of Kimball . . . ," 24 Sept. 1915, "McDowell County Honored," 3 Aug. 1917, "Mrs. Lucy Brown Successfully Operated on in Harrison's Hospital," 31 Aug. 1917, in *McDowell Times*; "Coal Company Shows Regard and Esteem for Negro Employee," *Welch Daily News*, 14 Nov. 1926.

8. "Hospital Moved to New Location," 7 Jan. 1916, and "Dr. Crichlow's Hospital Doing Good Work," 19 Oct. 1917, in *McDowell Times*.

9. See "Miss Delilah J. Price Operated on at Edwards Hospital in Bluefield," 24 Aug. 1917, "Returned from Edwards Hospital Improved," 26 Oct. 1917, and "The Lomax Hospital," 26 Feb. 1915, in *McDowell Times*; "The Colored People," *Bluefield Daily Telegraph*, 20 May 1920; "Negro Doctors Hold Interesting Meeting," 22 June 1917, "Dr. Whittico: Gone to Serve His Country," 31 Aug. 1917, "Dr. J. M. Whittico Receives Commission," 9 Nov. 1917, and "Mrs. Myra George: Undergoes Operation," 9 Apr. 1915, in *McDowell Times*; interview with Charles T. Harris, 18 July 1983.

10. "Jail Robber," 1 Jan. 1915, "My Clients are Always First," 9 July 1915, "J. K. Smith Ready to Help the Unfortunate," 3 Sept. 1915, " 'Jail Robber' Opens Down Town Office," 4 Feb. 1916, and "National Jail Robber Wins Celebrated Case," 29 Mar. 1918, in *McDowell Times*.

11. "Howard Harper for Legislature: Sketch of His Life," 9 June 1916, "Negro Lawyers form Organization," 17 Sept. 1917, "Negro Bar Association Hold[s] Successful Meeting," 28 Sept. 1917, "H. J. Capehart," 1 Jan. 1915, "William F. Denny," 1 Jan. 1915, and "S. B. Moon," 1 Jan. 1915, in *McDowell Times*; "The Colored People," *Bluefield Daily Telegraph*, 20 May 1920; Clerk of the Senate, ed., *West Virginia Legislative Hand Book* (Charleston, W.Va.: Tribune Printing Company, 1917, 1922, 1924, 1928, 1929, and 1931) (includes biographical data on attorneys Harper, Nutter, Capehart, and Hill); Thaddeus E. Harris Papers, Northfork, W.Va., McDowell County, Manuscript Division, William R. Perkins Library, Duke University; interviews with Lawrence Boling, 18 July 1983, Preston Turner, 26 July 1983, Pink Henderson, 15 July 1983, Lester and Ellen Phillips, 20 July 1983, and Roy Todd, 18 July 1983.

12. WVBNWS, *Biennial Report, 1921–22*, pp. 84–86.

13. *Fourteenth Census, 1920*, 4:1039–42; *Fifteenth Census, 1930*, 4:1741–43.

For reports on hotels, restaurants, and poolrooms, see WVBNWS, *Biennial Reports, 1921–22,* pp. 37–38, and *1923–24,* pp. 93–95.

14. WVBNWS, *Biennial Reports, 1921–22,* pp. 37–38, *1923–24,* pp. 93–95, *1925–26,* pp. 48–49, and *1929–32,* p. 46.

15. WVBNWS, *Biennial Report, 1923–24,* pp. 57–59.

16. See the column "The Colored People," *Bluefield Daily Telegraph,* 16 May 1920, 5 Aug. 1920, Sept. 1920, 4 Jan. 1921, 16 Nov. 1924, 16 Jan. 1926, 2 Dec. 1927, 3 Feb. 1928, and 28 Dec. 1930; S. R. Anderson to Justus Collins, 13 Aug. 1923, and L. Epperly to Collins, 22 Dec. 1923, in Series 1, Box 14, Folder 96, Justus Collins Papers, West Virginia Collection, West Virginia University.

17. "The Colored People," *Bluefield Daily Telegraph,* 16 May 1920, 4 Jan. 1921, and 16 Nov. 1924; Anderson to Collins, 13 Aug. 1923, in Series 1, Box 14, Folder 96, Justus Collins Papers; WVBNWS, *Biennial Reports, 1921–22,* pp. 87–88, *1923–24,* p. 80, *1925–26,* p. 118, and *1927–28,* p. 62.

18. *Fourteenth Census, 1920,* 4:1039–42; *Fifteenth Census, 1930,* 4: 1741–43; WVBNWS, *Biennial Reports, 1923–24,* pp. 29–36, *1925–26,* pp. 43–52, and *1929–32,* pp. 46–54.

19. WVBNWS, *Biennial Reports, 1923–24,* pp. 35–36, and *1925–26,* pp. 51–52; Clerk of the Senate, ed., *West Virginia Legislative Hand Book* (1931), p. 614; "Gary Colored News," *Welch Daily News,* 17 July 1925.

20. "The Bismark Restaurant and Pool Room," 13 Aug. 1915, and "Hotel Dixie," 18 Jan. 1918," in *McDowell Times.*

21. "Mr. and Mrs. Jas. Johnson," 1 Jan. 1915, "Restaurant," 9 Mar. 1917, "Grand Lecturer," 9 Mar. 1917, in *McDowell Times;* WVBNWS, "Hotels," *Biennial Report, 1921–22,* pp. 37–38; The First Baptist Church of Charleston, *The Bulletin,* 28 May 1922, in Charleston Branch Files, Box G-216, NAACP Papers; *The Bulletin,* newsclipping, ca. Jan. 1921, in Charleston Branch Files, Box G-215, NAACP Papers.

22. "Dr. A. S. Adams, Dentist," *McDowell Times,* 20 Apr. 1917.

23. "Miss Delilah Price Operated on at Edwards Hospital," 24 Aug. 1917, "The Alpha Hospital Charity Commission of Kimball," 24 Sept. 1915, "Dr. Crichlow's Hospital Doing Good Work," 19 Oct. 1917, and "Hospital Moved to New Location," 7 Jan. 1916, all in *McDowell Times.*

24. August Meier and Elliott Rudwick, "Attorneys Black and White: A Case Study of Race Relations within the NAACP," *Journal of American History* 62, no. 4 (Mar. 1976): 913–46; Carter G. Woodson, *The Negro Professional Man and the Community* (1934; rept., New York: Johnson Reprint Corporation, 1970), pp. 322–33; "William F. Denny," 1 Jan. 1915, "An Ex-Slave is Very Successful Attorney," 26 Feb. 1915 (reprint from the *McDowell Recorder*), "J. K. Smith, Ready to Help Unfortunate," 3 Sept. 1915, "National Jail Robber . . . Wins Celebrated Case," 29 Mar. 1918, "National Jail Robber," 24 May 1918, in *McDowell Times;* P. Ahmed Williams, in B. B. Maurer, ed., *Mountain Heritage* (Parsons, W.Va.: McClain Printing Co., 1980), "I Remember," pp. 183–87.

25. WVBNWS, *Biennial Report, 1921–22*, pp. 37–38; "Calhoun's Crowded Resort is Raided Twice in 48 Hours," 15 Jan. 1923 [1924], "Jail Sentence for A. L. Calhoun: Once Czar of Elkhorn," 18 Jan. 1924, in *Welch Daily News*.

26. For information on Keystone's fires during the war years, see "Put In a Fire Plug," 2 Feb. 1915, "Keystone Scene of Big Fire," 31 Dec. 1915, "Disastrous Fire Visits Keystone," 3 Mar. 1916, "Fire Threatens Half of Keystone," 21 July 1916, "Fire! Three Houses Destroyed," 4 Aug. 1916, and "Keystone Visited by Fearful Conflagration," 11 Jan. 1918, in *McDowell Times*. For the 1920s, see "Two Story Frame at Wilcoe Burns Down," 31 Dec. 1923, "Riverview Hotel at Clark Burns Down," 9 Jan. 1924, and "Eight Buildings Burned . . . in Center of Keystone," 8 Feb. 1924, in *Welch Daily News;* "Fire Destroys Seven Buildings," *McDowell Recorder*, 3 July 1929.

27. James T. Laing, "The Negro Miner in West Virginia" (Ph.D. diss., Ohio State University, 1933), pp. 281, 311, and 314; interviews with Leonard Davis, 28 July 1983, and Preston Turner, 26 July 1983.

28. WVBNWS, *Biennial Report, 1923–24*, p. 29; Laing, "The Negro Miner," pp. 286, 290, 312–15.

29. See chap. 5.

30. Abram L. Harris, *The Negro as Capitalist: A Study of Banking and Business among American Negroes* (Philadelphia: American Academy of Political and Social Sciences, 1936), pp. 46–61.

31. "News of Colored Folk," *Bluefield Daily Telegraph*, 15 Nov. 1924; WVBNWS, *Biennial Report, 1925–26*, p. 48, and *1929–32*, p. 46.

32. "Negro Fire Insurance Company," *McDowell Times*, 8 Oct. 1915; "Negroes Plan Big Ox Roast," *Raleigh Register*, 6 Nov. 1932.

33. "Address of Rev. R. H. McKoy," *McDowell Times*, 8 June 1917, and Attorney J. M. Ellis to Carter G. Woodson, 5 Nov. 1917, in Carter G. Woodson Papers, Reel 3, Library of Congress.

34. Dr. C. C. Barnett, Barnett Hospital of Huntington, to Dr. N. L. Barnett, Old City Hospital of Kansas City, 14 Sept. 1922, in private files of Captain Nelson L. Barnett, United States Air Force (retired), Huntington, West Virginia, copies in author's possession.

35. "Montcalm," 17 May 1918, "Hotel Liberty at Welch," 20 Sept. 1918, and "Mr. and Mrs. Jas. Johnson," 1 Jan. 1915, in *McDowell Times*.

36. "Dr. S. A. Viney is Claimed by Death," 7 May 1915, "The Alpha Hospital Charity Commission," 24 Sept. 1915, in *McDowell Times;* C. E. Stewart, administrative assistant, to Guy D. Goff, U.S. Senate, 8 Jan. 1930, in Series 3, Box 20, Folder 4, Governor H. D. Hatfield Papers, West Virginia Collection, West Virginia University; Clerk of the Senate, *West Virginia Legislative Handbook* (1916–31); interview with Pink Henderson, 15 July 1983.

37. "Hotel Dixie," 18 Jan. 1918, "W. D. Catus," 29 Mar. 1918, and "Two Free Dental Clinics," 28 Sept. 1917, in *McDowell Times*.

38. "Negro Lawyers to Form Organization," 17 Sept. 1917, "Negro Bar Association Hold[s] Successful Meeting," 28 Sept. 1917, "Citizens of Bluefield Coming to the Front," 26 Jan. 1917, in *McDowell Times;* WVBNWS, *Biennial Reports, 1921–22*, pp. 84–86, *1923–24*, pp. 58–59, and *1925–26*, p. 71.

39. T. Edward Hill to John J. Cornwell, 15 Nov. 1917, (reprinted in *Mc-Dowell Times*, 30 Nov. 1917); "Negro Lawyer on Legal Board of McDowell County," *McDowell Times*, 30 Nov. 1917.

40. "M'Dowell Co. Teacher's Institute," 1 Sept. 1916, "Teachers of Mercer Co. Conclude Successful Institute," 30 Aug. 1917, "Parents' Meeting," 1 Dec. 1916, "Honor Roll of Keystone-Eckman Graded School," 1 Jan. 1915, "Send the Children to School," 8 Sept. 1916, in *McDowell Times*.

41. Interviews with Pink Henderson, 15 July 1983, and Lester and Ellen Phillips, 20 July 1983; Laing, "The Negro Miner," pp. 462, 487; Ella W. Robinson, Asland, W.Va., to T. E. Harris, 3 Sept. 1924, in correspondence file, Thaddeus E. Harris Papers, Perkins Library, Duke University.

42. Laing, "The Negro Miner," pp. 462, 487.

43. Interviews with North Dickerson, 28 July 1983, Lawrence Boling, 18 July 1983, Preston Turner, 26 July 1983, Roy Todd, 18 July 1983, Andrew Campbell, 19 July 1983, and Charles T. Harris, 18 July 1983.

44. Interviews with Charles T. Harris, 18 July 1983, Andrew Campbell, 19 July 1983, and Pink Henderson, 15 July 1983; Laing, "The Negro Miner," pp. 295, 396, 397.

45. "The Adkin[s] District Teachers Appointed," 27 Aug. 1915, "Teachers for Browns Creek District, 1917–18," 31 Aug. 1917, "Teachers for Adkins District, 1917–18," 31 Aug. 1917, "Honor Roll of Keystone-Eckman Graded School," 1 Jan. 1915, "Prof. Barnett Resigns as Principal of the Gary Graded School," 8 Mar. 1918, in *McDowell Times*.

46. "Don't Favor Woman Suffrage, Its a Fake," 15 Jan. 1915, "Woman Suffrage Dead in New Jersey," 22 Oct. 1915, in *McDowell Times*.

47. WVBNWS, *Biennial Report, 1925–26*, pp. 114–18.

48. T. G. Nutter, "These Colored United States [Pt.] X: West Virginia," *The Messenger* 6, no. 2 (Feb. 1924): 44–48; E. Franklin Frazier, "Open Forum," *The Messenger* 6, no. 11 (Nov. 1924): 362–63. For a forceful call for more attention to the "shade of color" issue, see James O. Horton, "Urban Studies: Comment," in Darlene Clark Hine, ed., *The State of Afro-American History: Past, Present, and Future* (Baton Rouge: Louisiana State University Press, 1986), pp. 130–35; interview with Lawrence Boling, 18 July 1983; Laing, "The Negro Miner," pp. 463–64.

49. Interviews with North Dickerson, 15 July 1983, Lawrence Boling, 18 July 1983, Charles T. Harris, 18 July 1983, and William M. Beasley, 26 July 1983; James T. Laing, "The Negro Miner in West Virginia," *Social Forces* 14 (1936): 416–22.

50. Interview with Charles T. Harris, 18 July 1983; Laing, "The Negro Miner in West Virginia."

PART
4

Institutions, Culture, and Power

7

Religious Organizations

The changing Afro-American class structure shaped the war and postwar growth of black religious and fraternal organizations in southern West Virginia. In addition to reflecting the effects of racial exclusion, black migration, and the black miners' extensive participation in the coal economy, the rise of black institutions reflected the expansion of black leadership. Motivated by an expanding race consciousness as well as by their own desire for power, prestige, and economic position, black religious and fraternal leaders worked to adapt the black miners' southern cultural traditions to a new social context. As in the prewar years, black churches, fraternal orders, and mutual benefit societies would fail to fully reconcile the diverse socioeconomic and political interests within the black community. Yet, responding to the institutional effects of racial exclusion and class exploitation, they would repeatedly submerge their conflicts in the interest of racial unity. This chapter and the next explore these processes as they unfolded within the black coal-mining community between World War I and the onset of the Great Depression.[1]

With continuing black migration, proletarianization, and increasing racial segregation in southern West Virginia during World War I and the 1920s, the black church found increasingly fertile ground there. In its first biennial report of 1921–22, the Bureau of Negro Welfare and Statistics concluded: "The influence of church upon the life of the Negroes in West Virginia cannot be overestimated. It was the one uplifting agency that came with the Negroes who migrated from the South . . . and it has played a role vastly more important than is generally known in the moral and civil life of the race."[2] State-level membership in black religious organizations increased from no more than 15,000 in the prewar era to more than 21,800 in

1916 and to over 32,700 in 1926. The number of black churches increased from 345 in 1916 to 480 a decade later.[3]

Although the region's African Methodist Episcopal (AME), AME Zion, Colored Methodist Episcopal (CME), Presbyterian, and Holiness churches grew, the Baptist church retained its dominant position. In 1926, according to available county-level statistics, southern West Virginia blacks made up just under 50 percent of all Baptists in the region and well over 50 percent of all Baptists in Logan, McDowell, Mercer, and Raleigh counties. During the entire 1915–32 period, Baptists accounted for an estimated 70 percent of the state's black church members and 60 percent of the state's churches. The AME church, supplemented by a few AME Zion, CME, Presbyterian, and Holiness bodies, comprised the remainder.[4] Holiness and Pentecostal churches proliferated among northern black workers, but in southern West Virginia, the black Holiness Church of God and the Saints of Christ only accounted for two churches among them in the entire state in 1916, increasing merely to five in 1926. Given the spirited nature of black Baptist worship services, the Holiness and Pentecostal bodies made little headway in southern West Virginia. The AME Zion, CME, and Presbyterian churches fared little better; none exceeded thirteen congregations in the entire state by the late 1920s.

Continuing the deep religious traditions of their southern homes, black migrants to southern West Virginia soon joined established congregations or helped build new churches. Leonard Davis recalled that his family belonged to Baptist churches in Roanoke and Clifton Forge, Virginia, before migrating to southern West Virginia and joining the Baptist church at Leyland, Fayette County. Another black migrant, Pink Henderson, recalled attending a Baptist church in Jefferson County, Alabama, where he was baptized, his father served as a deacon, and his mother taught Sunday school before the family came to West Virginia and joined the Baptist church at Coalwood, McDowell County. Roy Todd, who served as the Sunday school secretary for a West Virginia Baptist church, originally belonged to a Baptist church in Alabama, where his father served as a deacon and was "well thought of." "We never left church out," he said.[5] "I always went to church," Andrew Campbell recalled. "We stayed in church all day on Sunday." North Dickerson, the West Virginia–born son of a black migrant, even claimed, "I was born in church." In the coalfields, another man stated simply, the church was "the only thing we had."[6]

The church established roots not simply among blacks who migrated from the South, but among workers who cut rights-of-way, built railroads, and, most importantly, loaded tons of bituminous coal. Throughout the period it was common for black men to work for the coal company and hold services "in the church on the hill," on company land. One black minister implied the connection between the church, black miners, and the coal economy: "This is indeed a great state . . . [with] its multitudinous grades of mineral. . . . so this means a great blessing to us, and above all we have great churches." The black church appealed to workers making the transition to a new industrial footing, and it certainly helped to reinforce a strong work ethic. "We should choose hard tasks in the Lord's service," Rev. W. R. Woodson titled one of his sermons. At the same time, the black church frequently drew upon its members' rural heritage, to express their expectations for a better life in the coalfields. As one sermon related, "In the morning sow the seed; in the evening withhold not thine hand."[7]

As elsewhere, blacks in the coalfields took growing pride in their churches, consistently struggling to improve the physical appearance of church buildings both inside and out. During the war years the *McDowell Times* reported numerous beautification campaigns. In cooperation with the cleanup campaign sponsored by the U.S. Coal and Coke Company at Gary, McDowell County, members of Rock Hill Baptist Church repainted their building so that it looked like new. Another Baptist church made "some needed and substantial improvements . . . among which was the installing of a modern set of oak pews which are second to none in this section of the state." In 1917, when Mt. Chapel Baptist Church of Keystone, McDowell County, rebuilt its building after a fire had destroyed it, the new edifice was reported to be "one of the finest and most handsomely built churches in the coal fields." In Lowe, Mercer County, Antioch Baptist Church was described as "the prettiest edifice in this section of the state." During the early and mid-1920s, the Rock Hill Baptist Church continued to target money for "exterior and interior" beautification. Other congregations must have done the same, for the phrase "beautiful church" was a recurring description of black churches in the region.[8]

However modest these church improvement efforts were, behind them stood the black coal-mining working class. To be sure, coal companies sometimes provided buildings for black churches (and white ones, too), but even when they did, they frequently delayed for as long as possible and then insisted that church members share the expense. In a letter to the owner of the Winding Gulf Colliery, the manager wrote: "We have fought this thing off for a long time, but I have put it up to the colored people to raise two hundred dollars in cash before we have to do anything. This may stall it for awhile longer. . . . It will involve an expense of eight hundred dollars when finally it is brought to a head." The money was soon raised, however, and the blacks in Winding Gulf gained a church.[9]

Paying off church mortgages and maintaining church buildings required fundamental sacrifice from black coal miners and their families. After special fund-raising events, as well as after regular services, the *Times* frequently reprinted lengthy columns of 5-, 10-, and 25-cent donations. During the war years, it enthusiastically reported detailed church-by-church accounts of fund-raising rallies and often noted that the giving was generous. On one occasion the First Baptist Church of Kimball raised $300; the St. James Baptist Church of Welch raised $260; and the Scott Street Baptist Church of Bluefield culminated an emergency fund-raising drive that netted $1,200. The members of Rock Hill Baptist Church at Gary also "turned out," the reporter stated, "and, as is their usual custom, brought out their substance and gave bountifully."[10] Although the black elite undoubtedly played a greater financial role in the Methodist Episcopal and Presbyterian churches, the black proletariat nonetheless played an important part, too, especially indirectly through its role in the black economy.

As black churches faced the brief economic depression that followed World War I, their fund-raising activities suffered, yet they persisted and, in some cases, escalated their efforts. In mid-1921, for example, following an intense fund-raising campaign at the Mt. Calvary Baptist Church in Princeton, the *Bluefield Daily Telegraph* reported, "The entire collection was donated to . . . erecting a new church building which will be dedicated on the fourth Sunday."[11] Unlike Mt. Calvary, however, most black churches merely survived the hard times.

With the economic upturn of the mid-1920s, fund-raising regained its momentum. As early as 1923, the Rock Hill Baptist Church opened a $7,000 building program. In a four-week campaign, the Sunday school alone contributed $700. The following year, after successful fund-raising efforts, Mt. Nebo Baptist Church in Kimball, McDowell County, planned dedication ceremonies for its new building. By the mid-1920s, the Scott Street Baptist Church had sponsored a rally that raised $1,700; the St. James Baptist

Church in Welch was planning a cornerstone ceremony for its new building; and the African Methodist Episcopal church in Welch had purchased a lot to "build a handsome [new] church structure."[12] None of this growth would have been possible without the numerous small contributions of the black miners.

Under the onslaught of the Great Depression, the role of proletarianization in the fortunes of black religious institutions was made even more explicit. By the early 1930s many congregations could no longer support their ministers, pay their debts, and contribute to regular fund-raising campaigns. Blacks steadfastly continued to mount financial rallies, though, seeking to sustain their religious institutions in the face of hard times. In 1928, for example, blacks at Micco, Logan County, sponsored a "Bean Carrying Contest" for "the benefit of the struggling Baptist church." In July 1932 in its "Local Colored News" column, the *Raleigh Register* reported "a depression rally" at the Ebenezer Baptist Church. Rally leaders urged men, women, and children to give 50, 25, and 10 cents, respectively. Seeking to retain their minister, in November 1932, members of St. Phillip's Baptist Church of Logan held a "Minister's Aid Church Rally."[13]

Despite fluctuations in the coal economy, between World War I and the early 1930s the church's role in the lives of southern West Virginia blacks increased. As suggested above, the development of black churches was related to the growth of a vigorous black ministry. The number of black ministers in the state increased from about 150 during the prewar years to over 230 in 1920, to over 310 in 1930 (table 6.2). Despite these increases, the growing number of black churches outdistanced the supply of black ministers by over 30 percent. In its 1921–22 biennial report, the BNWS noted that 178 churches, pastored by 95 ministers, attended an annual meeting of the West Virginia Baptist State Convention and explained, "The wide margin between the number of pastors and the number of churches is caused by a large number of preachers pastoring two or more churches."[14] Ministers usually preached at one church on the first and third Sundays and at another on the second and fourth Sundays. Some churches held Sunday services only once a month.

Black ministers helped to mediate not only the physical expansion of black churches, but the persistence and gradual transformation of Afro-American religious beliefs and practices. As black migration accelerated, black ministers deepened their appeals to the black spiritual and communal traditions of the rural South. In the winter of 1915, Rev. G. W. Woody preached a lively sermon at the Rock Hill Baptist Church. According to one observor, "he had such religious zeal and spiritual inspiration or fervor as characterized the early reformers and christian Pilgrims of the middle ages . . . and he preached with new life and vigor." Describing a sermon at the First Baptist Church of Kimball, the *Times* reported, "To say that Rev. Robinson preached an excellent soul-stirring sermon is putting it tamely." As in the prewar years, all were made to say, " 'Did not our hearts burn within us while he talked with us by the way?' " Rev. L. A. Watkins also preached "a most profound sermon," titled "Jesus is Passing." "His words were like coals taken from Jehovah's alter." "And before he had finished it seemed that Jesus was somewhere in the pulpit, for such rejoicing was never before witnessed."[15]

During the 1920s, the black church retained its strong emotional and spiritual appeal. In his weekly columns, S. R. Anderson frequently captured and repeated emotional content of black sermons. In mid-1921, for example, he discussed the need for spiritual conversion: "Wherefore as the Holy Ghost saith, today if ye will hear his voice, harden not your heart."[16] In March 1925 in the New River Field, members of Rev. Sherman's congregation heard "a soul-stirring sermon," from the text "Forget thou not thy Lord, thy God." In the evening he preached from the text, "Jesus Wept." During the late 1920s, the "Logan Colored News" reported five "soul-stirring sermons by well-known [black] gospel pulpiteers." And, under the growing impact of the Great Depression, at the Ebenezer Baptist Church in Beckley, Rev. P. F. King prepared a sermon on "The Power of Prayer," while the minister at the Scott Street Baptist Church in Bluefield prepared "a timely and gripping message."[17]

As in the prewar years, the greatest outpouring of spiritual fervor occurred at revivals. In January 1917 during a ten-day revival at the Scott Street Baptist Church, "Rev. J. B. Evans seemed at no time to have been at himself, so completely did he allow the spirit of God to handle him." In a revival at the Bluestone Baptist Church at Bramwell, "There was an outpouring of the Holy Ghost and men just couldn't help but to accept God," the church reporter stated. In November 1924, the "Colored" column of *The New River Company Employees' Magazine* reported that "the revival meeting held here was a success. . . . Rev. Bennett of Mt. Hope preached four stirring sermons." In 1923, 1928, and 1929, the "Logan Colored News" also reported spirited revival services.[18]

Revivals usually culminated in equally fervent baptismal ceremonies. In 1917 at the Bluestone River, "admist the shouts and songs

of a very large congregation lined up on both sides of the river . . .
eleven happy converts put on Christ by baptism." Black churches
often took in 35 or more persons at one time for baptism. On one
occasion, for example, a revival at the Scott Street Baptist Church,
Bluefield, Mercer County, resulted in 64 baptismal candidates; a
month later 46 of the 64 were actually baptized, the others apparently having moved to new locales or changed their minds. Following baptismal ceremonies, the converts reassembled at the local
church, where they received the "right hand of fellowship," in-
structions on the meaning of being a Christian, and "the Lord's
Supper." Throughout the 1920s Afro-Americans continued to line
small riverbanks to witness the baptism of new converts. During
the mid-1920s, however, as new, and frequently small, churches expanded, the baptismal ceremonies often retained their communal
character only if the church allowed the number of baptismal candidates to accumulate over several months or even a year. In late 1924
and early 1925, for example, revival services in two small churches
in the Winding Gulf Field netted only eight converts.[19]

Only funerals could vie with baptisms for emotional intensity
and communal atmosphere. At one of the many funerals reported
by the *McDowell Times*, "The great church was filled to overflowing
and all around on the outside were men and women pushing their
way as near the building as possible. . . . Women and men could be
seen all over the crowded church bathing their faces in tears while
constant outbursts of crying could be heard." In another instance,
the *Times* reported, "Many eyes were moist with tears as we said
peace be to his ashes and rest to his soul." In February 1924 the
Welch Daily News described the funeral of black miner John Wesley
Pompey as "the largest funeral ever held among the colored people
in this county. More than 1,000 persons were unable to get inside
the Vivian [McDowell County] church."[20] Emotion-laden funerals,
as well as sermons and baptisms, provided important occasions
for ministers to extend their influence over black congregations
while at the same time providing channels for communicants to express solidarity with each other. Equally important, they reinforced
the intensely spiritual and communal character of black cultural
traditions.

But however emotionally satisfying black sermons and religious
rituals may have been, they did not succeed on the basis of their
spiritual and communal qualities alone. During World War I and
the postwar period, black religious leaders heightened their appeals
to the intellectual and material side of life. Black sermons increas-

ingly showed more intellectual organization and content, containing clear and convincing messages based on carefully selected texts and scriptures. These sermons were described as "logical," "thoughtful," and "instructive" as well as lively and emotional. Even the most spirited of black ministers had "several unique, but deep, subjects" in his repertoire of sermons, which he handled "in masterly style," holding his "audiences spellbound throughout the services." At a meeting of the Winding Gulf Baptist Deacons Union, Rev. L. Epperson preached "a logical sermon." On the same occasion, Rev. W. H. Mitchell preached "an able and instructive sermon," entreating the congregation to "search the scriptures." In a sermon at the Memorial Baptist Church of Switchback, McDowell County, Rev. J. B. Evans "preached to a packed house" on the subject "A Present Opportunity to Reason with God," taking his text from Isaiah 1:18.[21]

Even as they rationalized their sermons, paving the way for the new ideas of the industrial age, black ministers advanced strict moral codes that reinforced traditional values. On one occasion Rev. C. H. Rollins preached from Proverbs 4:23: "Keep thy heart with all diligence; for out of it are the issues of life." Black ministers offered strong indictments against "sin," focusing on gambling, adultery, lying, stealing, dancing, and intemperance. In a sermon at the Eckman Baptist Church in McDowell County, Rev. J. W. Robinson condemned "that class of members who believe in card parties, wine tables and dancing halls." Such people, he said, were "too busy with the affairs of the world to attend church." At a meeting of the Bluestone Baptist Sunday School Union, Rev. R. W. Hill condemned parlor games as the first step toward gambling. Many professional gamblers, he maintained, "started this way and parents should encourage children along all lines of church work." During a fundraising event at the Scott Street Baptist Church, the minister spoke on the subject of alcohol, saying, "Look not upon wine when it is red and woe unto him that giveth his neighbor strong drink."[22]

Along with its condemnation of sin, however, the church consistently held out the chance for repentance.[23] The modern-day concern with color symbolism notwithstanding, spiritual redemption during this period was often summed up in this Bible verse "Though your sins be as scarlet, they shall be as white as snow; though they be red like crimson, they shall be as wool."[24] In keeping with the black religious traditions of the rural South, sermons in the postwar period frequently articulated a belief in heaven and an afterlife, especially as a reward for suffering endured for righteousness' sake on earth. In one revival sermon, the minister took his text from St. Matthew 25:46. "And these [the wicked] shall go away into everlasting punishment: but the righteous into life eternal." Another black minister exclaimed: "Fret not thy self because of evildoers, neither be thou envious against the workers of iniquity. For they shall soon be cut down like the grass, and wither like the green herb." In a funeral sermon, another black minister took his text from Revelation 2:10. "Fear none of those things which thou shalt suffer. . . . be thou faithful unto death, and I will give thee a crown of life."[25]

If black religious institutions strived to address the spiritual, moral, and intellectual demands of black life in the coalfields, they frequently spoke to its social realities as well. Excluded from the larger institutional, social, and cultural life of the region, blacks in southern West Virginia, as elsewhere, used the church as a social center, a political forum, and, especially, as a leadership training ground. Black church members formed and managed numerous church auxiliaries, including the Sunday school, choir, and boards of deacons and trustees. The dearth of black ministers, discussed above, gave Sunday school superintendents, deacons, and trustees broader leadership roles.[26]

More important, however, the church offered black women leadership opportunities. Black women consistently dominated the membership roster of black churches, making up nearly 57 percent of black Baptists in West Virginia in 1916. Ten years later, this percentage had slightly increased. Through the black Women's Baptist State Convention, the regional Baptist Women's District Convention, and a variety of local auxiliaries, women exercised a profound influence on the religious life of the black community. As elsewhere in black America, black churchwomen in southern West Virginia played a key role in fund-raising campaigns. During the war years the *McDowell Times* had praise for the district convention. "This convention is doing much good for the benefit of the race and the women. . . . They are strong advocates of the educational growth of our people and the immediate amount of spiritual and moral good being accomplished by them in their local work is being effectively felt and approved."[27]

The black church also served as a training ground for black youth. In 1915 Mt. Chapel Baptist Church founded the Dunbar Lyceum, which was to teach black youth how "to think quickly, perfect their talents, rid them of stage fright and make friends and acquaintances." The students gave speeches, recited poems, performed musical numbers, and discussed social issues. At one Lyceum meeting Dr. Joseph Brown discussed "health, sanitation, and the importance of cleanliness for the care of infants." In general, though, it was the Sunday school that played the main role in carrying out the educational, leadership, and training function of the church. In 1916 the Bluestone Baptist Sunday School Union celebrated its twenty-eighth anniversary. The gathering heard and discussed a variety of papers on the significance of the Sunday school in the life of the church, including "The Importance of Early Training of Children," "The Relationship of the Church to the Sunday School," and "The Deacons' Influence in the Sunday School." Some ministers encouraged youth to take an active role in all phases of church work, including regular Sunday services, midweek prayer sessions, and official business meetings. Through frequent Bible verse memory contests, black youth also absorbed the essential dogma and rhetoric of Afro-Christianity. On one occasion, first, second, and third prizes went to young people who recited 189, 178, and 125 Bible verses respectively.[28]

As leaders in the growth of the black church, many black ministers built well-deserved reputations for selfless service. They received accolades for their "sacrificial and conscientious service" and for their ability to rise "above the menial policies of a dollar as a passport in the world." When these men moved on to new churches, they sometimes left their old congregations with a fine record of achievements. When Rev. J. W. Coger resigned from the pastorate of the Northfork Baptist Church, he left the church "with money in the bank" with which to erect a new edifice. Similarly, as W. H. Mitchell resigned from the pastorship of the Wingfield Baptist Church, he took pride in the material progress of his working-class congregation: "Fifty-four laborers and families have bought homes of whom thirty are now happily situated in them and I hope that it will not be long before many more will be prepared to put their families in their [homes]."[29] Such ministers vouchsafed not only their reputations as "preachers—soul savers," but also their fame as pastors concerned with the material welfare of their parishioners.

Despite the tremendous commitment of black religious leaders, though, black churches everywhere faced growing competition from secular alternatives to religious culture. Bootlegging enterprises, dance halls, and gambling parlors multiplied in southern West Virginia and vied for the patronage of its growing black population. While black churchmen railed against sinful secular activities in their sermons, they often worried that they were losing the battle, a concern echoed by the *McDowell Times:* "You may announce that there will be a ball, a dance, a frolic, a German, and Lord only knows what that is, or anything like a 'shin-dig' and you will have a crowded house every time. They will be there regardless of admission at the door." One of "our good preachers," the *Times* lamented, was leaving Keystone because "the people don't show any disposition to support the church"—the church could not even pay its light bill. Moreover, some of the men would "buy liquor, drink it and get drunk and act the fool right in the very face of the church." During the early 1920s law officers discovered a thirty-gallon whiskey still near the black Baptist church at Superior, McDowell County. By the late 1920s the BNWS complained that there had been "a great falling off in church attendance, especially among the young people."[30]

Even so, in southern West Virginia, as elsewhere, there was substantial interaction and overlap between black religious and secular culture. The Harris Saxophone Orchestra of Kimball, directed by the tailor Ben Harris, frequently played at local dance halls and parties. Harris also directed the Rock Hill Baptist Church choir at Gary. The *Times* described it as perhaps "the best choir in the county," reporting that, with the way it sang, "no one could attend services at this place without feeling better." On one occasion, a dance hall at Northfork was literally transformed into a church in order to accommodate the revival services of a visiting evangelist. Nonetheless, black secular institutions such as dance halls provided the primary forums for cultural expression for a growing number of Afro-Americans, and the phenomenon generated deep concern among black ministers and middle-class black civic leaders. In its biennial report of 1927–28, the BNWS sought to aid black churches in their fight against secularization, proclaiming, "It is of the greatest importance that Negroes continue to have faith in the God of their fathers and mothers."[31]

In their failure to achieve a firmer grip over the lives of their congregants, black ministers were not entirely blameless. In their installation sermons and associational meetings, black ministers repeatedly urged each other to live upright lives before the people, but in practice they often did the opposite. In 1915 the *Times* reported that the people of Crozer Temple at Elkhorn were "alright, with the exception of one thing, and that is a leader who has been endowed with the Holy Spirit, and we pray how soon they may get a good honest man at this place." In the face of the brutality of company officials and local police, some local ministers urged blacks to "forgive" the company, "as it would jeopardize them as ministers in working among their people." One visitor responded to this line of preaching with a blistering rebuke. "For the apprehension of a few dollars," he said, "such so-called leaders" would "sell the[ir] moral, racial and ethical birthrights." "To control a church," he continued, they would "quell the political or civic rights of their people."[32]

Few black ministers fully disengaged themselves from the material comforts, power, and recognition that often came with their position. Because of the shortage of black preachers, some congregations went to great lengths to accommodate their pastors. Some able, and some not so able, black ministers exploited the shortage by taking the most lucrative posts and attempting to pastor several churches. Most black ministers received small salaries, but, as elsewhere in the South, were additionally rewarded by their congregations with gifts in kind. Taking these gifts into account, the support that black ministers in southern West Virginia received was greater than what the financial status of black miners would seem to suggest. In the spring of 1917, for instance, "The members and friends of Rev. Randolph, learning that he was soon to go to his conference . . . decided to compliment him with a fine suit of clothes. . . . a fine forty-dollar suit was handed to the distinguished divine." On one occasion, Rev. Crockett received everything "from a box of tooth picks to a barrel of flour." After a revival at Mora's Morning Star Baptist Church, Rev. E. G. Holcomb received "a pound party of meat, lard, sugar, coffee, tea, rice, and, in fact everything that goes to make life happy." One member gave the minister a twenty-dollar overcoat, while cash contributions came to sixteen-dollars.[33] After a nine-day revival, Rev. Coger was similarly feted. In his own words, "They put $32 in my hand, then gave me $53, making a total of [$85] in cash, which together with the pounding would total a long way over a hundred dollars."[34]

Black ministers had ample opportunity to exploit their churches, and some undoubtedly did just that, driving some parishioners to seek secular alternatives to the church. Yet, to their credit, most black ministers apparently received gifts in "appreciation" for "able service." When the congregation honored Rev. J. W. Crockett with "a large number of valuable presents," they made it explicit that they were "well pleased" with his service and "the upright life" he lived "in and before his people." Rev. T. J. Brandon received accolades upon his death despite his lack of formal training. "While he was not a college graduate nor a literary theologian, yet his preaching was believed in by all who heard him." Rev. T. H. Morton of East Gulf, Raleigh County, was described as a man who placed "sacrificial and conscientious service" first and was "above the menial policies of a dollar as a passport in the world."[35] Nonetheless, judging from the growing popularity of secular activities within the black community, perhaps too many ministers were in the habit of not following their own exhortations.

If black churches were challenged by the worldly orientation of many blacks, they faced even greater challenges from the growing social and cultural cleavages along gender and class lines that divided blacks. Although black women dominated church membership and contributed heavily to the financial support and general life of the church, they faced crucial gender-based limitations on their activities. Black women found few opportunities to serve as ministers since most black churches excluded them from ministerial service. Editor M. T. Whittico editorialized, "Women are needed to obey, sing, pray in private but not to preach except by a good clear Christian life. . . . To spread sunshine in the homes, churches, and societies . . . That's enough for women to do."[36]

Even worse a problem for the black church than gender inequality was inequality along class lines. The value of church property, the educational level of ministers, sermon styles, and decorum—all of these reflected important differences between the predominantly working-class Baptist churches and the slowly expanding, middle class–oriented AME and Presbyterian churches. According to available statistics for the 1920s, the AME church, with only about 20 percent of all black church members statewide, owned more than 30 percent of black church property. Other elite church bodies accounted for about 10 percent of all black church members and owned the remaining 30 percent of black church property.[37]

The Baptist minister became the principal target of the black elite's campaign for an educated black ministry. As early as 1915, a visiting minister captured the prevalent middle-class attitude: "The day of reckoning is approaching, when . . . the race shall demand cultured men to lead the race and demand a purer gospel than emotionalism and 'lung power,' and a silk hat and a long-tailed coat shall not be the passport of a preacher; yea, rather a good character and moral courage."[38] Although the number of educated black preachers had slowly increased since the prewar years, according to the BNWS's 1921–22 report, "Of the four hundred Negro ministers in West Virginia, less than fifty of them have had two years or more of standard college work, and less than one hundred have had

schooling equivalent to a standard high school course." Educated
black ministers, the bureau argued, would "create a healthy moral
sentiment which will result in driving out of the churches the ignorant, immoral, vicious and venal preachers who are hindrances to
the course of religion and the progress of the race."[39]

Although their numbers increased only slowly, it was the educated black ministers who introduced a more intellectual tone to
black churches and served elite congregations. Services at the black
Presbyterian and Methodist churches departed substantially from
the emotional tone of services at their Baptist counterparts. In his
sermon at the Ebenezer Presbyterian Church in Kimball, Rev. Coleman delivered a highly intellectual sermon. "This was not a sermon
that appealed to men's passions," the *Times* reported, "nor did it
cater to those emotional demonstrations that often make men de-
stroy church property, but it was a sermon that . . . appealed to
men and women's reasons and common sense." In a sermon at the
Excelsior Methodist Episcopal Church, the district superintendent
of the church took his audience "to avenues of higher thinking and
better living." When the *Times* compared services at elite churches
to working-class services (including funerals) it described them as
"full of logic and thoughtful in the extreme."[40]

Some Baptist churches, like the First Baptist Church of Charleston, gradually became elite over time. After arriving in southern
West Virginia in the prewar years, Rev. Mordecai W. Johnson continued his education, adding a divinity degree from the Rochester
Theological Seminary of New York in 1919 to his B.A. degrees from
Morehouse College in Atlanta and the University of Chicago. Under
Johnson's energetic leadership, the First Baptist Church of Charleston developed an expanding variety of social welfare auxiliaries and
a weekly news bulletin, supported by an extensive roster of black
business and professional advertisers. Even so, in contrast to their
Methodist and Episcopal counterparts, black ministers at the First
Baptist Church, even in their most thoughtful sermons, hoped to
prove themselves masters of emotional oratory, by closing their sermons "in a blaze of glory."[41]

Despite divisions along class, denominational, and racial lines,
black churches in southern West Virginia consistently worked to
heal disunity. Within particular faiths and across denominations,
Afro-Americans bridged divisions to create bonds between themselves and ties to the expanding local, state, and national black
community. As early as 1915, the *McDowell Times* declared the
need for an interdenominational meeting, especially in McDowell
County, in order to counteract "bigotry, egotism, jealousy, preju-

dice, envyings and right-down meaness." Sometimes black Methodist and Baptist churches held revival services together. In 1915 following a spirited joint revival service at Excelsior, both the Baptist and Methodist ministers involved were "perfectly satisfied with the additions to their churches." To provide music at the funeral services of a black physician, an "impromptu choir" was formed from members of five different churches that included AME, Baptist, and Presbyterian volunteers. Frequently, fund-raising events also involved interdenominational cooperation as black ministers preached in each other's pulpits on these occasions.[42]

In addition to expanding the Flat Top Baptist Association, the Mt. Olivet Baptist Association, and the Guyan Valley Association during World War I, Afro-Americans established two new associations, the Winding Gulf Baptist Association and the Mount Zion Primitive Baptist Association. By 1921, at least seven black associations made up the membership of the West Virginia Baptist Association, which participated in the National Baptist Convention. To some extent, the rise of new religious associations represented a splintering process. When the Winding Gulf Baptist Association began in 1917, the Flat Top Baptist Association contributed twelve of its twenty founding churches to it. Although there is little information on the split, the new association seemed to have helped unify the growing number of black churches in the Winding Gulf Field.[43]

The common practice of ministers visiting other churches promoted unity, too, on a regional, state, and national level. Under the sponsorship of several black churches, W. E. B. Du Bois spoke at the Lovely Zion Baptist Church in 1921. The *Bluefield Daily Telegraph* described his talk as "a brief, but vivid account" of the recent Pan-African Congress, held in Paris. "Dr. DuBois electrified his audience by the power of his matchless oratory," emphasizing the importance of "self-respect, race, pride and high ideals."[44] Rev. J. H. Adams, who had founded churches in southern West Virginia in the prewar era (including Lovely Zion), had moved to New York City by 1915. Through return visits, though, he kept close ties with southern West Virginia. The institutional ties of blacks in southern West Virginia extended even deeper into the South than the North. During the war years, Rev. C. T. Robinson of Birmingham, Alabama, conducted services at Berwind, McDowell County, and planned meetings at Davy.[45] Interstate church visitation facilitated the growth of the national black community, including the expanding industrial proletariat as well as the new bourgeoisie.

Black religious leaders also worked to link blacks to whites in an even broader ecumenical relationship. At a large revival meeting at

Pageton during the mid-1920s, among blacks in the capacity audience were "leading whites . . . including officials and professional men." Following a revival at Cinderella, Mingo County, the superintendent of the coal operation prepared a pool for baptizing "and everybody turned out. . . . The white people were there in large numbers and manifested a spirit of personal interest in the meeting." When an amateur cast of Ebenezer Presbyterian Church staged the moral drama "Finger of Scorn," nearly half of the capacity audience was white, including a leading merchant, the local postmaster, a dealer in pianos, organs, and sewing machines, and Rev. Charles Painter of the Kimball Methodist Episcopal Church South. At the conclusion of the performance, Rev. Painter paid high tribute to the black Presbyterian pastor for his work of racial uplift. In the Winding Gulf Field, until the black church at Pax, Fayette County, completed its building, white Methodists shared their facilities with the black congregation. On one occasion several whites attended the services, including the coal company superintendent and the bank boss. In the capital city of Charleston, a white minister spoke at the dedication of the new Metropolitan Baptist Church; he "touched and fired the hearts of the big audience" with the sincerity of his support.[46] Perhaps more so than elsewhere in the South, in southern West Virginia blacks and whites created significant forms of interracial fellowship. Their religious and cultural interactions certainly helped to curtail the extent of interracial conflict in coal-mining towns, even though, as in other facets of black life in the coalfields, the religious community was fragmented along color lines.

Interracial fellowship was a highly tenuous affair. Although whites spoke in black churches, for example, there is no evidence that black ministers spoke at white churches. In fact, as white workers, white elites, and the state increasingly coalesced around notions of black inferiority, racial segregation in the religious life of coal-mining communities intensified. Responding to these hostile social forces, as well as to their own expanding sense of race pride, Afro-Americans built their own churches and developed their own religious traditions. As elsewhere in industrial America, although their efforts were marked by cleavages along class and, to some extent, gender lines, blacks in the southern West Virginia coalfields successfully adapted the emotional, spiritual, and communal traditions they brought with them from the rural South to the growing rational, material, and individualistic dictates of the new industrial order.

NOTES

1. See Lawrence Levine, *Black Culture and Black Consciousness: Afro-American Folk Thought from Slavery to Freedom* (Oxford: Oxford University Press, 1977), chap. 3; Elizabeth R. Bethel, *Promiseland: A Century of Life in a Negro Community* (Philadelphia: Temple University Press, 1981), pp. 69–91, 136–44.

2. "Churches," in West Virginia Bureau of Negro Welfare and Statistics (WVBNWS), *Biennial Report, 1921–22* (Charleston, W. Va.), p. 77.

3. U.S. Bureau of the Census, *Religious Bodies, 1906* (Washington, 1910), 1:140, *1916* (Washington, 1919), 1:556, and *1926* (Washington, 1930), 1:722; WVBNWS, *Biennial Reports, 1921–22,* pp. 77–80, *1925–26,* and *1927–28,* respectively, 84–85, and 64–67. See also *Religious Bodies, 1916,* 2:100-101, 117, 496–500, and *Religious Bodies, 1926,* 2:130–39, 211–15, 995–1005.

4. *Religious Bodies, 1926,* 1:698–99.

5. Interviews with Leonard Davis, 28 July 1983, Pink Henderson, 15 July 1983, and Roy Todd, 18 July 1983.

6. Interviews with Roy Todd, 18 July 1983, Andrew Campbell, 19 July 1983, John L. Page, 14 July 1983, and North E. Dickerson, 28 July 1983. Cf. Levine, *Black Culture and Black Consciousness,* pp. 136–89, and Bethel, *Promiseland,* pp. 136–44.

7. "Winding Gulf Ministers and Deacons' Union," 19 Mar. 1915, "Bluestone Baptist Sunday School Union," 6 Oct. 1916, in *McDowell Times;* "Among the Colored People," *Bluefield Daily Telegraph,* 28 Nov. 1920, 2 Jan. 1921; "Logan Colored News," *Logan Banner,* 6 Apr. 1928; interview with North E. Dickerson, 28 July 1983; "On to Berwind," *McDowell Times,* 14 Sept. 1917; "Among Our Colored People," *The New River Company Employees' Magazine* (Nov. 1924): 11.

8. "Fourth Anniversary," 24 Aug. 1917, "Ministers and Deacons," 5 Nov. 1915, "Primitive Baptist People," 17 Aug. 1917, in *McDowell Times;* "Gary Colored News," 11 Dec. 1923, 2 Jan. 1924, in *Welch Daily News.* Also see "Among the Colored People," 3 July 1921, 1 Jan. 1925, in *Bluefield Daily Telegraph.*

9. "Rev. Ziegler," *McDowell Times,* 11 Jan. 1918; Yvonne S. Farley, "Homecoming," *Goldenseal* 5, no. 4 (Oct.-Dec. 1979): 7–16; George Wolfe, manager, to Justus Collins, owner, Winding Gulf Colliery Company, 31 Mar. and 3 Apr. 1917, in Series 1, Box 14, Folder 101, Justus Collins Papers, West Virginia Collection, West Virginia University.

10. "Church Rallies in Many Places," 11 June 1915; "Scott Street Baptist Church Set a Record," 13 July 1917, "Church Work in Bluefield," 18 July 1915, "Northfork M.E. Church Painted," 27 Aug. 1915, "Grand Rally at Excelsior," 3 Mar. 1916, "Successful Home Rally," 6 July 1917, "The Great Age Rally," 10 Aug. 1917, and articles from 28 May 1915, 4 June 1915, 7 Jan. 1916, 10 Aug. 1917, and 3 Mar. 1916, all in *McDowell Times;* "Among the Colored People," 3 July 1921, 1 Jan. 1925, in *Bluefield Daily Telegraph;* "Gary Colored," *McDowell Recorder,* 23 Jan. 1925; "Logan Colored News," *Logan Ban-*

ner, 6 Apr. 1928. For the financial connection between the black middle class and black workers, see chap. 6 above

11. "Among the Colored People," Bluefield Daily Telegraph, 3 July 1921.

12. "Gary Colored," 8 and 11 Dec. 1923, "Kimball Colored," 28 Jan. 1924, in Welch Daily News, "Among the Colored People," Bluefield Daily Telegraph, 1 Jan. 1925; "[Welch] Colored News," Welch Daily News, 14 and 15 July 1925.

13. "Logan Colored News," Logan Banner, 6 Apr. 1928, 9 Nov. 1932; "Local Colored News," Raleigh Register, 31 July 1932.

14. U.S. Bureau of the Census, Thirteenth Census of the United States, (Washington: 1913), 4:529–30, Fourteenth Census, 1920 (Washington, 1923), 4:1029–42, Fifteenth Census, 1930 (Washington, 1933), 4:1741–43; WVBNWS, Biennial Reports, 1921–22, pp. 77–80, 1923–24, pp. 63–64, 1925–26, pp. 84–86, and 1927–28, pp. 64–66; "Rev. J. W. Coger Called to Marytown," 22 Sept. 1916, "Called to Mt. Zion Baptist Church," 20 Oct. 1916, "Church," 22 Sept. 1916, "Church Directory," 5 and 10 Oct. 1916, 19 Jan. 1917, in McDowell Times, "Logan Colored News," Logan Banner, 18 Nov. 1927.

15. "Rock Hill Baptist Church Holds Good Service," 19 Feb. 1915, "Great Christian Revival at Cinderella," 4 June 1915, in McDowell Times.

16. "Among the Colored People," 3 July 1921, 16 Nov. 1924, and 6 Nov. 1932, in Bluefield Daily Telegraph.

17. "Among Our Colored People," The New River Company Employees' Magazine (Mar. 1925); "Logan Colored News," Logan Banner, 18 Nov. 1927; "Negro Activities," Raleigh Register, 6 Nov. 1932; "Among the Colored People," Bluefield Daily Telegraph, 6 Nov. 1932.

18. "Great Revival Just Closed," 26 Jan. 1917, "Pioneer Preacher Back in Coal Field," 29 Oct. 1915, in McDowell Times; "Pageton Holds a Big Community Meeting," Welch Daily News, 9 Feb. 1924; "Among Our Colored People," The New River Company Employees' Magazine (Nov. 1924); "Logan Colored News," 6 July 1923, 23 Mar. 1928, and 15 Mar. 1929, in Logan Banner.

19. "Eleven Happy Persons [I]mmersed in Bluestone River at Simmons," 2 Nov. 1917, "Great Revival," 26 Jan. 1917, "46 Persons Baptized," 2 Feb. 1917, 17 May 1918, in McDowell Times; The New River Company Employees' Magazine Nov. 1924, Mar. 1925.

20. For funeral accounts see McDowell Times, 7 May 1915, 23 July 1915, 30 July 1915, 24 Sept. 1915, and 23 July 1916; "News of Colored People," Bluefield Daily Telegraph, 2 Jan. 1921; "Enormous Crowd Attends Last Rites of Respected Colo[red] Citizen of Peerless," Welch Daily News, 6 Feb. 1924, "Logan Colored News," 18 Nov. 1927, 4 Nov. 1932, in Logan Banner.

21. "Evangelist," 9 Apr. 1915, "Winding Gulf Ministers and Deacons Union," 19 Mar. 1915, "Bluestone Baptist Sunday School Union," 9 Apr. 1915, in McDowell Times; "Among the Colored People," 22 Sept. 1920, 28 Nov. 1920, and 16 Nov. 1924, in Bluefield Daily Telegraph; "Logan Colored News," Logan Banner, 11 Nov. 1927.

22. "Winding Gulf Ministers and Deacons' Union," 19 Mar. 1915; "Bluestone Baptist Sunday School Union," 9 Apr. 1915; "Pastor['s] Anniversary and Rally," 4 June 1915; "Doctor D. C. Coleman," 3 Sept. 1915; "Look Not Upon Wine," 7 May 1915; "The Ministers and Deacons," 24 Sept. 1915, all in *McDowell Times;* "Among Colored People," 3 July 1921, 16 Nov. 1924, and 6 Nov. 1932, in *Bluefield Daily Telegraph;* "Logan Colored News," 6 July 1923, 23 Mar. 1928, and 15 Mar. 1929, all in *Logan Banner.*

23. "Winding Gulf Ministers and Deacons' Union," 19 Mar. 1915, "Bluestone Baptist Sunday School Union," 9 Apr. 1915, "The Evangelist Doing Great Work," 9 Apr. 1915, in McDowell Times, "Among Colored People," 3 July 1921, 16 Nov. 1924, and 6 Nov. 1932, in *Bluefield Daily Telegraph;* "Logan Colored News," 6 July 1923, 23 Mar. 1928, and 15 Mar. 1929, in *Logan Banner.*

24. "Bluestone Baptist Sunday School Union," 9 Apr. 1915, "Winding Gulf Ministers and Deacons Union," 19 Mar. 1915, "Great Revival Meeting at Excelsior," 5 Mar. 1915, in *McDowell Times;* "News of the Colored People," *Bluefield Daily Telegraph,* 16 Nov. 1924.

25. "Great Revival Meeting at Excelsior," 5 Mar. 1915, "Winding Gulf Ministers and Deacons' Union," 9 Mar. 1915, "The Ministers and Deacons," 24 Sept. 1915, in *McDowell Times;* "Among the Colored People," 3 July 1921, 16 Nov. 1924, and 6 Nov. 1932, in *Bluefield Daily Telegraph.*

26. "Winding Gulf Ministers and Deacons' Union," 19 Mar. 1915, "Baptists Install Pastor," 7 July 1916, "Sacred Concert at Rock Hill Baptist Church," 9 Apr. 1915, in *McDowell Times;* "Logan Colored News," 18 Nov. 1927, 6 Apr. 1928, and 15 Mar. 1929, in *Logan Banner.*

27. U.S. Bureau of the Census, *Religious Bodies, 1916,* 1:576–77, 2:100–101; *Religious Bodies, 1926,* 1:722–23, 2:130–39; "West Virginia Baptist Women's Convention," 20 Aug. 1915, "Baptist Women's District Convention is Held in Gary," 25 June 1915, "West Virginia [Baptist] Sunday School Convention Financial Rally Day," 3 Mar. 1916, and "Woman's Board Meeting a Success," 26 Jan. 1917, in *McDowell Times.* See also "Gary Colored News," *Welch Daily News,* 11 Feb. 1924, 14 July 1925.

28. "Dunbar Lyceum Notes," 5 Mar. 1915, "Dunbar Lyceum Hold[s] Big Meeting," 23 Apr. 1915, "A Successful Meeting," 7 Apr. 1916, "Bluestone Baptist Sunday School Union," 9 Apr. 1915, "A Successful Meeting, 7 Apr. 1916, and "Big Meeting at Marytown," 9 June 1916, in *McDowell Times;* "Churches," WVBNWS, *Biennial Report, 1921–22,* p. 78; "Logan Colored News," 18 Nov. 1927, 23 Mar. 1928, 6 Apr. 1928, and 15 Mar. 1929, in *Logan Banner;* "Among the Colored People," 12 June 1921, 3 July 1921, 16 Nov. 1924, and 6 Nov. 1932, in *Bluefield Daily Telegraph.*

29 "A Good Preacher," 13 Oct. 1916; "Rev. [C]oger Resigns Work at Northfork," 15 Dec. 1916; "Rev. Mitchell Tenders His Resignation," 19 Jan. 1917; "Rev. J. H. A. Cyrus an Able Man," 15 June 1917, all in *McDowell Times;* WVBNWS, *Biennial Reports, 1921–22,* pp. 77–80, *1923–24,* pp. 63–64, *1925–26,* pp. 84–86, and *1927–28,* pp. 64–66; interviews with Roy Todd,

18 July 1983, Andrew Campbell, 19 July 1983, and North E. Dickerson, 28 July 1983.

30. "Colored Folk Want Church in Keystone," *McDowell Times*, 15 Jan. 1915; "Thirty-Gallon Still Found Near Church," *Welch Daily News*, 21 Dec. 1923; WVBNWS, *Biennial Report, 1927–28*, pp. 66–67.

31. On the Columbia Orchestra, see the advertisement pages of the *McDowell Times*, 1915–18; "Rockhill Church Holds Good Service," 19 Feb. 1915, "Finger of Scorn: Play Before a Forty-Dollar House at Gary," 14 May 1915, "Rev. D. F. Turner at Northfork," 30 Nov. 1917, in *McDowell Times*; WVBNWS, *Biennial Report, 1927–28*, pp. 66–67.

32. "Baptists Install Pastor," 7 July 1916, "Installation Services," 16 Mar. 1917, "Ministers League," 11 Feb. 1916, "Winding Gulf Ministers and Deacons' Union," 19 Mar. 1915, "Bluestone Baptist Sunday School Union," 9 Apr. 1915 and 6 Oct. 1916, "An Ethical Conclusion," 25 June 1915, in *McDowell Times*; "Churches," WVBNWS, *Biennial Reports, 1921–22*, pp. 77–80, *1923–24*, pp. 63–64, *1925–26*, pp. 84–86, and *1927–28*, pp. 64–66.

33. "Rev. A. W. Randolph Remembered by His Members and Friends," 30 June 1916, "Rev. Crockett Stormed," 22 June 1917, "Rev. E. G. Holcomb, Thanks Good People of Mora," 9 Nov. 1917, in *McDowell Times*.

34. "Rev. J. W. Coger Thanks Galilee Baptist Church," *McDowell Times*, 26 Oct. 1917; "News of Welch Colored People," *Welch Daily News*, 4 Jan. 1924. See also "Gary Colored," *McDowell Recorder*, 23 Jan. 1925; "Superior Colored," *Welch Daily News*, 6 Dec. 1929; and "Logan Colored News," *Logan Banner*, 9 Nov. 1932.

35. "Rev. Crockett Remembered by His People," 15 Jan. 1915, "Preacher's Funeral," 30 July 1915, "Rev. W. C. Clements Greatly Remembered . . . at Coalwood," 4 June 1918, and "A Good Preacher," 13 Oct. 1916, in *McDowell Times*.

36. See "Don't Favor Woman Suffrage, Its a Fake," 15 Jan. 1915, "Dunbar Lyceum Holds Big Meeting," 23 Apr. 1915, in *McDowell Times*.

37. U.S. Bureau of the Census, *Religious Bodies, 1916*, 1:556; *Religious Bodies, 1926*, 1:722; WVBNWS, *Biennial Reports, 1921–22*, pp. 77–80, *1923–24*, pp. 63–64, *1925–26*, pp. 84–86, and *1927–28*, pp. 64–66.

38. "An Ethical Conclusion," *McDowell Times*, 25 June 1915.

39. WVBNWS, *Biennial Reports, 1921–22*, pp. 77–80, *1923–24*, pp. 63–64, *1925–26*, pp. 84–86, and *1927–28*, pp. 64–66.

40. "The District Conference," 3 Sept. 1915, "Doctor D. C. Coleman: Preacher's Able Sermon at Presbyterian Church," 3 Sept. 1915, "Conference of A.M.E. Church," 9 July 1915, "Church Work in Bluefield," 18 July 1915, "Grand Rally at Excelsior: A Huge Success," 3 Mar. 1916, and "Death of Mrs. Ada Williams," 27 Apr. 1917, in *McDowell Times*.

41. "Church Makes Good Showing: First Baptist at Charleston Holds Historical Anniversary Celebration," 18 June 1915, "Fiftieth Anniversary Celebration," 9 July 1915, in *McDowell Times*. See also First Baptist Church of Charleston, *The Bulletin*, 28 May 1922, in Box G-216, Charleston Branch Files, NAACP Papers; Joseph J. Boris, *Who's Who in Colored America*, vol. 1,

1927 (New York: Who's Who in Colored America Corp., 1927), pp. 108–9; Mary M. Spradling, ed., *In Black and White: A Guide to . . . Black Individuals and Groups* (Detroit: Gale Research Company, 1980), p. 517; Wilhelmina S. Robinson, *Historical Afro-American Biographies* (Cornwells Heights, Penn.: The Publishers Agency, Inc., under the auspices of the Association for the Study of Afro-American Life and History, 1978), pp. 215–16.

42. "Need of an Interdenominational Meeting," 12 Feb. 1915, "Great Revival Meeting at Excelsior," 5 Mar. 1915, "Dr. S. A. Viney is Claimed by Death," 7 May 1915, in *McDowell Times*; "Successful Rally," 17 Sept. 1915, "5th Anniversary," 31 Mar. 1916, "Help Rebuild Church," 3 Mar. 1916, "A Successful Meeting," 7 Apr. 1916, 25 Aug. 1916, 6 Oct. 1916, 23 Feb. 1917, and 13 Sept. 1918, all in *McDowell Times*; "News of the Colored People," *Bluefield Daily Telegraph*, 21 June 1921; "Logan Colored News," *Logan Banner*, 6 Apr. 1928; "Local Colored News," *Raleigh Register*, 3 July 1932.

43. "Ministers and Deacons' Union," 5 Nov. 1915, "Primitive Baptists Hold Important Meeting at Northfork," 14 May 1915, "Conference of A.M.E. Church," 9 July 1915, "Baptists Hold Big Meeting," 23 July 1915, "The District Conference," 3 Sept. 1915, "Mt. Olivet Baptist Association Meets," 28 July 1916, "Executive Board Meets," 28 July 1916, "Ministerial League," 25 Feb. 1916, "Great Meeting of the Baptists," 21 July 1916, "Flat Top Baptist Association," 20 July 1917, "New Association Organized," 21 Sept. 1917, "Primitive Baptist People Holds Second Annual Association in W.Va.," 17 Aug. 1917, "New Association Organized," 21 Sept. 1917, all in *McDowell Times*; WVBNWS, *Biennial Reports, 1921–22*, pp. 77–80, *1923–24*, pp. 63–64, and *1925–26*, pp. 84–86; "Elbert Colored News," 23 July 1925, "Gary Colored News," 14 and 17 July 1925, in *Welch Daily News*; "Logan Colored News," *Logan Banner*, 11 Nov. 1927, 23 Mar. 1928, 4 Nov. 1932.

44. "Dr. DuBois Lectures at Kimball," in "News of Colored People," *Bluefield Daily Telegraph*, 12 June 1921.

45. "Pioneer Preacher Back in Field," 29 Oct. 1915, "Robinson the Evangelist," 21 Apr. 1916, "Special Service in Keystone," 16 June 1916, "A Worthy Shepherd," 21 July 1916, "Rev. Hicks Pleased with Roanoke," 6 Oct. 1916, in *McDowell Times*. Also see "Logan Colored News," *Logan Banner*, 6 July 1923, 11 Nov. 1927.

46. "Pageton Holds a Big Community Meeting," *Welch Daily News*, 9 Feb. 1924, "Great Christian Revival at Cinderella," 4 June 1915, "Great Play: 'Finger of Scorn,' " 26 Feb. 1915, in *McDowell Times*. See also "Thacker Colored News," *Welch Daily News*, 30 Jan. 1924; "Logan Colored News," *Logan Banner*, 23 Mar. 1928.

8

Fraternal Orders

Closely aligned with black churches were black fraternal orders. Complete with marching band and full regalia, the fraternal order parades, thanksgiving services, and mutual benefit programs increased their importance in the lives of black workers in southern West Virginia in the 1915–32 period. While the parades, secret rituals, and religious services provided important social and cultural incentives for membership, fraternal insurance plans promised black miners protection against the vagaries of the proletarianization process. Yet, as elsewhere in black America during the war and postwar years, the black fraternal benefit programs were undermined by the rapid expansion of commercial insurance plans, the gradual growth of state employment compensation programs, and downswings in the coal economy.

Before their decline during the late 1920s, however, the fraternal orders played a key role, alongside the church, in transforming Afro-American institutional, cultural, and political life in the region. To help reinforce, and sometimes reconcile, their interest in both the spiritual and material welfare of their congregants, some black ministers joined the fraternal orders. Sometimes they even took leadership positions, and these enhanced their personal influence and economic standing. While serving the social welfare and cultural needs of the expanding black proletariat, the fraternal orders offered a substantial institutional framework for the expansion of the black elite. Black physicians, lawyers, and educators played a leading role in fraternal life.[1]

During the war years, the fraternal orders remained influential in the lives of southern West Virginia blacks. As in the prewar years, southern blacks who migrated to the region continued to join local fraternal bodies as well as churches. John L. Page migrated to southern West Virginia from Pembroke, Virginia, where his father belonged to the Knights of Pythias. In West Virginia the young Page joined a local chapter of the Ancient Free and Accepted Masons. When Roy Todd arrived in southern West Virginia from Alabama during the war years, he joined not only the Baptist Church but a local Masonic lodge as well. Originally from Ervington, Virginia, Walter H. Moorman became a member of both the Knights of Pythias and the Grand United Order of Odd Fellows in McDowell County. John M. Turner, from Floyd County, Virginia, soon joined the Masons and Odd Fellows in the Winding Gulf Field of Raleigh County.[2]

When Oscar Davis moved to southern West Virginia from Virginia, he joined the Knights of Pythias and discovered how important the material benefits of lodge membership could be when he lost a leg in a mining accident during the mid 1920s. Another black miner, born in Hickory, North Carolina, belonged to the United Order of Ethiopia, the Grand United Order of Odd Fellows, and the York Rite Masons upon his death in 1924. Miner and minister Wilford Dickerson, his son later recalled, held membership and offices in three fraternal orders: the Knights of Pythias, the Redmen, and the Masons, all of which provided benefit funds and insurance plans. Although the fraternal orders would decline as the new generation entered their coal-mining careers, until the late 1920s they retained a vital place in the lives of black coal miners and their families in southern West Virginia.[3]

By the mid-1920s, black membership in fraternal orders in West Virginia reached an estimated one-third of the state's total black population. As early as 1915, the Golden Rule Beneficial and Endowment Association expressed increasing optimism in its drive to become "the leading fraternal . . . organization of this state." During the war years, the organization had good reasons for optimism. In rapid succession Golden Rule established new lodges at Premier and Jenkinjones, McDowell County, in 1915; Pax, Fayette County, in 1916; and Bluefield, Mercer County, in 1917. Over a four-month period in 1918, one Golden Rule agent established five new lodges. The organization soon increased its membership from 5,500 in 1916 to 6,000 in 1917 and to 10,000 by the early 1920s, representing over two hundred subordinate lodges.[4]

The tremendous growth of Golden Rule was no exception. The Knights of Pythias, Odd Fellows, Masons, and Elks also opened new lodges during the war and postwar years. In the first half of 1916 alone, the Knights of Pythias added eight new lodges, bringing the total to seventy "strong lodges." At the nineteenth annual meeting of the state body, Burk's Garden Star Lodge of McDowell County won the order's first prize. It received $125 in gold for adding the largest number of new members. Similarly, the Odd Fellows reported "a flourishing condition" during the war years. Thomas Curry, grand district supervisor of the Elkhorn District of McDowell County, established fifteen new lodges, with over 700 members. In 1917, in recognition of his energetic and effective work, the West Virginia Odd Fellows awarded Curry first prize for the creation of new lodges.[5] The Odd Fellows increased their membership from 4,500 in 1921–22 to 8,471 in 1925–26, before dropping to 5,322 in 1927–28. While the Knights of Pythias also increased its membership during the 1920s, it peaked during the early 1920s, reaching over 7,500, before declining to 6,617 in 1925–26 and to 6,000 by 1927–28 (see table 8.1).

Although there is little data on the membership of the Elks and Masons during the war years, apparently by the early 1920s they had increased in prominence among black lodges in West Virginia. According to the BNWS, membership in black Masonic organizations—the Ancient Free and Accepted Masons and Heroines of Jericho and the Ancient Free and Accepted Masons and Eastern Star—rose from over 5,852 in 1921–22 to 6,100 in 1925–26, representing 188 subordinate lodges, before declining during the late 1920s. At the same time, the Improved Benevolent Protective Order of the Elks of the World increased from about 1,000 members in 1921–22 to nearly 2,000 in 1925–26, representing at least 20 subordinate lodges. Partly because of its small membership base, the Elks showed the most consistent growth. Whereas membership peaked in most organizations in 1925–26 or earlier, the Elks' membership peaked in 1927–28, at 5,000 members (see tables 8.1, 8.2).

No less than other facets of black life in the coalfields, the tremendous growth of black fraternal orders is not explained by migration alone. More significant, as suggested above, were the demographic and economic dynamics of the black working class's growth. In his 1922 report the grand chancellor of the Knights of Pythias explained the loss of 500 members over the previous year by pointing to the impact of the coal economy. "It is only going to be a short time before the coal strike and the railroad strike will be settled, and just as soon as those financial disturbances are adjusted times are going to pick up and I believe every man who desires to work will be able to find it. If that happy consummation is realized, there is no reason why we should not be able to get back every member we have lost this year and at the same time wonderfully increase our membership."[6]

TABLE 8.1
Membership in West Virginia Black Fraternal Orders, 1921–28

	1921–22		1923–24		1925–26		1927–28	
	Number	Percent	Number	Percent	Number	Percent	Number	Percent
Golden Rule Beneficial and Endowment Association	10,000	30.3	3,714	11.5	3,912	12.1	4,000	14.6
Knights of Pythias and Courts of Calanthe	7,515	22.8	7,252	22.5	6,617	20.6	6,000	21.9
Grand United Order of Odd Fellows and Households of Ruth	4,500	13.6	8,229	25.6	8,471	26.7	5,322	19.4
Ancient Free and Accepted Masons and Heroines of Jericho	3,840	11.6	4,450	13.8	3,700	11.5	N/A	N/A
Ancient Free and Accepted Masons and Eastern Star	2,012	6.1	2,350	7.3	2,400	7.4	2,000	7.3
Independent Order of St. Luke	3,851	11.6	4,625	14.3	5,000	15.5	5,000	18.3
Improved Benevolent Protective Order of the Elks of the World	1,052	3.1	1,519	4.7	1,982	6.1	5,000	18.3
Galilean Fishermen	190	0.5	N/A	N/A	N/A	N/A	N/A	N/A
Total	32,960	100.0	32,139	100.0	32,082	100.0	27,322	100.0

Source: West Virginia Bureau of Negro Welfare and Statistics, *Biennial Reports, 1921–22* (Charleston, W.Va.), p. 83, *1923–24,* p. 61, *1925–26,* p. 83, and *1927–28,* p. 71.

TABLE 8.2

Number of Subordinate Lodges, West Virginia Black Fraternal Orders, 1923–28

	1923–24		1925–26		1927–28	
	Number	Percent	Number	Percent	Number	Percent
Golden Rule Beneficial and Endowment Association	258	25.3	244	24.0	95	11.5
Knights of Pythias and Courts of Calanthe	240	23.5	252	24.8	265	32.3
Grand United Order of Odd Fellows and Households of Ruth	216	21.1	191	18.8	170	20.7
Ancient Free and Accepted Masons and Heroines of Jericho	126	12.3	113	11.1	N/A	N/A
Ancient Free and Accepted Masons and Eastern Star	55	5.3	75	7.3	60	7.3
Independent Order of St. Luke	112	10.9	119	11.7	110	13.4
Improved Benevolent Protective Order of the Elks of the World	12	1.1	20	1.9	119	14.5
Galileean Fishermen	N/A	N/A	N/A	N/A	N/A	N/A
Totals	1,019	100.0	1,014	100.0	819	100.0

Note: Data not available for 1921–22.

Source: West Virginia Bureau of Negro Welfare and Statistics, *Biennial Report, 1923–24* (Charleston, W.Va.), p. 83, *1925–26*, p. 83, and *1927–28*, p. 71.

With the rising membership of black coal miners, the fraternal orders reported growing financial success. During World War I, for example, Golden Rule established an initiation fee of $2.50, regular monthly dues of 50 cents, and a small monthly fee that varied with the extent of each member's insurance coverage. In 1916 the Golden Rule leadership enthusiastically reported that the association "is moving on. . . . Reports are coming into the office daily showing that old members are paying up and new members enrolling [in] nearly all of the subordinate associations." The organization raised $5,176 during that year, increasing the value of the real estate it held from $6,600 to $8,000. As black coal miners lost jobs in the postwar years, that value dropped to $6,000 in 1921–22; however, as black miners returned to work, it recovered and expanded, increasing from $15,000 in 1923–24 to $45,000 in 1927–28.[7] The Odd Fellows and Knights of Pythias improved their financial position even more than the Golden Rule did. The combined value of the real estate of the orders' subordinate bodies increased to over $70,000 during the mid-1920s.[8] The Masons, Elks, and a few other fraternal orders also improved their financial standing.[9]

As they did in the prewar years, the fraternal orders reinforced the spiritual and communal traditions of Afro-Americans. Official thanksgiving proclamations regularly entreated fraternal units to "meet in some convenient place, and in some appropriate manner thank Almighty God for His manifold blessings to our brotherhood in the year that has gone, and implore His protection and guidance in years that are to come."[10] In mid-1915, the Knights of Pythias of Keystone and Eckman, McDowell County, celebrated their annual thanksgiving at the Wingfield Baptist Church. The Pythians marched to the church in a parade behind the local Keystone-Eckman brass band. When dressed in full regalia, the fraternal brothers were sometimes described as resembling "soldiers ready for battle." In 1917, led by the Eckman-Landgraf Cornet Band, the Rising Sun chapter of the Golden Rule Association met at Lord's Hall in Keystone and marched to the Past-Time Theatre in Eckman. "Uniformly regaled" in the colors of their lodge, the *McDowell Times* reported, "It was composed of as fine a set of men as have been seen on the streets of Keystone." In 1925, the column "Gary Colored News" reported a similar parade, an annual event sponsored by the Elks, which the whole city enjoyed. The Elk marchers were led by mounted marshals and the Elbert-Filbert band. The marshals, arrayed in their "bright and sparkling regalia," presented "quite a pleasing spectacle."[11]

These Thanksgiving parades usually culminated at local churches, where members heard sermons and speeches by local black religious, fraternal, and civic leaders. Black leaders used the thanksgiving services to heighten black consciousness and racial solidarity. On such occasions, calls for racial unity, manhood, and strength emerged supreme. In a sermon before the Knights of Pythias, the Baptist minister, Rev. W. H. Mitchell "pointed out many of the [social] evils to be found in the coalfields and pointed out means for correcting them." He emphasized the value of racial unity, and the need for each man to constitute himself "the keeper of the other." Speaking before an annual thanksgiving gathering of Pythians, in 1917 Grand Chancellor L. O. Wilson took his text from Genesis 4:9: "And the Lord said unto Cain, where is Abel thy brother? And he said, I know not: Am I my brother's keeper?" For the next hour Wilson "dealt sledge-hammer blows on the fact that we are our brother's keeper."[12]

In a thanksgiving sermon before the Odd Fellows and their families, Rev. R. P. Johnson of the black Presbyterian church likewise emphasized racial solidarity. Like Rev. Mitchell, Johnson took his text from First Samuel, 4:9. "Be strong and quit yourselves like men . . . and fight." The fraternal addresses not only exhorted the brothers to be strong, but also expressed confidence in their ability to do so. One minister appealed to the men to "never say 'I can't,' but to have written over their doors—I can." Such encouragement of racial solidarity, strength, initiative, and confidence struck a deep and responsive chord among blacks in the coalfields. As one minister spoke on these themes, the *McDowell Times* reported, "it could be seen at once that he had the ear of every man, woman, boy and girl. The most rapt attention was paid him from the time he started till he closed." Likewise, despite searing heat, in mid-July 1925 the Elks packed the Baptist church at Gary to hear the principal speaker stress the virtues of "loyalty, fidelity, brotherly love and harmonious cooperation in all things."[13]

The fraternal parades, replete with colorful banners and flags, uniforms, music, and disciplined processions, along with the sermons that went with them, attracted broad public attention. Because they reinforced Afro-American spiritual and communal traditions, they were enormously attractive to black workers, who were making the transition from rural and semi-rural life to a new industrial setting. The fraternal orders also succeeded because they offered economic buffers against the vagaries of the proletarianization process. Perhaps more than anything else, they promised economic security against hard times. Moreover, the constant exposure of black coal miners to dangerous working conditions, the discriminatory policies of white insurance companies, and the dearth of employment opportunities for black women also worked to endear the fraternal orders to black workers.

The fraternal orders provided aid to members in distress and their families including unemployment, death, and sickness benefits. In 1916 the Baptist minister Rev. R. R. Henry praised the Knights of Pythias for "caring for the sick, burying the dead, relieving suffering and protecting and succoring widows and orphans." The Golden Rule Association announced that it was "not only a convenience," but "a necessity" in the lives of its members, aiding them "in time of sickness and death, furnishing the money in some cases to purchase the coffin before they could bury their dead, and pay[ing] all death claims in Thirty Days." By August 1916, Golden Rule had paid out $12,141 in sick claims and another $12,550 in death claims, all based upon a $2.50 initiation fee and a small monthly sum thereafter. Death claims alone reached $15,000 in 1917.[14] By the mid-1920s black fraternal orders in West Virginia had collectively disbursed nearly $250,000 in death, burial, sickness, and endowment benefits, revealing the growing economic importance of black fraternal insurance and mutual benefit programs.[15]

Along with black men, black women played a crucial role in the mutual benefit societies, through female auxiliaries of the Masons, Elks, Odd Fellows, and Knights of Pythias that expanded as their affiliated fraternal orders did. Black men increasingly praised the female auxiliary as a "very-important arm of the lodge." In 1915 the Masons at Williamson signaled this shift in attitude when they broke with tradition and invited women to attend their annual banquet. Under the continuing leadership of Mrs. Malinda Cobbs, the Independent Order of St. Luke increased its role in the fraternal life of the region. Assisted by her special deputy, Mrs. W. O. Moore, Cobbs traveled widely in southern West Virginia, promoting the order in the most remote coal-mining communities, including War, Excelsior, and Jenkinjones, McDowell County. Compared to other black fraternal orders, the Independent Order of St. Luke seems to have provided unusual opportunities for female leadership.[16]

Despite substantial gender and racial solidarity, the fraternal orders unfortunately mirrored larger patterns of socioeconomic inequality within the black community. In 1923–24, for example, the Knights of Pythias and the Odd Fellows and their auxiliaries made up 44.6 percent of fraternal bodies; yet, among subordinate lodges, the two orders accounted for over 70 percent of the value of lodge-owned real estate, 88 percent of lodge-owned property, and 60 percent of the cash on hand. This pattern of inequality was even stronger during the economic expansion of the mid-1920s. With 41.3 percent of the total membership in black fraternal orders and their auxiliaries (see table 8.1), and with 53 percent of all constituent bodies in 1927–28 (table 8.2), local chapters and auxiliaries of the Knights of Pythias and the Odd Fellows commanded over 94 percent of the value of real estate, about 60 percent of personal property, and over 75 percent of the cash on hand (tables 8.3 and 8.4).[17]

While the fraternal membership was predominantly working class, the leadership was dominated by black business and professional people. Black physicians, attorneys, educators, and influential ministers were most prominent in the Knights of Pythias and the Odd Fellows. During the war years, L. O. Wilson, the West Virginia state librarian, served as grand chancellor of the Knights of Pythias. Other state officers included the high-school principal and minister Rev. J. W. Robinson, grand vice chancellor, Kimball, McDowell County; the schoolteacher, C. W. Boyd, grand keeper of records, Charleston, Kanawha County; the physician Dr. N. L. Edwards, grand master of exchequer, Bluefield, Mercer County; the physician Dr. R. G. Harrison, grand medical register, Kimball, McDowell County; Rev. J. Turner, grand prelate, Kimberly, Fayette County; and the editor M. T. Whittico, grand lecturer, Keystone, McDowell County. Rev. J. W. Robinson replaced Wilson as grand chancellor in 1918; the Charleston attorney and prominent Elk T. G. Nutter occupied the post during the early 1920s. This office and others later changed hands, but the elite make-up of the Pythians' leadership continued.[18] The black bourgeoisie also dominated the leadership of the Odd Fellows, Masons, and Elks.[18]

Although elites dominated state and local chapters of the fraternal orders, at the local level, working-class blacks had greater access to leadership positions. In McDowell County, the list of officers of the Berwind Success Lodge Number 41, Knights of Pythias, included J. D. Hairston, a coal miner, and Pete Williams, also evidently a coal miner. The twelve-member Maybeury Star Lodge, Knights of Pythias, had mostly working-class officers. The *Times* reported, "They are at the heads of families, good church members and believe in educating their children."[19] The Golden Rule Beneficial and Endowment Association, though, provided perhaps the most liberal opportunities for working-class leadership. At its thirteenth annual meeting, for example, the coal miner, R. L. Benton,

TABLE 8.3
Value of Real Estate Held by Subordinate Bodies of West Virginia Black Fraternal Orders, 1921–28

	1921–22		1923–24		1925–26		1927–28	
	Dollar Amount	Percent	Dollar Amount	Percent	Dollar Amount	Percent	Dollar Amount	Percent
Golden Rule Beneficial and Endowment Association	6,000	4.2	N/A	N/A	N/A	N/A	N/A	N/A
Knights of Pythias and Courts of Calanthe	18,000	12.8	20,000	15.6	70,000	36.1	83,665	45.5
Grand United Order of Odd Fellows and Households of Ruth	58,900	42.1	75,000	58.8	90,000	46.5	90,000	49.0
Ancient Free and Accepted Masons and Heroines of Jericho	15,000	10.7	15,000	11.7	20,500	10.5	N/A	N/A
Ancient Free and Accepted Masons and Eastern Star	15,000	10.7	15,000	11.7	10,000	5.1	10,000	5.4
Independent Order of St. Luke	2,500	1.7	N/A	N/A	N/A	N/A	N/A	N/A
Improved Benevolent Protective Order of the Elks of the World	15,400	11.0	2,500	1.9	3,000	1.5	N/A	N/A
Galileean Fishermen	9,000	6.4	N/A	N/A	N/A	N/A	N/A	N/A
Totals	139,800	100.0	127,500	100.0	193,500	100.0	183,665	100.0

Source: West Virginia Bureau of Negro Welfare and Statistics, *Biennial Report, 1921–22* (Charleston, W.Va.), p. 83, *1923–24*, p. 83, *1925–26*, p. 61, *1925–26*, p. 83, and *1927–28*, p. 71.

TABLE 8.4
Cash on Hand of Subordinate Lodges, West Virginia Black Fraternal Orders, 1921–28

	1921–22		1923–24		1925–26		1927–28	
	Dollar Amount	Percent	Dollar Amount	Percent	Dollar Amount	Percent	Dollar Amount	Percent
Golden Rule Beneficial and Endowment Association	1,500	1.6	2,000	2.3	3,500	4.7	1,566	2.4
Knights of Pythias and Courts of Calanthe	29,000	31.9	15,000	17.8	25,000	33.8	25,000	38.4
Grand United Order of Odd Fellows and Households of Ruth	33,250	36.5	35,000	41.7	25,000	33.8	25,000	38.4
Ancient Free and Accepted Masons and Heroines of Jericho	19,300	21.2	22,500	26.8	7,250	9.8	N/A	N/A
Ancient Free and Accepted Masons and Eastern Star	6,000	6.6	5,000	5.9	7,000	9.4	7,000	10.7
Independent Order of St. Luke	1,800	1.9	2,300	2.7	2,700	3.6	3,700	5.6
Improved Benevolent Protective Order of the Elks of the World	N/A	N/A	2,000	2.3	3,500	4.7	2,700	4.1
Galileean Fishermen	N/A	N/A	N/A	N/A	N/A	N/A	N/A	N/A
Total	90,850	100.0	83,800	100.0	73,950	100.0	64,966	100.0

Source: West Virginia Bureau of Negro Welfare and Statistics, Biennial Report, 1921–22, (Charleston, W.Va.), p. 83, 1923–24, p. 61, 1925–26, p. 83, and 1927–28, p. 71.

delivered an address titled "How to Build up a Good Association." Benton "aroused and enthused everybody as nothing else," and "everybody went away talking about that milk and butter address." On a platform that included Professor R. P. Sims, president of Bluefield Collegiate Institute, Richard Hamm of Elkhorn, also evidently a coal miner, followed Benton and "kept the house in a roar of laughter at his original ideas of how to work in this order."[20] Although educated blacks probably treated their working-class counterparts condescendingly at such meetings, by extending its platform to coal miners, the Golden Rule Association strengthened the leadership role of black workers.

More than the other fraternal orders, Golden Rule also appealed to the religious traditions of Afro-Americans. Through the payment of claims in person, often by the president himself, the order vigorously publicized its insurance programs. In numerous churches throughout the region, the order paid claims before "very large crowd[s]," with Rev. McKoy offering "able, forceful and practical talk[s] on the merits of the institution, its far-reaching effects and the lasting good being accomplished by the society."[21] By highlighting tragedies that had befallen black families, these claim-paying ceremonies generated interest in the Golden Rule.

Nevertheless, however close the Golden Rule Association may have been to the black working class, its leadership and ideology reflected middle-class values. Golden Rule promoted the values of thrift, sobriety, and disciplined labor. "Live within your means," Rev. McKoy exclaimed in a sermon before the Rising Star Association of Golden Rule. "Our women and too many of our men are too much inclined to follow styles. Wear what you can pay for," he concluded, in an address that lasted "for one hour and 20 minutes." On another occasion, Rev. McKoy exhorted ministers, physicians, lawyers, teachers, and journalists to "invest a part of their money in colored enterprises," in order to "employ a greater number of our people than we are employing today."[22] In its emphasis on racial solidarity, self-help, and thrift, Golden Rule echoed a common theme of the black fraternal orders.[23]

Although thrift and racial solidarity were part of the black miners' broad constellation of survival strategies, the intensity of the elite campaign promoting them undoubtedly precipitated class conflicts within the fraternal orders. Although the precise evidence on this important issue is sparse, it is certain that most black coal miners found it exceedingly difficult to pay regular dues and insurance fees. Many were forced to cut their enrollments short. Even during the best of times, the black fraternal insurance plans operated on a highly fragile basis, unable to pay more than a minimum of death and injury benefits at any given time. During the war years, for example, one lodge found it difficult to meet its regular financial obligations, even to members in good standing. The leadership painfully reported: "For the past 12 months this lodge has been confronted with a number of serious embarassments. A number of deaths among members of this lodge have been the sad experiences of our members. Much sickness has claimed our attention. Thus it is that our financial treasury is not any fatter nor in a more favorable state of condition." In the spring of 1917 the grand lodge of the Knights of Pythias suspended several subordinate bodies for failure to meet their financial obligations.[24]

Despite the tremendous expansion of the fraternal orders during the war and postwar years, they gradually declined. The membership in black fraternal orders in West Virginia peaked at 32,960 in 1921–22 and gradually declined to 32,139 in 1923–24, 32,082 in 1925–26, and to 27,322 in 1927–28; thereafter, precise statistics are unavailable because of the effects of the Depression (see table 8.1). Reminiscent of what one historian has called "the heyday of the small, local mutual benefit society," the Golden Rule Beneficial and Endowment Association declined: "the larger and more strictly insurance society" taking its place.[25] More important, black fraternal orders in West Virginia were eroded not only by the rapid expansion of commercial insurance corporations, but also by the expansion of state workmen's compensation laws by the mid-1920s, by the continuing highly precarious economic status of black coal miners and their families, and especially by the onset of the Great Depression.

Throughout most of the 1920s, the BNWS lauded and sometimes exaggerated the role of the black fraternal orders as cushions against hard times in coal-mining towns. During the late 1920s and early 30s, however, no mention of the fraternal orders appeared in the bureau's reports, suggesting the orders' growing inability to meet the needs of the depression years. A black coal miner offered a bitter assessment of this process. Recalling the experiences of his father, Walter E. Moorman related: "During the Depression the Odd Fellows just like file bankruptcy. . . . The big fish ate up the little ones my daddy told me. So everybody higher up got all the money. Those down low didn't get anything, they got crumbs."[26]

During their most introspective and self-critical moments, black fraternal leaders sometimes admitted and even decried the exploitative dimensions of the fraternal orders. As early as 1917, in his address before the thirteenth annual meeting of the Golden Rule Association, Rev. McKoy condemned fraternal policies and practices that took unfair advantage of the black working class. "Too many of our educated people have manifested no interest in their illiterate brothers, further than to get from him the dollar." Likewise, in its 1927–28 biennial report, the BNWS for the first time admitted that "many of these so-called secret societies or fraternal orders have been dismal failures and that much of the hard earnings of poor deserving Negroes have been squandered."[27]

Despite their weaknesses, however, Afro-American fraternal orders played a crucial role in the larger community life of coal-mining towns. Excluded from white fraternal bodies, blacks found in their own fraternal organizations an important institutional alternative. Like churches, fraternal orders and their auxiliaries offered blacks access to leadership positions and a chance to exercise initiative and enjoy essential fellowship with their brothers and sisters. The various orders often shared the same buildings, contributed to common causes, and held joint meetings that sometimes took on the intensity of a crusade. In the winter of 1917, three men, including coal miner R. L. Benton, formed a committee and pushed for a unified interfraternity installation service in McDowell County. In addition to an "all-night dance," the committee proposed a program of speeches, featuring representatives from "every important fraternal order now in operation throughout this field."[28]

Echoing the black churches' experience, cooperation among the fraternal orders crossed state lines. During the war years, the West Virginia–based Golden Rule Association expanded into southwestern Virginia. In 1917, at Tazewell, Virginia, the association laid the cornerstone for a new building. During World War I the Charleston, West Virginia, attorney T. G. Nutter won a third term to national office as Grand Exalted Ruler of the Improved Benevolent Protective Order of the Elks of the World, U.S.A., after having received a plethora of letters from many states supporting his reelection. In 1918, another Charleston black, John Noel, an influential Odd Fellow, was elected Grand Master of the national organization. At the national parade and band competitions featured at the national meetings of the fraternal orders, West Virginia units sometimes won first prize.[29]

The fraternal orders also helped to stimulate a degree of interracial cooperation, especially among black and white elites. In 1918 when the Ninth District, Knights of Pythias, met at Holden, Logan

County, a white minister offered the welcome address, the white county prosecutor delivered a speech, and the white general manager of the Island Creek Coal Company attended the event, all giving "some encouraging remarks." In July 1925 at its annual memorial service, the Gary Elks invited colonel E. O'Toole, manager of the U.S. Coal and Coke Company, to serve as its guest speaker. He did not appear, but, in his absence, Claude Baugner, manager of the firm's store, the United Supply Company, gave a speech that "was well received." Above all, however, it was the fraternal parades that brought blacks and whites together. Accounts of parades frequently described the intermingling of blacks and whites along the parade routes: "men and women, boys and girls, both white and colored assembled on the sidewalks and hedges to see this parade."[30]

Substantial evidence of black-white amity notwithstanding, interracial fraternity was highly uneven, and it was often opportunistic on both sides of the color line. Coal companies viewed their support of the fraternal orders in the same way they viewed their support of black churches—as a mechanism to recruit and retain black workers. Their support was expressed through contributions as well as personal appearances at special meetings. For their part, black elites, while serving the needs of the expanding working class, also worked to enhance their own prestige and economic position by cementing ties with the larger white community. Nonetheless, like religious ecumenism in the southern mountains, interracial fraternity, inadequate as it was, still at least helped to prevent racial conflict in coal-mining towns.

During World War I and the immediate postwar years, black fraternal orders expanded in southern West Virginia along with black churches. Racial exclusion, patterns of black migration, increasing race consciousness, and the expansion of the black industrial working class all fueled this growth. In essence, though, black mutual aid societies and secret orders reflected the black community's search for economic security against the vagaries of the coal economy. As black coal miners increasingly lost their economic foothold during the late 1920s and early 1930s, like black religious institutions, black fraternal organizations declined, revealing their deep roots within the proletarianization process.

Although the fraternal membership was predominantly working class, black elites dominated leadership positions and used them as a platform for their own class values and to receive disproportionate personal rewards. Black workers, however, were not passive. They pursued their class, racial, and material interests within the framework of their own shifting spiritual and cultural needs. They used the fraternal order not only as a means of economic survival, but also as a means of adapting their cultural traditions to meet the new material and social demands of the expanding industrial system.

NOTES

1. For insight into black fraternal orders during the industrial period, see August Meier, *Negro Thought in America, 1880–1915: Racial Ideologies in the Age of Booker T. Washington* (Ann Arbor: University of Michigan Press, 1963), pp. 14–15, 136–38, and 141–44; Ivan H. Light, *Ethnic Enterprise in America: Business and Welfare among Chinese, Japanese, and Blacks* (Berkeley: University of California Press, 1972), pp. 152–60; Elizabeth R. Bethel, *Promiseland: A Century of Life in a Negro Community* (Philadelphia: Temple University Press, 1981), pp. 162–70; George C. Wright, *Life Behind a Veil: Blacks in Louisville Kentucky, 1865–1930* (Baton Rouge: Louisiana State University Press, 1985), pp. 132–35; Gunnar Myrdal, *An American Dilemma: The Negro Problem and American Democracy* (1944; rept., New York: Pantheon Books, 1962), 2:952–95.

2. Interviews with John Page, 14 July 1983, Roy Todd 18 July 1983, Walter E. and Margaret Moorman, 14 July 1983, and Charlotte P. Wallington, 21 July 1983.

3. Interviews with Leonard Davis, 28 July 1983, North Dickerson, 28 July 1983, and Lawrence Boling, 18 July 1983; "Enormous Crowds Attends Last Rites," *Welch Daily News*, 6 Feb. 1924; "Colored Lodges Scrap Over Burial Privilege," *McDowell Recorder*, 16 Jan. 1925.

4. "Golden Rule News," 12 Mar. 1915, 10 Mar. and 14 Apr. 1916, "New Year's Greetings: To the members of Golden Rule," 8 Jan. 1915, "Golden Rule People Hold 11th Annual Session at Bramwell," 4 June 1915, 9 June and 1 Dec. 1916, 12 Jan. 1917, "Golden Rule Hold Meeting," 16 Mar. 1917, "New Golden Rule in Keystone," 20 Sept. 1918, "Golden Rule Hold Annual Meeting," 1 June 1917, in *McDowell Times;* "Colored People," *Bluefield Daily Telegraph,* 16 May 1920; "Fraternal and Beneficial Societies," in West Virginia Bureau of Negro Welfare and Statistics (WVBNWS), *Biennial Report, 1921–22,* p. 83.

5. "Knights of Pythias Instituted at Beckley," 12 May 1916, "Proclamation No. 1: Grand Lodge Knights of Pythias," 25 Aug. 1916, "Knights of Pythias Proclamation 3," 2 Mar. 1917, "New Knights of Pythias Lodge," 3 Mar. 1916, "Pythian[s] Hold Big, Successful Meeting," 10 Aug. 1917, "Finds Lodges Prosperous," 19 May 1916, "Thomas Curry Wins Prize," 24 Aug. 1917, in *McDowell Times;* "Fraternal and Beneficial Societies," in WVBNWS, *Biennial Reports, 1921–22,* p. 83, and *1925–26,* p. 81.

6. "Grand Lodge Knights of Pythias in West Virginia . . . Proclamation No. 1," 10 Aug. 1922, Charleston, West Virginia Branch Files, Box G-215, NAACP Papers, Library of Congress.

7. "New Year's Greetings," 8 Jan. 1915, "Golden Rule Moving Ahead," 23 June 1916, "Golden Rule News," 25 Aug. 1916, in *McDowell Times;* WVBNWS, *Biennial Reports, 1921–22*, p. 83, *1923–24*, p. 61, *1925–26*, p. 83, and *1927–28*, p. 71.

8. "A Great Meeting," 20 Aug. 1915, "District Grand Lodge, G.U.O. of O.F. No. 31," 24 Aug. 1917, "Odd Fellows at Eckman," 27 Apr. 1917, in *McDowell Times;* WVBNWS, *Biennial Reports, 1921–22*, p. 83, *1923–24*, pp. 61, 83, *1925–26*, pp. 81–83, and *1927–28*, p. 71; "The Knights of Pythias Hold Successful Session," 11 Aug. 1916, "Proclamation No. 1: Grand Lodge Knights of Pythias," 25 Aug. 1916, "Pythians Hold Big Successful Meeting," 10 Aug. 1917, "Burk's Garden Star Lodge, No. 56: Making Great Headway," 7 July 1916, in *McDowell Times;* "Grand Lodge Knights of Pythias of West Virginia," Charleston, W.Va., Branch Files, Box G-215, NAACP Papers.

9. For data on the Masons and Elks, see "Masonic Reception," 12 Mar. 1915, "Grand Master A. P. Straughter Dead," 4 Feb. 1916, "Masons Meet," 30 June 1916, "Elks Ask Courts to Enjoin Negro Order," 1 Sept. 1916, "Elks 17th Convention: History-Making Event," 8 Sept. 1916, "I.B.P.O.E. of the World," 20 Sept. 1918, "Colored Masons Meet," 20 Sept. 1918, 2 Mar. 1917, in *McDowell Times;* "Gary Colored News," 12 and 24 Dec. 1923, 8 and 12 Jan. 1924, 1, 8, 11, and 13 July 1925, 6 Feb. 1924, in *Welch Daily News.*

10. See "Knights of Pythias Proclamation 3," *McDowell Times,* 2 Mar. 1917. Also see "Hemphill Colored Masons Install," *Welch Daily News,* 18 Dec. 1923; "Colored People," *Bluefield Daily Telegraph,* 16 May 1920, 15 June 1921, and 1 Jan. 1928.

11. "Grand Chancellor Attends Thankgsgiving Services," 4 June 1915, "Odd Fellows," 14 May 1915, "Big Turn Out of Odd Fellows," 18 May 1917, "Pythians Celebrate," 31 Mar. 1916, "Thanksgiving Services," 20 July 1917, in *McDowell Times;* "Gary Colored News," *Welch Daily News,* 11 and 13 July 1925; "Logan Colored News," *Logan Banner,* 15 Mar. 1929; "Negro Fraternal Orders Convene," *McDowell Recorder,* 24 July 1929.

12. "Grand Chancellor Attends Thanksgiving Services," *McDowell Times,* 4 June 1915; "Hemphill Colored Masons to Install," *Welch Daily News,* 18 Dec. 1923; "Knights of Pythias and Calanthes," *McDowell Times,* 25 May 1917.

13. "Big Turn Out of Odd Fellows," *McDowell Times,* 18 May 1917, "Gary Colored News," 11 and 13 July 1925, "Enormous Crowds . . . ," 6 Feb. 1925, in *Welch Daily News.*

14. "Thanksgiving Service Good," 4 Aug. 1916, "New Year's Greetings," 8 Jan. 1915, "Golden Rule News," 18 Aug. 1916 in *McDowell Times.*

15. "Masons Renew Contract with Bluefield Hospital," *McDowell Times,* 9 Apr. 1915; WVBNWS, *Biennial Reports, 1921–22* pp. 82–83, and *1927–28*, p. 71.

16. "Masonic Reception," 12 Mar. 1915, "District Grand Lodge, G.U.O. of O.F. No. 31," 24 Aug. 1917, "New K. of P. Lodge," 23 July 1915, "New Court of Calanthe Set Up [at] Jenkinjones," 20 July 1917, "Peter Ogden Day Celebrated at Tams," 12 Mar. 1915, "Odd Fellows Hold Big Meeting at Gary," 22 Dec. 1916, "The Knights of Pythias Hold Big, Successful Meeting," 10 Aug. 1917, "Knights of Pythias," 24 May 1918, "Big Turn Out of Odd Fellows," 18 May 1917, "Thanksgiving Service Good," 4 Aug. 1916, reports of the Independent Order of St. Lukes, 14 May 1915, 28 July 1916, 1 June 1917, 10 Aug. 1917, 31 Aug. 1917, and 12 Oct. 1917, all in *McDowell Times;* BNWS, *Biennial Reports, 1921–22,* p. 83, *1925–26,* pp. 61, 83, *1923–24,* pp. 59–62, *1927–28,* p. 71; "Gary Colored News," *Welch Daily News,* 1 and 6 July 1925.

17. WVBNWS, *Biennial Report, 1927–28,* p. 71.

18. "A Great Meeting," 13 Aug. 1915, "The Knights of Pythias," 11 Aug. 1916, "$1,000 Paid on Charleston Building," 17 May 1918, "John S. Noel, Grand Master of Odd Fellows," 13 Sept. 1918, "Grand Lodge Masons," 22 June 1917, in *McDowell Times;* "State Librarian," in John T. Harris, ed., *West Virginia Legislative Hand Book* (Charleston, W.Va.: The Tribune Printing Company, 1916), p. 809; "Grand Lodge of Knights of Pythias of West Virginia," 10 Aug. 1922, in W.Va. Branch Files, Box G-215, NAACP Papers.

19. *McDowell Times,* 4 Feb., 23 and 30 June 1916, 9 and 23 Mar., 27 Apr., and 13 July 1917, and 20 Sept. 1918.

20. Ibid., 12 Jan. and 4 June 1915, 1 Dec. 1916, 1 June 1917, and 8 Mar. 1918.

21. Ibid., 12 Feb. and 12 Mar. 1915, 25 Aug., 20 Oct., and 1 Dec. 1916.

22. Ibid., 20 July 1917, and "Address of Rev. McKoy," 8 June 1917.

23. "Thanksgiving Service Good," 4 Aug. 1916, "Thanksgiving Services," 20 July 1927, in *McDowell Times;* "Gary Colored News," *Welch Daily News,* 13 July 1925; WVBNWS, *Biennial Report, 1923–24,* p. 59.

24. "Pythians' Lodges Recently Visited by the Grand Lecturer," *McDowell Times,* 14 July 1916. See also *McDowell Times,* 28 July 1916, 2 Mar. 1917, and 26 Jan. 1917.

25. Meier, *Negro Thought in America,* p. 137.

26. WVBNWS, *Biennial Reports, 1921–22,* p. 83, *1923–24,* p. 61, *1925–26,* p. 83, and *1927–28,* pp. 70–71; interview with Walter and Margaret Moorman, 14 July 1983.

27. "Address of Rev. R. H. McKoy," *McDowell Times,* 8 June 1917; WVBNWS, *Biennial Report, 1927–28,* p. 69.

28. "Masonic Reception," 12 Mar. 1915, "Public Invited to Public Installation and Reception," 19 Jan. 1917, in *McDowell Times.*

29. "Bluegrass Association: Golden Rules of Tazewell Virginia," 27 July 1917, "Stands for Re-Election: Grand Chancellor T. G. Nutter to Again Head Elks," 18 July 1915, "John S. Noel, Grand Master of Odd Fellows," 13 Sept. 1918, in *McDowell Times.* See also *McDowell Times,* 27 Aug. 1915, 18 Aug. 1916, 22 June 1917, and 17 May 1918.

30. "Knights of Pythias," *McDowell Times*, 24 May 1918; "Gary Colored News," *Welch Daily News*, 13 July 1925; "Thanksgiving Services," 20 July 1917, "Pythians Hold Big Successful Meeting," 10 Aug. 1917, 14 May 1915, 31 Mar. 1916, and 18 May 1917, in *McDowell Times*; "Gary Colored News," *Welch Daily News*, 13 July 1925.

9

Proletarianization, Politics, and the
Limits of Black Power

Afro-American religious and fraternal organizations, intertwined
as they were with the changing black class structure, established
the leadership and institutional foundations for the political and
civil rights struggle of blacks in southern West Virginia. Because
West Virginia blacks, like blacks elsewhere in the border states,
retained the franchise,[1] the rise and expansion of the black coal-
mining proletariat offered unusual opportunities for black political leaders. Middle-class black leaders developed numerous black
Republican clubs through which they skillfully appealed to the socioeconomic, political, and cultural interests of the growing proletarian electorate. They also built interracial alliances with whites,
especially Republicans, though black Democratic clubs also slowly
emerged. Through the dual mobilization of black workers and white
allies, black politicians achieved favorable civil rights legislation,
court decisions, and policy changes. Nonetheless, while black miners united behind middle-class leaders, they also exhibited dissatis-
faction with the black bourgeois leadership, most dramatically in
their use of violence in the Winding Gulf Field and in the rise of the
Garvey Movement.

Although black coal miners soon discovered the limitations of violent action and Garveyism, nonetheless, both helped to stimulate
the vigorous expansion of the National Association for the Advancement of Colored People during the 1920s. The NAACP moved
increasingly to the forefront of black civil rights activism and represented the most important new political departure for southern
West Virginia blacks between World War I and the Great Depression. This chapter explores the electoral strategies of southern West
Virginia blacks, and the following chapter analyzes the emergence

and expansion of the Garvey movement and the NAACP and the increasing use of civil rights protest together with electoral strategies to achieve social change.

As the proletarianization of southern West Virginia blacks and increasing migration to the region coincided with the advent of woman's suffrage in 1920, the potential political power of blacks increased. The number of voting-age blacks increased from about 15,300 in 1910 to over 34,500 in 1920 and to almost 45,300 in 1930 (see table 9.1), increasing the potential pool of black voters by approximately 30,000—nearly a 200 percent increase. In McDowell County, where blacks were most heavily concentrated, the number of voting-age blacks rose from about 5,900 in 1910 to over 10,400 in 1920 and to 12,500 in 1930 (see table 9.2). As the second generation of white immigrants came of age and became eligible to vote, the black percentage of the potential voting pool dropped from 17.6 percent in 1910 to 15.5 percent in 1930, but a persistently large number of unnaturalized immigrants limited the importance of the immigrant vote. As late as 1930, for example, over 60 percent of the immigrants in southern West Virginia were unnaturalized, and in 1920 the figure was even higher, at about 80 percent.[2] Thus, throughout the 1915–32 period the black vote played a pivotal role in the political life of the region.

Black electoral activities revolved around the McDowell County Colored Republican Organization. Formed in 1904 and active throughout the remaining prewar years, the MCCRO increased its influence during World War I and the 1920s. In early 1915, its president, deputy sheriff J. E. Parsons, announced plans to strengthen the club and improve communication, so that "every Negro voter in the county may be reached in 24 hours." The *McDowell Times* repeatedly praised the MCCRO as the strongest black Republican club in the region and even in the country. On one occasion the black weekly exclaimed, "It is no secret that the organization will permit no avowed enemy of the Negro to get into office in McDowell county. It is true that some very unfair men occasionally get in but they sneak in as sheep." On the basis of race pride, the *Times* concluded, "Every Negro in McDowell county should help the officers make the organization as strong in this county as Tammany is in New York." Based partly upon the MCCRO's growing political influence, editor M. T. Whittico dubbed McDowell County "The Free State of McDowell."[3]

During the war years, the MCCRO kept its elite leadership structure. In August 1916 it reorganized, elected new officers, and chose

TABLE 9.1
Voting-Age Population of Southern West Virginia, 1910–30

	1910		1920		1930	
	Number	Percent	Number	Percent	Number	Percent
Blacks	15,327	17.6	34,577	16.0	45,283	15.5
Immigrants	11,485	13.1	16,147	7.5	14,516	5.0
All American-born whites	60,304	69.3	164,943	76.5	232,336	79.5
Total	87,116	100.0	215,667	100.0	292,135	100.0

Sources: U.S. Census Bureau, *Thirteenth Census of the United States, 1910*, (Washington, 1913), 3:1032–39; *Fourteenth Census, 1920*, (Washington, 1922), 3:1106–9; *Fifteenth Census, 1930*, vol. 3, pt. 2 (Washington, 1933), pp. 1274–77.

TABLE 9.2
Voting-Age Population of Southern West Virginia Blacks by County, 1910–30

County	1910		1920		1930	
	Number	Percent of County Total	Number	Percent of County Total	Number	Percent of County Total
McDowell	5,883	34.1	10,475	30.8	12,524	28.9
Mercer	2,009	18.5	3,550	14.7	4,312	14.0
Mingo	643	11.1	1,383	11.1	2,405	13.1
Logan	237	5.8	3,090	15.2	4,249	15.2
Fayette	3,488	22.3	5,506	18.8	6,492	18.4
Kanawha	2,120	9.7	5,548	8.9	7,694	9.1
Raleigh	866	11.8	3,648	18.1	6,072	18.7
Boone	48	2.0	426	6.1	391	3.5
Wyoming	33	1.4	951	14.1	1,144	12.0

Sources: U.S. Census Bureau, *Thirteenth Census of the United States, 1910* (Washington, 1913), 3:1032–39; *Fourteenth Census, 1920* (Washington, 1922), 3:1106–9; *Fifteenth Census, 1930*, vol. 3, pt. 2 (Washington, 1933), pp. 1274–77.

a new name—the People's Colored Republican Organization of Mc-Dowell County—although it continued to be known as the McDowell County Colored Republican Organization. The long-time black justice of the peace, Samuel Crider of Kimball, was elected president; attorney S. B. Moon, recording secretary; attorney W. H. Harris, corresponding secretary; Floyd Ross, a state officer in the Knights of Pythias, finance secretary; and Rev. A. D. Allen of English, chaplain. Elites also dominated the organization's special committees. Chairs of key committees, for example, included attorney T. Edward Hill, the constitution committee; editor M. T. Whittico, the nominating committee; and attorney S. B. Moon, the address to voters committee.[4]

During the 1920s, the elite character of the MCCRO persisted. Attorney T. Edward Hill was elected president in 1918 and reelected in 1920, serving two-year terms both times. In 1923 he relinquished the post to Dr. E. L. Youngue of Welch. Reporting on a 1924 state-level meeting of the MCCRO, the *Welch Daily News* claimed that "McDowell county colored leaders [Youngue and Hill] were the outstanding figures present at the big meeting in Charleston Saturday at which an agreement was reached as to a list of candidates for delegates to the [1924] Cleveland [Republican national] convention from this state."[5] Youngue retained the presidency until the late 1920s.

Although the MCCRO dominated black politics in southern West Virginia, black Republicans in other counties helped expand its influence. In 1916, for example, the *McDowell Times* praised Mercer County blacks for supporting MCCRO gubernatorial candidate Judge Ira Robinson. In a letter to the editor, the Fayette County attorney and former legislator J. M. Ellis endorsed the candidate. Through black leaders like Dr. James M. Whittico of Mingo County (the brother of the *Times's* editor) and W. F. Denny of Raleigh County (and *Times* columnist), blacks also retained strong commitment to the Republican party.[6]

In July 1926 a "rousing Republican rally" marked the formation of a "Colored Republican Club" at Holden, Logan County. According to the *Logan Banner*, more than three hundred men and women enrolled. Black political leaders, including the minister Arthur Eubanks, planned to establish additional Republican clubs at Earling and Mt. Gay, Logan County, but there is no evidence that they succeeded. The following year, a "Logan Colored News" columnist encouraged black Republicans to "make a strong pull . . . so that the battle of ballots . . . will see the dawn and breaking of a new political day in Logan county." On the eve of the 1932 local, state, and national elections, over seventy-five black Republicans met in Charleston. Representing black Republican constituencies in Mingo, Mercer, Fayette, Raleigh, Kanawha, Wyoming, Boone, and McDowell counties, black leaders reported "the work that had been done in their respective counties in [the] interest of the Republican ticket and gave assurance that the Negro voters in their counties were determinedly aroused as never before."[7]

Drawn almost exclusively from the ranks of the black elite, black political leaders skillfully appealed to the class and racial interests of black coal miners and their families.[8] They repeatedly emphasized beneficial labor legislation like the state's workmen's compensation law passed under Governor H. D. Hatfield. The *McDowell Times* editorialized, "It is a law that knows no man by the color of his skin, the te[x]ture of his hair nor by amount of money he owns."[8] Moreover, from its inception in 1921–22, the West Virginia Bureau of Negro Welfare and Statistics, itself a product of black political struggle, consistently protested the socioeconomic status of black miners, not only as a means of alleviating their plight, but also as a means of securing their votes. In its 1923–24 biennial report, the bureau boldly proclaimed, "Because of conditions not of the Negroes' making, politics has much to do with the condition of Negro schools, churches, homes, streets, roads through their little communities, law enforcement or the neglect on the part of officers to enforce the law, the attitude of the courts in dealing with him and his interests and, very frequently, whether Negroes are to be employed in large numbers and many other matters of vital importance to them." Although the bureau, since it was a state agency, avoided direct partisan appeals to black workers, in subsequent bienniums it pushed even harder to mobilize them.[9]

In its energetic efforts to mobilize the black electorate, the black political elite also tapped the religious traditions of black miners. Although black politicians generally condemned the emotionalism and fervor of working-class black religion, they repeatedly embellished their political appeals with borrowed religious rhetoric. In the columns of the Republican *McDowell Times*, the political use of religion was prominent. During one political campaign, the *Times* reported, "A regular old-time revival took place wherein many persons voluntarily came to the anxious seat of true Republicanism begging to be given a chance to confess their sins in having strayed after . . . idolatry, and asking to be allowed to enlist themselves in the course of the common people of West Virginia by being numbered among the faithful." The *Times* frequently referred to blacks who lived, talked, prayed, and preached Republicanism, while others were "baptized" and "rebaptized in Republicanism."[10]

Black politicians also borrowed from the cultural traditions of black fraternal orders. In the spring of 1916, black Republicans planned a parade of four hundred miners with caps and lamps, which had to be cancelled due to severe weather. In 1924 white Republicans sought the endorsement of attorney T. E. Harris, partly because he served as legal counsel for several black fraternal organizations, including the Improved Benevolent Protective Order of the Elks of the World. "This, of course, shows that he stands high among his own people," one campaigner stated.[11] Thus, in addition to church traditions, fraternal traditions were used to politically mobilize the predominantly working-class black electorate.

Given the black leaders' commitment to bourgeois values, their political appeals took on contradictory and even opportunistic overtones. Black electoral strategies sometimes revealed stark opportunism, not only in their manipulation of religious and cultural symbolism, but also in their manipulation of class and work relations. On the one hand, black political leaders sought to proletarianize the image of elite candidates. "I have seen him out in the mining camps mingling with the coal diggers whose horny hands were black with coal dust and callouses from swinging a pick and shovel," the *Times* described one gubernatorial candidate. On the other hand, black politicians sought to professionalize or deproletarianize the image of black workers, sometimes exaggerating their education, intelligence, and courage. Describing black miners as "thoroughly familiar with the great questions" of the day, attorney W. H. Harris exclaimed, "The men who delve into the subterranean caverns of the earth for 'black diamond' . . . are in open revolt . . . and are proclaiming from the house tops that neither threats, bribes nor intimidations shall deter them."[12] Although black miners were very aware of the forces that restricted their lives and did take courageous steps to secure justice, during electoral campaigns, black politicians sometimes painted an exaggerated portrait of them.

Although black elite spokesmen roundly condemned absenteeism, during elections they sometimes urged black miners to "take a day off" from work "and give the time as a thank offering to the Republican Party." In his bid for the state legislature, Attorney E. Howard Harper "told the miners not to hesitate to vote for [him and his partisans] . . . because of threats or intimidation, [and] that the coal companies would not discharge them, because they needed the service of [the] miner as badly as the miner needed money, and if by chance one should be discharged he could easily find employment elsewhere."[13] In this manner, black politicians encouraged and exploited the black miners' high turnover rate.

Despite substantial elements of opportunism in the black leaders' political appeals, intertwined as they were with the concrete class and racial subordination of Afro-Americans, they took on a certain congency and logic of their own. Within the framework of antagonistic racial and class relations in southern West Virginia, which affected both elite and working-class blacks, the overtures of black political leaders produced striking results. Black leaders succeeded in mobilizing increasing numbers of black voters. The *McDowell Times* frequently highlighted the role of workers in the formation of Republican clubs, if in condescending terms. "The pride of men's families, the records of deeds done for all the people. . . . are the things that moved 100 horny handed men of toil to come out and organize a Club." In reprints of letters and interviews with black coal miners, the *Times* also highlighted the role of black workers in the region's electoral activities. Responding to their own perception of their best interests as well as the injunctions of black politicians, some black miners expressed a resolve to vote their interests and, if necessary, move on to another job. In a *Times* interview, one miner declared: "We can labor anywhere. You [operators] all need us as bad as we need you."[14]

In their oral testimonies describing local political activity during World War I and the 1920s, many black coal miners recall a strong commitment among blacks to the Republican party. At the Winding Gulf Colliery operation in Raleigh County, Preston Turner modestly recalled, his father did not get involved in politics—"he was just a Republican all the way." The young Turner kept his parents' loyalty to the Republican party. "Democrats . . . never favored me . . . I got all my favors from the Republicans. . . . You deal with the people where you get your favors." The miner-minister Rev. Wilford Dickerson was "a straight Republican," his son recalled. "If you put a cow on the Republican ticket he would vote for the cow."[15]

Not all Afro-American political behavior was voluntary, however. As Walter and Margaret Moorman recalled, the proprietors of the Houston Colliery Company in McDowell County were Republicans; if employees failed to vote as the company instructed, they risked losing their jobs. "Miners and teachers," Walter Moorman said, "had to vote the same way." At Hemphill, McDowell County, Pink Henderson voted the Republican ticket because "you couldn't be a

Democrat and work in the mines." According to Lawrence Boling of Madison, Boone County, his father and "all" black miners were Republicans, because "all" the coal operators were Republicans. Coercion, however, sometimes involved the other major party in the region. In Logan County blacks apparently voted the "straight Democratic ticket," Roy Todd recalled, "because the Democrats ruled Logan County." Don Chafin, the notorious local sheriff enforced the vote. At a founding meeting of a black Republican club in 1926, a Logan County black man "told why he had been a Democratic worker in 1924. . . . He said he was beaten by Democratic henchmen and promised worse treatment if he did not turn Democratic." Even so, some blacks "played" both parties, Republican and Democratic. One black miner recalled that he sometimes secretly voted the Democratic ticket, while other registered black Republicans "never" voted a straight ticket, priding themselves on being "independent."[16]

Within the framework of such constraints, black politicians gained the support of black workers, and black political empowerment increased. The success of black political mobilization was most evident in black leaders' growing influence within the Republican party, in blacks' increasing presence in elective and appointive offices, and in the expansion of state-supported institutions for blacks. As early as 1915, blacks succeeded in modifying a proposed state primary bill whose provisions threatened to undercut their position within the state Republican party. The amended bill provided for the election of two committeemen from each state senatorial district and three committeemen at large. In exchange for their support, blacks demanded and secured the three at-large positions.[17]

During the 1920s, blacks were able to broaden their respresentation within the Republican party. As head of the Colored Bureau of the state Republican party, T. Edward Hill represented blacks on the Republican state executive committee. In McDowell, Fayette, Mingo, Raleigh, Wyoming, and Kanawha counties, blacks also made inroads on Republican county executive committees. During the early 1920s, four blacks served on the McDowell County committee: attorney E. Howard Harper of Keystone, attorney S. B. Moon of Wilcoe, John Thornton of Northfork, and James Hamilton of Powhatan. Another four blacks served on the Fayette County Republican executive committee, including the coal operator Matthew Buster of Montgomery, W. H. Banner of Boomer, P. A. Davis of Thayer, and T. W. Wade of Claremont. By the late 1920s, six blacks also served on the Kanawha County executive committee.[18] Moreover, as we will see, after receiving the franchise in 1920, black women also brought new vitality and strength to the black political struggle.

Linked to the expanding proletarian electorate, the black elite's growing influence within the Republican party was used to increase the black share of elective and appointive offices. During the war years the MCCRO received accolades for achieving the election of black justices of the peace, deputy sheriffs, constables, and town and city councilmen. In a tradition going back to the prewar period, the elective offices of justice of the peace and constable were the ones most persistently held by blacks. Competing in the election of 1916, several black candidates in McDowell County had served terms ranging from 4 to 20 years. In the Adkins district, Constable J. E. Whittle and Justice of the Peace C. C. Froe had served terms of 8 and 16 years, respectively. In the Northfork district, Constable John Claxton of Worth had served for 4 years, and Constable Cal Haines of the Elkhorn district had served for 16 years. In the Browns Creek district, Constable J. E. Richards and Justice of the Peace Samuel Crider (both of Kimball) had held office for 16 and 20 years, respectively. With few interruptions, Haines, Richards, Whittle, Froe, and Crider continued to serve through the mid- and late 1920s.[19]

By the late 1920s, Justice Samuel Crider had served more than 30 years. Understandably, Crider developed a strong reputation as unbeatable, in part because the Republican party had apparently agreed to elect blacks to certain local posts. "He is the unbeaten and unbeatable Justice of the Peace. . . . He will be the next colored Justice and there is no earthly power that can defeat him. . . . the whole people want him," the campaign literature frequently proclaimed. Crider was not only considered qualified, but was also thought to be an impartial dispenser of justice. "No man today, whether white or black, has a more complete record for fair dealing and the fulfillment of his oath by promise than Squire Samuel Crider."[20]

In addition to elected positions as constables and justices of the peace, Afro-Americans gained seats on city councils in Keystone, Kimball, Northfork, and Clark, McDowell counties and Montgomery, Fayette County. In 1915 seven blacks served on aldermanic councils in southern West Virginia. Eight served in 1921–22, and thereafter, through the 1920s, no less than six blacks served on city and town councils. The editor M. T. Whittico of Keystone, James Board of Kimball, and James George of Northfork all served unbroken aldermanic terms on their respective city councils from about 1918 through the 1920s. Other blacks served varying terms during the same period. Attorney H. J. Capehart, for example, served on the Keystone city council from about 1918 until 1924–25, when another black, Samuel Wade, replaced him for the duration of the 1920s.[21]

In their drive for elective offices, Afro-Americans turned their most forceful efforts toward the election of a state legislator. In the election of 1916 they succeeded, when attorney E. Howard Harper of Keystone received the Republican nomination and election to the West Virginia House of Delegates. Using a bloc voting strategy, blacks successfully exploited political divisions among whites. Forecasting victory for Harper in the primary, the *Times* chuckled, "There is no doubt there will be a lively scramble among several whites candidates for the honor of the places and no single man has any very large following at this time." Harper won one of four seats, competing against a field of six white candidates and one other black. He received more votes than the three whites and the black man put together; his nearest opponent lost by 1,000 votes.[22]

As noted in chapter one, Harper was born in Tazewell County, Virginia, and received his law degree from Howard University. Fifty-three years old in 1916, Harper figured prominently among the black elite. By mobilizing black support for white state and local officials, he consolidated his position within the Republican party during the prewar years. By 1916 he had "also gathered together some of this world's goods." Along with "having the finest residence" and owning "some very valuable property" in Keystone, Harper also owned and operated "a fine farm" in Kanawha County and another in Tazewell. Harper served in the legislative sessions of 1917 and 1925, and part of the 1927 session, before death cut short his third term.[23]

Although the evidence is thin, some southern West Virginia black coal miners apparently rose into the ranks of elected officials. Described as "one of the best miners in the Pocahontas Coal field," William Saddler served as justice of the peace in the Elkhorn district of McDowell County for several years. During most of the 1920s, miner R. L. Benton served on the school board of the Browns Creek district. In a sermon before the Odd Fellows, Rev. R. P. Johnson described Benton as as miner who had gained the confidence of his race as well as the coal operators. After his electoral victory in 1926, the *Welch Daily News* reported that Benton "was given a large majority" in his election to the board.[24]

Black coal miners achieved their highest political office, however, when the coal miner John V. Coleman of Fayette County was elected to the House of Delegates in 1918. Born in 1874 in Summers County, West Virginia, Coleman received his public school education in Fayette County, where he pursued a coal-mining career. At the regular session of the 1919 legislature, he served on the forestry and conservation committee and on the penitentiary, labor, and medicine and sanitation committees as well. During his tenure, Coleman also introduced an anti-lynching bill, but it failed to pass.[25] Like black elite politicians, black coal miners who won elective office placed racial equity high on their political agenda.

Although black coal miners sometimes won important elections, elite blacks of substantial education and training like E. Howard Harper, Harry J. Capehart, T. Edward Hill, and others dominated the political life of the region and held the most lucrative and prestigious positions. Harper was the first black to serve in the West Virginia legislature since the 1909 session. His election in 1917 initiated an unbroken pattern of black elite legislators holding office throughout the 1915–32 period. In 1918 when coal miner John V. Coleman entered the statehouse, southern West Virginia sent not one, but three, blacks to the state legislature, including two graduates of the Howard University law school. The Keystone, McDowell County, attorney Harry J. Capehart succeeded Harper, and the Charleston attorney T. G. Nutter won election in Kanawha County. Nutter, through his powerful position as grand chancellor of the West Virginia Knights of Pythias, developed a strong presence in the Kanawha County Republican party and managed to gain reelection in 1920 and 1922. Capehart used the powerful McDowell County Colored Republican Organization to launch his bid for the state legislature. Before entering the state legislature in 1918, he had served as secretary of the MCCRO, city assessor of Keystone for two terms, and Keystone city councilman.[26]

In 1928, McDowell County elected T. Edward Hill—lawyer, publisher, and former head of the Bureau of Negro Welfare and Statistics—to the state legislature. A graduate of Howard University, Hill had built a solid political base in the county. Serving as director of the BNWS until 1927, Hill occupied a variety of business and political posts: business manager of the *McDowell Times* since 1911, secretary of the West Virginia Negro Bar Association since its founding during World War I; president of the MCCRO between 1918 and 1921; and director of the Colored Voters Division, Republican State Committee from 1920 to 1928.[27]

Finally, completing the roster of elite black legislators, in 1930 young black attorney Stewart A. Calhoun of McDowell County was elected to the House of Delegates. As noted in chapter 6, Calhoun was born in Keystone and received his law degree from Howard University. A member of four fraternal orders—the Elks, Odd Fellows, Knights of Pythias, and the Independent Order of St. Luke—Calhoun opened his law practice in 1925. In rapid succession, he was soon elected Keystone city attorney, city councilman for two terms, and finally state legislator. Calhoun served on the legislature's judiciary, education, labor, insurance, and election committees.[28]

Before 1920, although black women (like all women) were excluded from the franchise, they played a significant part in black electoral politics. Recognizing the growing political importance of black women, in 1916 the MCCRO appointed three women to the newly created Civic Committee, which was charged with investigating the larger social welfare and community issues affecting Afro-Americans.[29] In 1916 black women also played a key, if informal, role in the formation of Kimball's "colored" Republican club. Although women were barred from the club's first meeting, their support thoroughly impressed a *McDowell Times* partisan. "Great crowds of beautifully gowned ladies waving banners and applauding vociferously thronged the streets around the club. . . . The ladies being so enthusiastic, the club has decided to hold public session at sometime in the near future to which all the ladies will be invited." Kimball had developed a reputation as the largest black voting precinct of McDowell County, and the *Times* soon reported "a strong organization of [Republican] women under the leadership of that tireless worker and astute politician Miss Maggie Anderson." Unfortunately, little biographical information on her is available.[30]

Following the suffrage amendment of 1920, black women increased their involvement in political affairs. When black legislator E. Howard Harper died in 1927, his wife, Mrs. Minnie Buckingham-Harper, was appointed to serve out his term, upon the enthusiastic and unanimous recommendation of the McDowell County Republican executive committee and the MCCRO.[31] When Governor Howard M. Gore appointed Mrs. Harper, she gained the distinction of being "the first woman of the Negro Race to become a member of a legislative body in the United States."[32] Although black women were far less successful than black men at winning elections, as they gained increasing influence in the Republican party, they began to campaign for local public office. In 1923, a black woman, Mrs. William Drewery, was elected to the city council of Clark, McDowell County.[33] She retained her seat through the late 1920s. However, the main role of black women in politics continued to be supporting the election of black men.

Based on the growing political potential of the black working class, blacks not only escalated their campaign for elective office, but also redoubled their efforts to gain appointive posts. In 1922 the Welch attorney Arthur G. Froe was appointed the recorder of deeds for the District of Columbia. At a state meeting of black Republicans, Froe later explained that the black voters in West Virginia "constituted a power that demanded recognition in both the state and nation." In recommending Froe for the recorder's job, one of the highest federal appointments held by blacks during the period, President Warren G. Harding agreed. The "colored voters of West Virginia, holding the balance of power feel that they are entitled to recognition," Harding stated. In his nomination letter to the president, West Virginia senator Davis Elkins described Froe as "an able lawyer" and "a colored man of the highest standing in the Southern part of West Virginia." In another letter to the president, the black politician Thomas W. Fleming of Cleveland, Ohio, wrote, "Mrs. Fleming and I have known Mr. Froe for years and I can say that in his appointment, you have selected a colored man of the very highest character and ability and one whom I am sure will do his work well."[34]

According to the Froe family historian, Mrs. Jessie M. Thomas, local Republicans supported Froe's move to Washington in order to circumvent his political demands at the local level. Nonetheless, since the national Republican party usually reserved the recorder of deeds office for an influential black Republican of national stature, the recorder's job was a coveted patronage position. Among some veteran employees of the office, who had served under other recorders, Froe soon developed a reputation as "the best of the lot." Indicative of the important role of southern West Virginia blacks in national Republican politics, when Arthur G. Froe left the recorder's position in 1930, another southern West Virginia black, Charles E. Mitchell of West Virginia State College, was soon appointed U.S. minister to Liberia. Born in St. Michaels, Maryland, in 1870, Mitchell had served as an instructor and business manager at WVSC from 1910 to 1930.[35]

Although federal patronage carried a great deal of prestige it did little to expand economic opportunities for blacks in southern West

Virginia during the 1920s. To broaden their opportunities in the public sector, Afro-Americans escalated their fight against racial inequality in state governmental, educational, and social welfare institutions. They waged a consistent two-front battle: to increase appropriations to established black institutions and to build new institutions to cover needs as yet unmet. On both fronts, blacks achieved substantial results. In addition to appropriations for established black institutions like West Virginia State College and Bluefield Collegiate Institute (as noted in chapter 5), they obtained a variety of new state-supported social welfare institutions such as the Denmar Tuberculosis Sanitarium, the West Virginia Colored Insane Asylum, the West Virginia Colored Deaf and Blind School, the State Industrial School for Colored Boys, the State Industrial School for Colored Girls, the State Home for Aged and Infirm Colored Men and Women, and the Bureau of Negro Welfare and Statistics.[36]

Black legislators from southern West Virginia either introduced themselves the legislation that gave rise to these reforms or else lobbied for its introduction by their white Republican allies. Indeed, their alliance with the Republican party partly explains their success on the state and local level. Republicans dominated West Virginia politics through World War I and the 1920s. With the exception of the Democrat John J. Cornwell, elected to the governorship in 1916, Republicans controlled the state's political machinery. Even during Cornwell's four-year term, Republicans controlled both houses of the legislature and passed legislation that undermined Cornwell's control over state government. From the beginning of his tenure, as one state historian has noted, Cornwell "was forced to work with Republicans," a development that redounded to the benefit of blacks.[37]

While blacks were fortunately allied with the dominant political party, only their own careful organization and resolve fully explains their success in the political arena. To be sure, Afro-Americans worked within the traditional constraints of racial segregation and demanded "separate but equal" access to state funds. Yet they rejected the notion of segregation as a badge of black inferiority. In every struggle for a new all-black institution, black leaders repeatedly pinpointed racial exclusion and discrimination as the principal rationale for their demands. For cultural reasons, they also consistently reiterated their belief that black professionals were better equipped than whites to serve the growing social welfare needs of black clients.

Their activities demonstrated that racial segregation, like other dimensions of white racism, was by no means a static phenomenon. It was shaped not only by the initiatives of an antagonistic state and white citizenry, but also by the political demands of blacks themselves. It was the blacks' demand that they be included rather than excluded that made West Virginia's system of racial discrimination at least less destructive than it might have been. The activities of blacks on their own behalf demonstrated that the racial status quo was formed by a dual process that involved the political and cultural demands of blacks as well as the racial policies of a hostile state and society.[38] Above all, the political activism of blacks reflected the dynamics of black proletarianization. Only the expansion of the black coal-mining proletariat fully explains the growing political potential of West Virginia blacks. This potential together with the rise of a vigorous black leadership, led to black empowerment.

The political struggle of blacks in southern West Virginia was by no means a purely local or state one. It involved a great deal of cooperation with blacks in other parts of the nation, North and South. Blacks throughout the country, along with black politicians in southern West Virginia, attacked the Democratic party, decrying its unjust segregationist policies and its disfranchisement of southern blacks. In a 1916 article, attorney W. H. Harris urged blacks in West Virginia, Kentucky, and other border states where blacks retained the franchise "to organize and attack southern representation, disfranchisement, jim crowism and segregation. Let us support no man who will not pledge himself to actively oppose these iniquitous measures."[39]

During the early 1920s when Arthur G. Froe was being considered for the federal recorder position, he received letters of endorsement from Afro-Americans in the North and South that not only supported him, but also stressed what his appointment would symbolize for his race. C. B. Johnson of Greenville, South Carolina, wrote that Froe's appointment "gives increased hope and courage to millions of my people, to know [that] the door of opportunity is not entirely closed against them." In another letter, a northern supporter echoed Johnson: "I feel sure that the colored people in every part of the country will appreciate his appointment to this high office."[40] That the recorder's job, a low-level federal position, took on such symbolic recognition among blacks also suggests how little they could hope to achieve in national politics, even under the banner of their Republican allies.

Despite the notable political successes of southern West Virginia blacks, a variety of forces hampered black political unity in the region. Conflicts evolved within the Republican party, particularly during primary elections, as competing members of the black elite sought the party's endorsement. These conflicts were sometimes abrasive and highly debilitating. During the primaries, white Republicans usually encouraged several blacks to contend for the same office, "thereby insuring defeat of all" and "causing the responsibility of the elimination of the Negro from elective office to rest upon the Negro himself." Black politicians frequently criticized their White Republican allies, calling them de facto Democrats. "Democrats kick, burn, disfranchise, lynch, segregate and Jim Crow us with our eyes wide open and tell us to our face that they have no love for us, while many of our Republican Friends (?) do the same thing in disguise—behind our backs."[41]

Primary elections placed blacks in the midst of hostile white Republican factions. In the gubernatorial primary of 1916, for example, the MCCRO split between the Judge Ira Robinson faction and the Abraham Lilly faction. Chairman J. E. Parsons, the well-known attorney H. J. Capehart, and the popular agricultural extension worker R. W. White supported Lilly. The black forces for Robinson, who was endorsed by the incumbent governor, H. D. Hatfield, were led by attorney and future BNWS director T. Edward Hill, M. T. Whittico of the *McDowell Times,* and the popular attorney and *Times* columnist W. H. Harris. Each faction organized mass meetings and appealed to the predominantly working-class electorate. The Robinson faction continually played up the Hatfield administration's aid to black institutions and passage of the workmen's compensation law, while the Lilly forces emphasized imperfections in the law and the need for more "efficient" administration.

Evidently most black miners supported Robinson as the candidate in closer tune with their interests. Although he lost to Democrat John J. Cornwell in the general election, Robinson won the Republican nomination for governor. He carried virtually every precinct in McDowell County, outdistancing his opponent by nearly 3,000 votes. In January 1916, one black miner wrote, "I have heard enough about Judge Robinson to make me know that he is the man for governor." When the Robinson forces won the battle, most black Republicans reunited behind the party's candidate, but a handful of influential black political figures, including MCCRO chairman J. E. Parsons, crossed over to the Democratic party in the general election in protest.[42] If factionalism sometimes created political opportunities, such as chances for electing blacks to the state legislature, just as frequently it undermined black political progress.

Interparty strife also posed critical problems for black political unity. Buoyed by the national election of Woodrow Wilson, in 1916 Democrats captured the governor's office and won influential positions in various counties in southern West Virginia. Governor John J. Cornwell conducted a thoroughgoing purge of black Republican appointees to the state bureaucracy, firing some blacks and reducing the salaries of others. He also slashed appropriations for black institutions. Black Republicans were especially bitter over the firing of L. O. Wilson, the black state librarian, from a black patronage position with deep prewar roots. The Democrat-controlled house finance committee cut general educational appropriations, which hurt whites but fell especially hard on blacks. It reduced the senate's appropriations for West Virginia State College by $3,500 while defeating a $40,000 building proposal for Bluefield Collegiate Institute, "notwithstanding the fact that three and four girls sleep in a room."[43] Black teachers, who were mostly women, were especially vulnerable to the shifting political fortunes of blacks. As new partisans entered office, politically active black teachers were frequently fired or transferred to unfavorable locations.[44]

Although few blacks belonged to the Democratic party before the late 1920s, Democrats gained a slowly increasing black following in southern West Virginia. In 1928 the national Democratic committee spearheaded the formation of "Colored Smith Clubs." In West Virginia, Dr. C. F. Hopson of Charleston was elected state chairman, with E. L. Powell, a high-school principal and agent of the Supreme Life and Casualty Insurance Company, serving as executive secretary and member of the Democratic National Advisory Committee. Earl B. Dickerson, a Chicago attorney and regional director of the "Colored Smith Clubs," reported a gradually increasing coterie of black Democrats in the Mountain State.[45] By 1932, under the leadership of I. J. K. Wells, state chairman of the "Colored Democratic" campaign, the Democratic party had staged over thirty rallies among blacks in the southern mountain region including Kanawha, Raleigh, Logan, Wyoming, Fayette, Mingo, and McDowell counties.[46] In order to justify his support of the Democratic party in 1932, Wells identified his cause with Democratic black leaders of national stature. "Why are most all of our papers [including the *Pittsburgh Courier*] and such leaders as Dr. Du Bois, Kelly Miller, . . . Wm. Pickens, and Walter White refusing to support the Republican Party and are encouraging us if we are not right?"[47] Although blacks in West Virginia mainly voted Republican in the elections of 1932, Democrats made important inroads among the black electorate in southern West Virginia.

While the vicissitudes of two-party politics shaped the black political experience in the region, gender issues also influenced the political struggle of Afro-Americans there. When black women gained the vote and joined the MCCRO during the 1920s, they escalated their political demands—but always within the established framework of proper gender roles. They demanded the secretary's seat as a female prerogative and waged a progressively aggressive campaign to capture the slot. By 1929 this struggle had become the most potent issue dividing the MCCRO along gender lines. The women unsuccessfully supported their own Memphis T. Garrison in the bitterly fought contests of 1926 and 1928, while most men supported the male incumbent.[48] Despite the efforts of these women to abide by the sexist notion of certain prescribed roles for men and women, including exploiting the idea that the secretarial job was a female preserve, they were still denied access to leadership. Their fight reveals gender conflict as yet another obstacle in the Afro-American quest for racial solidarity.

Although important socioeconomic and ideological issues underlay the political divisions within the black community, they unfortunately often erupted into destructive personal confrontations. In his regular columns in the *Times*, attorney W. H. Harris frequently ridiculed the intellectual and behavioral characteristics of his opponents. When the well-known local criminal defense attorney James Knox Smith, who was a former slave, delivered a speech supporting Lilly, Harris described the address as "minstrel-like" and of the "slave quarters" variety. Such personal attacks intensified in the case of blacks who defected to the Democratic party. The *McDowell Times* often dropped consideration of the issues altogether and mounted concerted attacks on the presumed moral, intellectual, mental, and physical characteristics of black Democrats.[49]

Intraracial conflicts certainly weakened the political struggle of Afro-Americans in southern West Virginia, but it was the complex interplay between the forces of class and race, along with vagaries of two-party politics, that undercut the effectiveness of black politics. When blacks supported unpopular candidates, they faced cruel recrimination from white partisans that sometimes cost them their jobs, housing, and civil rights. Dependent on the coal company for the basic necessities of life, black coal miners living in company towns were especially vulnerable. When William Saddler, the coal-miner justice of the peace, opposed his employer's candidate in the gubernatorial primary of 1916, for example, he lost his job and was refused credit at the company store.[50]

Fortunately, as blacks and whites increasingly collided in the electoral arena, an obverse pattern of political cooperation developed. Although interracial alliances undoubtedly involved a mix of selfish socioeconomic and political motivations on both sides of the color line, at least it led black and white Republicans to consistently interact, and sometimes even closely. During political campaigns, blacks and whites frequently shared the same speaking platforms. When Governor H. D. Hatfield traveled to McDowell County, campaigning on behalf of Judge Robinson during the war years, he not only spoke on the same platform with blacks but also visited the offices of the *McDowell Times.* When he left the governor's office in 1916, blacks presented him with a gold watch as a token of their friendship and appreciation; one supporter exclaimed, "That is ONE white man I'd fight for!"[51]

During the 1920s, Hatfield continued his fruitful relationship with southern West Virginia blacks. When he ran for a U.S. Senate seat in 1928, his friendship with blacks paid handsome dividends: he won by only 1,000 votes, and blacks had voted overwhelmingly Republican. Hatfield praised his black supporters, not only for their political contributions to the Republican party, but also for their public and private accomplishments. In 1930 he recommended two black attorneys for federal appointments. "I can recommend both of these men with a great deal of enthusiasm and say that they stand as an equal in their profession to those who have arrived at the highest attainments at the bar." Through Hatfield's recommendation, attorney H. J. Capehart became a special assistant to the U.S. district attorney for the southern district of West Virginia, and, as noted earlier, Charles E. Mitchell of West Virginia State College was appointed U.S. minister to Liberia. Such instances of blacks holding federal office suggested strong bonds between blacks and white Republicans like Hatfield.[52]

Unfortunately, the amicable relationship that developed between blacks and their white allies was insufficient to stem the countervailing pattern of white resistance to black advancement. During the entire 1915–32 period, besides the Whitney and Whitfield lynchings, one of the most violent interracial confrontations was one that grew out of Republican party conflict. In 1916, as elsewhere in the region, blacks in the Winding Gulf Field found themselves in the middle of the Robinson and Lilly factions. George Wolfe, manager of the Winding Gulf Colliery Company, supported Robinson; many, if not most, Raleigh County blacks supported Lilly. On the afternoon of the election, a fight broke out between blacks and whites and was quelled by the police, who arrested two blacks and held them in the local jail.[53]

Fearing a lynching, an angry group of black men attacked the jail, killed one white officer and wounded others, and freed the men. "All of these colored people in Raleigh county are more [or] less armed, and they have been quietly buying up ammunition for the past several days," Wolfe reported to Winding Gulf's owner, Justus Collins. "In my opinion the Robinson-Lilly race for nomination for Governor has seriously effected some of the colored people. You cannot send for a nigger and sit him down in the executive mansion and plot with him to over-throw the white people without evil results." The county sheriff, whose son had narrowly escaped injury in the affair, was also "naturally very bitter," according to Wolfe. "He wants to show . . . that they cannot bunch up together and shoot up a bunch of deputies to liberate a couple of three-by-four coons."[54]

Police officers and privately employed security men soon arrested nearly forty black men, including the two who had been freed from jail. Two of the blacks involved were hastily tried and sentenced to life imprisonment; others were gradually released. Only the company's extensive dependence on black labor curbed the extent of white reprisals. From the outset, Wolfe urged caution to Justus Collins: "I want to handle this matter as quietly as we can so that we will suffer as little as possible in the ways of loss of men. Heaven knows, it is going to cost us a lot anyway." Wolfe feared that his effort to discipline black workers would cause "a good many of the good reliable colored people" to "get out of the county and go elsewhere."[55]

The racial violence at Winding Gulf underscored the precarious status of blacks within the party of their allies. It also revealed critical limitations on the black elite's appeal to the proletarian electorate: at a crucial moment, the grievances of black coal miners would not be contained within the regular channels of electoral politics. Although the Winding Gulf confrontation was not part of a long-term deliberately violent strategy for social change, it did demonstrate that black coal miners could consider collective violence and use it, not only in defense, but also as a preemptive response to racial inequality. During the 1920s, sparse evidence suggests, the black coal miners' willingness to use violence in defense of their civil rights continued. As the Ku Klux Klan escalated its activities during the early 1920s, for example, some black workers resolved to repel violence with violence. At Crozer, McDowell County, when "the white members of the organization [periodically] planted their fiery cross on the hill," Laing discovered, "each time the Negroes got their rifles and shot it full of holes."[56]

Yet, as the swift and sweeping white reprisals in the Winding Gulf incident revealed, blacks' efforts to redress their grievances through violence were fraught with peril. The critical limitations of both electoral and violent strategies for social change precipitated the search for more effective modes of political struggle. During the early postwar years, the nationalistic Garvey movement and the NAACP civil rights campaign would move increasingly to the forefront of black politics, while protest strategy, although it had roots in the prewar era, would now receive greater organizational support and take on greater force.

NOTES

1. See George C. Wright, *Life Behind a Veil: Blacks in Louisville, Kentucky, 1865–1930* (Baton Rouge: Louisiana State University Press, 1985); Nicholas C. Burckel, "Progressive Governors in the Border States: Reform Governors in Missouri, Kentucky, and Maryland, 1900–1918" (Ph.D. diss., University of Wisconsin, 1971); August Meier, *Negro Thought in America, 1880–1915* (Ann Arbor: University of Michigan Press, 1963); Paul Lewinson, *Race, Class and Party: A History of Negro Suffrage and White Politics in the South* (1932; rept., New York: Russell and Russell, 1963); V. O. Key, *Southern Politics in State and Nation* (New York: A. A. Knopf, 1949).

2. "Great Work for Future: Colored Republican Organization Doing Great Work," 26 Feb. 1915, editorial page, 26 Mar. 1915, "Hand-Picked Committee is Called," 31 Mar. 1916, W. H. Harris, Jr., "Reorganization of the McDowell County Colored Republican Club," 21 July 1916, W. H. Harris, Jr., "McDowell Republican Organization Should be Social as Well as Political," 4 Aug. 1916, "Together We Stand: Divided We Fall" and editorial page, 12 Mar. 1915, "Whittico Dead," 23 June 1939, in *McDowell Times;* "Negroes Form Slate: Ask Representation at National Meet" 15 Jan. 1923 [1924], "Republican Majority in McDowell County Over 6,000," 3 Nov. 1926, *Welch Daily News,* "McDowell County Colored Republican Organization Re-elects Dr. Youngue Head: Hill Endorsed for Legislature," *McDowell Recorder,* 23 Oct. 1929. See also "Republican Speaking—Mr. Colored Man," flyer and enclosure, W. L. McMillan to R. L. Thornton, in Department of Justice, Record Group No. 60, Straight Numerical File No. 182363, National Archives.

3. U.S. Census Bureau, *Thirteenth Census of the U.S., 1910* (Washington, 1913), 3:1032–39; *Fourteenth Census, 1920* (Washington, 1922), 3:1106–9; *Fifteenth Census, 1930*, vol. 3, pt. 2 (Washington, 1933), pp. 1274–77.

4. "M'Dowell Republican Organization," 4 Aug. 1916, "Strong Organization Formed," 18 Aug. 1916, "Announces Committees," 25 Aug. 1916, in *McDowell Times*.

5. John T. Harris, ed., *West Virginia Legislative Hand Book* (Charleston, W.Va.: The Tribune Printing Company, 1929), p. 201; "To Issue Call," *McDowell Times*, 8 Mar. 1918; "Negroes Form Slate: Ask Representation at National Meet," *Welch Daily News*, 15 Jan. 1923 [1924]; "McDowell County Colored Republican Organization Re-elects Dr. Youngue Head," *McDowell Recorder*, 23 Oct. 1929.

6. "Mercer County Negroes Strong for Robinson," 17 Mar. 1916, "Fare Thee: Goodbye Cousin Abe," 24 Mar. 1916, "Mingo County Strong for Republican Ticket," 3 Nov. 1916, "Raleigh County News," 28 Apr. 1916, in *McDowell Times*.

7. "Colored Republican Clubs to be Formed at Holden," 16 July 1916, "Logan Colored News," 18 Nov. 1927, 4 Nov. 1932, in *Logan Banner*.

8. "Ask Who and What Kind of Men Receive Your Votes," 3 Dec. 1915, "Why Abe Lilly Can't Win," 14 Apr. 1916, "A Social Gathering," 24 Mar. 1916, 7, 14, and 21 Jan. 1916, 5 and 19 May 1916, in *McDowell Times*; "Negroes Form Slate," 15 Jan. 1923, "Republican Majority in McDowell County Over 60,000," 3 Nov. 1926, in *Welch Daily News*; "McDowell County Colored Republican Organization Re-elects Dr. Youngue Head," *McDowell Recorder*, 23 Oct. 1929.

9. West Virginia Bureau of Negro Welfare and Statistics (WVBNWS), *Biennial Reports, 1921–22*, pp. 5–8, *1923–24*, pp. 80–81.

10. "A Social Gathering," 24 Mar. 1916, "Substantial Improvements Winding Gulf Collieries Company," 13 Oct. 1916, in *McDowell Times*. Some politically active black ministers reinforced the political use of religion. On the political role of the black minister Rev. C. H. Mitchell, see W. H. Hallanan, member for West Virginia, Republican National Committee, to H. D. Hatfield, U.S. senator, 10 Dec. 1919, Hatfield to Hallanan, 13 Dec. 1929, Hallanan to Colonel Floyd E. Cunningham, State Road Commissioner, 10 Dec. 1929, in Series 3, Box 20, Folder No. 3, H. D. Hatfield Papers, West Virginia University, West Virginia Collection.

11. "Triumphant Tour of Judge Ira E. Robinson," *McDowell Times*, 26 May 1916; "Colored Lodge Men Send in Donation for Harding Fund," *Welch Daily News*, 8 Jan. 1924; S. H. Thompson to Col. Guy D. Goff, 20 Feb. 1924, and Joseph M. Trigg, Washington, D.C., to T. E. Harris, 21 Feb. 1924, in Thaddeus E. Harris Papers, Northfork, W.Va., Manuscript Division, William R. Perkins Library, Duke University.

12. "Hatfield-Robinson Republican Club," 14 Jan. 1916, "Judge Robinson Is Ideal Campaigner," 24 Mar. 1916, W. H. Harris, "Why Abe Lilly Can't Win," 14 Apr. 1916, in *McDowell Times*.

13. "Triumphant Tour of Judge Ira E. Robinson," 14 Apr. 1916, "Colored Republicans Take Notice," 14 July 1916, *McDowell Times*.

14. "The Kimball Meeting, 14 Jan. 1916, "Hatfield-Robinson Republican Club," 14 Jan. 1916, "Judge Robinson Is Ideal Campaigner," 24 Mar. 1916, "Administration Won a Miner's Argument," 26 May 1916, in *McDowell Times*.

15. Interviews with Preston Turner, 26 July 1983, North E. Dickerson, 28 July 1983, Walter and Margaret Moorman, 14 July 1983, Pink Henderson, 15 July 1983, Roy Todd, 18 July 1983, and Lawrence Boling, 18 July 1983; "Colored Republican Club to be Formed at Holden," *Logan Banner*, 16 July 1926.

16. Interviews with Moorman, Henderson, Todd and Boling (same dates as in n. 15); "Colored Republican Club," *Logan Banner*, 16 July 1926.

17. "Necessity of Watchfulness," *McDowell Times*, 19 Feb. 1915. See also "Negroes Form Slate: Ask Representation at National Meet," 15 Jan. 1923 [1924], "Republican Majority in McDowell County . . . ," 3 Nov. 1926, "Large Number of Rallies . . . In County," 1 Nov. 1928, "Taylor Declines to Debate Lilly on Negro Record," 1 Nov. 1928, "Dr. Hatfield and General Conley Speak in McDowell . . . ," 3 Nov. 1928, "Enthusiasm of Yesterday . . . ," 5 Nov. 1928, and "McDowell County Voters," 6 Nov. 1928, in *Welch Daily News*; "McDowell County Colored Republican Organization . . . , " *McDowell Recorder*, 23 Oct. 1929.

18. Harris, ed., *West Virginia Legislative Reference Hand Book (1929)*, p. 201; "Civic Relations," in WVBNWS, *Biennial Reports, 1921–22*, pp. 62–68, *1923–24*, pp. 80–88, *1925–26*, pp. 132–42, and *1929–32*, pp. 40–45.

19. Harris, ed., *West Virginia Legislative Reference Hand Book*, p. 201; civic and political reports, in WVBNWS, *Biennial Reports, 1921–32*; "Resolutions . . . Fiftieth Anniversary Celebration," 9 July 1915, "Biggest and Best Justice in State," 24 Mar. 1916, in *McDowell Times*; "McDowell County Colored Republican Organization," *McDowell Recorder*, 23 Oct. 1929.

20. "Resolutions," 9 July 1915; "Biggest and Best Justice," 24 Mar. 1916, in *McDowell Times*; WVBNWS, *Biennial Report, 1925–26*, pp. 132–39.

21. "Resolutions," 9 July 1915; "Biggest and Best Justice," 24 Mar. 1916, *McDowell Times*; civic and political reports, WVBNWS, *Biennial Reports, 1921–32* (same as in n. 19 above); "McDowell County Colored Republican Organization," *McDowell Recorder*, 23 Oct. 1929.

22. Harris, ed., *West Virginia Legislative Reference Hand Book* (1917), p. 737 and (1928), p. 220; "Negro Elected to the Legislature," 24 Nov. 1916, "Howard Harper for Legislature," 16 June 1916, "Attorney Moon on Legislature," 17 Sept. 1915, in *McDowell Times*.

23. Harris, ed., *West Virginia Legislative Hand Book* (1917), p. 737, (1928), p. 220; "Negro Elected to the Legislature," *McDowell Times*, 24 Nov. 1916.

24. "Strong-Arm Method Disfranchise Elkhorn District," 25 Feb. 1916; "Fired," 16 Mar. 1916; "Governor Called Out Militia Upon Request of Citizens," 16 June 1916; and "Necessity of Watchfulness," 19 Feb. 1915; "A Hopeless Desperate Fight," 21 Apr. 1916; 18 May 1917, all in *McDowell Times*; "Republican Majority," *Welch Daily News*, 3 Nov. 1926.

25. Harris, ed., *West Virginia Legislative Reference Hand Book* (1919), p. 790; "Anti-Lynching Law," in WVBNWS, *Biennial Report, 1921–22*, pp. 73–76.

26. Harris, ed., *West Virginia Legislative Reference Hand Book* (1919), p. 790, (1920), pp. 241, 258, (1922), p. 147, and (1924), p. 140. For additional biographical data on black legislators, see chaps. 1 and 6 above.

27. Ibid. (1929), p. 201, and (1931), p. 614. See also chaps. 1 and 6.

28. Ibid.

29. "Strong Organization Formed," *McDowell Times*, 18 Aug. 1916.

30. "Gathering of the Clans of Kimball," 17 Mar. 1916, "Triumphant Tour of Judge Ira E. Robinson," 14 Apr. 1916, 31 Mar. 1916, in *McDowell Times*.

31. Harris, *West Virginia Legislative Hand Book* (1928), p. 221; B. A. Mills of Keystone to W. E. B. Du Bois, 1 July 1928, Reel 27, W. E. B. Du Bois Papers, Library of Congress.

32. Harris, *West Virginia Legislative Hand Book* (1928), p. 221.

33. WVBNWS, *Biennial Reports, 1923–24*, pp. 80–88, *1925–26*, pp. 132–42, and *1927–28*, pp. 43–47.

34. Presidential case file no. 51, Commissioners of the District of Columbia, folder no. 39, Arthur Froe, Warren G. Harding Papers, Library of Congress; Office of the Recorder of Deeds, reel 50, series 1, Calvin Coolidge Papers, Library of Congress; "Negroes Form Slate," *Welch Daily News*, 15 Jan. 1923 [1924], President's Office to W.Va. Senator Davis Elkins, 5 Dec. 1921, Davis Elkins to Harding, 27 Jan. 1922, Thomas W. Fleming to Harding, 6 Feb. 1922, in Harding Papers.

35. "Froe Booster Here," *Baltimore Afro-American*, 17 July 1926, newsclipping, recorder of deeds, reel 50, Coolidge Papers; Mrs. Jessie M. Thomas, "The Moon and Froe Families," West Virginia Conference on Black History, Charleston, W.Va., Apr. 1988; *Register of the Department of State*, 1 Jan. 1931 (Washington, 1931), pp. 51, 199–200.

36. For the legislative histories of state-supported black institutions, see *McDowell Times*, 19 and 26 Jan., 2 Feb. 1917; WVBNWS, *Biennial Reports, 1921–22*, pp. 1–15, 69–72, *1923–24*, p. 76, and *1925–26*, pp. 105–6. See also the corresponding reports of the West Virginia State Board of Control (WVSBC), *Biennial Reports, 1916–31* (Charleston, W.Va.), Harris, *West Virginia Legislative Hand Book* (1921), p. 288.

37. Otis K. Rice, *West Virginia: A History* (Lexington: University Press of Kentucky, 1985), pp. 216–19.

38. Cf. Howard N. Rabinowitz, *Race Relations in the Urban South, 1865–1890* (New York: Oxford University Press, 1978).

39. "The Negro as a Soldier and as a Citizen," *McDowell Times*, 30 June 1916. On the same theme, see other *Times* articles by attorneys Harris and Moon and the black agricultural extension agent R. W. White: "The Issue Discussed," 24 Mar. 1916, "Political, Economic Independence of the Negro," 3 Mar. 1916, "Primary: Is Here to Stay," 14 July 1916, all by W. H. Harris; "Democracy's 'Little David,' " 25 Aug. 1916, "The New Americanism," 5 May 1916, "The Stage 'Sittings,' " 25 Feb. 1916, by S. B. Moon; and R. W. White, "National Political Conditions," 12 Nov. 1915.

40. C. B. Johnson, principal of Union High School, to Harding, 7 Feb.

1922, Fleming to Harding, 6 Feb. 1922, and Rev. H. Milton Mickens, pastor of the AME church of Huntington, W.Va., to Harding, 4 Feb. 1922, in presidential case file no. 51, folder no. 39, Harding Papers; "Negroes Form Slate," *Welch Daily News*, 15 Jan. 1923 [1924]; Arthur G. Froe to Edward T. Clark, 12 Nov. 1924, reel 50, series 1, Coolidge Papers.

41. "Differences Between Democrats and Republicans Toward the Negro," 22 Oct. 1915, "Together We Stand," 12 Mar. 1915, "Strong-Arm Methods," 25 Feb. 1916, and "Fired," 16 Mar. 1916, "Governor Called Out Militia upon Request of Citizens," 16 June 1916, in *McDowell Times*.

42. "Hand Picked Committee," 31 Mar. 1916, Harris, "Reorganization," 21 July 1916, and "McDowell Republican Organization," 4 Aug. 1916, "Hatfield-Robinson Republican Club," 14 Jan. 1916, "Mr. Lilly Speaks," 7 Jan. 1916, " 'Cousin Abe' and 'Aunt Amanda,' " 7 Jan. 1917, "Serious Blunder," 31 Dec. 1915, Harris, "Dr. Joseph E. Brown Presides at Lilly Funeral at Keystone," 26 May 1916, "We Told You So," 30 Mar. 1917, "Substantive Improvements," 13 Oct. 1916, editorial page, 29 Sept. 1916, "Negro Democrat Now Known," 6 Oct. 1916, "An Open Letter from the Good Citizens' League to Negro Supporters of Democracy," 20 Oct. 1916, "McDowell County Official Vote by Precincts," 8 Dec. 1916, T. Edward Hill, "Negro Democrat Interviewed," 23 Feb. 1917, "The Kimball Meeting," 14 Jan. 1916, "Judge Robinson Is Ideal Campaigner," 24 Mar. 1916, "Administration Won a Miner's Argument," 26 May 1916, all in *McDowell Times*.

43. "White Man Appointed Librarian," 30 Mar. 1917, "We Told You So," 30 Mar. 1917, "Cut Negroes," 2 Mar. 1917, in *McDowell Times*; "McDowell County Colored Republican Organization," *McDowell Recorder*, 23 Oct. 1919; Harris, *West Virginia Legislative Hand Book* (1916), p. 809.

44. P. Ahmed Williams, "I Remember," in B. B. Maurer, ed., *Mountain Heritage* (Parsons, W.Va.: McClain Printing Company, 1980), pp. 183–87.

45. For data on black Democratic clubs, see "Watch Them," 8 Sept. 1916, "Negro Democrat Interviewed," 23 Feb. 1917, in *McDowell Times;* "Form Colored Smith Clubs," *Raleigh Register*, 13 Sept. 1928; Mrs. E. L. Powell, NAACP secretary, to William Pickens, 29 Apr. 1923, NAACP Branch Files, MacDonald, W.Va., Box G-218, in National Association for the Advancement of Colored People Papers, Library of Congress.

46. "Negroes Plan Big Ox Roast," and "Negro Democrats See Great Victory," both in *Raleigh Register*, 6 Nov. 1932; "Roosevelt Sweeps Nation . . . McDowell Continues Safely in Republican Column," *Welch Daily News*, 9 Nov. 1932; "Democrats Sweep Nation, State, and County," *Logan Banner*, 9 Nov. 1932; "Democrat Ticket Sweeps to Victory: Mercer County Democratic Candidates Are Victorious," *Bluefield Daily Telegraph*, 9 Nov. 1932; "Roosevelt Sweeps Nation: Demos Take Raleigh by Big Margin," *Raleigh Register*, 9 Nov. 1932; "Fayette All Democratic: Every Republican on County Ticket Defeated," *Raleigh Register*, 11 Nov. 1932.

47. "Negroes Plan Big Ox Roast," *Raleigh Register*, 6 Nov. 1932.

48. "McDowell County Colored Republican Organization," *McDowell Recorder*, 23 Oct. 1929.

49. W. H. Harris, "Dr. Joseph Brown Presides . . . ," 26 May 1916, "Reorganization," 21 July 1916, editorial page, 19 Sept. 1916, "Negro Democrat Now Known," 6 Oct. 1916, "An Open Letter," 20 Oct. 1916, editorial page, 29 Sept. 1915, "An Open Letter from the Good Citizens' League to Negro Supporters of Democracy," 20 Sept. 1916, all in *McDowell Times*.

50. "Differences Between Democrats and Republicans Toward the Negro," 22 Oct. 1915, "Together We Stand," 12 Mar. 1915, "Strong Arm Methods," 25 Feb. 1916, "Fired," 16 Mar. 1916, "Governor Called Out Militia upon Request of Citizens," 16 June 1916, in *McDowell Times*.

51. "Gov. Hatfield in Keystone," 12 Nov. 1916, "Armageddon of Lillyism Capitulates," 28 Apr. 1916, in *McDowell Times*.

52. H. D. Hatfield to Herbert Hoover, 21 Jan. 1930, Hatfield to T. G. Nutter, 21 Jan. 1930, Hatfield to H. J. Capehart, 21 Jan. 1930, biographical sketches of Nutter and Capehart, 21 Jan. 1930, in series 3, box no. 20, folder no. 4, Hatfield Papers; "Gov. Hatfield Received Watch in Token of Negroes Friendship," 9 Mar. 1917, and "Governor Hatfield," 23 June 1916, in *McDowell Times*; WVBNWS, *Biennial Reports, 1929–32*, p. 44; *Register of the Department of State, Jan. 1, 1931* (Washington, 1931), pp. 51, 199–200.

53. George Wolfe, manager, to Justus Collins, owner, Winding Gulf Colliery Company, 7 and 8 June 1916, in Series 1, Box 14, Folder 96, Justus Collins Papers, West Virginia University, West Virginia Collection.

54. Wolfe to Collins, 7 and 8 June 1916, Justus Collins Papers.

55. Wolfe to Collins, 7 and 8 June 1916, Justus Collins Papers; "3 Killed, and 2 Hurt in Election Day Riot . . . Colored Rioters Under Arrest," 8 June 1916, "Thirty-Seven in Jail on Riot Complicity Charge," 15 June 1916, "Thirty-Two Indicted for Winding Gulf Outrage," 6 July 1916, "Two Rioters Sentenced to Life Terms in State Pen," 20 July 1916, "Ed Cook Must Serve Life Term, Says Supreme Court," 28 Feb. 1918, all in *Raleigh Register*.

56. James T. Laing, "The Negro Miner in West Virginia" (Ph.D. diss., Ohio State University, 1933), pp. 488–89. For additional information on the Ku Klux Klan in McDowell County, see "The People (McDowell County)," in West Virginia Writers Project, Box 67, Folder 1, West Virginia Collection, West Virginia University.

10

The UNIA, The NAACP, and the Search for Political Alternatives

Garvey

In their struggle for social justice, black coal miners increasingly turned toward the Garvey movement, led by the Universal Negro Improvement Association (UNIA), and toward the National Association for the Advancement of Colored People. Through local branches and affiliates of the UNIA and NAACP, black miners supported a broad struggle that went beyond the limits of electoral politics. Yet, unlike their counterparts farther South, southern West Virginia blacks were able to capitalize on their vote power and work within the framework of conventional politics. This strategy enabled them to implement many of their civil rights objectives through legislation. Nonetheless, like other facets of black life in the coalfields, the Afro-American search for political alternatives was characterized by a complex pattern of racial and class fragmentation as well as solidarity.

The rise of the Garvey movement in southern West Virginia, as elsewhere in America, highlighted the black workers' growing impatience with racial inequality. T. E. Crumbey, a Logan County member of the UNIA expressed their pent-up grievances. "There are only certain kinds of work he is allowed to do. . . . He may be hungry and have money for food, but there are thousands of places in this country where he may not eat, because he is black. If he goes to certain places of amusement, he is segregated as if by contact he might contaminate the rest of the patrons."[1]

By the mid-1920s, no less than eight local divisions or chapters of the UNIA had emerged in southern West Virginia. The Garvey movement was especially strong in McDowell, Kanawha, Raleigh, and Fayette counties. The range of dues-paying members was much greater in small company towns than in larger commercial centers. The capital city chapter had a dues-paying membership of only 6 to 19 persons, while the chapter membership in the small coal towns of Capels, Coalwood, and Sprague, ranged in size from 20 to 51, 10 to 59, and 14 to 31 people, respectively. Moreover, a comparative assessment of available officer lists reveals new names different from the established roster of elite black leaders— undoubtedly coal miners. Emphasizing race pride and the need for black self-determination, Garvey's ideology of "Race First" struck a responsive chord among large numbers of black workers in the coalfields.[2]

What little evidence there is documenting the specific programs and activities of the UNIA in West Virginia suggests that Garveyites perceived the limitations of the prevailing political strategies and promoted pan-African unity as a means of effecting black liberation. They also read the *Negro World*, attended local meetings, and listened to various speakers.[3] Black women also participated in the expanding Garvey movement, serving as secretaries and members of local chapters, and sometimes they even dominated the program at local meetings. At one Charleston division rally, after the meeting opened with prayer and the singing of the division's song, one woman took the speaker's platform to offer fund-raising suggestions, and another read from volume I of the *Philosophy and Opinions of Marcus Garvey*. A third woman warned the gathering, "We will make a great mistake if we step out of the path of the Universal Negro Improvement Association."[4]

Blacks in southern West Virginia publicly expressed their faith in Marcus Garvey and his ideas. In his February 1926 letter to the editor of the *Negro World*, T. E. Crumbey credited Garvey with awakening blacks to the "real meaning of freedom." "The Honorable Marcus Garvey realized a long time ago that Negroes are a long way from being free men. Many Negroes never knew this until he told them. He has awakened thousands. The Negro is awake for good. . . . Garveyism has become their password of success." As late as November 1930, the Charleston division reported a two-night mass meeting, featuring an address titled, "Awakening." The members, the division reporter said, "were awakened as never before. . . . Some members living 15 miles away did not go home, but just remained in the city till the next session night. We had a splendid house. It was one hundred percent U.N.I.A."[5]

Like other blacks around the nation, blacks in the coalfields sometimes spoke of Marcus Garvey as "a Moses." They perceived him as a kind of messenger of universal racial cooperation and liberation from injustice. "Providence has sent us a Moses who is no less a person than the Hon. Marcus Garvey," W. J. Childs of the Charleston UNIA wrote to the editor of the *Negro World*. Afro-Americans in the coalfields also confirmed their solidarity with the cause of African liberation. "To reap the full fruits of this great plan of racial unity," wrote Childs, "men of courage, ability and integrity must volunteer to lay the foundation of nationhood upon the so-called dark continent of Africa." Yet Childs affirmed the value of Afro-Americans' citizenship, and he worked to adapt the pan-African theme to the reality of black life in southern West Virginia and America. "There need be no wholesale exodus from our present homelands. Our blood is in the soil, and we have paid for our rights even if we do not possess them. We have paid with sacrifice on the bloody field of honor and in ample contribution to the material and spiritual development of this nation."[6]

Even as blacks grasped for a nationalistic alternative to electoral strategies for social change, they retained their demands for economic equality and the freedom to fully exercise their rights as American citizens. Moreover, the persistent electoral political orientation of Afro-Americans, marked by strong collaboration with white allies, limited the effectiveness of the separatist response. It is no wonder, then, that the civil rights campaign of the NAACP would soon dominate the black workers' freedom struggle in the southern mountains.

As black workers confronted the limitations of the Garvey movement, the NAACP supplanted the UNIA and emerged at the center of the black miners' struggle for equal rights. More than any other organization, it helped to link the black proletariat to the larger civil rights campaign. Although the NAACP was a nonpartisan body, working closely with black elected and appointed officials, it played a crucial role in the expansion of state-supported black institutions, the curtailment of white mob violence, and the growing protection of blacks under the law. In their struggle for racial justice, however, Afro-Americans were not alone. Civil rights leaders, besides helping to unite middle- and working-class blacks, also cultivated and retained a tiny core of white allies.

Founded in 1909 in New York City, the NAACP steadily increased in influence during the postwar years. The number of branches grew from less than 100 before the war to more than 400 in cities and towns throughout the nation in 1921.[7] During World War I the NAACP had no presence in southern West Virginia; by 1932 it had nearly a dozen branches and affiliates (see table 10). Except for Boone, each county had at least one viable branch and sometimes less viable ones. One exasperated organizer exclaimed that "it is awful hard for us . . . to add members fast. . . . [For] every little town want one Association in the[i]r town."[8]

Formed in 1918, the Charleston, Kanawha County, branch of the NAACP emerged as the pioneer chapter in the region and the strongest one. The Charleston branch had its roots in the militant West Virginia State Civic League (WVSCL), founded in September 1915 under the leadership of Rev. I. V. Bryant of Huntington, attorney Brown W. Payne of Raleigh County, and Dr. F. M. Gamble of Charleston.[9] In conjunction with the NAACP's national campaign, during the spring and summer of 1918 the WVSCL launched a series of mass protests against the racist film *The Birth of a Nation*. The protests culminated in the formation of the Charleston NAACP, which soon took the place of the WVSCL at the forefront of the civil rights struggle in southern West Virginia. The Charleston branch grew from 56 charter members in 1918 to well over 1,000 by the mid-1920s, when it "was never in better spirits," its president reported. Because of its substantial financial contributions, the Charleston branch regularly appeared on the NAACP's national "Honor Roll." In 1930, national board chairwoman Mary White Ovington declared, "It is impossible to think too highly of the Charleston branch and of the splendid support it always gives."[10]

TABLE 10

Southern West Virginia Branches of the National Association for the Advancement of Colored People, 1918–32

	Year Chartered	County
Charleston	1918	Kanawha
Bluefield	1918	Mercer
Beckley	1920	Raleigh
Gary	1921	McDowell
Mt. Hope	1921	Fayette
Williamson, Mingo, et al.	1923	Mingo
Keystone	1925	McDowell
Logan	1927	Logan
Winona	1927	Fayette
Montgomery	1931	Fayette
Glen Rogers	1932	Wyoming

Source: West Virginia Branch Files, Boxes G-214 through G-217, National Association for the Advancement of Colored People Papers, Manuscript Division, Library of Congress.

From 1918 through 1921, the pastor of Charleston's First Baptist Church, Rev. Mordecai Johnson, served as president of the Charleston branch. Under his leadership, business and professional people dominated the chapter's work. Of 56 charter members, 31 were professional, clerical, and business people, and the remainder was comprised of a variety of skilled and unskilled laborers. Under Johnson's successor, attorney T. G. Nutter, the Charleston branch retained its elite leadership structure.[11] Nonetheless, the branch was able to expand during the early 1920s only by appealing to the black working class. R. C. McIver, a baggage agent for the City Taxi Company, served as a very influential and effective membership captain. Although Rev. Johnson later split with him over policy issues, he once described McIver as a man of "remarkable energy" and enthusiasm, well-suited for the mass-membership campaign in the Kanawha-New River Field.[12]

The Charleston NAACP was soon followed by branches in Bluefield, Beckley, Gary, Keystone, Logan, and other cities and towns. Described by one local organizer as "the hot bed of the K.K.K.," Logan County was the scene of an especially enthusiastic drive to establish NAACP chapters. In a letter to the national office, Rev. F. Thomas wrote, "I am in Logan Co. W.Va. and you know that I want the greatest organization of our race here in this county."[13] In some small coal towns, organizers had difficulty raising the minimum of 50 members required to establish a branch charter. In many of these cases, the small branch simply affiliated with a major branch. Attached to the Logan County branch, for example, were the affiliates of Slagle, Peach Creek, Yolyn, Amherstdale, MacBeath, Kistler, and Lundale, to name only a few. A typical small branch, the Gary branch was chartered in 1921 and over the years increased from 60 to over 300 members by 1925. That year the Gary branch remitted nearly $350 to national headquarters and helped the Bluefield branch raise $1,000 for an important local civil rights case.[14] Despite their size, the small branches and affiliates gave significant financial support to local and national programs.

From the beginning, unlike the Charleston branch, the other West Virginia chapters were predominantly working class, and women played a prominent role in them. Black workers made up between 60 and 80 percent of the charter members of the Gary, Logan, Mt. Hope, and Winona branches. Although the small black elite controlled all the major leadership posts, skilled workers also held influential positions, including the electrician H. Ball, who was president of the Logan branch, and the carpenter S. R. Jackson, who was secretary of the Winona chapter.[15] Black women made up over 30 percent of all charter members and held important offices, too. At its beginning in 1921, and through the 1920s, the Gary branch elected the schoolteacher Memphis Tennessee Garrison as Secretary. In 1925 the Keystone branch included the religious leader Mrs. Mattie Thornton, vice president; the teacher Ida Whittico, secretary; and another teacher, Helen M. James, treasurer. Black women in the Charleston chapter served as secretary, assistant secretary, treasurer, and director of youth activities. In Mingo County, Mary Hairston was elected vice president of the Williamson branch in 1923 and president in 1926. Since black coal miners were often on the job for long hours, in 1932 one branch president, Rev. J. Y. Brown, advised the local to "elect competent women as officers." The chapter soon met and elected one woman vice president and another secretary.[16]

In the fight for equal protection before the law, the NAACP, like the Republican clubs discussed in chapter 9, worked to mobilize not only the economic resources of the black community, but its spiritual and cultural resources as well. Rev. Mordecai Johnson promoted the NAACP as "an instrument for the achievement of a Christian objective." Thousands of black miners, he believed, would support the NAACP, "if they once get the vision of the Association as an arm of God." The national office reinforced local efforts to mobilize the black church behind the civil rights campaign. When the Gary branch suggested that a national officer reschedule his visit because "this little town (is) in the midst of a Baptist revival," he replied, "Can you not get some person to tactfully suggest to the preacher that they suspend their services for that evening and come out and help us to do the Lord's work in stopping lynchings, segregation, etc.?"[17]

The NAACP launched a broad attack on race prejudice and discrimination in the coalfields. Its targets included organs of public opinion, especially the press; the criminal justice system, including official and unofficial violence and intimidation; and publicly financed educational and social welfare institutions. Organized assaults on injustice on these fronts sometimes resulted in favorable state legislation, court decisions, and public policy changes. Although the NAACP played the leading role in the struggle, black institutions like the *McDowell Times*, the McDowell County Colored Republican Organization, and the Bureau of Negro Welfare and Statistics played crucial supporting roles and sometimes even took principal parts. These shifts reflect the complex interplay of protest and electoral strategies for social change in the southern mountains.

As suggested above, it was protest against the anti-black film *The Birth of a Nation* that gave impetus to the rise of the Charleston NAACP. In early 1918, when movie houses advertised and scheduled showings of the film in several area towns and cities, Charleston blacks held a mass meeting at Garnet High School "to protest the forthcoming production." When two theaters in McDowell County scheduled the film, blacks "protested vigorously against its appearance and contemplated legal action." Using the MCCRO as a base, black leaders appealed to the State Executive Council of Defense, which was comprised of the Democratic Governor John J. Cornwell, other state elected officials, and the black auxiliary council of defense. They won a major victory when the state council prohibited the showing of films that tended "to create race friction, for the duration of the war."[18]

When the State Executive Council of Defense dissolved in the early postwar years, blacks pushed for state legislation that "would forever prohibit the showing of such pictures." Under increasing pressure from his black constituency, Republican state senator J. W. Luther of McDowell County introduced a bill "barring pictures and plays from the state tending to create race friction."[19] In February 1919, without a dissenting vote, the state legislature passed the bill, and Governor Cornwell signed it into law. The act provided that "it shall be unlawful for any person, corporation or company to advertise, exhibit, display or show any picture or theatrical act in any theatre or other place of public amusement or entertainment within this state which shall in any manner . . . result in arousing prejudice, ire or feelings of one race or class of citizens against any other race or class of citizens." Violations of the law carried penalties of $100 to $1,000, at the discretion of the court, and violators could be ordered to spend up to thirty days in jail. Although local theaters soon challenged the law, blacks successfully used the new statute to ban further showings of *The Birth of a Nation*. In April 1925 the state supreme court upheld the law. T. G. Nutter, the Charleston NAACP attorney, reported to national headquarters: "Won Smashing Victory—Supreme Court This Morning—When Court Decided Unanimously Against Showing of Birth of A Nation—Case Fought Through Common Pleas Circuit and Supreme Courts."[20]

Afro-Americans waged an equally vigorous offensive against racist reporting. Although the NAACP attacked unfair journalistic practices, it was the *McDowell Times* and the Bureau of Negro Welfare and Statistics that waged the most consistent campaign against local white papers. Both frequently attacked the white press for playing up black crime while downplaying black accomplishments. Throughout the 1920s the BNWS urged white newspapers to change their editorial policies on blacks. "If the newspapers could be induced to stop using 'Negro' in the headlines in reporting crimes committed by members of that race, they would remove a source of great harm to the Negro race and an element which breeds ill will." Crimes committed by Jews, Italians, Englishmen, and other white ethnic groups, the bureau argued, were not "published in the headlines and seldom mentioned in the body of the article."[21] From World War I through the mid-1920s numerous newspapers, responding to black protests, initiated weekly "Colored News" columns, in which the positive side of black life in coal-mining towns received detailed treatment.[22] Although no white papers changed their racially biased policies to the satisfaction of blacks, some nonetheless made important modifications, recognizing that blacks represented a lucrative market.

Blacks aimed their most vigorous protests against mob violence and summary justice, and the Ku Klux Klan became a major target of their efforts. Civil rights leaders worked to end the Klan's secrecy, emphasizing its potential for inciting race war. Take "the cowls" from over its head, T. Edward Hill exclaimed, "and the danger of crime being committed in its name and in similar regalia will be removed." In 1919 when a white mob lynched two black miners in Logan County, the infant Charleston NAACP pushed for an official investigation to bring the perpetrators to justice. When white law enforcement officials resisted its efforts, the branch would not "let the matter rest."[23] Although its efforts proved fruitless in bringing the lynchers to justice, the local NAACP exhibited its resolve to protect blacks against mob violence and summary justice.

In the Harry Lattimar rape case of 1921, the Charleston NAACP won a major victory. It appealed the case to the West Virginia Supreme Court, which overturned the lower court's guilty verdict and death sentence, granted Lattimar a new trial, and ordered a change of venue from Mingo to Wayne County. Although Lattimar was not fully exonerated, he escaped the death penalty.[24] In 1925 the Gary and Bluefield branches successfully defended Payne Boyd in the Mercer County Court. Boyd was a black man unjustly accused of murdering a white man. When an all-white jury returned a guilty verdict against him and sentenced him to hang, the local NAACP branches escalated their defense efforts, obtained a change of venue, introduced evidence proving Boyd's innocence, and secured his release. In 1930 the Logan Branch quickly expended most of its funds fighting another murder case.[25]

Although the NAACP waged an energetic campaign against civil rights violations, it achieved only partial success. Within the highly charged racial climate of the coalfields, the NAACP faced a difficult dilemma: first and foremost, it sought to prevent mob violence, but it also sought to encourage the use of the formal legal system by advocating the severe prosecution of offenders found guilty in a court of law. The NAACP strove to convince whites that it did not condone black criminal behavior but, in the process, risked exposing blacks accused of crimes to an unjust legal process. In the Leroy Williams rape case, for example, the NAACP publicly proclaimed: "We condemn without reservation the barbarous, inhuman and fiendish assault against Mrs. H. W. Stephens, of Edgewood, Monday morning, December 12, 1921, and call upon the constituted authorities *to prosecute without mercy* the author of that crime against society, with due regard to law" (my italics). With its position widely circulated in the white press, the NAACP reported, "The [r]eaction was immediate and the town became absolutely quiet and the talk of lynching ceased."[26]

The NAACP later appealed for a commutation of Williams's death sentence to life imprisonment, emphasizing the mob atmosphere in which the accused was tried. There was, the NAACP argued, a "high tensive state of public mind that precluded that calm and deliberate approach to the trial of such an inhuman offense nine days after its commission. . . . there is a surprising general feeling among the people that Leroy Williams should not hang."[27] Although the NAACP lost the appeal and was unable to prevent the state's unjust execution of Williams, it had at least helped to prevent mob violence.

The struggle against racial inequality in the coalfields culminated in a campaign for a state anti-lynching law. Following the war, the black coal miner and state legislator John V. Coleman introduced the "first anti-lynching bill ever introduced" into the West Virginia legislature. Following the Whitney-Whitfield lynching, the anti-lynching campaign gained greater momentum, despite attempts by white citizens and lawmakers to assure blacks that "it is very seldom that a lynching occurs in West Virginia."[28] In 1921, however, following a brutal white-on-white lynching, West Virginia passed an anti-lynching statute. Introduced by black delegate H. J. Cape-

Coal, Class, and Color

hart of McDowell County, the statute established a penalty of not less than one year imprisonment, nor more than ten years for each offense.[29] Although these sanctions were lenient, the passage of the West Virginia anti-lynching law represented a major victory for the NAACP, black politicians, and black workers, especially given the failure of the national campaign for federal anti-lynching legislation at this time.

While the white-on-white lynching facilitated the success of the West Virginia anti-lynching campaign, the law was nonetheless a product of black activism. More specifically, it represented the increasing growth of black civil rights protests and electoral activities and their joint strategic use. The expanding network of state-supported black institutions similarly reflected this development. In 1918, for example, the Charleston NAACP protested against the state's plan to house black deaf, mute, and blind children at the West Virginia Collegiate Institute "without proper facilities and instructors." Rather than appropriate money for a black facility, the state attempted to transfer the children to Maryland, where proper facilities for blacks allegedly existed. When the state of Maryland unexpectedly rejected the children and sent them back, the NAACP and black political leaders joined together and escalated their protests. Their combined efforts led to the creation of the West Virginia School for Colored Deaf and Blind in 1919.[30]

Although the combination of black protest and electoral activities generally produced an ironic reinforcement of racial segregation in coal-mining towns, Afro-Americans effectively used it to push for integrated juries in county courts. During World War I, Fayette County blacks advanced an eloquent defense of black jury duty: "Whereas, two hundred thousand of the flower of Negro manhood are now offering their lives for the preservation of the ideals of democracy . . . we stultify ourselves in attempting to carry the ideals of democracy across the [R]hine when they do not obtain on the banks of the New and Kanawha Rivers." In 1919 the West Virginia Supreme Court handed down a historic decision mandating the selection of black jurors in the state's courts of law.[31]

Despite the supreme court's favorable ruling, blacks had to continue their fight for inclusion on juries into the 1920s because local courts resisted the change in the law. In its 1921–22 biennial report, the BNWS urged jury commissioners in all counties with an appreciable black population to hear "the pleas of Negroes for members of their race on juries to pass upon the causes vital to their life, liberty and property." In the following biennium, the bureau reiterated its plea that jury commissioners "place the names of Negroes in the jury box" and that they "be drawn for service on grand and petit juries." Such protests produced results in Kanawha, Raleigh, and McDowell counties, where a tradition of black jury service emerged.[32] Although the evidence is inconclusive, integrated juries must have made a difference in the outcome of black criminal cases. For example, in a McDowell County assault case involving a young black man and a young white female, the presence of five blacks on the jury of twelve evidently prevented the death sentence from being handed down.[33]

In its celebrated public library case, the Charleston NAACP launched a direct assault against racial discrimination in the capital city. In 1928 when the city of Charleston established a segregated branch of the public library, the Charleston NAACP filed a lawsuit against the city. State law, the NAACP argued, provided for segregated schools, but not for segregated public libraries. When the circuit court upheld the position of the Charleston Board of Education, the NAACP appealed to the state supreme court. Under the leadership of black attorneys T. G. Nutter and Clayton E. Kimbrough, Sr., the NAACP won the appeal. Its victory was by no means complete, though, for the supreme court ruled that "the Board of Education may provide separate departments for white and colored persons in the library building."[34] Despite the partial nature of this victory, Afro-Americans had gained important legal ground in mitigating the effects of institutionalized racism in southern West Virginia.

The Afro-American civil rights campaign was not entirely dominated by males. Black women were prominent among the NAACP membership and officer lists, as noted above, and proved to be a vital force in the civil rights struggle. The Gary chapter produced the finest example of female leadership, Secretary Memphis Tennessee Garrison, who emerged as the crucial mainstay of the chapter's various programs. Under her dynamic leadership, the Gary chapter developed a large range of local projects, and even national ones such as the national headquarter's annual Christmas Seal Campaign, which she spearheaded.[35] In addition to the favorable publicity the campaign garnered, with its motto, "Merry Christmas and Justice for All," contributions totaling $300 to $400 were soon being netted annually. In 1929 Garrison won the coveted Madame C. J. Walker Gold Medal Award for her contributions to the civil rights cause. It is no wonder that she was later dubbed "Miss Civil Rights of West Virginia."[36]

If the Afro-American civil rights struggle was not an entirely black male–dominated effort, neither was it an entirely black effort. It also garnered significant white support. The white Mingo County attorney Thomas West played a key role in the NAACP's legal defense efforts. In the Harry Lattimar rape case, West helped to gain a change of venue and a reduced sentence for the accused. In the Henry Grogan rape case, West appealed to the American Civil Liberties Union and again assisted the Charleston NAACP's legal defense committee. Attorney West, the Charleston branch later reported, had not received "one cent of pay, the money we have raised going toward the enormous expense of the case." Moreover, in one case, the Charleston branch reported, "Mr. West made a strong fight over bitter opposition. His life was threatened for trying to save the Negro and he has been severely criticized by the [white] citizens of Mingo county, but he did not swerve for a minute from his duty."[37]

Through the sponsorship of concerts, plays, and nationally renowned speakers, including W. E. B. Du Bois, Roland Hayes, and Clarence Darrow, the NAACP promoted interracial cooperation, and sometimes the color line dropped temporarily. When black tenor Roland Hayes performed in Charleston, the BNWS enthusiastically reported, "There were about as many White people as Negroes present seated without regard to races, equally as well dressed, as well behaved and as clean, and they all seemed to enjoy the music of the great black singer."[38] In 1928, a visit by the famous white attorney Clarence Darrow, the NAACP lawyer in the celebrated Ossian Sweet case, was likewise a huge success.[39]

Interracial cooperation was nevertheless a fragile affair in southern West Virginia. As black civil rights leaders escalated their campaigns, they lost white friends and alienated potential white recruits. From 1919 to 1922 the West Virginia secretary of state, Houston G. Young, was an important white member and supporter of the Charleston NAACP. However, when the NAACP asked Governor Morgan to commute the death sentence of Leroy Williams to life imprisonment, Young withdrew his support from the body, declaring, "I cannot belong to a society or help to contribute as long as its organization officially fails to endorse the carrying out of the extreme penalty provided by law in such cases."[40] Such occurrences underscored the highly tenuous and unequal nature of black-white alliances in the region. Indeed, few whites were members of the numerous southern West Virginia chapters of the NAACP.

If a dearth of dependable white allies weakened the civil rights struggle, internal conflict unfortunately also took its toll. As in the case of the power struggle within the MCCRO discussed in chapter 9, Afro-Americans in the NAACP understandably fought over prestigious leadership positions. From its inception, the Charleston branch was plagued by internal rivalry. A faction led by the painting contractor and decorator I. M. Carper and the agricultural extension agent R. W. White clashed with another faction, led by Rev. Mordecai Johnson and the grocer C. H. James.

Johnson and James were actively involved in protests against *The Birth of A Nation,* and they expected to take first charge of the new Charleston branch. They claimed that Carper and others lacked "full public confidence by reason of their conduct in public affairs." The Carper faction vigorously counterargued that it deserved the charter because it had organized first and had held itself "out to the public in such capacity." Although the Carper group had in fact met first, national headquarters chartered the Johnson group and urged Carper to cooperate with it.[41] Although the two factions eventually met, resolved their differences, and officially launched the Charleston NAACP, their acrimonious intraracial battle for leadership had delayed and marred the new chapter's formation. Intraclass rivalry among the elite, however, was not the only conflict to stalk the Charleston branch.

During the early 1920s, as the Charleston branch escalated its appeal to black workers, interclass conflicts emerged. In 1921, R. C. McIver, the captain of the Charleston NAACP membership drive mentioned in chapter 9, charged the local with discrimination in the "distribution of recognition." Chafing under the elite's apparent exploitation of his services, McIver sought permission to establish a second chapter. In a letter to Walter White of the national office, Rev. Mordecai Johnson confirmed McIver's exploitation. "When I consented to his appointment as a captain . . . I was conscious of the danger involved, but I was willing to risk the danger in order that we might use his remarkable energy for the good of our cause. . . . The direction in which his zeal sometimes drives his intelligence and worth requires constant community scrutiny, criticism and oftimes stoppage."[42] Although the NAACP rejected McIver's request for a second branch, his efforts revealed substantial friction between elite and working-class blacks. McIver's ambitions later took him to Logan County, where he settled and again became the center of a major NAACP controversy.

In 1927 McIver and his associates proposed a second NAACP branch for Logan County and precipitated a major intraracial working-class confrontation. The official Logan County branch under the leadership of President H. Ball, an electrician, was headquartered in the town of Omar. Coal miners from Omar made up over 90 percent of the charter members. McIver and his associate Jefferson Crouder proposed a branch in the city of Logan, emphasizing the inconvenience of traveling to Omar, some ten miles away. The NAACP's national director of branches, Robert Bagnall, vigorously opposed having two chapters in Logan County. To outmaneuver McIver, Ball himself proposed and led the relocation of the Logan County headquarters to Logan.

Ball, referring to his rival McIver as a newcomer of no more than five or six months' residence, repeatedly emphasized the need to organize the surrounding coal communities like Omar. "Our people live in the outskirts of the town, and in coal company camps, all places leading into Logan. So you see no two branches here are going to succeed." Ball also argued another reason for denying McIver a charter: "One of them is sure to fail to keep up the quota of memberships required by the organization. As members come and go in the coal fields, all the time."[43]

As some analysts of black civil rights activism in a later context have noted, disunity could serve a positive function by stimulating warring factions to greater organizational effort in the achievement of complementary goals. Yet intraracial fragmentation—compounded by the precarious socioeconomic foundation of the black community—weakened the civil rights offensive in southern West Virginia and hampered the pace of social change during the 1920s. The NAACP's chapters were rooted so deeply in the proletarianization process that some were quite short-lived. In 1927 the Winona and Ansted branch and its affiliates finally received a charter, after nearly two years of effort to meet the minimum qualifications. Within two years, however, the branch formally disbanded because of a downturn in the coal industry. In 1927 organizers of the branch at Glen Rogers, Wyoming County, reported, "The reason we have not been able to organize is because work is very slow at present, but as work get better . . . we will be able to organize."[44]

The history of the NAACP's Logan branch, which was organized during the late 1920s, not only highlights the destructive impact of the Great Depression on the NAACP, but also suggests the relationship between proletarianization and the regional civil rights campaign. In March 1928, as sporadic unemployment rose and black miners were increasingly on the move in search of jobs, President Ball reported that the Logan branch was largely inactive.[45] With their incomes declining, black people in Logan County found it increasingly difficult to meet their civil rights commitments. "They promise to do but fail at the last to bring the money," Ball informed the national office in 1929. In early 1932, he reported even greater failure and financial instability, "owing to the mine running only one and two days a week." When the national office launched its 1932 Emergency Fund Campaign, Logan accepted a pledge of $25; it could raise only $12.75. "We are doing the best we can under the present condition of work in this field";[46] indeed, considering the county's depressed economic condition, the Logan branch's commitment to the civil rights struggle was remarkable. Even so, as the depression took an increasing toll on the livelihood of black miners, NAACP memberships continued to decline, numerous associations and affiliates became defunct, and other chapters formally disbanded. The Great Depression made the connection between proletarianization and the civil rights campaign clear.

Notwithstanding the economic hardships to come, however, the NAACP's rise and expansion after World War I represented the fullest exercise of black political power that southern West Virginia had yet seen. At a time when most southern blacks were disfranchised, West Virginian Afro-American civil rights and political leaders increasingly combined protest with legislative reforms. They led the expansion of state-supported black institutions, curbed lynchings, and brought blacks increasingly, if tenuously, under the protection of the law, using the support of white allies.

Yet the success of the civil rights campaign was incomplete, plagued by staunch white resistance and fraught with internal conflicts along class lines. In the broader context of industrial change, however, the political and civil rights struggles of blacks in southern West Virginia reveal, in sharp relief, how complex a process black industrial working-class formation was. It involved not only economic, demographic, and cultural change, but also changes in the balance of power and in the ability of blacks to influence the state. Given the tremendous obstacles that the black proletariat faced, through their organizations like the MCCRO, the NAACP, and the UNIA, black coal miners in southern West Virginia exercised a real influence on the larger political system. As the depression and subsequent social and technological changes in the coal industry undercut the basis of their livelihood, blacks would find their cultural and political traditions facing greater challenges in the decades ahead. Fortunately, the 1915-32 generation bequeathed a rich legacy. How well the next generation would be able to draw upon it must be the subject of another study.

NOTES

1. T. E. Crumbey, Stirrat, W.Va., to editor, "The Negroes Are a Long Way from Being Free," *Negro World*, 6 Feb. 1926.

2. Universal Negro Improvement Association, Parent Body, Division Lists, 1925–26, courtesy of Robert A. Hill, editor, the Marcus Garvey and UNIA Papers, University of California-Los Angeles; Robert A. Hill, ed., *The Marcus Garvey and Universal Negro Improvement Association Papers* (Berkeley: University of California Press, 1986), 4:654–68; Judith Stein, *The World of Marcus Garvey: Race and Class in Modern Society* (Baton Rouge: Louisiana State University Press, 1986); Tony Martin, *Race First: The Ideological and Organizational Struggles of Marcus Garvey and the Universal Negro Improvement Association* (Westport, Conn.: Greenwood Press, 1976).

3. Divisional reports, "Beckley, W.Va.," 15 Aug. 1925, "Charleston, W.Va.," 28 May 1927, 9 July 1927, in *Negro World*.

4. "Charleston, W.Va.," *Negro World*, 9 July 1927.

5. Crumbey, "The Negroes," 6 Feb. 1926, "Charleston, W.Va. Enjoys One Hundred Per Cent U.N.I.A.," 29 Nov. 1930, in *Negro World*.

6. W. J. Childs, Charleston UNIA to editor, "Black Men Must Answer the Call of Africa," *Negro World*, 9 Mar. 1929.

7. Charles Flint Kellogg, *NAACP: A History of the National Association for the Advancement of Colored People*, vol. 1, *1909–1920* (Baltimore: Johns Hopkins Press, 1967); John Hope Franklin and Alfred A. Moss, Jr., *From Slavery to Freedom: A History of Negro Americans* (1947; rept., New York: Alfred A. Knopf, 1988), pp. 288–89; August Meier and Elliot Rudwick, *From Plantation to Ghetto* (1966; rept., New York: Hill and Wang, 1976), pp. 87–89; Allan H. Spear, *Black Chicago: The Making of a Negro Ghetto, 1890–1920* (Chicago: University of Chicago Press, 1967), pp. 227–31.

8. For information on other local branches, see West Virginia Branch Files, Boxes G-213 through G-217, NAACP Papers; Rev. J. Y. Brown to NAACP headquarters, 22 Sept. 1932, Glen Rogers Branch Files, Box G-217, NAACP Papers, Manuscript Division, Library of Congress; Rev. F. Thomas to William Pickens, 29 Sept. 1924, Pickens to Thomas, 29 Sept. 1924, H. C. Ball, president Logan branch, to Pickens, director of branches, 12 Mar. 1928, Pickens to Ball, 14 Mar. 1928, Logan Branch Files, Box G-217, NAACP Papers.

9. "Civil League Organized," 13 Aug. 1915, "Civil League to Meet in Charleston," 17 Sept. 1915, "Civic League is Perfected," 24 Sept. 1915, "General Secretary, W.Va. State Civic League," 8 Oct. 1915, "Negroes in Fayette County," 6 Sept. 1918, in *McDowell Times*; West Virginia Bureau of Negro Welfare and Statistics (WVBNWS), *Biennial Reports, 1921–22*, pp. 72–73, 89–90, *1925–26*, pp. 140–41.

10. "Application for Charter," 4 June 1918, "Annual Report of the Charleston Branch," June 1921, Rev. Mordecai Johnson to Walter White to Johnson, 25 May 1918 and 21 Jan. 1921, White to Johnson, 27 May 1918, White to Edward C. Lewis, Charleston branch secretary, 20 June 1918, "Financial Statement of the Charleston Branch NAACP," 1 Jan. 1922–1 Jan. 1923, secretary, NAACP headquarters, to T. G. Nutter, 29 May 1928, Mary White Ovington, chair of board, to Nutter, 18 Nov. 1930, Charleston Branch Files, Box G-215, NAACP Papers.

11. "Application for Charter," 4 June 1918, T. G. Nutter to William Pickens, 2 Feb. 1925, "Committee Assignments," annual report of the Charleston branch, June 1921, Nutter to White, 2 Oct. 1930, Charleston Branch Files, Box G-215, NAACP Papers.

12. R. C. McIver to NAACP headquarters, 7 Jan. 1921, White to McIver, 12 Jan. 1921, Johnson to White, 21 Jan. 1921, "Note on Church Affiliations," Charleston Branch Files, Box G-215, NAACP Papers.

13. Rev. J. Y. Brown to NAACP headquarters, 22 Sept. 1932, Glen Rogers Branch Files, Box G-217, NAACP Papers; Rev. F. Thomas to William Pickens, 29 Sept. 1924, Pickens to Thomas, 29 Sept. 1924, H. C. Ball, president of Logan branch, to Pickens, director of branches, 12 Mar. 1928, Pickens to Ball, 14 Mar. 1928, Logan Branch Files, Box G-217, NAACP Papers.

14. For documentation on other branches, see West Virginia Branch Files, Boxes G-214 through G-217, NAACP Papers; "Application for Charter," 20 Dec. 1921, "Snatched from Gallows by Wartime Finger Prints: Payne Boyd, Defended by West Va. N.A.A.C.P., to Go Free," 30 Oct. 1925 (news release), M. T. Garrison, secretary, to Walter White, 21 Oct. 1925, White to Thomas G. Howard, President, Bluefield Branch, 3 Oct. 1925, Gary Branch Files, Box G-216, NAACP Papers.

15. "Applications for Charters: 20 Dec. 1921," Gary Branch Files, Box G-216; "Applications for Charters: 30 Mar. 1927," Logan Branch Files, Box G-217; "Applications for Charters: 16 Mar. 1921," Mt. Hope Branch Files; and "Applications for Charters: 11 Apr. 1927," Winona Branch Files, all in Branch Files, NAACP Papers.

16. "Application for Charter, 1925" C. H. W. to Butler, 10 Nov. 1925, Keystone Branch Files, Box G-217, NAACP Papers; Edward Lewis, secretary, to National Headquarters, 3 Dec. 1918, Lewis to Ovington, 7 Jan. 1922, Charleston Branch Files, Box G-215, NAACP Papers; Rev. J. Y. Brown to Robert Bagnall, 9 Nov. 1932, Glen Rogers Branch Files, Box G-217, NAACP Papers; Mary Hairston to Walter White, 10 Apr. 1926, James Weldon Johnson to Hairston, 14 Apr. 1926, Williamson Branch Files, Box G-218, NAACP Papers, Gary Branch Files, Box G-216, NAACP Papers.

17. M. T. Garrison to William Pickens, 8 and 12 Oct. 1928, Pickens to Garrison, 11 Oct. 1928, Gary Branch Files, Box G-216, NAACP Papers; Rev. Mordecai Johnson to W. E. B. Du Bois, 5 Mar. 1918, Charleston Branch Files, Box G-215, NAACP Papers.

18. Rev. M. Johnson to Walter White, 23 Mar. 1918, Charleston Branch Files, Box G-215, NAACP Papers; "General Legislation Urged by Negroes," in WVBNWS, *Biennial Report, 1921–22*, pp. 72–73.

19. WVBNWS, *Biennial Report, 1921–22*, pp. 72–73; John T. Harris, ed., *West Virginia Legislative Hand Book* (Charleston, W.Va.: The Tribune Printing Company, 1920), p. 158.

20. "West Virginia Supreme Court Bars 'Birth of Nation' Film," 10 Apr. 1925 (news release), "Won Smashing Victory," telegram from T. G. Nutter, president, Charleston branch, to James Weldon Johnson, 3 Apr. 1925, Charleston Branch Files, Box G-215, NAACP Papers.

21. "White Press and the Negro," *McDowell Times*, 22 Jan. 1915; WVBNWS, *Biennial Reports 1921–22*, p. 52, *1923–24*, pp. 78–80, and *1925–26*, pp. 114–18. For an NAACP attack on racist reporting, see "Report of Charleston NAACP," Dec. 1921, Charleston Branch Files, Box G-215, NAACP Papers.

22. See "The Colored News" columns of local newspapers, especially the *Welch Daily News, Logan Banner, Bluefield Daily Telegraph, McDowell Recorder,* and the *Raleigh Register;* "Newspapers and Inter-racial Co-operation," in WVBNWS, *Biennial Report, 1925–26*, pp. 114–18.

23. For full citations about the lynching, see n. 1, chapter 5. See also "A Cowled and Gowned Danger," in WVBNWS, *Biennial Report, 1921–22*, pp. 52–54, "Klansmen Perform Last Rites at Green Funeral," *Charleston Mail*, ca. 1921, (newspaper clipping), application blank, Knights of the Ku Klux Klan, ca. 1921, all in Charleston Branch Files, Box G-215, NAACP Papers.

24. E. C. Lewis to Walter White, 19 Dec. 1922, White to Lewis, 16 Dec. 1922, Lewis to White, 13 Dec. 1922, all in Box G-215, and "The NAACP," in *The Bulletin*, 18 May 1922, all in Charleston Branch Files, Box G-216, NAACP Papers.

25. Memphis T. Garrison to James Weldon Johnson, 21 Aug. 1925, Winifred L. Webb to Garrison, 24 Aug. 1925, "Cleveland Boyd on Witness Stand," newsclippings, *Bluefield Daily Telegraph*, ca. 1925, "Interest [in] Murder Case is Intense," newsclippings, *Bluefield Daily Telegraph*, 6 Feb. 1925, "Snatched From Gallows By Wartime Finger Prints," NAACP news release, all in Gary Branch Files, Box G-216, NAACP Papers; Logan Branch Files, correspondence, 1930, Box G-217, NAACP Papers.

26. E. C. Lewis to headquarters, "Crime is Condemned by Colored Organization," newsclipping, *Charleston Gazette*, ca. 12 Dec. 1921, "Report of Charleston Branch NAACP," Dec. 1921, Walter White to T. G. Nutter, 28 Feb. 1922, "A Negro Woman," letter to editor, newsclipping, *New York Age*, n.d., *Cincinnati Post*, newsclipping, 23 Feb. 1922, "Young Quits Association for Effort in Negro's Behalf," newsclipping, 25 Feb. 1922, all in Charleston Branch Files, Box G-215, NAACP Papers. See also n. 2, chapter 5.

27. "Report of the Charleston Branch NAACP," Dec. 1921, "Crime is Condemned by Colored Organization," newsclipping, *Charleston Gazette*, ca. 12 Dec. 1921, Charleston Branch Files, Box G-215, NAACP Papers.

28. WVBNWS, *Biennial Reports, 1921–22*, pp. 73–76, and *1923–24*, pp. 96–98.

29. Ibid. For information about the white-on-white lynching, see "Confessed Wife Slayer Lynched," *Raleigh Register,* 29 July 1920.

30. WVBNWS, *Biennial Reports, 1921–22,* pp. 73–76, *1923–24,* pp. 96–98; Lewis to secretary, NAACP headquarters, 23 Oct. 1918, Charleston Branch Files, Box G-215, NAACP Papers; WVBNWS, "West Virginia Colored Deaf and Blind School," *Biennial Report, 1921–22,* pp. 70–71; West Virginia State Board of Control (WVSBC), "West Virginia Schools for the Colored Deaf and Blind," *Biennial Report, 1928–30* (Charleston, W.Va.), pp. 318–33.

31. "Negroes for Jury Duty," 1 Sept. 1916, "Negroes of Fayette County," 6 Sept. 1918, in *McDowell Times.* Also see "Colored Contingent Will Go to Camp Lee Tuesday," 25 Oct. 1917, "Back to 'Ol Virginny' Go Negroes to Enter Training," 1 Nov. 1917, "130 White Men to Go . . . 86 Colored to Precede Them," 6 June 1918, in the *Raleigh Register;* Harry A. Ploski and James Williams, eds., *The Negro Almanac: A Reference Work on the Afro-American,* 4th ed. (New York: Bellwether Publishing Company, 1983), p. 25. Cf. Richard Bardolph, ed., *The Civil Rights Record: Black Americans and the Law, 1849–1970* (New York: Thomas Y. Crowell Company, 1970), pp. 63–64.

32. WVBNWS, "The Courts," *Biennial Report, 1921–22,* pp. 76–77; WVBNWS, *Biennial Report, 1923–24,* p. 98.

33. "Negro is Placed on Trial Today in Assault Case," 28 July 1925, "Jury in Watt Wall Case Recommends Mercy," 29 July 1925, in *Welch Daily News.* See also WVBNWS, *Biennial Reports, 1925–26,* pp. 110–14, and *1927–28,* pp. 56–61.

34. Nutter to William T. Andrews, special legal assistant, NAACP headquarters, 28 Feb., 15, 20, and 28 Mar., 21 Apr., and 28 May 1928, Andrews to Nutter, 21 May, 1 and 7 Mar. 1928, R. S. Spillman, member and attorney of Charleston Board of Education, to Nutter, 27 Feb. 1928, "Resolutions, Charleston Board of Education," 13 Oct. 1927, "The Board of Education of the Charleston Independent School District: Minutes of A Special Meeting," 21 Feb. 1928, "Charleston, W.Va. N.A.A.C.P. Ready to Fight Jim Crow Library," news release, NAACP headquarters, telegram, Nutter to James Weldon Johnson, 19 May 1928, "Anderson H. Brown, Et Al. vs. the Board of Education of Charleston Independent School District, 1928," transcript, State Supreme Court of Appeals, West Virginia, Case No. 6294, all in Charleston Branch Files, Box G-215, NAACP Papers.

35. Memphis T. Garrison, "Annual Report of the Gary W.Va. Branch . . . Year Ending December 31, 1925," Garrison to William Pickens, 21 Aug. 1925, director of branches to Garrison, 30 Apr. 1925 and 14 Jan. 1928, Garrison to Robert Bagnall, 1 Feb. 1927, in Gary Branch Files, Box G-216, NAACP Papers; "Gary Colored News," *Welch Daily News,* 12 Dec. 1923.

36. "N.A.A.C.P. Christmas Seal Profits Exceed Those of Previous Years," "Mrs. Garrison Reports Large Sale of N.A.A.C.P. Christmas Seals," Bagnall to Ovington, 26 Feb. 1930, Bagnall to White, 26 Feb. 1930, Garrison to Bagnall, telegrams 4 and 7 Dec. 1927, Garrison to Bagnall, 24 Sept., 4 Oct. 1929, 11 Feb. and 29 Oct. 1930, Bagnall to Garrison, 25 Sept. 1929, 6 Nov.

1930, in Gary Branch Files, Box G-216, NAACP Papers; Edward Cabbell to Joe W. Trotter, Jr., 1987.

37. "Report of the Charleston Branch," 18 Feb. and 19 June 1920; Walter White to T. G. Nutter, 2 Feb. 1922, 17 and 24 Apr. 1924, Nutter to White, 28 Jan. 1922, Nutter to attorney Thomas West, 28 Jan. 1922, White to E. C. Lewis, 19 Dec. 1922, Lewis to White, 18 May 1921, 19 Dec. 1922, White to Lewis, 5 Oct. and 16 Dec. 1922, "The N.A.A.C.P.," *The Bulletin*, 18 May 1922, in Charleston Branch Files, Box G-215, NAACP Papers. Also see n. 16 above and n. 3 of chapter 5.

38. WVBNWS, *Biennial Report, 1923–24*, p. 78.

39. Sarah Meriwether Nutter to James Weldon Johnson, 23 Feb., 1928, Johnson to S. M. Nutter, 24 Feb. 1928, T. G. Nutter to Johnson, 17 Feb. 1928, T. G. Nutter to White, 21 Apr. 1924, "Darrow Had Great Meeting in Charleston, W.Va.," news release, national headquarters, all in Charleston Branch Files, Box G-215, NAACP Papers; WVBNWS, *Biennial Report, 1921–22*, pp. 51–52; John Hope Franklin, *From Slavery to Freedom: A History of Negro Americans* (1947; rept., New York: A. A. Knopf, 1967), pp. 483–84; Meier and Rudwick, *From Plantation to Ghetto* pp. 241–43.

40. H. G. Young, W.Va. secretary of state, to T. G. Nutter, 24 Feb. 1922, Nutter to Young, 25 Feb. 1922, Charleston NAACP to Governor E. F. Morgan, 21 Feb. 1922, all in Legal Files, Box D-2, NAACP Papers; "Young Quits Association for Effort in Negro's Behalf," newsclipping, 25 Feb. 1922, in Charleston Branch Files, Box G-215, NAACP Papers.

41. Walter White to Rev. Johnson, 21 Mar., 4 Apr., and 27 May 1918, Johnson to White, 23 Mar., 25 May 1918, R. W. White, W.Va. Dept. of Agriculture, to Walter White, ca. 12–16 Mar. 1918, Walter White to R. W. White, 4 Apr. 1918, all in Charleston Branch Files, Box G-215, NAACP Papers.

42. R. C. McIver to NAACP headquarters, 7 Jan. 1921, White to McIver, 12 Jan. 1921, Johnson to White, 21 Jan. 1921, "Note on Church Affiliations," in Charleston Branch Files, Box G-215, NAACP Papers.

43. See Jefferson Crouder, Logan, W.Va., to Bagnall, 16 May 1927, Bagnall to Ball, 14 May, 12 July 1927, Ball to Bagnall, 6 Mar., 6 July 1927, in Charleston Branch Files, Box G-217, NAACP Papers.

44. See John Bracey, August Meier, and Elliot Rudwick, eds., *Conflict and Competition: Studies in the Recent Black Protest Movement* (Belmont, Calif.: Wadsworth Publishing Company, 1971), pp. 1–64; Winona Affiliate to NAACP Headquarters, Dec. 1925, "Application for Charter," 15 Apr. 1927, C. O. Love to Bagnall, 27 Jan. 1929, Winona Branch Files, Box G-218, NAACP Papers; W. H. Pierson to Bagnall, 31 Oct. 1927, Bagnall to Pierson, 4 Nov. 1927, Glen Rogers Branch Files, Box G-217, NAACP Papers.

45. H. C. Ball to James Weldon Johnson, 12 Mar. 1928, William Pickens to Ball, 14 Mar. 1928, in Logan Branch Files, Box G-217, NAACP Papers.

46. Ball to Bagnall, ca. 27 June 1929, Bagnall to Ball, 2 July 1929, Ball to Roy Wilkins, 22 Feb. 1932, Ball to Bagnall, 30 May 1929, 17 Mar. 1930, 16 May 1932, in Logan Branch Files, Box G-217, NAACP Papers.

Conclusion: Toward a Proletarian Synthesis in Black History

The history of African-American life and labor in southern West Virginia from 1915 to 1932 reveals the significance of class, race, and region in the development of black America. Black miners worked in a multiethnic labor force and joined white workers in the United Mine Workers of America, but they were also southern blacks who made the transition from agriculture to industry. Rural poverty, southern injustice, and the labor demands of the coal industry underlay the black migration to West Virginia and the rise of the black coal-mining proletariat. Black miners, however, by utilizing family, friend, and community networks, became another force behind the proletarianization process, acting as agents in their own industrial transformation. Nonetheless, the racist attitudes and practices of white industrialists, workers, and the state relegated blacks to the bottom of the expanding coal labor force. The dynamics of race, class, and region, although they varied in intensity over time and between regions, shaped the experiences of black workers virtually everywhere in twentieth-century America.[1]

With parallels elsewhere in industrial America, racial stratification in the labor force influenced the expansion of racial inequality in the larger community life of coal-mining towns. Perhaps more than in the coal-mining labor force, in the social, cultural, and institutional life of the region, whites developed a firmer consensus on the race question that transcended their class and ethnic differences and treated blacks as genetically inferior to whites or, at the very least, "socially" inferior to them. Racism increased as a popular white mentality, peaking in the immediate postwar years through the early 1920s. It was during this period that racism resulted in the lynching of two blacks, inspired the proliferation of Klu Klux Klan units, blocked equal protection before the law, encouraged biased journalism, and retarded the growth of essential educational, legal, medical, and social welfare services for blacks.

Black miners developed a broad range of responses to the intensification of racism in the coalfields. Their actions displayed a complex mixture of class and racial consciousness that cogently addressed their precarious position between the hostile forces of white capital, labor, and the state. They honed their skills and efficiency in the production of coal; moved frequently in search of better mines, higher pay, and better working conditions; cemented sporadic alliances with white workers; and, most important, established racial solidarity with the expanding black elite. While racial solidarity itself was limited by internal conflicts along class lines, the black elite provided an increasing array of business, professional, and institutional services to black workers and their families, as reflected in the rapid growth of black churches, fraternal orders, and political and civil rights organizations. These developments were not unique to southern West Virginia, however. They were part of a larger process: the making of black America during the industrial era.[2]

Despite numerous parallels, black coal-mining life deviated from black life elsewhere in industrial America. A variety of wage earners in construction, transportation, trade, and manufacturing comprised the black proletariat in many sections of the urban North and South. In contrast, coal-mining regions offered few employment opportunities outside the mines. The coal industry dominated the regional economy and expanded within a geographical and social environment that was neither strictly rural nor urban. More important, unlike urban patterns of Afro-American labor, in southern West Virginia coal workers were highly dispersed and lightly supervised. The unpredictable underground terrain made direct supervision by foremen difficult and gave miners substantial independence in their daily work routines. Although undercutting machines virtually eliminated the skilled pick-and-shovel miner, coal miners had to be skilled in using dynamite, judging atmospheric conditions, checking the safety of roof supports, and correcting a variety of potential hazards. To be sure, coal operators employed a variety of mechanisms for exploiting the labor force, including company stores and company-controlled towns. Yet black workers, by controlling certain aspects of the work process, were nonetheless somewhat more independent than their urban counterparts, who faced the ubiquitous presence of foremen, and their rural counterparts, who had to cope with the coercive and exploitative methods of southern agriculture.[3]

On the eve of World War I, a large black coal-mining working class had already fully emerged in southern West Virginia. It had also experienced a tremendous transformation of attitudes and behavior, characterized by the increasing shift from the socioeconomic and cultural imperatives of southern agriculture to the corresponding imperatives of industrial capitalism. Mining skills increasingly supplanted old agricultural ones, and the spiritual and communalistic traditions of rural blacks underwent a gradual reorientation under the new materialistic, rationalistic, and individualistic dictates of coal-mining towns. Hence, the events of World War I and the 1920s intensified processes that were already well underway.

In northern industrial cities like Cleveland, Detroit, and Milwaukee, World War I represented a sharp break with the past. For the first time in northern history, black men made the transition from domestic and personal service work, common labor, and agricultural jobs into the industrial workplace.[4] The rise of the black proletariat in the antebellum era in southern cities predated the rise of the black coal-mining work force and grew along with it. Black workers in the urban South were not only common laborers, but also brick masons, carpenters, and blacksmiths.[5] On the eve of World War I, however, following the classical Marxist formulation of the proletarianization process, as they became industrial workers, black artisans lost their previous autonomy as independent producers. At the same time, the black coal-mining proletariat in southern West Virginia dramatically expanded, swelled by blacks who had previously been sharecroppers, farm laborers, saw mill hands, and railroad workers in the southern economy. Nonetheless, in confirmation of conventional Marxist interpretations, the proletarianization of Afro-Americans in the coalfields was a highly exploitative process, marked by extensive racial, as well as class, inequality.[6]

As residents of a border state, West Virginia blacks faced fewer legal restrictions than their kinsmen farther south. They retained the franchise, as did blacks in Kentucky, Maryland, and Missouri, and they continued to exercise substantial political influence. Black politicians, by appealing to the black miners' need for a broad range of social welfare, educational, and legal services, gained election to the West Virginia House of Delegates, and three black men (one a coal miner) served in the 1918 legislative session. Black legislators

achieved a state anti-lynching law, a state statute banning the showing of racially inflammatory films like *The Birth of a Nation,* a variety
of new all-black, state-supported social welfare institutions, and appropriations for the expansion of established black schools, colleges, and social services, which alleviated some of the demeaning
features of West Virginia's system of racial discrimination. The exercise of black power at the state and local level in West Virginia
paralleled the rise of black political influence in large northern cities
like Chicago, New York, and Cleveland as the Great Migration accelerated. Blacks in West Virginia made greater political strides than
many of their counterparts living in the urban North and West did,
including blacks in Evansville, Indiana, St. Paul, Milwaukee, and
San Francisco, cities where the black population remained relatively
small despite sharp increases during World War I and the early
1920s.[7]

As the black population expanded in southern West Virginia,
however, black political leaders failed to contain working-class political behavior within the confines of electoral politics. When Raleigh
County black miners resorted to violence during World War I, they
demonstrated the limitations of black electoral activities and precipitated a search for political alternatives. Some blacks in the region
turned toward the nationalistic Garvey movement, forming several
chapters of the Universal Negro Improvement Association through
which they affirmed their faith in Garvey's vision of a universal
brotherhood of black people. Most blacks, however, like blacks elsewhere in the United States, increasingly turned toward the NAACP,
with its militant civil rights campaign. Coupled with electoral struggles, the NAACP's equal rights campaign moved to the forefront of
black political life in southern West Virginia. Although protest and
electoral campaigns were especially successful in southern West
Virginia, they were nonetheless part of a growing national pattern.[8]

Compared to black coal miners farther north and south, black
miners in southern West Virginia secured a firm position in the coal
industry. In the North black miners remained small in number and
highly dispersed, making it impossible for them to wage successful
political struggles like West Virginia blacks. During the late nineteenth and early twentieth centuries, employers recruited Southern,
Central, and Eastern European immigrants, rather than blacks, to
work in the mines of Illinois, Indiana, Ohio, Iowa, Pennsylvania,
and northern West Virginia. Strong white labor unions developed
with racist policies that helped to exclude blacks from northern
mines. In order to resist white workers' demands for higher pay and

better working conditions, northern coal operators gradually began to employ black workers, first hiring some as strikebreakers. Paradoxically, northern black miners soon joined white union workers and spearheaded a vigorous tradition of interracial unionism.[9] Northern black labor leaders later aided the UMWA's campaign to organize nonunionized black and white miners in southern West Virginia.

If blacks were largely excluded from northern mines, they dominated the coal labor force in the Birmingham district of Alabama. Yet a variety of forces weakened their position in the Deep South and made them more vulnerable to the exploitive dimensions of industrial capitalism than their counterparts in southern West Virginia. They faced the abusive contract and convict labor systems, political disfranchisement (reinforced by vicious racial violence, including lynchings and race riots), and a racially discriminatory wage scale that placed black earnings distinctly below those of whites for the same work.[10] These conditions helped to drive many Alabama miners to southern West Virginia. Although black miners there occupied the lowliest positions in the coal labor force compared to whites, they forged comparatively greater opportunities in West Virginia than their black counterparts elsewhere. They gained a solid footing in the coal mines, received equal pay for equal work, and confronted fewer lynchings and incidents of mob violence. Able to vote, they also waged a vigorous and largely successful political struggle for recognition of their human and civil rights.

As suggested by the foregoing analysis, this book should help to sharpen our comparative perspective on Afro-American life in the era of the Great Migration. It documents the growth of the black coal-mining proletariat, explores the impact of class formation on the community life of coal-mining towns, and points toward a proletarian synthesis in Afro-American history. By locating the black coal miners' experience within a particular geographical and historical context, by analyzing that experience within the multiple frameworks of class, race, and region, and by treating black miners as central actors in the larger drama, *Coal, Class, and Color* should also help us transcend the debilitating debates over the nature of interracial unionism in the UMWA, the representativeness of national black labor leaders like Richard L. Davis, and, most of all, the primacy of class versus race in shaping the black miners' experience.[11] Ultimately, as historical sociologist Edna Bonacich recently notes, "The issue isn't a choice between the dominance of race or class, or the way in which the two intertwine complexly, but rather the way in which capitalist development shaped the interests and actions of various class-race segments, and how those interests and actions in turn shaped the directions capitalist development took."[12]

Indeed, tied closely to the socioeconomic, demographic, technical, political, and cultural dynamics of industrial capitalism, the black miners' experience dovetailed with national and international working-class and social history. By World War I, as labor historian David Montgomery notes, "an industrial core, throbbing with manufacturing activity at continually rising levels" had emerged in the United States, Western Europe, and parts of Eastern and Southern Europe. A large rural periphery surrounded the core, encircling its urban centers, and witnessed the increasing onslaught of industrial capitalism, which fueled the rise of a new industrial working class. While the Third World of Asia, Africa, and Latin America lay beyond the rural periphery of the European continent, their economies and societies were likewise increasingly integrated into the world capitalist economy.[13]

In various regions of the world, then, industrial capitalism shaped the emergence and expansion of an industrial working class. At the same time, as suggested by the experiences of black coal miners in southern West Virginia, by taking a hand in shaping their own experience, workers played an active role in shaping the course of capitalist development. Linked to the larger national and international political economy, the black experience in southern West Virginia thus takes on broader significance. It transcends regional, subregional, and national boundaries and suggests the need for greater theoretical and methodological cross-fertilization on all levels of social and labor history. Only through broad conceptual interchanges will we be able to appreciate the particularistic and universalistic aspects of the way capitalist development shaped class, race, and nationality and was in turn shaped by them. Only then will we be able to fully comprehend the interconnectedness of the human experience through time and across boundaries of class, region, nationality, and race.

NOTES

1. William H. Harris, *The Harder We Run: Black Workers since the Civil War* (New York: Oxford University Press, 1982), pp. 51–94; Philip S. Foner, *Organized Labor and the Black Worker, 1619–1973* (New York: International Publishers, 1974), pp. 120–87; Gavin Wright, *Old South, New South: Revolutions*

in the Southern Economy since the Civil War (New York: Basic Books, 1986), pp. 177–97; Sterling D. Spero and Abram L. Harris, *The Black Worker: The Negro and the Labor Movement* (1931; rept., New York: Atheneum, 1968), pp. 128–81.

2. James Grossman, *Land of Hope: Chicago, Black Southerners, and the Great Migration* (Chicago: University of Chicago Press, 1989), chap. 5; Earl Lewis, *At Work and at Home: Blacks in Norfolk, Virginia, 1910–1945* (Berkeley: University of California Press, forthcoming), chap. 5; Peter Gottlieb, *Making Their Own Way: Southern Blacks' Migration to Pittsburgh, 1916–30* (Urbana: University of Illinois Press, 1987), pp. 183–215; Dennis Dickerson, *Out of the Crucible: Black Steelworkers in Western Pennsylvania, 1875–1980* (Albany: State University Press of New York, 1986), pp. 101–17; Joe William Trotter, Jr., *Black Milwaukee: The Making of an Industrial Proletariat, 1915–45*, pp. 80–144; George C. Wright, *Life Behind a Veil: Blacks in Louisville, Kentucky, 1865–1930* (Baton Rouge: Louisiana State University Press, 1985), pp. 123–55; Douglas H. Daniels, *Pioneer Urbanites: A Social and Cultural History of Black San Francisco* (Philadelphia: Temple University Press, 1980), pp. 106–75.

3. Wright, *Old South, New South*, pp. 156–97; Grossman, *Land of Hope*, chap. 7; Lewis, *At Work and at Home*, chaps. 3, 4; Wright, *Life Behind a Veil*, pp. 213–20; Gottlieb, *Making Their Own Way*, pp. 89–116; Trotter, *Black Milwaukee*, pp. 41–66; Kenneth Kusmer, *A Ghetto Takes Shape: Black Cleveland, 1870–1930* (Urbana: University of Illinois Press, 1976), pp. 65–90; Allan H. Spear, *Black Chicago: The Making of a Negro Ghetto, 1890–1920* (Chicago: University of Chicago Press, 1967), pp. 129–66.

4. Grossman, *Land of Hope*, chap. 7; Gottlieb, *Making Their Own Way*, pp. 89–116; Trotter, *Black Milwaukee*, pp. 41–66; Kusmer, *A Ghetto Takes Shape*, pp. 65–90; Spear, *Black Chicago*, pp. 129–66.

5. Wright, *Old South, New South*, pp. 156–97; Lewis, *At Work and at Home*, chaps. 3 and 4; Wright, *Life Behind a Veil*, pp. 213–20; Howard Rabinowitz, *Race Relations in the Urban South, 1865–1890* (New York: Oxford University Press, 1978), pp. 68–73; Peter J. Rachleff, *Black Labor in the South* (Philadelphia: Temple University Press, 1984), pp. 3–12.

6. Charles Tilly, *As Sociology Meets History* (New York: Academic Press, 1981), chap. 7; T. B. Bottomore, trans. and ed., *Karl Marx: Selected Writings in Sociology and Social Philosophy* (New York: McGraw-Hill Book Company, 1964).

7. Darrel E. Bigham, *We Ask Only a Fair Trial: A History of the Black Community of Evansville, Indiana* (Bloomington: Indiana University Press, 1987), pp. 194–214; Trotter, *Black Milwaukee*, pp. 115–44; David V. Taylor, "Pilgrim's Progress: Black St. Paul and the Making of an Urban Ghetto, 1870–1930" (Ph.D. diss., University of Minnesota, 1977); Daniels, *Pioneer Urbanites*, pp. 162–75.

8. John Hope Franklin and Alfred A. Moss, *From Slavery to Freedom: A History of Negro Americans* (1947; rev. ed., New York: Alfred A. Knopf, 1988), pp. 286–309; Mary Berry and John Blassingame, *Long Memory: The Black Experience in America* (New York: Oxford University Press, 1982) pp. 150–76;

August Meier and Elliott Rudwick, *From Plantation to Ghetto* (1966; rev. ed., New York: Hill and Wang, 1976), pp. 232–53.

9. Ronald L. Lewis, *Black Coal Miners in America, 1780–1980* (Lexington: University Press of Kentucky, 1987), pp. 79–98; Darold T. Barnum, *The Negro in the Bituminous Coal Mining Industry* (Philadelphia: University of Pennsylvania Press, 1970); Dorothy Schweider, *Black Diamonds: Life and Work in Iowa's Coal-Mining Communities* (Ames: Iowa State University Press, 1983); Dorothy Schweider, Joseph Hraba, and Elmer Schweider, *Buxton: Work and Racial Equality in a Coal-Mining Community* (Ames Iowa: Iowa State University Press, 1987); Herbert Gutman, "The Negro and the United Mine Workers of America: The Career and Letters of Richard L. Davis and Something of Their Meaning, 1890–1900," in *Work, Culture, and Society in Industrializing America: Essays in American Working-Class and Social History* (New York: Vintage Books, 1977), pp. 121–208; Stephen Brier, "The Career and Letters of Richard L. Davis Reconsidered: Unpublished Correspondence from the National Labor Tribune,"*Labor History* 3 (Summer 1980): 420–29.

10. Lewis, *Black Coal Miners in America*, pp. 13–75; Daniel Letwin, "Race, Ideology, and the 'Labor Problem' in the Coal Fields of Birmingham, Alabama, 1916–1922" (unpublished paper presented at Lowell Conference on Industrial History, October 1988).

11. Gutman, "The Negro and the United Mine Workers of America," pp. 121–208; Brier, "The Career and Letters of Richard L. Davis Reconsidered," 420–29; Herbert Hill, "Myth-Making as Labor History: Herbert Gutman and the United Mine Workers of America," *International Journal of Politics, Culture, and Society* 2, no. 2 (Winter 1988): 132–200; Stephen Brier, "In Defense of Gutman: The Union's Case," *International Journal of Politics, Culture, and Society* 2, no. 3 (Spring 1989): 382–95; David A. Corbin, *Life, Work, and Rebellion in the Coal Fields: The Southern West Virginia Miners, 1880–1922* (Urbana: University of Illinois Press, 1981), especially chap. 3, "Class over Caste: Interracial Solidarity in the Company Town."

12. Edna Bonacich, "Capitalist and Racial Oppression: In Search of Consciousness," in Jerry Lembcke and Ray Hutchison, eds., *Research in Urban Sociology*, vol. 1, *Race, Class, and Urban Change* (Greenwich, Conn.: JAI Press, Inc., 1989), pp. 181–94.

13. David Montgomery, *The Fall of the House of Labor: The Workplace, the State, and American Labor Activism, 1865–1925* (Cambridge: Cambridge University Press, 1987), pp. 70–71. Also see John H. M. Laslett, *Nature's Noblemen: The Fortunes of the Independent Collier in Scotland and the American Midwest, 1855–1889* (Los Angeles, Calif.: Institute of Industrial Relations, 1983); John H. M. Laslett, "The Independent Collier: Some Recent Studies of Nineteenth-Century Coal-Mining Communities in Britain and the United States," *International Labor and Working Class History*, no. 19 (Spring 1982): 18–27; Brian Peterson, "Reports: Methodological Approaches to Comparative Mining History," *International Labor and Working Class History*, no. 9 (May 1976): 3–6; John Benson, *British Coalminers in the Nineteenth Century: A Social History* (New York: Holmes and Meier, 1980).

Essay on Primary Sources

This study is based upon a variety of state and federal censuses, special reports, newspaper accounts, manuscript collections, oral interviews, and selected secondary accounts. For secondary accounts, readers are referred to the preface and chapter endnotes and to three very helpful collections of essays and bibliographical works: William H. Turner and Edward Cabell, *Blacks in Appalachia* (Lexington: University Press of Kentucky, 1985); Robert F. Munn, *The Coal Industry in America: A Bibliography and Guide to Studies*, 2d ed. (Morgantown: West Virginia University Library, 1977); and Harold M. Forbes, *West Virginia History: A Bibliography and Guide to Research* (Morgantown: West Virginia University Press, 1981).

FEDERAL AND STATE SOURCES

United States census reports—covering such vital demographic and social facts as population size, age, sex, state of birth, marital status, and education by county, race, and ethnicity—provide the primary statistical data for this study. In addition to the regular decennial reports, several special censuses have proved useful, including *Negroes in the United States, 1920–32* (1935; rept., New York, 1966), *Religious Bodies, 1906, 1916, and 1926* (Washington, 1910, 1919, and 1930), and *Families*, vol. 4 (Washington, 1933). The published congressional hearings that were conducted during and after large-scale labor violence in southern West Virginia were a rich source of data. Based on interviews with coal operators and miners from a variety of ethnic and racial backgrounds, the hearings offer insight into the phenomenon of interracial unionism, as well as the white coal operators' perceptions and treatment of black workers. See especially, U.S. Senate, *West Virginia Coal Fields: Hearings Before the Committee on*

Education, vol. 1 (Washington, 1921) and U.S. Senate, *Conditions in the Coal Fields of Pennsylvania, West Virginia, and Ohio: Hearings Before the Committee on Interstate Commerce* (Washington, 1928).

Housed at the West Virginia Collection, West Virginia University, and at the Department of Culture and History, Division of Archives, in Charleston, the records of various state departments offer socio-economic data on blacks in the coalfields. From the turn of the century through the early 1930s, the annual reports of the State Department of Mines feature statistics on the coal labor force listed by county, ethnicity, and race. These reports allow us to analyze the changing social composition of the coal labor force, including its responses to the volatile upturns and downturns of the coal economy. Although uneven in its coverage, for several years the State Department of Mines gathered statistics on fatal and serious nonfatal accidents by race and ethnicity for the state and sometimes for individual counties. These data provide keen insight into the specific working conditions of laborers in many underground and surface occupations.

The biennial reports of the West Virginia Bureau of Negro Welfare and Statistics provide the most comprehensive source of information on blacks in West Virginia. From its beginning in 1921, the BNWS, under the authority of the West Virginia State Board of Control, published comprehensive biennial reports on black economic, social, institutional, and political developments throughout the state. These reports include substantial data by county permitting close analysis of changing patterns of black life during the 1920s and early 1930s. Indeed, for assessing the dynamic interplay between changes in the black labor force and transformations in black community life, the records of the BNWS are singular. Their only drawback is that they must be carefully corroborated (where possible) through a wide array of other official records, from which a great deal of the data were derived.

The West Virginia State Board of Control supervised a variety of segregated social welfare institutions. These include the Department of Negro Schools, the West Virginia Collegiate Institute (West Virginia State College), Bluefield Colored Institute (Bluefield State College), the State Home for Aged and Infirm Colored Men and Women, the West Virginia Industrial School for Colored Boys, the West Virginia Industrial School for Colored Girls, and the Denmar Tuberculosis Sanitarium. The Co-operative Extension Service, under the State Department of Agriculture, and the State Department of

Health both employed black agents and submitted reports by race. Although they are not organized by race and ethnicity, the records of the State Road Commissioner and the reports of the State Commissioner of Prohibition are also helpful. Finally, the *West Virginia Legislative Hand Book, Manual and Official Register,* published annually, provides a list of black elected and appointed officials, replete with photos and biographical sketches on West Virginia's black legislators.

NEWSPAPERS

Newspapers offer essential information on black life in southern West Virginia. The local black weekly the *McDowell Times* is by far the most important. Next to the BNWS, it is the best written source on black coal-mining life because of its extensive coverage of the socioeconomic, political, and cultural life of blacks in the region. Under the headings of particular coal-mining communities, one finds advertisements of black business and professional people, reports of local churches and fraternal orders, editorials and news accounts illuminating race relations, and detailed stories on black political, social welfare, educational, and civil rights activities. For charting the complex interplay of class, race, and region, the *Times* is invaluable. Although the paper got its start at the turn of the century, extant copies of the paper (obtainable on microfilm through the West Virginia Department of Culture and History) unfortunately are only available for the years 1913 to 1918 and for the late depression years and early 1940s. A variety of daily and weekly white newspapers, however, through regular "Colored News" columns, help fill the gap.

Several white newspapers developed special columns covering local black life. Although the white press otherwise played up black crime and helped popularize white racism, these black news columns, usually under the editorship of aspiring black journalists, at least highlighted black achievements and helped balance the usual racially biased reporting. Especially useful are the *Welch Daily News, Logan Banner, Bluefield Daily Telegraph, McDowell Recorder,* and the *Raleigh Register.* Most disappointing in this respect are the Democratic and Republican papers, *The Charleston Gazette* and *The Charleston Daily Mail.* Extant issues of other newspapers illuminate specific aspects of black life in the region: for the important relationship between blacks and the United Mine Workers of America, see the *United Mine Workers Journal;* for the Garvey movement, the division reports and letters to the editor of the *Negro World;* and for the relationship between blacks in northern and southern West Virginia, the *Pioneer Press.*

MANUSCRIPT AND ARCHIVAL COLLECTIONS

Manuscript and archival collections offer a wealth of information on black coal-mining life and labor. At the National Archives in Washington, D.C., the records of the U.S. Coal Commission, the U.S. Department of Labor, and the U.S. Department of Justice proved especially useful. The files of the Coal Commission contain useful statistical and descriptive data on the composition of the labor force, housing conditions, and the number and quality of schools, churches, and recreational facilities. The records of the Department of Labor include data on the labor recruitment activities of coal companies and helpful published studies as well. Two studies, one by the Women's Bureau and the other by the Children's Bureau, were particularly helpful for this book: *Home Environment and Opportunities of Women in Coal-Mine Workers' Families* (Washington, 1925) and *The Welfare of Children in Bituminous Coal Mining Communities in West Virginia* (Washington, 1923). The records of the U.S. Department of Justice provide invaluable data on the Great Migration. At the request of the U.S. attorney general, federal attorneys in various parts of the South submitted detailed reports of black population movement from the rural South into a variety of industrial regions including southern West Virginia. These records clearly illuminate the role of black kin and friendship networks in influencing black migration and employment.

Housed at West Virginia University, the West Virginia Collection contains the papers of Justus Collins, a major coal operator and employer of black labor. The owner of the Winding Gulf Colliery Company, Collins frequently corresponded with management officials on the position of blacks in the mines and in the community. This correspondence includes data on women, schools, and the outbreak of racial violence during World War I. The papers of Ulysses G. Carter, also in the West Virginia Collection, are also informative. Carter was a black educator who offered mine safety classes to black workers during the 1930s. His papers contain important speeches and newsclippings touching on black life in the 1920s.

Also in the West Virginia Collection is the *The New River Company Employees' Magazine,* 1924–30. It provides fascinating data on the day-to-day activities of black miners under its column titled

"Among Our Colored." Useful information on black involvement in the political and labor struggles of the region, although sparse, is found in the papers of Republican governor and U.S. senator H. D. Hatfield, Democratic governor John J. Cornwell, and the white labor leader Van Amberg Bittner, all in the West Virginia Collection. Finally, West Virginia University is the repository of the Storer College Papers. Storer College, located at Harpers Ferry in the northeastern section of West Virginia, was the state's first institution of higher education for blacks. The college's records reveal how it declined as West Virginia State College, and then Bluefield State College, opened in the southern part of the state and grew in influence.

The records of the National Association for the Advancement of Colored People contain the most complete manuscript collection on blacks in southern West Virginia. Housed at the Library of Congress, Washington, D.C., the NAACP Papers include material from more than a dozen southern West Virginia branches and affiliates that were active during the 1920s and early 1930s. In addition to documenting civil rights and political activities, the NAACP branch files provide details on the economic and social conditions of blacks as well. Offering substantial quantitative and qualitative data on black men and women in the NAACP, these records help to document the crosscurrents of class, race, culture, and power in coal-mining communities. Since local branches and affiliates conducted regular fund-raising campaigns, the correspondence between local offices and national headquarters are sometimes replete with commentary on employment conditions in the mines, highlighting the connection between the black miners and the civil rights campaign. The Gary and Logan branches are especially illuminating on this score. For reports of the NAACP national field secretary and the NAACP's national department of branches, see also Randolph Boehm, ed., *Papers of the NAACP, pt. 1, 1909–1950: Meetings of the Board of Directors, Records of Annual Conferences, Major Speeches, and Special Reports* (Frederick, Md.: University Publication of America, 1982).

Although less useful than the NAACP Papers, other manuscript collections at the Library of Congress provide helpful information. The National Urban League papers contain valuable materials on the migration process, especially the "Early Surveys: Migration Study, Birmingham Summary." They also contain correspondence on racial inequality in company housing policy in southern West Virginia. For information on the Welch, McDowell County, attorney

Arthur G. Froe, who served as the recorder of deeds for the District of Columbia, the Warren G. Harding and Calvin Coolidge presidential papers are indispensable. They offer information on Froe's appointment to office, his government service, his national connections, and his ties with black and white constituents in southern West Virginia.

In addition to Louis R. Harlan's various books (cited in the endnotes), the Booker T. Washington collection is invaluable for documenting the enduring prewar link between Washington and his old hometown in Malden, Kanawha County. The papers of W. E. B. Du Bois and Carter G. Woodson also contain important, if limited, correspondence between these national figures and black workers, and especially black elites, in southern West Virginia. The Washington, Du Bois, and Woodson collections are located in the Library of Congress. The Du Bois Papers there focus especially on Du Bois's years as editor of the NAACP's *Crisis* magazine. Du Bois's private papers are at the University of Massachusetts at Amherst. Finally, the parent-body division lists of the Universal Negro Improvement Association (in the Schomburg Collection of the New York Public Library) shed light on the Garvey movement in southern West Virginia. Under the editorship of Robert Hill, portions of these papers are now available in volume 4 of *The Marcus Garvey and Universal Negro Improvement Association Papers* (Berkeley: University of California Press, 1986). These lists should be used in conjunction with the division reports of the *Negro World*.

ORAL INTERVIEWS

For understanding the perspective of black coal miners, the most important resource is their own recollections, along with those of their wives and children. While my criteria for selecting the interviewees was partly practical (dependent on the availability, health, and consent of possible participants), I made a decided effort to capture variability as well as representativeness within the group. I conducted oral interviews with 29 individuals, including 16 coal miners (one white), 4 railroad men (some of whom had mining experience); and 9 women (wives and daughters of coal miners). Although most of the interviewees were born in states covering a broad cross-section of the upper and lower South, a few were born in West Virginia, reflecting the rise of a new generation of black coal miners and their families. No matter what the origin of the interviewees, though, their experiences all reflected the tendency of blacks within the region to move frequently.

The interviewees include the following persons: William Beasley, Lawrence Boling, Pearl Brannon, Andrew Campbell, James Cook, Leonard Davis, Anita Dickerson, North Dickerson, Geraldine Freeman, Willie Freeman, Charles T. Harris, Pink Henderson, Harold Hobson, Sidney Lee, Margaret V. Moorman, Walter E. Moorman, Mary Q. Morris-Goode, John L. Page, Ellen Phillips, Lester Phillips, Isabella Scott, Roy Todd, Thelma O. Trotter, Preston Turner, Charlotte Wallington, George Watkins, Cecil L. Williams, Salem Wooten, and Thornton W. Wright. Supplementary oral interviews of black miners can be found in the West Virginia Collection, in *Goldenseal* (the quarterly publication of the West Virginia Department of Culture and History), and in James T. Laing's "The Negro Miner in West Virginia" (Ph.D. diss., 1933).

MISCELLANEOUS SOURCES

Visual materials recording black life in the coalfields can be found in the photo archives of West Virginia University in Morgantown and the Eastern Regional Coal Archives in Bluefield, West Virginia. These photo collections shed light on the work of coal mining as well as community life in coal towns. For understanding the prewar religious experience of blacks in southern West Virginia, the personal files of retired U.S. Air Force captain Nelson L. Barnett, Jr., are helpful. They contain obituaries, sermons, and correspondence between black ministers and their families. A 1924 essay by the Charleston attorney T. G. Nutter mainly featured southern West Virginia blacks. This highly illuminating essay was illustrated with twenty-eight photos of prominent black business and professional men and women. See "These 'Colored' United States [Pt.] X: West Virginia," *The Messenger* 6, no. 2 (Feb. 1924): 44–48. For a critical response to Nutter's article, see E. Franklin Frazier, "Open Forum," *The Messenger* 6, no. 11 (Nov. 1924): 362–63.

The papers of black attorney Thaddeus E. Harris, housed at Duke University (Manuscript Division, the William R. Perkins Library), are also useful for documenting the lives of black professional people in the Mountain State. The Harris papers contain extensive correspondence between the attorney T. E. Harris and his wife. The study of black women in the coalfields is also aided by Minnie Holly Barnes, *Holl's Hurdles* (Radford, Va., 1980), a brief autobiography of a black schoolteacher; the Peters Sisters, *War Poems* (1919), a short volume of poems written by two sisters during World War I; Ahmed Williams, "I Remember 'The Free State of Mc-Dowell,' " in B. B. Maurer, *Mountain Heritage,* 4th ed. (Parsons, W.Va., 1980), firsthand statements on black women and other features of life in McDowell County; and Kitty B. Frazier and Diana Simmons, "Fannie Cobb Carter (1872–1973)," a manuscript about the black teacher, social worker, and administrator of the West Virginia State Home for Colored Girls, in Barbara Matz and Janet Craig, eds., *Missing Chapters: West Virginia Women in History* (West Virginia Women's Commission et al., 1983). The local historian Mrs. Jessie M. Thomas of Gary, McDowell County, is also an invaluable resource for research on blacks in southern West Virginia.

Index

John Mercer Langston and the Fight for Black Freedom, 1829–65
William and Aimee Lee Cheek

The Old Village and the Great House: An Archaeological and Historical
Examination of Drax Hall Plantation, St. Ann's Bay, Jamaica
Douglas V. Armstrong

Black Property Owners in the South, 1790–1915
Loren Schweninger

The Sociogenesis of a Race Riot: Springfield, Illinois, in 1908
Roberta Senechal

Coal, Class, and Color: Blacks in Southern West Virginia, 1915–32
Joe William Trotter, Jr.

Reprint Editions

King: A Biography
David Levering Lewis SECOND EDITION

The Death and Life of Malcolm X
Peter Goldman SECOND EDITION

Race Relations in the Urban South, 1865–1890
Howard N. Rabinowitz, with a Foreword by C. Vann Woodward

Race Riot at East St. Louis, July 2, 1917
Elliott Rudwick

W. E. B. Du Bois: Voice of the Black Protest Movement
Elliott Rudwick

The Negro's Civil War: How American Negroes
Felt and Acted during the War for the Union
James M. McPherson

Lincoln and Black Freedom: A Study in Presidential Leadership
LaWanda Cox

Slavery and Freedom in the Age of the American Revolution
Edited by Ira Berlin and Ronald Hoffman

Upheaval in the Quiet Zone:
A History of Hospital Workers' Union, Local 1199
Leon Fink and Brian Greenberg

Labor's Flaming Youth:
Telephone Operators and Worker Militancy, 1878–1923
Stephen H. Norwood

Another Civil War:
Labor, Capital, and the State
in the Anthracite Regions of Pennsylvania, 1840–68
Grace Palladino

Coal, Class, and Color:
Blacks in Southern West Virginia, 1915–32
Joe William Trotter, Jr.